T0207488

Communications
in Computer and Information Science   1878

Editorial Board Members

Joaquim Filipe ⓘ, *Polytechnic Institute of Setúbal, Setúbal, Portugal*
Ashish Ghosh ⓘ, *Indian Statistical Institute, Kolkata, India*
Raquel Oliveira Prates ⓘ, *Federal University of Minas Gerais (UFMG),
Belo Horizonte, Brazil*
Lizhu Zhou, *Tsinghua University, Beijing, China*

Rationale

The CCIS series is devoted to the publication of proceedings of computer science conferences. Its aim is to efficiently disseminate original research results in informatics in printed and electronic form. While the focus is on publication of peer-reviewed full papers presenting mature work, inclusion of reviewed short papers reporting on work in progress is welcome, too. Besides globally relevant meetings with internationally representative program committees guaranteeing a strict peer-reviewing and paper selection process, conferences run by societies or of high regional or national relevance are also considered for publication.

Topics

The topical scope of CCIS spans the entire spectrum of informatics ranging from foundational topics in the theory of computing to information and communications science and technology and a broad variety of interdisciplinary application fields.

Information for Volume Editors and Authors

Publication in CCIS is free of charge. No royalties are paid, however, we offer registered conference participants temporary free access to the online version of the conference proceedings on SpringerLink (http://link.springer.com) by means of an http referrer from the conference website and/or a number of complimentary printed copies, as specified in the official acceptance email of the event.

CCIS proceedings can be published in time for distribution at conferences or as post-proceedings, and delivered in the form of printed books and/or electronically as USBs and/or e-content licenses for accessing proceedings at SpringerLink. Furthermore, CCIS proceedings are included in the CCIS electronic book series hosted in the SpringerLink digital library at http://link.springer.com/bookseries/7899. Conferences publishing in CCIS are allowed to use Online Conference Service (OCS) for managing the whole proceedings lifecycle (from submission and reviewing to preparing for publication) free of charge.

Publication process

The language of publication is exclusively English. Authors publishing in CCIS have to sign the Springer CCIS copyright transfer form, however, they are free to use their material published in CCIS for substantially changed, more elaborate subsequent publications elsewhere. For the preparation of the camera-ready papers/files, authors have to strictly adhere to the Springer CCIS Authors' Instructions and are strongly encouraged to use the CCIS LaTeX style files or templates.

Abstracting/Indexing

CCIS is abstracted/indexed in DBLP, Google Scholar, EI-Compendex, Mathematical Reviews, SCImago, Scopus. CCIS volumes are also submitted for the inclusion in ISI Proceedings.

How to start

To start the evaluation of your proposal for inclusion in the CCIS series, please send an e-mail to ccis@springer.com.

Aurona Gerber · Marijke Coetzee
Editors

South African Institute of Computer Scientists and Information Technologists

44th Annual Conference, SAICSIT 2023
Pretoria, South Africa, July 17–19, 2023
Revised Selected Papers

 Springer

Editors
Aurona Gerber ⓘ
University of the Western Cape
Cape Town, South Africa

Marijke Coetzee ⓘ
North-West University
Auckland Park, South Africa

ISSN 1865-0929   ISSN 1865-0937 (electronic)
Communications in Computer and Information Science
ISBN 978-3-031-39651-9   ISBN 978-3-031-39652-6 (eBook)
https://doi.org/10.1007/978-3-031-39652-6

© The Editor(s) (if applicable) and The Author(s), under exclusive license
to Springer Nature Switzerland AG 2023

This work is subject to copyright. All rights are reserved by the Publisher, whether the whole or part of the material is concerned, specifically the rights of translation, reprinting, reuse of illustrations, recitation, broadcasting, reproduction on microfilms or in any other physical way, and transmission or information storage and retrieval, electronic adaptation, computer software, or by similar or dissimilar methodology now known or hereafter developed.
The use of general descriptive names, registered names, trademarks, service marks, etc. in this publication does not imply, even in the absence of a specific statement, that such names are exempt from the relevant protective laws and regulations and therefore free for general use.
The publisher, the authors, and the editors are safe to assume that the advice and information in this book are believed to be true and accurate at the date of publication. Neither the publisher nor the authors or the editors give a warranty, expressed or implied, with respect to the material contained herein or for any errors or omissions that may have been made. The publisher remains neutral with regard to jurisdictional claims in published maps and institutional affiliations.

This Springer imprint is published by the registered company Springer Nature Switzerland AG
The registered company address is: Gewerbestrasse 11, 6330 Cham, Switzerland

Preface

This volume of Springer CCIS (CCIS 1878) contains the revised accepted research papers of SAICSIT 2023, the *44th Conference of the South African Institute of Computer Scientists and Information Technologists*. SAICSIT 2023 was held from 17 to 19 July 2023 at the 26 Degrees South Bush Boho Hotel in Muldersdrift, South Africa. The theme of the conference was *Connect to be the Future.*

The power of face-to-face time has been proven time and again and for any community to flourish, all members must flourish. The past few years have demonstrated our connectedness as the Covid-19 pandemic spread worldwide. On the plus side, our interconnectedness supports innovation and creativity, leading in many cases to more success for individuals and organisations. The strength of weak ties is a well-known social network concept. We all benefit from accessing new and non-redundant information through those ad hoc connections we usually do not see in our everyday interactions. Unfortunately, large groups are becoming less interconnected in our world of remote interaction, and we should aim to address these challenges as Computing scholars.

The role of the 44th SAICSIT conference was to connect the computing community so that innovation and creativity can flourish. The SAICSIT conference aims to provide a space to meet and exchange ideas on addressing the challenges of the fast-evolving digital future.

This SAICSIT 2023 proceedings book contains 18 full research papers organised in their respective Computer Science and Information Systems research tracks. These submissions were included for presentation in the program of SAICSIT 2023. With more than 58 papers submitted and 54 submissions in total sent out for review, the acceptance rate for full research papers for this CCIS volume is 33%. In the Information Systems track, 36 submissions were sent out for review and 13 were accepted for this volume of Springer CCIS, amounting to an acceptance rate of 36%. In the Computer Science track, 18 submissions were sent out for review, and 5 were accepted for this volume of Springer, amounting to an acceptance rate of 28%. The review process was rigorous with every paper receiving at least three substantive reviews from an expert program committee with more than 20 national and international affiliations. The track chairs managed the review process and supported the authors to revise their papers to the quality results that are published in this proceedings. We want to express our gratitude to the track chairs and program committee reviewers for their hard work and dedication. Thank you to the authors of all the submitted papers for sharing their research results. We hope the opportunity to participate in SAICSIT 2023 will have a lasting impact on the quality and productivity of the future research in our scholarly community.

We also acknowledge the enthusiasm and outstanding contributions of the local organisers of SAICSIT 2023, the School of Computer Science and Information Systems at the North-West University in South Africa. The administration, faculty, and staff of the North-West University, as well as our conference organiser, Mongoose C&D, supported the planning and execution of the conference. Thank you to everyone who contributed to the success of SAICSIT 2023.

June 2023   Aurona Gerber
                                                                          Marijke Coetzee

SAICSIT 2023 Organisation

General Chair

Marijke Coetzee   North-West University, South Africa

Computer Science Co-chairs

Tiny du Toit   North-West University, South Africa
Hein Venter   University of Pretoria, South Africa

Information Systems Co-chairs

Sunet Eybers   University of South Africa, South Africa
Roelien Goede   North-West University, South Africa
Mathias Mujinga   University of South Africa, South Africa

Publication Co-chairs

Aurona Gerber   University of the Western Cape and CAIR, South Africa
Marijke Coetzee   North-West University, South Africa

SAICSIT 2023 Programme Committee

Computer Science Track

Adedayo, Oluwasola Mary   University of Winnipeg, Canada
Bosman, Anna   University of Pretoria, South Africa
Brink, Willie   Stellenbosch University, South Africa
Chavula, Josiah   University of Cape Town, South Africa
Dlamini, Moses   University of KwaZulu Natal, South Africa
Du Toit, Tiny   North-West University, South Africa
Ezugwu, Absalom   North-West University, South Africa

Folorunsho, Olaiya	Federal University Oye Ekiti, Nigeria
Furnell, Steven	University of Nottingham, UK
Gutierrez-Cardenas, Juan	Universidad de Lima, Peru
Hazelhurst, Scott	University of the Witwatersrand, South Africa
Hutchison, Andrew	Google, Switzerland
Isong, Bassey	North-West University, South Africa
James, Steven	University of the Witwatersrand, South Africa
Klein, Richard	University of the Witwatersrand, South Africa
Kotzé, Eduan	University of the Free State, South Africa
Lubbe, Heinke	North-West University, South Africa
Machanick, Philip	Rhodes University, South Africa
Marais, Patrick	University of Cape Town, South Africa
Meyer, Thomas	University of Cape Town and CAIR, South Africa
Moodley, Deshendran	University of Cape Town, South Africa
Morgenrood, Nathan	North-West University, South Africa
Nel, Stephan	Stellenbosch University, South Africa
Olivier, Martin	University of Pretoria, South Africa
Pilkington, Colin	University of South Africa, South Africa
Potgieter, Linke	Stellenbosch University, South Africa
Sanders, Ian	University of the Witwatersrand, South Africa
Serfontein, Rudi	North-West University, South Africa
Simmonds, Rob	University of Cape Town, South Africa
Suleman, Hussein	University of Cape Town, South Africa
Tait, Bobby	University of South Africa, South Africa
Timm, Nils	University of Pretoria, South Africa
Tucker, Bill	Stellenbosch University, South Africa
Van Alten, Clint	University of the Witwatersrand, South Africa
van der Merwe, Annette	North-West University, South Africa
Van der Merwe, Brink	Stellenbosch University, South Africa
van Zijl, Lynette	Stellenbosch University, South Africa
Venter, Hein	University of Pretoria, South Africa
Wa Nkongolo, Nkongolo	University of Pretoria, South Africa
Watson, Bruce	Stellenbosch University, South Africa
Zugenmaier, Alf	Hochschule München, Germany

Information Systems Track

Adebesin, Funmi	University of Pretoria, South Africa
Adeliyi, Timothy	University of Pretoria, South Africa
Campher, Susan	North-West University, South Africa
Chimboza, Tendani	University of Cape Town, South Africa
Chipangura, Baldreck	University of South Africa, South Africa

da Veiga, Adele	University of South Africa, South Africa
Davids, Zane	University of Cape Town, South Africa
De Wet, Lizette	University of the Free State, South Africa
Eybers, Sunet	University of South Africa, South Africa
Gcora-Vumazonke, Nozibele	University of Pretoria, South Africa
Gerber, Aurona	University of the Western Cape and CAIR, South Africa
Goede, Roelien	North-West University, South Africa
Hattingh, Marie	University of Pretoria, South Africa
Kotzé, Eduan	University of the Free State, South Africa
Kritzinger, Elmarie	University of South Africa, South Africa
Kroeze, Jan H.	University of South Africa, South Africa
Kruger, Neels	North-West University, South Africa
Le Roux, Daniel	Stellenbosch University, South Africa
Malele, Vusi	North-West University, South Africa
Matthee, Machdel	University of Pretoria, South Africa
Mawela, Tendani	University of Pretoria, South Africa
Mennega, Nita	University of Pretoria, South Africa
Mujinga, Mathias	University of South Africa, South Africa
Ncube, Zenzo Polite	University of Mpumalanga, South Africa
Olaitan, Olutoyin	Walter Sisulu University, South Africa
Oluwadele, Deborah	University of Pretoria, South Africa
Parry, Douglas	Stellenbosch University, South Africa
Piderit, Roxanne	University of Fort Hare, South Africa
Pillay, Komla	University of Johannesburg, South Africa
Pretorius, Henk	University of Pretoria, South Africa
Prinsloo, Tania	University of Pretoria, South Africa
Seymour, Lisa	University of Cape Town, South Africa
Smit, Danie	University of Pretoria and BMW, South Africa
Smit, Imelda	North-West University, South Africa
Smuts, Hanlie	University of Pretoria, South Africa
Steyn, Riana	University of Pretoria, South Africa
Tait, Bobby	University of South Africa, South Africa
Taylor, Estelle	North-West University, South Africa
Turpin, Marita	University of Pretoria, South Africa
van der Merwe, Mac	University of Pretoria, South Africa
Van Staden, Corné	University of South Africa, South Africa
Wa Nkongolo, Mike	University of Pretoria, South Africa
Weilbach, Lizette	University of Pretoria, South Africa

Contents

Computer Science Track

Matching Production and Test Files:
A Comparison of Filename
and Statement-Based Approaches

Gerald Kipruto Kirui[ID] and Stephen Phillip Levitt[(✉)][ID]

University of the Witwatersrand, Johannesburg, South Africa
stephen.levitt@wits.ac.za

Abstract. Accurate matching of test and production files plays a critical role in the analysis and evaluation of Test-Driven Development (TDD). However, current approaches often yield unsatisfactory results due to their reliance on filename-based matching. The purpose of this study is to compare the performance of a statement-based matching algorithm with the traditional filename-based approach. A comprehensive evaluation was conducted using 500 tests from 16 open-source Java projects, wherein the weighted F1-scores of both methods were assessed. Subsequently, the 95% confidence intervals were determined using a pseudosample size of 500. The statement-based approach achieved a 95% confidence interval of [0.6815, 0.7347], while the filename-based method had a notably lower interval of [0.1931, 0.2459]. These results demonstrate the superior performance of the statement-based matching algorithm, providing a more accurate and reliable solution for matching test and production files in TDD research. In conclusion, the statement-based matching algorithm significantly outperforms the filename-based method, which will benefit TDD research by offering a more accurate method of matching production files to test files.

Keywords: Traceability Links · Assertion Analysis · F1-Score

1 Introduction

Test-Driven Development or Test-Driven Design (TDD) is a software development practice in which automated tests are written prior to production code in an incremental, iterative manner with the sole purpose of delivering quality code [4].

Researchers who are interested in software testing are often interested in matching test code files with the corresponding production code files that are being tested, since TDD requires tests to be written at a certain point in time with respect to production code.

In the case of empirical TDD studies, this matching allows researchers to use file commit timestamps to determine when tests are written with respect to the production code being tested. Code coverage as an indicator of TDD

© The Author(s), under exclusive license to Springer Nature Switzerland AG 2023
A. Gerber and M. Coetzee (Eds.): SAICSIT 2023, CCIS 1878, pp. 3–18, 2023.
https://doi.org/10.1007/978-3-031-39652-6_1

is insufficient, as it includes no timing information regarding when tests are written. Most researchers take it for granted that matching a test file to its target production files by comparing filenames is reasonably accurate. In this paper, we investigate the accuracy of such a method and propose an alternative, more accurate approach.

Section 2 discusses related work and outlines the problem statement. Sections 3 and 4 describe the methods of operation of the filename-based and statement-based matching algorithms, respectively. Sections 5 and 6 explain metrics to analyze the performance of the algorithms and strategies to quantify the confidence level in the performance measured, respectively. Section 7 provides and discusses the results. Lastly, Sect. 8 concludes the paper.

2   Background

2.1   Related Work

Zaidman et al. [15] investigated the co-evolution of production code and test code using three projects (two open-source projects and one industrial project). They analyzed commit behavior, the relative growth of production code and test code, and test coverage evolution over time. The authors concluded that TDD can be detected as the simultaneous committing of production code and associated test code in a VCS.

Borle et al. [1] compared the productivity and code quality of GitHub projects that use TDD to varying degrees. They created a TDD or TDD-like set (experimental) and a non-TDD set (control). The degree of TDD variation was allowed in two ways: the difference in commit timestamps between production code and test code, and class coverage. The authors analyzed the commit velocity of test-production file pairs and found that only 0.8% of Java projects strictly practice TDD and that there is no observable benefit from using TDD.

Kochhar et al. [5] conducted a study to determine the presence or absence of test cases in 50,000 GitHub projects. They found that 57.34% of projects did not have any tests, and 90% of projects had fewer than 100 tests. Projects with tests were larger in size than those without, with a weak positive correlation between the size of a project and the number of tests. There was also a negative correlation between the size of a project and the number of tests per LoC.

Hanhela [3] investigated the use of the test-first approach in open-source projects. The author found that only 5% of test-production file pairs were "test-first", while 61% were "test-with" and 34% were "test-last". The majority of projects (74%) had at least one test file, and 52% had at least one test-production file pair committed either before or with the production file. The author concluded that since the majority of test files are committed with their corresponding production files, they were likely written around the same time, and the test-first approach is not widely used in open-source projects.

Wang et al. [13] investigated the co-evolution of production code and test code. They analyzed 975 open-source Java projects to determine the factors that affect whether test code should be updated. From the results, they proposed a machine-learning-based approach, SITAR, to predict the test code that requires an update when its corresponding production code is modified. After evaluating SITAR on 20 popular Java projects, they found that it obtained an average precision and recall of up to 81.4% and 76.1%, respectively, in a within-project setting.

Van Rompaey et al. [12] evaluated six strategies that resolve traceability between production code and test cases, namely naming convention, fixture element types, static call graph, last call before assert, lexical analysis, and co-evolution. To determine the baseline for traceability, they requested developers to manually select units under test that link to a given set of test cases from three projects, namely JPacman, ArgoUML, and Mondrian. The performance of each strategy was then determined via applicability and accuracy by comparing the output to the baseline. They concluded that the strategy based on naming convention yielded high precision and recall, although they note that it may be project-dependent. The authors recommended combining the strategies to improve traceability resolution.

White et al. [14] presented TCTracker, an approach to establish test-to-code traceability at the method-level and at the class-level. TCTracker combines multiple static and dynamic techniques to address the shortcomings of using a single technique for test-to-code traceability. They evaluated TCTracker on a dataset of traceability links that was manually curated from four open-source projects. They found that TCTracker performs better than any individual technique in establishing traceability links between tests and production code.

2.2   Problem Statement

Zaidman et al. [15] used the similarity of filenames to match a single test file to a single production file. Borle et al. [1] used a regular expression that matches imports from testing frameworks to check if a repository includes test files. They matched one test file to only one production file by checking if their filenames differed by the case-insensitive string "test". Kochhar et al. [5] identified test files by evaluating whether a file's name contains the string "test". Hanhela [3] matched one test file to only one production file according to the similarity in their filenames, i.e., the test file's name starts with the name of the production file and ends with the word "Test". Wang et al. [13] paired a production class with its corresponding test class by checking if the test filename differed from the production filename only by the string "Test" in the test filename. Van Rompaey et al. [12] established that linking a test case to its corresponding production file(s) by checking if they differ by the string "Test" can yield high precision and recall, depending on project guidelines. White et al. [14] noted that the techniques based on naming conventions yielded low recall.

Many test files are left unpaired when undertaking a purely name-based approach when matching test files and production files. For instance, suppose a project has three production files called Circle.java, Rectangle.java, and Triangle.java and one test file called PerimeterTest.java, which tests the implementation of the perimeter function in each of the production classes. If the traditional filename-based matching algorithm were used to match the three production files to the test file, it would fail since the filenames are not defined similarly in order to explicitly link `PerimeterTest.java` to the production files. A statement-based matching algorithm would overcome this problem as it would not depend on the filenames but rather on the classes being instantiated in the test file. Moreover, the strategy used by most researchers to match tests to production files does not take into account integration tests because integration tests involve testing multiple software units as a combined entity [11] and it is not clear which unit the integration test should be named after.

This paper will introduce a strategy for matching a test file to its target files at statement-level granularity by linking assert statements in test code to the public methods of production classes that are tested by the assert statements.

3   Matching Files via Filenames

The filename-based algorithm checks if a filename contains the string "test" to determine if it is a test file. It checks if the production filename is at least 80% similar to the test filename after all filenames are converted to lowercase and "test" is removed from the test filename. Python's `difflib.SequenceMatcher` is used to match strings given a threshold and is based on the Ratcliff-Obershelp algorithm [7]. The similarity ratio is given by 2 * M/T where M is the sum of the matches and T is the sum of the lengths of the original strings. Refer to Fig. 1: The production file `AnnotationValidatorFactory` would be matched to the test file `AnnotationsValidatorTest` because the similarity ratio is equal to 2 * (10 + 9)/(20 + 26) which is equal to 0.82.

Fig. 1. Similarity between `annotationsalidator` and `annotationvalidatorfactory`

4   Matching Files via Assertions

The statement-based matching algorithm differs from the filename-based matching algorithm in that it analyzes source code line-by-line to match files, rather than matching files based on their filenames.

4.1   Distinguishing Between Tests and Production Files

PyDriller [8] is used to obtain a full list of production and test files in a project. To label a file as a test file, two factors are considered: whether the source code includes at least one assert statement and whether there is at least one import from JUnit or TestNG, since they are the most popular testing frameworks [16]. The first regular expression in Listing 1.1 matches the assert statements used by the test frameworks. The second regular expression captures all the imports used in a file; the resultant list must be filtered by checking if the string "junit" or "testng" is part of the import, which would indicate that testing is performed in the file in question.

```
1 r"assert(Equals|That|ThatThrownBy|Same|NotSame|NotNull|Null
      |True|ArrayEquals|Throws|False|Timeout)\s*\("
2 r"import\s*.*;"
```

Listing 1.1. Regular expressions to determine whether a file is a test file

A file is considered a test file only if it has at least one match result for each of the regular expressions in Listing 1.1. Otherwise, it is considered a production file. The key subsystems utilized by the statement-based matching algorithm are depicted in Fig. 2 below.

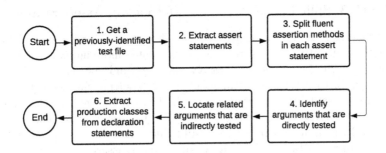

Fig. 2. Flow diagram of the statement-based matching algorithm.

4.2   Block 2: Extract Assert Statements

Block 2 takes test code as input and outputs a list of assert statements used in the test code. This block serves to isolate the parts of the test code that have a direct link to the production classes being tested. Assertion methods take objects of classes as arguments, and these could be direct instantiations of production classes or instantiations of third-party classes. A third-party class is a class that is provided by a third-party library or framework, which is a piece of software that is created and maintained by a separate organization or individual. Consider the test function in Listing 1.2, which verifies the behaviour of the add function from the Complex class from Apache Commons Math [10]. Given this test function, block 2 will return the array in Listing 1.3.

```
1 @Test
2 public void testAddComplexNumbers() {
3     Complex a = new Complex(3, 4);
4     Complex b = new Complex(1, -2);
5     Complex expectedResult = new Complex(4, 2);
6     Complex result = a.add(b);
7
8     assertEquals(expectedResult, result);
9 }
```

Listing 1.2. Testing the Complex class from Apache Commons-Math

```
1 [
2     "assertEquals(expectedResult, result);"
3 ]
```

Listing 1.3. Output of block 1 given Listing 1.2

4.3   Block 3: Split Fluent Assertion Methods in Assert Statements

A fluent assertion method is a method that allows one to chain multiple assertions together such that the entire assert statement is more human-readable and expressive [6]. The functions isNotEmpty, hasSize and contains in the assert statement in Listing 1.4 are examples of fluent assertion methods. Block 3 is responsible for splitting the assertion methods with the goal of isolating the arguments in each assertion method. It takes a list of assert statements obtained from block 2 as input and returns the split fluent assertion methods. The element in the array in Listing 1.4 is an example of an assert statement that uses fluent assertion methods. When it is passed to block 3, the output is given by Listing 1.5.

```
1 [
2     "assertThat(numbers).isNotEmpty().hasSize(5).contains(4)
      ;"
3 ]
```

Listing 1.4. An example of an assert statement that uses fluent assertion methods

```
1 [
2     "assertThat(numbers)",
3     "isNotEmpty()",
4     "hasSize(5)",
5     "contains(4)"
6 ]
```

Listing 1.5. The output of block 3 given Listing 1.4 as input

Notice that the block isolates each fluent assertion method from the assert statement by splitting them into separate elements.

4.4   Block 4: Identify Directly-Tested Arguments

Block 4 identifies the arguments used in the split assertion methods. It takes the split assertion methods of an assert statement as input and returns the arguments within these methods because some of the arguments may be objects instantiated by production classes, thus providing a clear link between the test file and a production file. The array of elements in Listing 1.6 is an example of an input to block 4. The corresponding output is given by Listing 1.7. Notice that only the arguments that are valid object names (firstList and secondList) are returned, whereas primitive data types and methods invoked by objects (such as 9 and getSize respectively) are discarded.

```
1  [
2      "assertThat(firstList)",
3      "isNotEmpty()",
4      "hasSize(secondList.getSize())",
5      "contains(9)"
6  ]
```

Listing 1.6. An example of split assertion methods and their arguments

```
1  [
2      "firstList",
3      "secondList"
4  ]
```

Listing 1.7. Output of block 4 given Listing 1.6 as input

4.5   Block 5: Locate Directly and Indirectly Tested Objects

Block 5 is responsible for identifying *and* locating the positions and names of object references within the code that have dependencies on the object references that are directly tested in assert statements. By taking into account the names of objects passed directly into assert statements (the output of block 4), it conducts a comprehensive analysis of the test code to determine all relevant relationships between objects. To achieve this, block 5 pinpoints the connections between different objects in the code, as one object could be the return value of another object.

Block 5 takes two parameters as input and returns one entity. The two parameters are the test file parsed as text and all the object references that are directly tested. The output is a set of the very same directly tested object references as well as all the object references they depend on. This is achieved by splicing the declaration statements associated with each object reference and then extracting the object from which it was instantiated, if it exists. Note that for each newly discovered object, there may exist yet another object from which it is instantiated. Hence, this subsystem is executed recursively until all the object references (both directly and indirectly tested) are identified. Consider Listing

1.8 for an example of the action of block 5. Note that Line 7 in Listing 1.8 represents the continuation of the test in the same fashion, i.e., the creation of objectC, objectD, etc.

```
1  @Test
2  public void someTestFunction() {
3      ProductionClassA objectA = new ProductionClassA();
4
5      ProductionClassB objectB = objectA.someFunctionA(1,
       someParameterA);
6
7      // Test continues ...
8
9      ProductionClassZ objectZ = objectY.someFunctionY(
       someParameterX);
10
11     assertNotNull(objectZ);
12 }
```

Listing 1.8. A test function where the object being tested is dependent on other objects

```
1 [
2     "objectA", "objectB", ..., "objectY", "objectZ"
3 ]
```

Listing 1.9. Output of block 5 given Listing 1.8 and "objectZ" as input

Notice that although objectZ is the only object that is directly tested, all other objects that it depends on for its creation are also returned by block 5. This is because the test would have failed if there were any issues during the creation of the other objects. Hence, the other objects are considered to be tested, albeit indirectly.

4.6   Block 6: Extract Production Classes from Declaration Statements

Block 6 is responsible for extracting the production classes from the declaration statements. Before the extraction, it identifies the lines of code that contain the declaration statements for all the names of objects that are directly or indirectly tested in an assert statement. Block 6 takes as input a collection of tested objects (the output of block 5) and a complete set of production classes in a project. It returns a subset of the production classes that appear in at least one declaration statement.

To achieve this, block 6 gets the positions of the directly and indirectly tested objects in the parsed test file from block 5. Then, for each position, a part of the parsed test code is extracted via string slicing. The extracted substring is the declaration statement corresponding to the object whose position was provided. The start of each substring is the last newline character ("\n") before the given position, and the end of each substring is the first semi-colon (";") after the given position. Lastly, each substring is analyzed to check for the presence of production class names.

Consider Listing 1.10: the `testPolynomialFunction` method examines the behavior of two distinct polynomial function classes, `PolynomialFunction` and `PolynomialFunctionLagrangeForm` from Apache Commons Math. Initially, a `PolynomialFunction` object named `func` is instantiated using an array of coefficients $\{1, -2, 1\}$, representing the polynomial $f(x) = (x-1)^2$. The method computes the value of this polynomial at $x = 2.0$, storing the result in the variable `resultOne`. Next, a `PolynomialFunctionLagrangeForm` object called `lagrange` is created, utilizing arrays of x-coordinates $\{-1, 0, 1\}$ and corresponding y-coordinates $\{2, 1, 0\}$. The method then calculates the value of the Lagrange polynomial at $x = 2.0$ and assigns it to the variable `resultTwo`. Finally, the test function employs assert statements to validate the correctness of both polynomial evaluations. Listings 1.11, 1.12 and 1.13 show the output of each block from 2 to 6 upon analyzing this test code. The positions of object names identified by block 5 are indicated in yellow in Listing 1.10.

```
1  public void testPolynomialFunction() {
2      double[] coeffs = {1, -2, 1};
3      PolynomialFunction func = new PolynomialFunction(
       coeffs);
4      double resultOne = func.value(2.0);
5
6      double[] x = {-1, 0, 1};
7      double[] y = {2, 1, 0};
8      PolynomialFunctionLagrangeForm lagrange = new
       PolynomialFunctionLagrangeForm(x, y);
9      double resultTwo = lagrange.value(2.0);
10
11     assertThat (resultOne).isEqualTo(1.0)
12             .and (resultTwo).isEqualTo(-1.0);
13 }
```

Listing 1.10. Testing the behaviour of classes from Apache Commons-Math

```
1  ["assertThat(resultOne).isEqualTo(1.0).and(resultTwo).
      isEqualTo(-1.0);"] // block 2
2  ["assertThat(resultOne)", "isEqualTo(1.0)", "and(resultTwo)
      ", "isEqualTo(-1.0)"] // block 3
3  ["resultOne", "resultTwo"] // block 4
4  ["resultOne", "resultTwo", "func", "lagrange"] // block 5 -
      all object names associated with the test
5  [96, 268, 332, 433, 146, 344, 381, 158] // block 5 -
      corresponding positions of the object names
```

Listing 1.11. The output of block 2 - 5

```
1  [
2      "double resultOne = func.value(2.0);",
3      "PolynomialFunction func = new
4      PolynomialFunction(coeffs);",
5      "double resultTwo = lagrange.value(2.0);",
6      "PolynomialFunctionLagrangeForm lagrange = new
7      PolynomialFunctionLagrangeForm(x, y);"
8  ]
```

Listing 1.12. Declaration statements extracted by block 6

```
1  [
2      "PolynomialFunction",
3      "PolynomialFunctionLagrangeForm"
4  ]
```

Listing 1.13. Production classes identified by block 6

5 Performance Metrics: Precision, Recall and F1-Score

A true positive (TP) production file selection is when a production class is accurately identified by the algorithm in a test file, while a false positive (FP) production file selection is when the algorithm falsely reports that a production class is tested. A false negative (FN) production file selection is when a production class is tested by a test file, but the algorithm fails to identify it. The performance of the file matching algorithms on a single project is determined using precision (ρ), recall (λ) and F1-score (ψ) according to the expressions below:

$$\rho = \frac{TP}{TP + FP} \tag{1}$$

$$\lambda = \frac{TP}{TP + FN} \tag{2}$$

$$\psi = 2 \cdot \frac{\rho \cdot \lambda}{\rho + \lambda} \tag{3}$$

The ground truth (a set of production files that are truly tested) for a single test file was determined by manually analyzing each file and recording the tested production classes. The manual analysis was done by a single individual; a script that randomly samples one test file per execution was used. After every execution, the script also provided a subset of production filenames that appear in the test file (that may or may not be tested). The individual then manually looked through the code to determine which production files from the subset were actually tested by the test file. The TP, FP, and FN values were evaluated by running a script that compared the output of the algorithms to the ground truth. For a more general indication of the performance of the file matching algorithms, multiple projects were analyzed. Hence, the weighted precision, weighted recall, and weighted F1-score were used to represent the overall performance, where the weight is determined by the number of test files in each project. If there are n projects with ω_i tests in the ith project, then the weighted precision ($\bar{\rho}$), weighted recall ($\bar{\lambda}$), and weighted F1-score ($\bar{\psi}$) are given by the following expressions:

$$\bar{\rho} = \frac{\sum\limits_{i=1}^{n} \omega_i \cdot \rho_i}{\sum\limits_{i=1}^{n} \omega_i} \tag{4}$$

$$\bar{\lambda} = \frac{\sum\limits_{i=1}^{n} \omega_i \cdot \lambda_i}{\sum\limits_{i=1}^{n} \omega_i} \tag{5}$$

$$\bar{\psi} = \frac{\sum\limits_{i=1}^{n} \omega_i \cdot \psi_i}{\sum\limits_{i=1}^{n} \omega_i} \tag{6}$$

6   Bootstrap Confidence Intervals

The weighted F1-score was chosen to represent the overall performance of the matching algorithms. The greater the number of test files used to evaluate the performance of the matching algorithms, the greater the confidence level in the weighted F1-score, but it is impossible to collect an infinite number of test files. Hence, the bootstrap confidence interval for the weighted F1-score was chosen to quantify the level of certainty in the performance of the matching algorithms when a given sample size is used. It is a method for estimating the certainty in the weighted F1-score due to sampling variation by resampling the dataset with replacement and computing the weighted F1-score for each bootstrap sample. The confidence interval provides a range of likely values for the true population value of the weighted F1-score. There are three main steps for determining the confidence interval of a metric [2]:

1. Create a distribution based on K bootstrapped samples for the statistic u.
2. Sort the values in ascending order.
3. The lower bound of the $100\ (1-2\alpha)$ percent confidence interval is the $K\ \alpha^{th}$ value, and the upper bound is the $K\ (1-\alpha)^{th}$ value in the sorted distribution.

K represents the number of pseudosamples that are generated from the original sample, u represents the statistic of interest (e.g., mean), and α represents a variable that determines the confidence level (e.g., if α equals 0.025, then the confidence level is 95%). Bootstrap confidence intervals are valuable in this study as they inform the reader of the confidence in the reported performance of the algorithm.

7   Results and Discussion

The performance of the statement-based and filename-based matching algorithms was evaluated using 500 tests from sixteen open-source Java projects. Figure 3 shows the F1-scores of the two matching algorithms for each Java project. Table 1 shows the weighted performance metrics of the matching algorithms. Table 2 shows a summary of the statistics related to the F1-score of the Java projects.

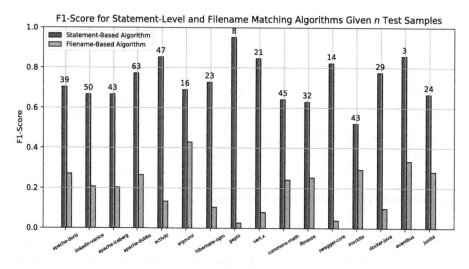

Fig. 3. F1-scores for the statement-based and filename-based matching algorithms given n test samples from different Java projects.

Table 1. Weighted performance metrics for the matching algorithms.

Matching Algorithm	Weighted Precision ($\bar{\rho}$)	Weighted Recall ($\bar{\lambda}$)	Weighted F1-Score ($\bar{\psi}$)	Weighted Accuracy
Statement-Based	0.8667	0.6114	0.7170	0.7427
Filename-Based	0.4947	0.1401	0.2180	0.3803
Performance Improvement	+0.3720	+0.4713	+0.4990	+0.3624

The statement-based matching algorithm's weighted precision (86.67%) is 37.2% points higher than the filename-based matching algorithm's weighted precision (49.47%). Practically, this means that the statement-based matching algorithm has a 37.2% higher likelihood of correctly identifying tested production files while minimizing the inclusion of untested production files. Similarly, the statement-based matching algorithm's weighted recall (61.14%) exceeds

Table 2. Summary of statistics across the 16 Java Projects

Matching Algorithm	Min	Max	Variance
Statement-Based	0.5206	0.9517	0.0121
Filename-Based	0.0256	0.4286	0.0129

the filename-based matching algorithm's weighted recall (14.01%) by 47.13% points. This indicates that the statement-based matching algorithm has a 47.13% higher likelihood of capturing tested production files, significantly reducing the chances of missing such files compared to the filename-based matching algorithm. Regarding the F1-score, the statement-based matching algorithm's weighted F1-score (71.70%) is 49.9% points higher than the filename-based matching algorithm's weighted F1-score (21.80%). This suggests that the statement-based matching algorithm has a 49.9% better balance between precision and recall, making it more effective at accurately identifying tested production files while minimizing both false positives and false negatives. In practical terms, these percentage differences imply that the statement-based matching algorithm is far more effective at matching test files to production files, resulting in more accurate and reliable outcomes if it is used for TDD research. However, it incurs higher spatial and time complexity, requiring more computer memory and operations, leading to a longer processing time.

Consider the performance of the algorithms on the project Gephi: the extreme performance difference between the algorithms may be due to the sampled tests being integration tests, as each test tests an average of ten production files; hence, the chosen test filename does not match any one particular production file. Since the statement-based matching algorithms analyzes source code instead of filenames, its performance is not affected in the way that the filename-based matching algorithm is affected. Notice the relatively poor performance of the statement-based matching algorithm with respect to Mockito. Mockito, as a mocking framework, is designed to simplify the process of creating mocks and stubs for unit testing [9], making it highly likely that its own tests rely on the features it provides, such as dependency injection, mocking, and stubbing. Mockito's own tests primarily consist of unit tests that focus on testing individual components in isolation, using mocks and stubs to replace external dependencies. Although some integration tests might be employed to ensure proper functioning of components when interacting with each other, the primary focus is on unit testing with mocks and stubs, allowing the Mockito development team to ensure the framework's reliability and correctness while maintaining a fast and efficient testing process. Since the statement-based matching algorithm's method of operation does not detect the use of mocks or stubs, this may explain its relatively poor performance with respect to Mockito.

The difference between the upper bound and lower bound values (expressed as a percentage) for the 95% confidence interval of the weighted F1-score for both matching algorithms is displayed in Fig. 4. Table 3 shows upper bound and lower bound values using a sample size of 10 and 500.

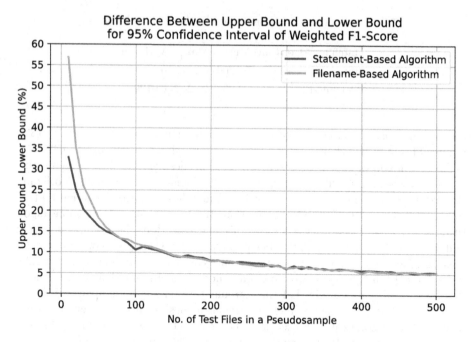

Fig. 4. Difference between the upper bound and lower bound for the 95% confidence interval of the weighted F1-score for the matching algorithms

Table 3. Upper bound and lower bound values for the weighted F1-score for the matching algorithms for 10 test samples and 500 test samples

Matching Algorithm	$\bar{\psi}_{upper}$ ($n = 10$)	$\bar{\psi}_{lower}$ ($n = 10$)	$\bar{\psi}_{upper}$ ($n = 500$)	$\bar{\psi}_{lower}$ ($n = 500$)
Statement-Based	0.8952	0.5676	0.7347	0.6815
Filename-Based	0.7501	0.1816	0.2459	0.1931

Pseudosample sizes ranging from 10 to 500 in increments of 10 were used to generate the plot. At a pseudosample size of 500, the 95% confidence interval of the statement-based matching algorithm is [0.6815, 0.7347] and that of the filename-based matching algorithm is [0.1931, 0.2459]. This suggests that, regardless of the specific sample size used, the statement-based matching algorithm is more likely to provide more accurate matches between test files and production files due to its higher weighted F1-score confidence interval. Moreover, the differences in the lower bounds (0.4884) and the upper bounds (0.4888) indicate a substantial performance gap in favor of the statement-based matching algorithm. This consistent superiority of the statement-based matching algorithm's confidence intervals suggests that it is more favourable to use for matching test files to production files in most scenarios.

7.1   Threats to Validity

This study may have limitations due to a sample size of 500 tests from sixteen projects, although this was mitigated by the use of the bootstrap confidence interval. The implementation of the filename-based algorithm from prior literature could not be obtained; there could be variations in the performance between the algorithm implemented for this study and the algorithm in prior research. The manual analysis of test files to determine which production classes are tested may have also introduced human error. To reduce the manual labour and the chance of human error in determining the production classes that are tested, a script was used to simply list the production classes that appear anywhere in the test code. This reduced the likelihood of incorrect classification of tested production classes. The statement-based matching algorithm may be affected when applied to new datasets that rely heavily on mocks or stubs, as it was not designed to consider the presence of mocks or stubs. The external validity of the findings may be constrained because of the use of open-source Java projects since software projects written in different languages or in different contexts may have different testing or programming styles. TDD involves writing tests prior to production code, and the statement-based matching algorithm can be used to detect the use of TDD. However, other aspects, such as the time difference between committing tests and production files, need to be taken into account to accurately detect the use of TDD. Hence, the statement-based matching algorithm alone may not accurately assess whether TDD is being practiced since it analyzes only one aspect of TDD.

8   Conclusion

This paper has proposed a statement-based matching algorithm. It consists of six blocks: block 1 gets a previously-identified test file; block 2 extracts assert statements; block 3 splits fluent assertions; block 4 identifies directly tested arguments; block 5 identifies directly and indirectly tested objects; and block 6 extracts production classes from declaration statements. The statement-based matching algorithm was shown to be more accurate, as it has a weighted F1-score of 0.7170 and a 95% confidence interval of [0.6815, 0.7347], whereas the filename-based matching algorithm has a weighted F1-score of 0.2183 and a 95% confidence interval of [0.1931, 0.2459]. The improved accuracy will benefit future TDD research as it can be used as a more accurate way to check if a project has used TDD, increasing the validity of the conclusions drawn by researchers. Future work will extend the statement-based matching algorithm to detect static classes in addition to instance classes, thereby improving recall.

References

1. Borle, N., Feghhi, M., Stroulia, E., Grenier, R., Hindle, A.: Analyzing the effects of test driven development in GitHub. In: 2018 IEEE/ACM 40th International Conference on Software Engineering (ICSE), pp. 1062–1062. IEEE (2018)
2. Cohen, P.R.: Empirical Methods for Artificial Intelligence, vol. 139. MIT Press, Cambridge (1995)
3. Hanhela, J.: Usage of test-driven development in open source projects. Ph.D. thesis, Master's thesis Jari Hanhela Spring (2015)
4. Janzen, D., Saiedian, H.: Test-driven development concepts, taxonomy, and future direction. Computer **38**(9), 43–50 (2005)
5. Kochhar, P.S., Bissyandé, T.F., Lo, D., Jiang, L.: Adoption of software testing in open source projects-a preliminary study on 50,000 projects. In: 2013 17th European Conference on Software Maintenance and Reengineering, pp. 353–356 (2013). https://doi.org/10.1109/CSMR.2013.48
6. Leotta, M., Cerioli, M., Olianas, D., Ricca, F.: Fluent vs basic assertions in java: an empirical study. In: 2018 11th International Conference on the Quality of Information and Communications Technology (QUATIC), pp. 184–192. IEEE (2018)
7. Ratcliff, J.W., Metzener, D.E.: Pattern-matching-the gestalt approach. Dr Dobbs J. **13**(7), 46 (1988)
8. Spadini, D., Aniche, M., Bacchelli, A.: Pydriller: python framework for mining software repositories. In: Proceedings of the 2018 26th ACM Joint Meeting on European Software Engineering Conference and Symposium on the Foundations of Software Engineering, pp. 908–911 (2018)
9. Spadini, D., Aniche, M., Bruntink, M., Bacchelli, A.: To mock or not to mock? an empirical study on mocking practices. In: 2017 IEEE/ACM 14th International Conference on Mining Software Repositories (MSR), pp. 402–412. IEEE (2017)
10. The Apache Software Foundation: Apache Commons Math GitHub Repository. https://github.com/apache/commons-math. Accessed 2022
11. Thomas, D., Hunt, A.: Mock objects. IEEE Softw. **19**(3), 22–24 (2002). https://doi.org/10.1109/MS.2002.1003449
12. Van Rompaey, B., Demeyer, S.: Establishing traceability links between unit test cases and units under test. In: 2009 13th European Conference on Software Maintenance and Reengineering, pp. 209–218. IEEE (2009)
13. Wang, S., Wen, M., Liu, Y., Wang, Y., Wu, R.: Understanding and facilitating the co-evolution of production and test code. In: 2021 IEEE International Conference on Software Analysis, Evolution and Reengineering (SANER), pp. 272–283. IEEE (2021)
14. White, R., Krinke, J., Tan, R.: Establishing multilevel test-to-code traceability links. In: Proceedings of the ACM/IEEE 42nd International Conference on Software Engineering, pp. 861–872 (2020)
15. Zaidman, A., Rompaey, B., Deursen, A., Demeyer, S.: Studying the co-evolution of production and test code in open source and industrial developer test processes through repository mining. Empirical Softw. Eng. **16**, 325–364 (2011). https://doi.org/10.1007/s10664-010-9143-7
16. Zerouali, A., Mens, T.: Analyzing the evolution of testing library usage in open source java projects. In: 2017 IEEE 24th International Conference on Software Analysis, Evolution and Reengineering (SANER), pp. 417–421. IEEE (2017)

Focused Crawling for Automated IsiXhosa Corpus Building

Cael Marquard[✉][iD] and Hussein Suleman[iD]

University of Cape Town, Cape Town, Western Cape, South Africa
cael.marquard@gmail.com, hussein@cs.uct.ac.za

Abstract. IsiXhosa is a low-resource language, which means that it does not have many large, high-quality corpora. This makes it difficult to perform many kinds of research with the language. This paper examines the use of focused Web crawling for automatic corpus generation. The resulting corpus is characterised using statistical methods: its vocabulary growth has been found to fit Heaps' Law, and its word frequency has been found to be heavy-tailed. In addition, as expected, the corpus statistics did not match expectations from non-agglutinative languages.

Keywords: Corpus · IsiXhosa · Web Crawling · Low Resource Languages

1 Introduction

IsiXhosa is a low-resource language, meaning that there are few large, high-quality corpora available for research purposes. This makes it difficult to perform many kinds of research with the language, such as the testing of novel information retrieval algorithms, the training of machine-learning models on isiXhosa, and corpus linguistics research.

Web crawling is the process of visiting pages on the Internet and then recursively visiting the pages that they link to, in order to build a view of the content on the Web. The Web has been used in the past as a source for corpus building for isiXhosa and other languages, as it contains many freely-accessible documents. Other methods of building corpora include paying participants to answer prompts [3], or manually curating collections of documents for inclusion. These methods require more time and money in comparison to Web crawling, which can be done as a largely automated process. Therefore, Web crawling arguably may be used to address the lack of isiXhosa corpora in a cost-effective manner and enable further research with the language. Additionally, a corpus of documents obtained from the Web is likely to be more representative of the kind of documents that an isiXhosa Web search engine would need to process, and thus may be more suited to information retrieval research in Web indexing.

Focused crawling is an optimised approach to Web crawling, which is applied when the aim is to retrieve only pages that satisfy specific criteria [7]. While

© The Author(s), under exclusive license to Springer Nature Switzerland AG 2023
A. Gerber and M. Coetzee (Eds.): SAICSIT 2023, CCIS 1878, pp. 19–31, 2023.
https://doi.org/10.1007/978-3-031-39652-6_2

broad Web crawling may require large amounts of storage, bandwidth, and CPU time, focused Web crawling uses fewer resources, meaning it can be applied at a lower cost. The broad Web crawling approach has been modified through a directing algorithm that decides which links to crawl and how, in order to maximise the number of relevant pages crawled per total number of pages crawled. The focused crawler decides to save a page or crawl links based on the number of isiXhosa sentences found on the page. This is ascertained using a language identification algorithm, which estimates the probability that a given piece of text is written in isiXhosa.

This research sought to investigate this approach to corpus building. In particular, the following research question was posed:

To what degree is it possible to build a high quality isiXhosa corpus automatically through focused Web crawling?

To answer this question, a corpus of isiXhosa documents was collected using focused Web crawling. This resulting corpus has been analysed and compared to linguistic benchmarks such as Heaps' [19] and Zipf's laws [15] in order to characterise the text. The resulting metrics are compared to other corpora, both in isiXhosa and in other languages. The veracity of the isiXhosa language identification approach has been manually verified, and the sites included have been categorised as well as classified as likely machine translated or likely human-written. The source-code of the crawler and the analysis tools is provided as a Git repository, hosted on GitHub.[1] This paper is based on research conducted as part of coursework undertaken by the first author.

2   Related Works

Barnard et al. [3] built a corpus of South African languages by recording the utterances of speakers in response to prompts generated from pre-existing corpora. With this manual approach, an isiXhosa corpus of 56 h of speech (136 904 words) was constructed, in addition to similar length corpora for the other languages targeted by the researchers.

As an alternative to manual approaches, focused crawling has been applied to building corpora of specific languages [13,14]. In the case of Swiss German (GSW), over 500 000 sentences were collected over a period of approximately three months [13]. The algorithm used to direct the crawler was remarkably simple—if the page had more than two GSW sentences on it, outgoing links were also crawled.

By comparison, Corpulyzer uses a more complex seeding and directing algorithm [18]. The process begins with filtering the Common Crawl Corpus[2] to extract only the web pages in the target language. Then, sites are prioritised based on the percentage of target-language content found on the site as a whole, and on its individual pages.

---

[1] Source code available at https://github.com/Restioson/isixhosa-crawler.
[2] https://commoncrawl.org/.

Focused crawling has been proposed in order to capture documents most relevant to a given topic [7]. The initial crawler design proposed by Chakrabarti et al. [7] relies on breaking down Web pages into a taxonomy based on their topic. This, however, does not suit the application of focused crawling to language-specific corpus building, as it is unclear how the output of a language identification algorithm could fit into a topic taxonomy.

Gaustad and Puttkamer's dataset [9] is an example of a corpus of isiXhosa created from the Web. The original dataset was obtained by randomly selecting documents from official South African government websites, and then using an existing language identification tool in order to filter them. This approach is similar in that it also uses documents from the Web, but it is limited to one website, and will not crawl links from government websites to other sites in order to find more documents.

Crawling in combination with language identification has been applied to the task of collecting isiXhosa documents for the purpose of building an isiXhosa search engine [11]. However, the approach taken by Kyeyune [11] was to use a broad, undirected crawl and filter the documents using language identification after the fact. Using a focused crawling approach, it is hypothesised that documents can be more efficiently crawled from the web than by using a broad crawl, as many non-isiXhosa pages could be filtered out, leading to a higher harvest rate.

In order to decide whether to save a page or not, the language in which the page is written must be identified. There are many pre-existing language detection software packages such as Lingua[3], but many of them suffer from a lack of coverage of South African languages, which can lead to issues such as confusing text in Chichewa for text in isiXhosa. Since Chichewa and isiXhosa are not mutually intelligible, this kind of error is not acceptable. Fortunately, there are other approaches to classifying South African languages, such as using rank order statistics [8], which perform far better at this task. In the end, the NCHLT South African Language Identifier [16] was chosen, since it is fairly accurate, is provided as pre-built software, and is simple to interface with.

The corpus gathered by the crawler may be characterised through a variety of statistical measures. Zipf's law predicts that, in a corpus sufficiently large, the rth most common term will have frequency proportional to $\frac{1}{r^\alpha}$, where $\alpha \approx 1$ [2,15]. Heaps' law predicts that, in a corpus sufficiently large, the vocabulary size of the corpus will grow with respect to its total size in words N according to the power law $k \times N^\beta$, with k and β being parameters to the curve [2,19]. These predictive models have been shown to hold for the vast majority of languages. Thus, the quality of the corpus can also be judged by how well these laws hold.

IsiXhosa is an agglutinative language. This means that each word may consist of several, clear-cut morphemes [1]. Morphemes are the smallest unit of words which carry meaning [17]. Many of the methods for analysing corpora are based on languages which are not agglutinative, such as English. Hence, they may not work as well for a language like isiXhosa. Thus, instead of segmenting the corpus

---

[3] https://github.com/pemistahl/lingua.

on word boundaries for analysis, it may make sense to segment the corpus by word and then by each morpheme in each word (morphological decomposition). Another approach could be to segment the corpus into n-grams, which are character sequences n characters long [12]. N-grams have been used before to identify the language of a given text, and it has been suggested that Zipf's law holds for n-gram frequency in corpora [5].

3   Methodology

3.1   Design of Crawler

The crawling application itself is comprised of three main components:

1. **Seeding.** The seeding algorithm is responsible for creating a list of pages used by the crawler to begin its search.
2. **Language identification.** This allows the crawler to ascertain if a certain page is written in isiXhosa and should be added to the corpus.
3. **Direction.** This allows the crawler to decide which pages to crawl and in what order.

The crawler was written in Python using the Scrapy[4] framework. Scrapy is a mature framework for writing Web crawlers in Python and has many utilities for controlling the crawling process, such as automatically respecting `robots.txt` and rate-limits in order not to be a burden to the websites included in the corpus. The source code of the crawler is available on GitHub[5].

Seeding Process. To begin the crawling process, the algorithm was supplied with a list of initial URLs from which to begin the recursive search of the graph of Web pages.

Linder et al. [13] leverage Google search for the creation of a list of seed URLs. By generating combinations of Swiss German words, Google's indexed archive was searched for documents likely to contain Swiss German. Medelyan et al. [14] used a similar approach, adapted to their more specific criteria, which included both topic and language.

A similar approach was used for the isiXhosa crawler, in which single isiXhosa words (from the dataset of the IsiXhosa.click live dictionary[6]) were searched through Google's Custom Search JSON API[7]. URLs were kept as seeds if the returned snippet was identified to be isiXhosa and they were not contained within the blocked sites list. It was hypothesised that higher quality seeds could be generated this way, since pages that happened to contain a heteronym of an isiXhosa word but no isiXhosa text would be excluded, speeding up the initial

---

[4] https://scrapy.org/.
[5] https://github.com/Restioson/isixhosa-crawler.
[6] https://isixhosa.click.
[7] https://developers.google.com/custom-search/v1/overview.

stages of the crawl. Additionally, the website of I'solezwe lesiXhosa[8] was included manually in the seed list, as it is a well known hub of isiXhosa content.

Sites in the block list were machine translated sites, dictionary websites, sites with isiXhosa content in navigation elements only, and sites from the WikiMedia projects[9]. The WikiMedia projects were excluded, since these sites are available as public data downloads and are organised by language, which therefore makes them uninteresting to crawl. Although, they may have links to other isiXhosa language material which is not available as public data downloads, they were excluded so as to streamline the seeding process, with the assumption that these materials would be linked elsewhere on the internet, too.

In order to comply with Google's rate limit of 100 searches per day, the API was queried four times on four separate days, each time with a new, random set of words, selected with replacement. The seed URLs were then deduplicated, and sites in the block list removed. In total, 235 unique seed URLs were gathered.

Language Identification. First, the human readable text from each page was scraped using the BeautifulSoup library[10]. Then, NLTK [4] was used to tokenize the text into sentences, using the Punkt algorithm [10]. Since an isiXhosa sentence tokenizer was not available within NLTK, the English model was used. Because isiXhosa also terminates sentences with the same punctuation marks as English, this was not anticipated to be an issue. Sentences were then split into subdivisions of 300 characters using the standard library text wrapping function since, if the sentence is too long, it is rejected by the language classifier. After this, the segmented sentences were sent to the language classifier and deemed to be isiXhosa if the classifier had a confidence value of at least 0.5 and isiXhosa was the most likely language determined for the text.

Direction. Based on the hypothesis that isiXhosa pages link to other isiXhosa pages more often than a random page links to an isiXhosa page, the prevalence of isiXhosa text on the page can be used to determine whether the pages it links to should be crawled or not. This is similar to the approach that was used by Linder et al. [13]—pages that had at least one Swiss German sentence had their links crawled.

Separate heuristics were used to decide whether to save a page and whether to crawl a given link. A page was saved if it contained over five isiXhosa sentences, or over 40% of its sentences were in isiXhosa. Sites known to be using the GTranslate[11] machine translation plugin were excluded. This plugin is very widely used on the web in order to provide automated translations of content on websites. However, since the translation quality is often quite poor, sites containing text translated by GTranslate were excluded. A site was determined to be using GTranslate if an HTML comment starting with "delivered by GTranslate" was present in the document.

---

[8] https://isolezwelesixhosa.co.za.
[9] https://wikimediafoundation.org/our-work/wikimedia-projects/.
[10] https://crummy.com/software/BeautifulSoup/.
[11] https://gtranslate.io/.

All links from a page were added to a list to be crawled if the page contained at least one isiXhosa sentence. Additionally, links would be added to the list if the anchor text of the link was identified as isiXhosa, or if it included the substring "xhosa". This was to account for pages that were written in English or other languages, but had links to isiXhosa versions of the page. Links were prioritised in the crawl if they contained "xhosa" or had their anchor text written in isiXhosa. Otherwise, they were assigned default priority. This likely did not affect the result of the crawl since, by the end, the sites were crawled almost completely.

The list of links was filtered to remove websites in the block list before being added to the crawl queue.

4   Analysis

4.1   Basic Statistics and Validation

The crawler was run from 29 September to 20 October 2022. Table 1 lists some basic statistics about the corpus obtained.

Table 1. Basic statistics of the corpus.

Pages	202 646
Total words	75 807 261
Unique words	672 460
Total sentences	4 663 036
Unique sentences	1 002 714
Websites	90

The largest five domains (containing the most isiXhosa documents) crawled are listed in Table 2, along with the number of documents obtained from each, the category of the website, and whether it was determined as being machine translated.

Table 2. The top five sites in the corpus, ranked by number of documents

Domain	Pages	Category	Machine translated
seals.ac.za	107 021	Academic	No
jw.org	67 888	Religious and News	No
churchofjesuschrist.org	10 696	Religious	No
fundza.mobi	4 814	Literature	No
isolezwelesixhosa.co.za	3 882	News	No

It is worth noting that out of the five top sites, two of the websites are religious. Out of the top 15, six are religious. Specifically, these sites contain isiXhosa translations of the Bible, as well as other texts about Christianity. This could be one of the reasons for the high number of duplicate sentences in the corpus—each website may be hosting the same translation of the Bible.

Jw.org in particular contains translations of religious text, but it also contains (religious) isiXhosa news media, so it has been categorised as both religious and news. The largest domain, seals.ac.za, contains mostly documents from the SEALS Digital Commons[12], which is a collection of academic output from Eastern Cape universities. According to the 2011 census [6], isiXhosa is the most common first language in the Eastern Cape, so it is no surprise that Eastern Cape universities produce much of the isiXhosa content available on the internet.

4.2   Statistical Distributions of the Corpus

The text in the corpus was evaluated using standard corpus characterisation techniques and compared against benchmarks such as Zipf's law and Heaps' law [2,15,19]. It can then be evaluated whether the corpus fits general expectations of natural language corpora. This was done by plotting the data against manually selected Zipf's and Heaps' curves. In order to evaluate the corpus, the order of the documents in the corpus was randomized using the shuf program from the GNU Core Utilities, and it was then passed to a utility written to process the JSON Lines format output by Scrapy[13]. Since the raw data was very large (22GB), it was processed in parallel, with each document being sent to a worker thread. In order to parallelise the language identification process, the NCHLT classifier server [16] was launched 12 times—one instance per logical CPU core on the machine used for analysis.

Agglutinativity of IsiXhosa. It should be noted that since isiXhosa is an agglutinative language, relying on word segmentation may yield results inconsistent with broad expectations, since the number of distinct words is likely to be higher, given that meaning is often created by appending morphemes to words in a sentence. Therefore, in addition to a standard word-based analysis, a modified trigram-based analysis has also been performed, which segments the text into character n-grams of length three [5,12].

Duplicate Texts. Since many websites crawled contain the same headers and footers, it was expected that many sentences would be duplicated across the corpus. Since isiXhosa translations of the Bible was a notably large source of documents in the corpus, this increases the likelihood of duplicate sentences occurring in the corpus.

---

[12] https://vital.seals.ac.za/vital/access/manager/Index.

[13] https://scrapy.org/.

A simple duplicate check based on case-insensitive sentence-level equality reveals that only 22% of the sentences (1 002 714) in the corpus are unique (which represents roughly 19% of the corpus's overall word count). However, duplicates are not uncommon in online data sources and many potential uses for crawled corpora, such as search enginge indexing algorithms, exploit this fact. Hence, despite the potential to skew the analysis, the duplicate sentences have been included in the dataset.

Zipf's Law. Zipf's law is a predictive model that estimates that, in a sufficiently large corpus, each word has a frequency in the text that is inversely proportional to its rank [2, 15]. For example, the second most common word is estimated to occur roughly half as frequently as the first most common word. The harvested corpus can be compared to this idealised frequency falloff curve in order to determine whether it matches this general benchmark of word usage.

When word frequency and rank is plotted on a log-y graph (Fig. 1), it can be seen that the frequency of a word versus its rank fits a heavy-tailed distribution.

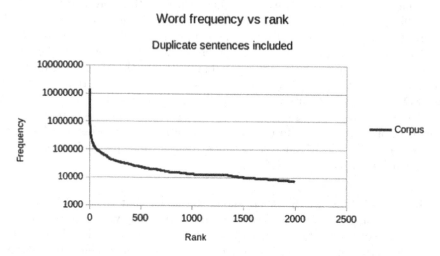

Fig. 1. Curve for the corpus on a log-y graph, including duplicate sentences.

Token-to-Type Ratio. The Token-to-Type ratio (TTR) of the corpus can be measured in order to estimate lexical variety in the corpus. The TTR of a given corpus can be calculated as the corpus size in words divided by the number of unique words in the corpus [2]. This ratio can be computed for the corpus in order to compare its lexical variety to other corpora.

When duplicate sentences are present in the corpus, the lexical variety appears to grow slowly with the corpus size (Fig. 2). However, when they are excluded, the lexical variety grows much faster. The TTR of the full corpus is

21.5 when duplicate sentences are removed. This is quite different to the figure obtained in the work by Ali et al. [2], which has a TTR of 27.17 for English and 26.71 for Arabic at 800 000 words. By comparison, the isiXhosa corpus obtained has a TTR of 4.81 with duplicate sentences excluded or 11.81 with duplicate sentences included at a corpus size of 800 014 words. This could be due to the fact that isiXhosa is an agglutinating language, meaning that a higher lexical variety is expected.

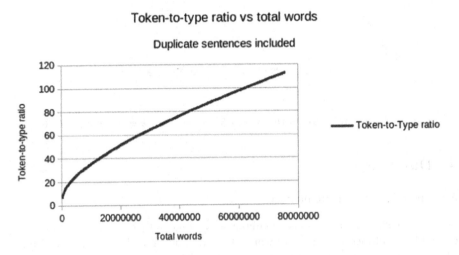

Fig. 2. Token-to-Type ratio vs corpus size in words

Heaps' Law. Heaps' law is a predictive model for estimating the size of the vocabulary of a given corpus. For a corpus of size N words, with k and β being parameters to the curve, the size of the vocabulary v is estimated to be $k \times N^{\beta}$ [2, 19]. Typically, k will be between 10 and 100, while β will be approximately 0.5 [2]. The vocabulary growth of the corpus can be modelled and then compared with a Heaps' curve of suitable parameters k and β in order to ascertain if the corpus fits the estimated trend.

The corpus's vocabulary growth fits the prediction of Heaps' law very well, as can be seen in Fig. 3. The values of K and β are within the typical ranges of $10 \le k \le 100$ and $\beta \approx 0.5$ [2].

However, Heaps' law does not predict the growth of the number of unique trigrams in the corpus well. As seen in Fig. 4, the growth of the number of unique trigrams does not seem to fit a power graph.

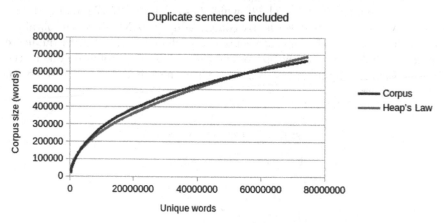

Fig. 3. Heaps' law graph of the corpus for words with $k = 96$ and $\beta = 0.46$

5   Discussion

5.1   Effects of Agglutination

Since isiXhosa is an agglutinative language in which subjects, objects, and verbs can all be combined into a single word, it is possible that Zipf's and Heaps' laws are not good predictors of the statistics of isiXhosa corpora. For instance, in English, the five most common words are "the", "be", "and", "of", and "a" [20]. The articles "the" and "a" are missing from isiXhosa, as it does not use articles. The other words are translated to isiXhosa using grammatical constructs, which are affixed to other words in the sentence. Specifically, "be" is translated using the copulative concord, "of" is translated using the possessive concord, and "and" is translated using the prefix "na", possibly in conjunction with the auxiliaries "kunye" or "kwaye", though it is mostly present on its own. The absence of these common words as separate words could contribute to the distribution of word frequency in the corpus being not perfectly Zipfian.

In order to account for the agglutinativity of isiXhosa, terms may be segmented in other ways, such as by n-grams or morphologically. When the text is decomposed into trigrams instead of words, the distribution is even less Zipfian. This could be due to the fact that there is a finite (and relatively small) number of total possible trigrams. This may therefore contribute to the tail of the distribution being heavier than would be expected for words, which would change the shape of the distribution and may explain why it does not match a Heaps' power law graph. Morphological decomposition may represent a more interesting way to segment the text, but this is still the subject of research in isiXhosa.

It may be that some of these statistical models do not hold for isiXhosa text. If this is the case, then it is likely that they would also not hold for languages closely related to isiXhosa, such as the Nguni languages isiZulu, siSwati, and isiNdebele.

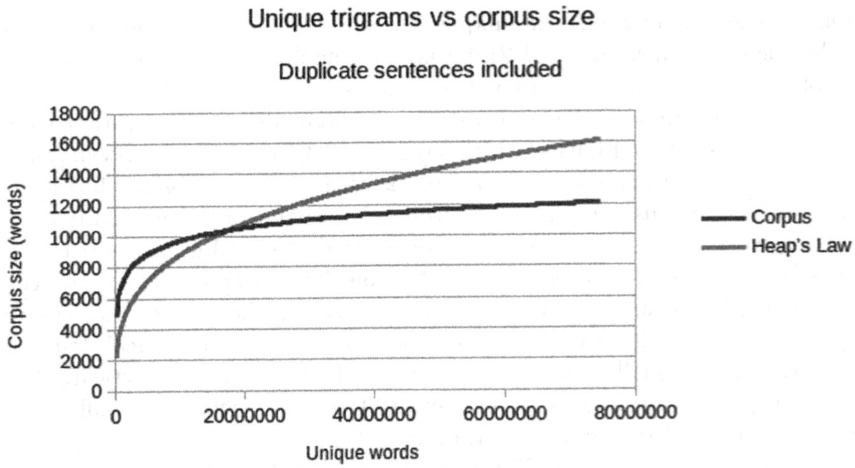

Unique trigrams vs corpus size

Duplicate sentences included

Fig. 4. Heaps' law graph of the corpus for trigrams with $K = 70$ and $\beta = 0.3$

Indeed, Barnard et al. [3] found that, for an isiXhosa corpus of 136 904 words, 29 130 unique words occurred. This represents a Token-to-Type ratio of 4.7. In comparison, when sentences are deduplicated, the corpus obtained through Web crawling had a Token-to-Type ratio of 3.7 at a size of 129 462 words. These values are much closer to each other than the values obtained by Ali et al. [2] for Arabic and English.

5.2   Effect of Seed URLs on Final Crawl

Only four new domains (4.54% of all domains) were discovered that were not included in the list of seed URLs. These domains accounted for only 0.098% of documents in the corpus. One of these domains (jw-cdn.org) was the Content Delivery Network (CDN) for another one of the sites (jw.org). This accounted for 196 documents, whereas the other new domains only accounted for one document each. This further demonstrates that sites on the isiXhosa web are likely to link either to themselves or websites that they are directly affiliated with, but not external, unaffiliated websites.

Therefore, the seed URLs greatly determined which websites ended up being crawled in the end. This suggests that the isiXhosa web is sparse and fairly difficult to discover. This may mean that a focused crawl is not the best approach to discover new websites containing isiXhosa content, although it is a good fit for extracting isiXhosa documents from known hubs of isiXhosa.

6   Conclusions and Future Work

Through the use of a focused Web crawling algorithm, a corpus of isiXhosa documents has been collected, totalling 202 646 documents containing 4 million sentences, 1 million of which are unique. The corpus matches various statistical models, such as Heaps' law and Zipf's law. It should, however, be noted that some of the analysis methods may not be suited to isiXhosa, given that it is an agglutinative language. The websites crawled were also almost entirely determined by the list of seed URLs, which suggests that focused Web crawling may be a good strategy to extract content from known isiXhosa websites, but is not a good strategy for discovering new websites that contain isiXhosa content.

Future work may investigate alternative statistical distributions to better fit isiXhosa data. This could then be extended to other isiXhosa corpora and corpora in related languages, such as isiZulu, to explore if these characteristics are unique to isiXhosa or if they apply to languages similar in grammatical structure and lexicon. Additionally, future work may attempt to verify analytically how well the corpus fits Zipfs' and Heaps' laws if it is large enough and sufficiently similar in characteristics to other corpora.

Some of the deviations from Zipf's and Heaps' laws may be due to the agglutinative nature of the isiXhosa language, as has been discussed. Therefore, future work may aim to segment the corpus morphologically and then ascertain whether it fits these models more closely.

Since the seed URLs made up 95.45% of all sites in the corpus, the seeding approach may be refined in future to yield better results for future crawls. While the WikiMedia projects' pages were excluded from this research, future work could investigate the possibility of using them to assist in generating the list of seed URLs.

Acknowledgements. This research was partially funded by the National Research Foundation of South Africa (Grant number: 129253) and University of Cape Town. The authors acknowledge that opinions, findings and conclusions or recommendations expressed in this publication are that of the authors, and that the NRF accepts no liability whatsoever in this regard.

References

1. Aikhenvald, A.Y.: Typological distinctions in word-formation. In: Shopen, T. (ed.) Language Typology and Syntactic Description, vol. 3, 2 edn., pp. 1–65. Cambridge University Press (2007). https://doi.org/10.1017/CBO9780511618437.001
2. Ali, M., Mohammed, Suleman, H.: Building a multilingual and mixed Arabic-English corpus. In: Proceedings of Arabic Language Technology International Conference (ALTIC), Alexandria, Egypt (2011)
3. Barnard, E., Davel, M., van Heerden, C., Wet, F., Badenhorst, J.: The NCHLT speech corpus of the South African languages, pp. 194–200 (2014)
4. Bird, S., Klein, E., Loper, E.: Natural Language Processing with Python: Analyzing Text with the Natural Language Toolkit. O'Reilly Media, Inc. (2009)
5. Cavnar, W., Trenkle, J.: N-gram-based text categorization. In: Proceedings of the Third Annual Symposium on Document Analysis and Information Retrieval (2001)
6. Census in brief. Statistics South Africa, Pretoria (2011). https://www.statssa.gov.za/census/census_2011/census_products/Census_2011_Census_in_brief.pdf

7. Chakrabarti, S., Berg, M., Dom, B.: Focused crawling: a new approach to topic-specific web resource discovery. Comput. Netw. **31**, 1623–1640 (2000). https://doi.org/10.1016/S1389-1286(99)00052-3

8. Dube, M., Suleman, H.: Language identification for South African bantu languages using rank order statistics. In: Jatowt, A., Maeda, A., Syn, S.Y. (eds.) ICADL 2019. LNCS, vol. 11853, pp. 283–289. Springer, Cham (2019). https://doi.org/10.1007/978-3-030-34058-2_26

9. Gaustad, T., Puttkammer, M.J.: Linguistically annotated dataset for four official South African languages with a conjunctive orthography: IsiNdebele, isiXhosa, isiZulu, and Siswati. Data Brief **41**, 107994 (2022). https://doi.org/10.1016/j.dib.2022.107994, https://www.sciencedirect.com/science/article/pii/S2352340922002050

10. Kiss, T., Strunk, J.: Unsupervised multilingual sentence boundary detection. Comput. Linguist. **32**(4), 485–525 (2006). https://doi.org/10.1162/coli.2006.32.4.485, https://aclanthology.org/J06-4003

11. Kyeyune, M.J.: IsiXhosa search engine development report. Technical report CS15-01-00, University of Cape Town (2015). https://pubs.cs.uct.ac.za/id/eprint/1035/

12. Lecluze, C., Rigouste, L., Giguet, E., Lucas, N.: Which granularity to bootstrap a multilingual method of document alignment: character n-grams or word n-grams? Procedia - Soc. Behav. Sci. **95**, 473–481 (2013). https://doi.org/10.1016/j.sbspro.2013.10.671

13. Linder, L., Jungo, M., Hennebert, J., Musat, C.C., Fischer, A.: Automatic creation of text corpora for low-resource languages from the internet: the case of swiss German. In: Proceedings of the 12th Language Resources and Evaluation Conference, pp. 2706–2711. European Language Resources Association, Marseille (2020). https://aclanthology.org/2020.lrec-1.329

14. Medelyan, O., Schulz, S., Paetzold, J., Poprat, M., Markó, K.: Language specific and topic focused web crawling. In: Proceedings of the Fifth International Conference on Language Resources and Evaluation (LREC 2006), pp. 865–868. European Language Resources Association (ELRA), Genoa (2006). http://www.lrec-conf.org/proceedings/lrec2006/pdf/228_pdf.pdf

15. Piantadosi, S.T.: Zipf's word frequency law in natural language: a critical review and future directions. Psychon. Bull. Rev. **21**(5), 1112–1130 (2014)

16. Puttkammer, M., Hocking, J., Eiselen, R.: NCHLT South African language identifier (2016). https://repo.sadilar.org/handle/20.500.12185/350. Accepted: 2018-02-05T20:22:40Z Publisher: North-West University

17. Sims, A., Haspelmath, M.: Understanding Morphology, 2 edn. Routledge (2010). https://doi.org/10.4324/9780203776506

18. Tahir, B., Mehmood, M.A.: Corpulyzer: a novel framework for building low resource language corpora. IEEE Access **9**, 8546–8563 (2021). https://doi.org/10.1109/ACCESS.2021.3049793

19. van Leijenhorst, D., van der Weide, T.: A formal derivation of heaps' law. Inf. Sci. **170**(2), 263–272 (2005). https://doi.org/10.1016/j.ins.2004.03.006, https://www.sciencedirect.com/science/article/pii/S0020025504000696

20. Zhukovskyi, S.: Word frequency list of American English (2010). https://www.academia.edu/29501273/Word_Frequency_List_of_American_English

Zero-Day Threats Detection for Critical Infrastructures

Mike Nkongolo[1(✉)] and Mahmut Tokmak[2]

[1] University of Pretoria, Hatfield 0028, South Africa
mike.wankongolo@up.ac.za
[2] Mehmet Akif Ersoy University, Burdur, Turkey
mahmuttokmak@mehmetakif.edu.tr

Abstract. Technological advancements in various industries, such as network intelligence, vehicle networks, e-commerce, the Internet of Things (IoT), ubiquitous computing, and cloud-based applications, have led to an exponential increase in the volume of information flowing through critical systems. As a result, protecting critical infrastructures from intrusions and security threats has become a paramount concern in the field of intrusion detection systems (IDS). To address this concern, this research paper focuses on the importance of defending critical infrastructures against intrusions and security threats. It proposes a computational framework that incorporates feature selection through fuzzification. The effectiveness and performance of the proposed framework are evaluated using the NSL-KDD and UGRansome datasets in combination with selected machine learning (ML) models. The findings of the study highlight the effectiveness of fuzzy logic and the use of ensemble learning to enhance the performance of ML models. The research identifies Random Forest (RF) and Extreme Gradient Boosting (XGB) as the top-performing algorithms to detect zero-day attacks. The results obtained from the implemented computational framework outperform previous methods documented in the IDS literature, reaffirming the significance of safeguarding critical infrastructures from intrusions and security threats.

Keywords: Zero-day threats · Fuzzy logic · Feature selection · Machine learning · UGRansome · Critical infrastructures

1 Introduction

Recent advances in technologies such as the Industrial Internet of Things (IIoT), wireless systems, and the Web of Things (WoT) have raised some threats that endanger the authenticity, trustworthiness, and cybersecurity of various critical infrastructures. Critical infrastructures are any vital entities (banking, energy, telecommunications, etc.) that are so important to a country's daily operations that their disruption would have disastrous consequences for the country's security and daily operations [1]. Companies can employ an array of countermeasures, such as firewalls, anti-virus programs, anti-malware technologies, and intrusion

© The Author(s), under exclusive license to Springer Nature Switzerland AG 2023
A. Gerber and M. Coetzee (Eds.): SAICSIT 2023, CCIS 1878, pp. 32–47, 2023.
https://doi.org/10.1007/978-3-031-39652-6_3

prevention techniques, to defend themselves against malicious incursions [2]. An Intrusion Detection System (IDS) is acknowledged as one of the most effective tools for securing critical infrastructures from suspicious behavior among all security protocols [3]. This article describes a machine learning (ML) strategy that used fuzzy logic to protect critical infrastructures from unknown network attacks. The following ML techniques were considered: extreme gradient boosting (XGB), extra-trees (ET), decision trees (DT), random forest (RF), naive Bayes (NB), and support vector machines (SVM). The NSL-KDD and UGRansome datasets were also used to assess the performance of the models described in the study [3]. The first one might be thought of as a legacy dataset that contains outmoded properties that have not changed since it was created in 1990. The latter might be viewed as a unique and novel dataset of zero-day threats that was developed in 2021 by Mike Nkongolo et al. [4–6]. A 0-day exploit is an unknown malicious intrusion [7] that can damage critical infrastructures. The penetration occurs without being detected by the IDS. As a result, IDS vendors have zero days to develop keys to recognize them [6]. This makes 0-day intrusion a serious security threat for any critical infrastructure. Consequently, to safeguard critical infrastructures from 0-day exploits, this study employed the UGRansome and NSL-KDD datasets, which underwent a fuzzy-based feature selection process, to develop a computational framework. Furthermore, the implementation of the feature selection (FS) technique is crucial in the proposed computational framework to ensure that only the best (most optimal) patterns are chosen for the modeling process. Moreover, the fuzzy logic's selection criteria used the ET classifier. In the experiment, four feature vectors were produced by the fuzzy-based feature selector for the multi-class and binary classification processes. The modeling technique made use of the four attribute vectors. Using those four specific features, this study evaluated the models' performance and contrasted the findings with those of existing ML methods. The experimentation proved that the classifiers under consideration work better when fuzzy logic is used for FS. The rest of this article is divided into the following sections: The related work is described in Sect. 2; experimental datasets are outlined in Sect. 3; and the background of the ML models are introduced in Sect. 4. Sections 5 outlines the proposed computational framework. An explanation of the findings is included in Sect. 6 which also includes experimental setups. This study report is concluded in Sect. 7.

2   Related Works

The NSL-KDD dataset was utilized by Zhang et al. [8] to develop a deep learning-based IDS architecture. In the study, the authors developed an auto-encoder technique to choose the most pertinent features that the deep neural network (DNN) used for classification. The auto-encoder-based DNN model's performance was evaluated using the accuracy, recall, precision, and F1 score. The findings showed that the auto-encoder enhanced the DNN classification performance with 79.74% accuracy, 82.22% precision, 79.74% recall, and 76.47% F1-score. To increase the detection accuracy, the authors may have added extra parameters to the DNN architecture. Tama et al. [9] provided a two-step methodology for intrusion detection systems (TSE-IDS). The TSE-IDS uses a variety of FS techniques in the first stage, including particle swarm optimization (PSO), ant colony algorithm (ACO), and genetic algorithm (GA). Based on the results from the pruning tree (REPT) model, the fitness criterion was able to extract a feature set from the original data. The bagging technique was used as part of an ensemble learning scheme in the second step. The UNSW-NB15 and NSL-KDD datasets were used in the experimentation. Moreover, the binary classification configuration was taken into account. Some of the metrics, including precision, accuracy, and sensitivity, were used to assess the effectiveness of their methods. The tests showed that, for the NSL-KDD dataset, TSE-IDS achieved 85.797% accuracy, 88.00% precision, and 86.80% sensitivity. Using the UNSW-NB15 dataset, the TSE-IDS achieved accuracy, sensitivity, and precision values of 91.27%. However, the TSE-IDS was not tested with a multi-class configuration. A comparison of the SVM with rule-based classifiers was performed by Sarumi et al. [10]. A filter and wrapper-based FS approach was used for each of those models. The NSL-KDD and UNSW-NB15 datasets were utilized to evaluate the Apriori and SVM's performance. By concentrating on the NSL-KDD results, it was shown that a filter-SVM could achieve 77.17% accuracy, 95.38% recall, and 66.34% precision. The accuracy, recall, and precision of the filter-Apriori approach were 67.00%, 57.89%, and 85.77% respectively. In contrast, the wrapper-SVM obtained a precision of 68%, an accuracy of 79.65%, and a recall of 98.02%. A precision of 85%, an accuracy of 68.6%, and a recall of 58.81% were achieved using the wrapper-Apriori. Most of the research articles discussed in the IDS literature used the legacy NSL-KDD dataset. This research argues that NSL-KDD data does not include 0-day attack properties due to missing patterns to address current network concerns. In addition, this dataset presents different categories of malicious patterns that have changed and evolved. Similarly, the UNSW-NB15 dataset is not strongly correlated to realistic network behaviors and cannot be used to study unknown malware. However, Suthar et al. [4] introduced a novel dataset named Emotet and recommended UGRansome for ransomware detection. On another front, Maglaras et al. [11] reported the UGRansome performance in a cloud-based optimization setting for 0-day threats recognition to protect critical infrastructures from malicious intrusions [12]. More recently, Tokmak [6] compared the performance of the deep forest model with SVM, NB, RF, and DNN algorithms on the UGRansome and NSL-KDD datasets. The range of the obtained results was between 87% to 99%. In the experiments, the UGRansome proved its efficacy in categorizing three predictive classes of 0-day concerns such as anomaly (A), signature (S), and synthetic signature (SS). In addition, the deep forest achieved more successful results with the following algorithms: DNN (97%), RF (97%), and SVM (96%). As such, our research agrees with Shankar et al. [5] and Rege and Bleiman [1] who have recently recommended UGRansome to be used in the recognition of unknown networks attacks like ransomware and zero-day attacks.

3   Experimental Datasets

The NSL-KDD dataset is utilized in this study to evaluate the effectiveness of the suggested fuzzy-based computational model [2]. It is a popular corpus in the IDS field compared to the UGRansome dataset. It has served as the foundation for numerous ML-based IDS studies. R2L, normal, U2R, Probe, and DoS traffic trace categories are all included in the NSL-KDD corpus [2]. The NSL-KDD has two subsets: the NSL-KDD Train and the NSL-KDDTest+ [2]. The NSL-KDD was split into the NSL-KDD-Train+ and NSL-KDD-Val. Furthermore, 20% of the overall NSL-KDD-Train set is made up of the NSL-KDD-Val which has 80% of the original training data. The chosen models were computed on the NSL-KDD-Train+ partition, the trained models were evaluated using the NSL-KDD-Val, and the technique was tested using the NSL-KDD-Test+. The validation stage ensures that the algorithms used are not prone to overfitting ML models [2]. The features that make up the NSL-KDD attributes are shown in Table 1. Table 2 presents the distribution of the values for each threat category for each subset. In this study, the NSL-KDD is compared to the UGRansome dataset [3, 4, 12]. However, the proposed fuzzy-based framework's performance was evaluated using the UGRansome data.

Table 1. A description of the features in the NSL-KDD dataset

No	Name	No	Name
f1	Protocol	f2	Service
f3	Flag	f4	Duration
f5	Bytes	f6	Error rate
f7	Urgent	f8	Hot
f9	Failed logins	f10	Dst count
f11	Logins	f12	Dst srv count
f13	Num compromised	f14	Root shell
f15	Su attempted	f16	Num root
f17	Num shell	f18	Access file
f19	Outbound cmds	f20	Host login

The UGRansome dataset is a comprehensive anomaly detection dataset that encompasses multiple attack categories, including Signature (S), Anomaly (A), and Synthetic Signature (SS). In addition, the dataset was divided into two partitions, namely, the UGRansome19Train and UGRansome-Val. The UGRansome-Val represents 30% of the entire UGRansome19Train which constitutes 70% of the original training data. The selected ML models were computed on the UGRansome19Train partition, the validation set was utilized to evaluate the trained models while the UGRansome18Test was mainly used for testing purposes. The UGRansome validation step guarantees that the ML classifiers used in the experiments are not prone to overfitting.

Table 2. Distribution of subsets in the NSL-KDD dataset

Dataset	Normal	DoS	Probe	R2L	U2R	Total
KDDTrain	57,343	35,927	10,656	895	42	115,973
KDDTrain+	40,494	24,478	7,717	649	42	84,480
KDDVal	15,849	10,449	1,939	146	10	21,493
KDDTest+ Full	8,711	6,458	1,754	1,421	100	22,544

The dataset includes three categories and their respective labels (S, SS, and A). Each predictive class has been labeled to include 0-day threats such as Locky, CryptoLocker, advanced persistent threats (APT), SamSam, and Globe [3]. Table 3 presents the UGRansome design as it was used to test and train the fuzzy-based FS model [3]. The values distribution per attack categories for each data subset is outlined in Table 4.

Table 3. A description of the features in the UGRansome dataset

No	Name	Type	No	Name	Type
f1	SS	Categorical	f2	Cluster	Numeric
f3	S	Categorical	f4	A	Categorical
f5	Spam	Categorical	f6	BTC	Numeric
f7	Blacklist	Categorical	f8	Bytes	Numeric
f9	Nerisbonet	Categorical	f10	USD	Numeric
f11	UDP scan	Categorical	f12	JigSaw	Categorical
f13	SSH	Categorical	f14	Port	Numeric
f15	DoS	Categorical	f16	CryptoLocker	Categorical
f17	Port scanning	Categorical	f18	WannaCry	Categorical

Table 4. Distribution of subsets in the UGRansome dataset

Dataset	A	S	SS
UGRansome19Train	40,323	25,822	9,656
UGRansomeVal	11,869	9,439	1,736
UGRansome18Test	4,701	3,408	6,954
Total	56,893	38,669	18,346
Average	19, 964	12,889	6,115

4   Machine Learning Background

A DT is a hierarchical structure that uses a series of if-else conditions to make decisions or predictions [2]. The mathematical formulation involves defining the splitting criteria and calculating impurity measures such as Gini Index or Entropy.

1. **Splitting Criteria:** Let D be the dataset at a particular node of the DT, and X be the feature set. The splitting criteria aim to find the best feature and threshold value that maximizes the separation of classes or reduces impurity [2]. For a binary split, the splitting criterion can be defined as:

$$Splitting_{criterion}(D, X) = argmax_{Gain}(D, X) \qquad (1)$$

Where Gain(D, X) represents the gain obtained by splitting the dataset D based on feature X.

2. **Entropy:** The Entropy (H) is computed as follows:

$$H(D) = -\sum p_i \times log(p_i)$$

In this study, a DT has been used to address the UGRansome multi-class classification problem, as shown in Fig. 1. The root node, intermediate node, and leaf node of the UGRansome's data structure have been demonstrated.

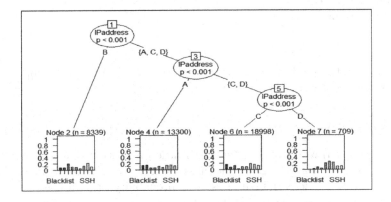

Fig. 1. DT of the UGRansome dataset

Figure 1 involves the use of a DT to classify 0-day threats based on IP addresses of the UGRansome dataset [3,12]. The root node represents the IP address, which is divided into four classes (A, B, C, and D) based on the presence of malicious activity [3]. The tree is recursively split at intermediate nodes until the final prediction (Blacklist and SSH attacks) is reached. The leaf nodes represent the final predictions made by the DT algorithm.

4.1 Tree-Based Ensemble Classifiers

The tree-based ensemble classifiers XGBoost, ET, and RF are selected and used in this study. DTs are the building blocks utilized in these algorithms.

The RF is an ensemble learning algorithm that combines multiple DTs to make predictions [12]. Each DT in the RF is built on a different subset of the training data and uses a random selection of features. The final prediction is generally made by aggregating the predictions of all the individual trees [3]. The RF algorithm leverages the diversity and collective decision-making of multiple DTs to improve the overall prediction accuracy and generalization capability [2]. Extra Trees (ET), or extremely randomized trees, further randomizes the DT splits compared to traditional DTs. The mathematical formulation is similar to the DT, but the splitting criteria involve additional randomization [2,6]. In turn, XGBoost is an ensemble-based ML technique that utilizes multiple DTs [2] by combining the outputs of weak learners through gradient boosting. The implementation involves the following objective function and the update rule:

1. **Objective Function:**

$$Obj(\Theta) = L(y, y_*) + \gamma(f), \tag{2}$$

where L is the loss function, y is the true labels, y_* is the predicted labels, $\gamma(f)$ is the regularization term for the model complexity, and θ represents the model parameters.

2. **Update Rule:**

$$f_t = f_{(t-1)} + \psi \times h_{t(x)}, \tag{3}$$

where f_t is the prediction at iteration t, ψ is the learning rate, $h_{t(x)}$ is the weak learner at iteration t, and x is the input data.

4.2   Naive Bayes

Naive Bayes (NB) is a probabilistic classification algorithm that assumes independence between features given the class variable [3]. The mathematical formulation involves calculating the posterior probability of each class given the input features. Given a dataset D with N samples and K classes, and an input feature vector $X = (x_1, x_2, ..., x_m)$, the mathematical formulation of NB can be expressed as follows:

1. **Prior Probability:**

$$P(C_k) = \frac{N_k}{N} \tag{4}$$

where $P(C_k)$ represents the prior probability of class C_k, N_k is the number of samples in class C_k, and N is the total number of samples.

2. **Likelihood:**

$$P(X|C_k) = P(x_1|C_k) \times P(x_2|C_k) \times ... \times P(x_m|C_k) \tag{5}$$

where $P(X|C_k)$ represents the likelihood of observing the feature vector X given class C_k.

4.3   Support Vector Machine

Support vector machine (SVM) is a supervised ML algorithm that can be used for both classification and regression tasks [3]. In the case of binary classification, the mathematical formulation of SVM involves finding an optimal hyperplane that separates the data into two classes while maximizing the margin between the classes [12]. The formulation can be represented as follows: Given a dataset $D = (x_1, y_1), (x_2, y_2), ..., (x_N, y_N)$, where x_i represents the input feature vector of dimension d, and y_i represents the corresponding binary class label (-1 or +1), the objective function of the SVM formulation aims to find a hyperplane characterized by the weight vector w and bias term b, which separates the data points with maximum margin. This function can be formulated as:

$$minimize : (\frac{1}{2}) \times ||w||^2 + C \times \sum (max(0, 1 - y_i \times (w^T \times x_i + b))) \quad (6)$$

where $||w||^2$ represents the L2-norm of the weight vector w, C is a regularization parameter that controls the trade-off between maximizing the margin and minimizing classification errors, and the second term represents the hinge loss function that penalizes misclassifications [2]. The SVM formulation includes the following constraints:

$$y_i \times (w^T \times x_i + b) \geq 1 - \epsilon_i, \forall\ i = 1, 2, ... N \quad (7)$$

$\epsilon_i \geq 0$, for i = 1, 2, ..., N; where ϵ_i represents the slack variable that allows for the presence of some misclassified or margin-violating samples. The decision function for classifying new input data x can be defined as:

$$f(x) = sign(\sum (\alpha_i \times y_i \times K(x_i, x)) + b) \quad (8)$$

where $K(x_i, x)$ represents the kernel function that computes the similarity or dot product between the support vectors x_i and the new input data x. The final SVM model is determined by the values of the weight vector w, the bias term b, and the support vectors obtained during the training process.

5   The Proposed Fuzzy-Based Framework

The proposed method for fuzzy logic-based feature selection (FL-based FS) involves the following steps:

1. **Define the Universe of Discourse:** Let U be the universe of discourse representing the set of all possible features. Each feature x belongs to U, i.e., $x \in U$.
2. **Define Fuzzy Sets:** Identify the fuzzy sets that represent different degrees of relevance or importance of features. Let A_i be a fuzzy set associated with feature x_i, where i = 1, 2, ..., N. A_i is defined by a membership function $\mu_i(x_i)$, which assigns a degree of membership between 0 and 1 to each feature x_i.

3. **Assess the Relevance or Importance of Features:** Determine the degree of relevance or importance of each feature based on a specific criterion or objective [13]. This can be done by evaluating the membership function $\mu_{i(x_i)}$ for each feature x_i. The membership function may consider various factors, such as statistical measures to determine the degree of relevance [13].

4. **Rank Features:** Once the degrees of relevance or importance are obtained for all features, the algorithm ranks them in descending order based on their membership values [13]. The ranking indicates the relative significance of each feature in contributing to the desired criterion or objective [13].

5. **Select the Subset of Features:** Choose a threshold or a predetermined number of features to select from the ranked list. Features with higher membership values above the threshold are considered more relevant and selected for further analysis or modeling.

6. **Perform ML:** Use the selected subset of features as input variables for the ML algorithms. The FS process aims to improve the model's performance by reducing dimensionality and focusing on the most informative features [7].

The proposed FL-based FS has been illustrated in Algorithm 1. Moreover, the FL was computed in various stages to select the list of pertinent features $(V = v_1, v_2, v_3, v_4; g_1, g_2, g_3, g_4)$ used in the classification process. Table 5 gives information on the selected feature vector and the length of each vector.

Algorithm 1. Fuzzy Logic-based Feature Selection

Require:
  1: Input features $X = \{x_1, x_2, \ldots, x_n\}$
  2: Triangular membership function parameters a, b, c
Ensure:
  3: Selected features X_{selected}
  4: **function** FUZZYFEATURESELECTION(X, a, b, c)
  5:     Normalize input features X
  6:     Calculate membership degrees $\mu(x; a, b, c)$ for each feature $x \in X$
  7:     Initialize feature importance scores $I = \{0, 0, \ldots, 0\}$
  8:     **for** $i = 1$ to n **do**
  9:         **for** $j = 1$ to n **do**
 10:             $I[i] \leftarrow I[i] + \mu(x_j; a, b, c)$
 11:     Sort features based on importance scores in descending order
 12:     $X_{\text{selected}} \leftarrow$ top-ranked features from X based on I
 13:     **return** X_{selected}

The approach utilized a triangular membership function characterized by three parameters, namely a, b, and c. This membership function assigned a value between 0 and 1 based on how close the data point is to the center (b) of the triangular function. The general form of a triangular membership function

$(\mu(\text{x}))$ is:

$$\begin{cases} \frac{b-a}{x-a} & \text{if } a \leq x \leq b, \\ \frac{c-x}{c-b} & \text{if } b \leq x \leq c, \\ 0 & \text{otherwise,} \end{cases} \quad (9)$$

where μ represents the membership value for a data point x in the UGRansome fuzzy set. The proposed framework consists of components for data preparation, feature selection, modeling, and evaluation. The numerical/categorical inputs of the experimental datasets are normalized (scaled) during the data preparation/pre-processing phase. The Min-Max scaling function shown in Eq. 10 was computed [2].

$$v_{scaled} = \frac{v_n - min(v_n)}{max(v_n) - min(v_n)} \quad (10)$$

This procedure makes sure that the input data stays between [0, 1].

Performance Metrics

The evaluation metrics employed to assess the models developed in this study include precision (PR), recall (RC), accuracy (AC), F1-score (F1S), and empirical error:

$$PR = \frac{TP}{TP + FP} \quad (11)$$

$$RC = \frac{TP}{TP + FN} \quad (12)$$

$$AC = \frac{TP + TN}{TP + TN + FP + FN} \quad (13)$$

$$F1S = 2 \times \frac{PR \times RC}{PR + RC} \quad (14)$$

$$Error = \frac{FP + FN}{TP + TN + FP + FN} \quad (15)$$

Those metrics were calculated using the Confusion Matrix (CM) [5]:

$$CM = \begin{bmatrix} TN & FP \\ FN & TP \end{bmatrix}$$

There are four key categories to consider in the matrix: True Negative (TN) refers to the accurate identification of regular network patterns as non-malicious, while True Positive (TP) represents the correct identification of intrusions as malicious activities [3]. On the other hand, False Positive (FP) items are non-intrusive activities that are mistakenly categorized as intrusions [12]. Lastly, False Negative (FN) encompasses hostile network patterns that are incorrectly labeled as normal or non-malicious [1]. The F1S is the harmonic mean of the PR and RC. Additionally, the receiver operating characteristic (ROC) curves for each selected method were also computed. The ROC curve was used to calculate the area under the curve (AUC) of each model. The AUC's range is restricted to [0, 1], and values closer to 1 indicate a successful classification method.

6   Results

The experimentation was carried out using two classification procedures such as the binary and multi-class classification processes. Five labels from the NSL-KDD dataset were taken into consideration during both processes (DoS: 4, Probe: 3, U2R: 2, R2L: 1, and Normal: 0). For the UGRansome dataset, three labels were taken into consideration (SS: 2, S: 1, and A: 0).

6.1   Binary Classification Results

The RF algorithm, which uses $v_2 - v_4$ and has a validation accuracy (VAC) value of 99.8%, has the highest performance values in terms of VAC. The DT had an accuracy rate of 89.1% and had the highest testing accuracy (TAC) values. The DT used v_3 to achieve a VAC of 99.8%, PR of 95.0%, RC of 80.6%, and F1S of 87.0%. The classifier that produced the highest performance results in terms of PR was the RF, which used $v_1 - v_4$ to achieve a VAC rating of 99.9%. Similar to this, the best NB model achieved a score of 80.6% in terms of TAC. When compared to the NSL-KDD dataset, the experiment shows a modest performance improvement with the UGRansome dataset. The ROC curves produced by each model (XGB, ET, RF, SVM, DT, and NB) were displayed to assess the effectiveness of the classification process using the AUC metric. The feature vectors v_1, v_3, and v_4 produced similar outcomes. The baseline classifiers (NB and SVM) on the other hand, obtained AUCs of 62% and 64%, respectively. In conclusion, tree-based models had the best binary classification performance. The AUCs measurements found in Fig. 2 provide evidence in favor of this performance. The plot on the left side shows the ROC curves of each model tested and trained with the NSL-KDD. The plot on the right shows the ROC curves of each model tested and trained with the UGRansome.

6.2   Multi-class Classification Results

The XGB had the highest TAC value, with a score of 89.8% using g_2 (Table 6). Moreover, the classifier that produced the highest performance values in terms of VAC was the RF, which used $g_1 - g_4$ and had a VAC value of 99% (Table 6). The CM depicts that selected models were successful in identifying attack types such as anomaly (A), DoS, probe, normal, signature (S), and synthetic signature (SS) in both datasets (Fig. 3). Figure 3 portrays the overall classification results. A comparative analysis with existing methodologies of the IDS literature has been illustrated in Table 7.

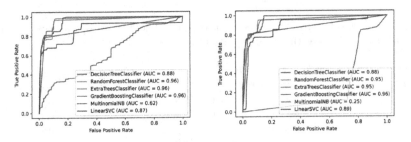

Fig. 2. ROC curve analysis of each model using extracted features

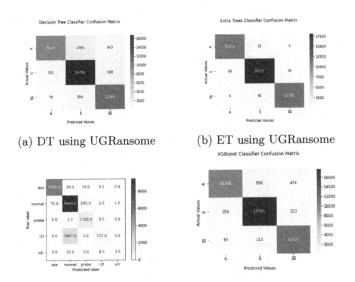

(a) DT using UGRansome

(b) ET using UGRansome

(c) NSL-KDD classification using (d) UGRansome classification us-
XGB   ing XGB

Fig. 3. Classification results for the UGRansome and NSL-KDD

The proposed methodology outperformed works presented in Table 7 due to the fuzzy logic that acted as a feature selector approach. The proposed methodology surpassed results obtained by Zhang et al. [8], Tama et al. [9], Sarumi et al. [10], Tokmak [6], and Lobato et al. [14].

Table 5. Selected features using the FL procedure. These features/patterns are found in both datasets in detecting zero-day attacks.

Dataset	Vector	Length	List of features	0-day detection?
NSL-KDD	v_1	11	logged in, flag	Yes
			num access file, num outbound cmds	Yes
	v_2	9	dst host srv diff host rate	Yes
			src bytes	Yes
	v_3	9	num access files, is guest login	Yes
			same srv rate	No
	v_4	10	protocol type, flag	Yes
			land	No
			same srv rate	No
UGRansome	v_1	11	Locky, CryptXXX	Yes
			CryptoLocker, EDA2	Yes
			Globe	Yes
	v_2	9	S	Yes
			B, C, D	No
	v_3	20	Blacklisting	Yes
			1GZKujBR, 8e372GN, Crypt	Yes
			WannaCry, CryptoLocker, EDA2	Yes
			Globe	Yes
	v_4	14	UDP	No
			TCP	No
			B	No
			Blacklisting, SSH	Yes
NSL-KDD	g_1	14	duration, service, urgent, files	Yes
			access, outbound	Yes
	g_2	19	attempted, root, shells, access files count, srv count, error rate,	Yes
			src bytes	Yes
	g_3	20	rate, rv rate, host count	Yes
			same srv rate	No
	g_4	10	protocol type, flag	Yes
			land	No
			same srv rate	No
UGRansome	g_1	13	1DA11mPS, 1NKi9AK5	Yes
			1GZKujBR, 1AEoiHY2	Yes
			Globe	Yes
	g_2	9	S	Yes
			17dcMo4V, 1KZKcvxn	Yes
	g_3	20	1BonuSr7, 1sYSTEMQ	Yes
			18e372GN, 1Clag5cd, 1DiCeTjB	Yes
			1Lc7xTpP, WannaCry, CryptoLocker, EDA2	Yes
			NoobCrypt	Yes
	g_4	14	DMALocker	Yes
			NoobCrypt	Yes
			CryptoLocker20	Yes
			Blacklisting, SSH	Yes

Table 6. Binary classification performance results obtained from the UGRansome dataset

Classifier	Vector	VAC	TAC	PR	RC	F1S
NB	v_1	84.2%	78.6%	77.4%	61.5%	74.7%
XGB	v_1	98.3%	86.0%	95.1%	75.2%	86.0%
ET	v_1	98.6%	85.4%	96.0%	77.0%	85.6%
RF	v_1	99.9%	87.5%	96.5%	78.5%	86.4%
SVM	v_1	90%	80%	94%	63%	75%
DT	v_1	**99.3%**	86.8%	96.1%	78.6%	85.3%
NB	v_2	**90.5%**	**80.2%**	95.3%	63.6%	74.7%
XGB	v_2	99.2%	86.3%	96.1%	75.3%	84.4%
ET	v_2	99.0%	86.1%	95.3%	74.4%	84.8%
RF	v_2	**99.9%**	87.4%	96.3%	76.7%	85.1%
SVM	v_2	91.1%	**88.8%**	89.1%	77.8%	84.1%
DT	v_2	99.1%	88.4%	95.3%	**80.4%**	87.8%
NB	v_3	88.9%	**80.4%**	93.1%	61.4%	73.3%
XGB	v_3	99.7%	86.1%	96.0%	74.1%	82.6%
ET	v_3	99.6%	86.4%	95.3%	73.4%	82.6%
RF	v_3	**99.9%**	87.4%	97.4%	76.6%	85.8%
SVM	v_3	95.1%	80.4%	90.1%	65.2%	76.4%
DT	v_3	**99.9%**	**90.1%**	96.3%	85.9%	88.7%
NB	v_4	88.3%	80.6%	98.1%	60.8%	74.1%
XGB	v_4	99.5%	87.3%	96.3%	77.5%	86.3%
ET	v_4	99.8%	88.8%	96.5%	78.4%	86.6%
RF	v_4	**99.9%**	87.3%	97.6%	76.4%	85.3%
SVM	v_4	**96%**	81%	91%	66%	77%
DT	v_4	99%	**89.0%**	95.8%	80.7%	87.1%

Table 7. Comparative analysis with previous studies

No	Author	Method	Accuracy	Advantage	Limitation
1	Zhang et al. [8]	DNN	82%	True positive rate	Biases
2	Tama et al. [9]	FS	91%	True negative rate	Data normalization
3	Sarumi et al. [10]	SVM	98%	Classification	Empirical error
4	Suthar et al. [4]	FS	–	Internet protocol	Weak evaluation
5	Tokmak [6]	DL	97%	PSO	Feature scaling
6	Kasongo [2]	GA	98%	FS	Legacy data
7	Lobato et al. [14]	SVM	90%	0-day detection	False positive/negative

6.3   Zero-Day Attack Prediction

The proposed framework exhibited promising performance in predicting advanced persistent threats (APTs), including the notorious Razy attack (Fig. 4). However, it did not demonstrate its effectiveness in effectively countering such threats, which are known for their sophisticated and evolving nature [3,12]. This discussion underscores the significance of detecting unknown attacks, such as EDA (Fig. 4). To enhance its capabilities, the proposed framework should be expanded to include real-time monitoring and adaptive defense mechanisms, enabling proactive protection against zero-day attacks [15]. In future work, the authors intend to explore the application of a heuristic feature selection technique specifically for zero-day threat detection.

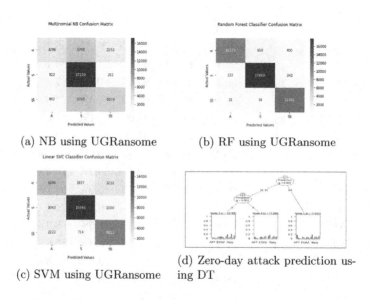

(a) NB using UGRansome

(b) RF using UGRansome

(c) SVM using UGRansome

(d) Zero-day attack prediction using DT

Fig. 4. Classification and prediction using the UGRansome

7   Conclusion

This paper presents a computational framework for defending critical infrastructures against intrusions and security threats. It incorporates feature selection through fuzzification and evaluates the effectiveness using machine learning models with the NSL-KDD and UGRansome datasets. The study demonstrates the superior performance of fuzzy logic and ensemble learning in detecting zero-day attacks, outperforming previous methods in intrusion detection systems.

References

1. Rege, A., Bleiman, R.: A free and community-driven critical infrastructure ransomware dataset. In: Onwubiko, C., et al. (eds.) Proceedings of the International Conference on Cybersecurity, Situational Awareness and Social Media. Springer Proceedings in Complexity, pp. 25–37. Springer, Singapore (2023). https://doi.org/10.1007/978-981-19-6414-5_2
2. Kasongo, S.M.: Genetic algorithm based feature selection technique for optimal intrusion detection. Preprints (2021)
3. Nkongolo, M., Van Deventer, J.P., Kasongo, S.M.: Ugransome1819: a novel dataset for anomaly detection and zero-day threats. Information **12**(10), 405 (2021)
4. Suthar, F., Patel, N., Khanna, S.: A signature-based botnet (emotet) detection mechanism. Int. J. Eng. Trends Technol. **70**, 185–193 (2022)
5. Shankar, D., George, G.V.S., Janardhana Naidu, J.N.S.S., Madhuri, P.S.: Deep analysis of risks and recent trends towards network intrusion detection system. Int. J. Adv. Comput. Sci. Appl. **14**(1) (2023)
6. Tokmak, M.: Deep forest approach for zero-day attacks detection. Innov. Technol. Eng. 45–56 (2022). ISBN 978-625-6382-83-1
7. Nkongolo, M., van Deventer, J.P., Kasongo, S.M.: The application of cyclostationary malware detection using Boruta and PCA. In: Smys, S., Lafata, P., Palanisamy, R., Kamel, K.A. (eds.) Computer Networks and Inventive Communication Technologies. Lecture Notes on Data Engineering and Communications Technologies, vol. 141, pp. 547–562. Springer Nature Singapore, Singapore (2023). https://doi.org/10.1007/978-981-19-3035-5_41
8. Zhang, C., Ruan, F., Yin, L., Chen, X., Zhai, L., Liu, F.: A deep learning approach for network intrusion detection based on NSL-KDD dataset. In: 2019 IEEE 13th International Conference on Anti-counterfeiting, Security, and Identification (ASID), pp. 41–45. IEEE (2019)
9. Tama, B.A., Comuzzi, M., Rhee, K.-H.: TSE-IDS: a two-stage classifier ensemble for intelligent anomaly-based intrusion detection system. IEEE Access **7**, 94 497–94 507 (2019)
10. Sarumi, O.A., Adetunmbi, A.O., Adetoye, F.A.: Discovering computer networks intrusion using data analytics and machine intelligence. Sci. Afr. **9**, e00500 (2020). https://www.sciencedirect.com/science/article/pii/S2468227620302386
11. Maglaras, L., Janicke, H., Ferrag, M.A.: Combining security and reliability of critical infrastructures: the concept of securability, p. 10387 (2022)
12. Nkongolo, M., Van Deventer, J.P., Kasongo, S.M., Zahra, S.R., Kipongo, J.: A cloud based optimization method for zero-day threats detection using genetic algorithm and ensemble learning. Electronics **11**(11), 1749 (2022)
13. Javaheri, D., Gorgin, S., Lee, J.-A., Masdari, M.: Fuzzy logic-based DDoS attacks and network traffic anomaly detection methods: classification, overview, and future perspectives. Inf. Sci. (2023)
14. Lobato, A.G.P., Lopez, M.A., Sanz, I.J., Cardenas, A.A., Duarte, O.C.M., Pujolle, G.: An adaptive real-time architecture for zero-day threat detection. In: 2018 IEEE International Conference on Communications (ICC), pp. 1–6. IEEE (2018)
15. Nkongolo, M., van Deventer, J.P., Kasongo, S.M., van der Walt, W.: Classifying social media using deep packet inspection data. In: Ranganathan, G., Fernando, X., Rocha, Á. (eds.) Inventive Communication and Computational Technologies. LNNS, vol. 383, pp. 543–557. Springer, Singapore (2022). https://doi.org/10.1007/978-981-19-4960-9_43

A Verification Tool for Real-Time Task Schedulability Analysis

Madoda Nxumalo[1,2]([✉]) [iD], Nils Timm[1] [iD], and Stefan Gruner[1] [iD]

[1] Department of Computer Science, University of Pretoria, Pretoria, South Africa
{mnxumalo,ntimm,sg}@cs.up.ac.za
[2] Department of Computer Science, University of Eswatini, Kwaluseni, Eswatini
manxumalo@uniswa.sz

Abstract. We present a tool that implements a spotlight abstraction technique for model checking the schedulability of real-time tasks in operating systems. We present the implemented model checking approach, tool features, usage, and a performance evaluation of the tool. The model checking approach applies spotlight abstraction that partitions the task queue under schedulability analysis into a so-called 'spotlight' and a 'shade' to combat the state-space complexity. Iteratively, the schedulability analysis of the spotlight is undertaken over an abstract model of the system under consideration. In each iteration, the tasks from the shade are brought to the spotlight, and model checking can proceed until a decisive schedulability result is obtained. Empirical results for the schedulability analysis of real-time tasks showed that definite model checking results can be obtained within reasonable run-time.

Keywords: Timed Automata · Model Checking · Three-Valued Abstraction · Schedulability

1 Introduction

This paper presents the implementation of an abstraction technique that enables the efficient *model checking of schedulability properties* of real-time operating systems (RTOS). *Schedulability analysis* determines whether a given set of real-time tasks under a particular scheduling policy can meet all of its deadline constraints.

Spotlight abstraction [Schrieb et al., 2009] is used to partition the task queue under schedulability analysis into a so-called 'spotlight' and a 'shade'. The spotlight consists of a predefined number of tasks at the front of the queue which allows for the construction of an abstract model with a small-sized state space. The remaining tasks are kept in the shade. Iteratively, the schedulability analysis of the spotlight is undertaken over an abstract system model. If the model checking results are inconclusive more tasks from the shade are brought to the spotlight and the subsequent iteration of model checking proceeds. An inconclusive result (also called a partial result) occurs when the abstract task-set in the

© The Author(s), under exclusive license to Springer Nature Switzerland AG 2023
A. Gerber and M. Coetzee (Eds.): SAICSIT 2023, CCIS 1878, pp. 48–60, 2023.
https://doi.org/10.1007/978-3-031-39652-6_4

spotlight has been resolved to be schedulable by the model checker, however, the schedulability of the remaining tasks in the shade is not yet decided. The iterations are repeated until a decisive schedulability result is obtained.

Our tool TVMC supports the schedulability analysis under the non-preemptive 'first in first out' (FIFO), the priority-based dynamic 'earliest deadline first' (EDF), the 'longest remaining time first' (LRTF) and the 'highest response ratio next' (HRRN) policies of scheduling for a uniprocessor system. We also present experimental results that compare the performance of TVMC against the Uppaal [Larsen et al., 1997] platform-based RTLib [Shan et al., 2016] and the Timestool [Amnell et al., 2003]. The empirical results focus on whether the schedulability property holds for the analysed task set, the execution times of each experiment, and the *sizes of the problems* such as the state space of the abstract model and queue sizes.

2   Related Work

UPPAAL [Larsen et al., 1997, David et al., 2009] is a widely used framework for model checking, validation, and verification of real-time systems. It supports various types of problems, including schedulability analysis [Ahn et al., 2016] and planning in robot systems [Foughali and Hladik, 2020, Mikucionis et al., 2010]. RTLIB [Shan et al., 2016] is a library of tools that contains Uppaal templates that describe the behavior of real-time systems schedulers. The templates are loaded into UPPAAL and then the schedulability properties are verified on the UPPAAL platform. RTLIB templates are for task models that describe hard real-time systems, weakly hard real-time systems, and sporadic task models. Hard real-time systems adhere to strict deadlines such that a failure to meet a single deadline leads to a system failure. A weakly hard real-time system is tolerate its met and missed deadlines to a clearly specified a bounded window of time. Sporadic real-time tasks are hard and reoccur at any random instant.

The TIMESTOOL [Amnell et al., 2003, Fersman et al., 2002] is a front-end for UPPAAL that implements schedulability analysis of real-time tasks. It supports the schedulability analysis for task sets that implement preemptive and non-preemptive scheduling policies such as rate monotonic, and earliest deadline scheduling policies. TIMESTOOL, UPPAAL and TVMC are all based on model checking algorithms adopted from [Bengtsson and Yi, 2003].

TIMESTOOL and UPPAAL support multiple features, e.g. simulations, compile error handling, and several scheduling policies. The difference between UPPAAL and TIMESTOOL is that the latter is specialized in the verification of schedulability analysis while the former model checks different types of properties, e.g. mutual exclusion, for various types of real-time problems. TIMESTOOL even implements code synthesis to compile the model into executable code. Our tool supports four scheduling policies, and it offers the verification of real-time schedulability analysis for larger task-sets.

Rather than using timed automata models of real-time systems behavior to verify schedulability properties, some tools develop and implement frameworks. A recently proposed schedulability analysis tool is SET-MRTS [Chen

et al., 2022] which provides a framework to implement the schedulability analyses. The schedulability test collection and toolkit SCHEDCAT [Brandenburg
and Gul, 2016] provides a framework of the kernel that contains reusable components which can be adapted for different types of schedulability tests. Unlike
SCHEDCAT, SET-MRTS provides a fully developed framework that integrates
all utilities for schedulability tests. Cheddar [Singhoff et al., 2004] is another
framework to perform schedulability analysis which provides tools to verify if
models of the real-time system meet their time constraints.

3   Technical Details

In an iterative approach, *spotlight abstraction* [Schrieb et al., 2009] is applied to a
queue that contains the real-time tasks to be analysed. This queue is partitioned
into two sets called 'spotlight' and 'shade' [Timm, 2013]. Figure 1 shows the
two portions; the spotlight and the shade. Algorithm 1 implements the spotlight
abstraction technique in TVMC. The time complexity of Algorithm 1 is $O(n^2)$.
In the first iteration, Lines 4–7 of the algorithm select the first k tasks at the
front of the queue as the spotlight.

The shade of the first iteration contains the tasks that would be extracted
from the queue after the spotlight tasks have been scheduled. Lines 8–10 create one abstract task that summarises the properties of the tasks in the shade
in an approximative manner. The concrete spotlight tasks together with the
summarising abstract task now form an abstract queue, as shown in Fig. 2.

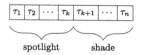

Fig. 1. A queue with n tasks

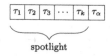

Fig. 2. Queue from Fig. 1 in abstract form

Algorithm 1 3vSpotAbstraction

Input: k, q, Π;

1: $\varphi = $ **true**;
2: $visited = A = \emptyset$;
3: **while** $(q \neq \emptyset)$ **do**
4:    **for** $(\tau_i \in q[0, k])$ **do**
5:       $p = q.pop()$;
6:       $q'.add(p)$;
7:    **end for**
8:    **if** $(q \neq \emptyset)$ **then**
9:       $q'.add(\tau_\alpha)$;
10:    **end if**
11:    $A.addAll(q')$;
12:    $nta = buildNTA(A, \Pi)$;
13:    $\varphi' = abstractProperty(A)$;
14:    $\varphi = 3vChecker(nta, \varphi', visited)$;
15:    **if** $(\varphi == $ **false**$)$ **then**
16:       **return** not schedulable;
17:    **end if**
18: **end while**
19: **return** schedulable;

From the abstract queue and the processor, an abstract system is modeled as a network of timed automata in Line 12. Timed automata Alur [1994] are used as the system models in the TVMC tool, which are finite-state machines extended with continuous real-valued variables (clocks) used to measure time delays. The abstract system model is a parallel composition of timed automata, one for each concrete task (e.g. Figure 3) belonging to the spotlight, one for the processor (Fig. 5), and one for the abstract task (Fig. 4).

Figure 5 shows a standard processor model that is *in use* when a task has acquired the processor, and that is *available* after the processor released a task. Figure 3 shows a model of a typical concrete task with $\{init, inQueue,$ *Run, Terminate, Error*$\}$ states. The associated actions are $\{enqueue, acquire,$ *release, abort, requestNew*$\}$. The variables x and y are deadline and execution time constraints, respectively. $x = (c_i \leq D_i)$ is the proposition that the clock valuation c_i is not greater than the deadline D_i. $y = (e_{t_i} \leq W_i)$ is the proposition that the execution time e_{t_i} is not greater than the worst-case execution time (WCET) W_i. The timed-automation model of the abstract task $\tau_\alpha = (O_\alpha, W_\alpha, D_\alpha, P_\alpha)$ is shown in Fig. 4. This model summarizes the properties of the tasks in the shade. The abstract task τ_α is a tuple consisting of the minimum occurrence O_α, minimum least WCET W_α, minimum deadline D_α, and minimum period P_α of the tasks in the shade. Since it is an *abstract* task, it does not execute and reach a *Run* state, instead, it reaches a *Pause*$_\alpha$ state that causes the model checker to pause and allow the iterative algorithm to load more tasks from the concrete queue into the abstract queue.

Line 13 defines the schedulability property for the tasks in the abstract queue. In line 14 of Algorithm 1, the schedulability property of the abstract system

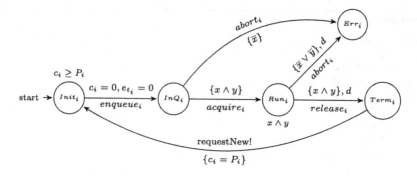

Fig. 3. A task model τ_i

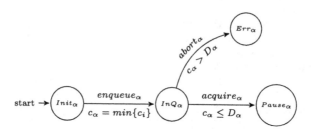

Fig. 4. An abstract task model τ_α

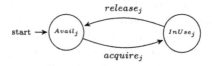

Fig. 5. A processor model π_j

model is verified, using Algorithm 2. This model checking algorithm is a modified version of the standard forward reachability analysis algorithm [Bengtsson and Yi, 2003]. The modifications made on the model checking algorithm accommodate *Pause* behavior required by the abstract task τ_α (see Lines 12–16 of Algorithm 2). The potential behaviour of the tasks in the shade is coarsely abstracted and represented by τ_α in the abstract system model.

In Lines 15 to 18, Algorithm 1 decides whether to initiate the next iteration or to terminate based on the model checking result. The complexity of Algorithm 2 is $O(n^2)$. The maximum complexity for algorithms that executes the DBMs is $O(n^3)$ [Lu et al., 2012]. An example of a DBM algorithm for constraint satisfaction, i.e., $z \not\models \varphi$ has a complexity of $O(n^2)$. If the model checker returns an inconclusive result, then the abstraction algorithm transfers more tasks from the shade to the spotlight and updates the concrete and abstract task models accordingly. After the update, the next iteration of model checking can proceed. These iterative steps are repeated until

---

Algorithm 2 3vChecker

Input: $nta, \varphi', visited$

1: $z = nta(\langle l_0, Z_0 \rangle)$;
2: $wait = paused = \emptyset$
3: $wait.add(\langle l_0, Z_0 \rangle)$;
4: **while** $(wait \neq \emptyset)$**or**$(paused == \emptyset)$ **do**
5:    $z = wait.pop()$;
6:    **if** $(z \not\models \varphi')$ **then**
7:       **return false**;
8:    **end if**
9:    **if** $(Z \not\subseteq Z', \forall \langle l, Z' \rangle \in visited)$ **then**
10:       $visited.add(z)$;
11:       **for** $\langle l', Z' \rangle : \langle l, D \rangle \rightarrowtail \langle l', D' \rangle$ **do**
12:          **if** $(l' \notin Pause_\alpha)$ **then**
13:             $wait.add(z')$;
14:          **else**
15:             $paused.add(z)$;
16:          **end if**
17:       **end for**
18:    **end if**
19: **end while**
20: **return true**;

---

a definite schedulability result (*true* or *false*) is obtained. This approach reduces the whole model checking problem into smaller sub-problems by exploiting the order of operations on queues. In the performance evaluation, we will show that the abstraction-based approach enables significantly better model checking runtimes in comparison to an approach that analyses the concrete system directly.

By means of a running example adopted from [Stallings, 2011, Chap. 10] we demonstrate how TVMC works. Consider a queue q with five tasks where it has to be determined whether all tasks are schedulable under the EDF policy. A task is characterized by the quadruple $\tau = (Occurrence, WCET, deadline, period)$, where $WCET$ denotes the *worst case execution time* and $Occurrence$ stands for the arrival time. The concrete queue is given by $q = \{\tau_A, \tau_B, \tau_C, \tau_D \tau_E\}$ with $\tau_A = (10, 20, 110, 110)$, $\tau_B = (20, 20, 20, 20)$, $\tau_C = (40, 20, 50, 50)$, $\tau_D = (50, 20, 90, 90)$, and $\tau_E = (60, 20, 70, 70)$. Moreover, the input parameter $k = 3$ is the maximum number of spotlight tasks in each iteration. Based on the EDF queuing policy the queue gets re-ordered to $q = \{\tau_B, \tau_C, \tau_E, \tau_D, \tau_A\}$. The first three tasks at the front of q form the *spotlight* and they are placed in an abstract queue. The remaining tasks τ_D and τ_A form the *shade*. The parameters of the shade tasks are used to generate one abstract task $\tau_\alpha = (40, 20, 70, 70)$. The parameters of τ_α are formed by the *minimum* occurrence, *minimum* period, *minimum* WCET, and *minimum* deadline of the parameters of τ_D and τ_A. From the spotlight tasks and the abstract task, i.e., $q_a = \{\tau_B, \tau_C, \tau_E, \tau_\alpha\}$, an abstract timed automaton is generated using the parallel composition of timed automata consisting of a model of the processor and models of each task in q_a.

The model checking algorithm, whose input parameters are the abstract timed automaton A_a and the abstract task queue q_a, is invoked. The abstract timed automaton is explored over q_a. While the model checking algorithm runs, the spotlight tasks τ_B, τ_C, τ_E are removed from q_a and it is verified that these tasks will terminate within their deadlines. When the clock valuation of the abstract task is 80, then the abstract task which represents the shade will be at the front of q_a. Once the abstract task is removed from q_a, the $Pause_\alpha$ state is reached, the current model checking run is paused and the subsequent iteration is initiated in order to consider the tasks in the shade.

In the second iteration, the remaining two tasks are placed in an updated abstract queue $q'_a = \{\tau_D, \tau_A\}$, and an updated abstract timed automaton A'_a is generated accordingly. Eventually, the model checking algorithm resumes exploring A'_a. It will be verified that both τ_D and τ_A will terminate within their specified deadlines. The tool then returns that the original task queue q is schedulable since all tasks reached the *terminate* state and none reached the *error* state.

4   Features of the Tool

We now highlight the features of our tool (TVMC). Model checking schedulability of real-time task-sets using *iterative spotlight abstraction* is the major feature of the tool. If the queue is not divided into a spotlight and a shade, then the tool can also model check a concrete scheduler queue. However, *directly* model checking the abstract task queue is limited to task-sets with a maximum size of five tasks. For larger task sets, the direct approach fails due to exhaustion of memory. The tool supports schedulability checking under the following scheduling policies: FIFO, EDF, LRTF, and HRRN.

The tool works with the following inputs: The user provides the task-set either via a prepared text file or via a randomly generated task-set. By selecting the randomly generated task-set, the size of the task-set must be specified as an input. If the task-set is obtained from a text file, then the file name is a required parameter. Refer to Fig. 6 for an example of the input task-set file. The input task-set is an array whose list entries are the tasks. Each task is a class object that is characterized by variables representing the name of the task, the WCET, the deadline, and the period. An additional input parameter is the selection of the scheduling policy to be applied. The tool accommodates the task arrival times of the tasks in the task-set. By default, all the tasks have an arrival time of zero. In the input example, see Fig. 6, the occurrence of all the tasks is 0. The user is also required to input the maximum size of the spotlight queue that will be enforced by the abstraction algorithm in each iteration. If the user wants to verify the schedulability property of an input task-set without enforcing the spotlight abstraction technique, the user simply sets the input maximum size of the spotlight queue to be the size of the input task-set.

Upon the start of the schedulability analysis, the task-set is sorted as per the chosen scheduling policy and printed in an output file. In each iteration of model checking, the tasks in the spotlight and in the shade are printed. Furthermore, the

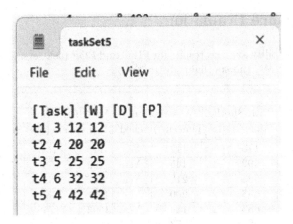

Fig. 6. An example of the input text file.

size, i.e., the number of states and transitions, of the abstract timed automaton that is formed by the spotlight tasks is also printed and saved in an output file. Once the tool has terminated, with a definite schedulability result (*true* or *false*), the time required for the analysis is written into an output file. The tool also reports if the task-set is schedulable or not. If the task-set is not schedulable then a counterexample is printed into an output file. Figure 7 displays an example of an output file for the input task-set in 6. The first couple of lines in Fig. 7 show the number of clocks, states and transitions for each spotlight abstraction iteration. Then the number of spotlight abstraction iterations, the schedulability result, and the execution times are also printed. The tool is available in Github[1] where the source code, user guide, experiments, and other related documentation can be found.

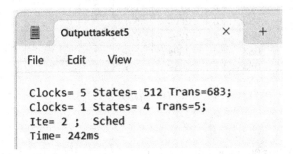

Fig. 7. An example of the output file.

[1] https://github.com/MadodaNxumalo/TVMC-On-RTOS.

5   Performance Evaluation

Table 1. Schedulability analysis results for FIFO and EDF task-sets: TVMC (spotlight abstraction) vs TVMC (no spotlight abstraction).

FIFO							
	With Spotlight Abstraction				No Abstraction		
Tasks	Trans/Ite	Ite	Time(ms)	Sched?	Trans	Time(ms)	Sched?
3	115	1	112	Yes	115	75	Yes
4	492	1	145	Yes	492	166	Yes
5	683	2	212	Yes	2085	458	Yes
6	683	2	200	Yes	8794	3350	Yes
7	683	2	183	Yes	36935	71765	Yes
8	683	2	273	Yes	*	*	*
9	683	3	225	Yes	*	*	*
11	683	3	300	No	*	*	*
13	683	4	326	Yes	*	*	*
16	686	4	396s	No	*	*	*
20	683	5	481s	Yes	*	*	*

(a) FIFO

EDF							
	With Spotlight Abstraction				No Abstraction		
Tasks	Trans/Ite	Ite	Time(ms)	Sched?	Trans	Time(ms)	Sched?
3	115	1	64s	Yes	115	68s	Yes
4	492	1	136s	Yes	492	165s	Yes
5	683	2	150s	Yes	2085	399s	Yes
6	683	2	191s	No	8794	3066s	No
7	683	2	195s	Yes	36935	69549s	Yes
8	683	2	213s	Yes	*	*	*
9	683	3	272s	Yes	*	*	*
11	683	3	260s	No	*	*	*
13	683	4	328s	Yes	*	*	*
16	683	4	339s	No	*	*	*
20	683	5	541s	No	*	*	*

(b) EDF

This section presents the empirical results of applying our approach to verify schedulability properties. Our tool is compared against the well-established TIMESTOOL and the Uppaal platform-based RTLIB to analyze FIFO and EDF queues. The experiments were run on an Intel i7 at 2.30 Ghz processor running on Windows. We show the execution times and the 'factual' schedulability results (true/false) of the analysis. The models were generated using a pseudo-random task-set generating approach [Bertout et al., 2014]. TIMESTOOL and

Table 2. Schedulability analysis results for FIFO and EDF task-sets: TVMC (spotlight abstraction) vs TIMESTOOL vs UPPAAL-RTLIB

FIFO

Tasks	Iterations	Spotlight Abstraction		Times Tool		Uppaal-RTLib	
		Time	Sched?	Time	Sched?	Time	Sched?
2	1	0s121	Yes	1s10	Yes	0s007	Yes
3	1	0s79	Yes	1s13	Yes	0s009	Yes
5	2	0s232	Yes	1s27	Yes	0s013	Yes
7	2	0s216	Yes	30s21	Yes	0s024	Yes
9	3	0s258	Yes	20m12s71	EBA	0s055	Yes
11	3	0s289	Yes	2m34s21	EBA	N/A	N/A
13	4	0s351	Yes	4m55s30	EBA	N/A	N/A
15	4	0s371	No	9m31s01	EBA	N/A	N/A
20	5	0s405	Yes	12m34s41	EBA	N/A	N/A
50	6	7s062	No	N/A	N/A	N/A	N/A
100	7	13s785	No	N/A	N/A	N/A	N/A
200	6	29s377	No	N/A	N/A	N/A	N/A
500	10	76s189	No	N/A	N/A	N/A	N/A

(a) FIFO

EDF

Tasks	Iterations	Spotlight Abstraction		Times Tool		Uppaal-RTLib	
		Time	Sched?	Time	Sched?	Time	Sched?
2	1	0s31	Yes	1s23	Yes	0s007	Yes
3	1	1s10	Yes	1s10	Yes	0.006	Yes
5	2	2s27	Yes	12m02s67	Yes	0s030	Yes
7	2	1s86	Yes	9m01s03	SCL	0s044	Yes
9	3	3s18	No	10s35	SCL	0s055	No
11	3	3s27	Yes	10s55	SCL	N/A	N/A
13	4	3s21	Yes	20s44	SCL	N/A	N/A
15	4	4s41	No	8m11s12	SCL	N/A	N/A
20	5	4s178	Yes	15m33s43	SCL	N/A	N/A
50	9	9s217	No	N/A	N/A	N/A	N/A
100	11	15s931	No	N/A	N/A	N/A	N/A
200	7	33s740	No	N/A	N/A	N/A	N/A
500	13	78s650	No	N/A	N/A	N/A	N/A

(b) EDF

RTLIB do not support scheduling under the policies HRRN and LRTF. Therefore, these policies are not considered in the performance evaluation.

The practical bottleneck of the tool is that it cannot generate timed automata for abstract task-sets with sizes larger than 7. This challenge is highlighted by the experimental results in Table 1 where spotlight-abstraction-based model checking is compared to model checking without abstraction. In the table, the maximum spotlight queue size is 4 tasks in each iteration. "Trans/ite" stands for number of transitions per iteration. (∗) denotes that experiment runs did not terminate due to space explosion. Notably, as the size of the tasksets increase, the execution times of the experiments also increase exponentially for the no-abstraction approach. Meanwhile, the execution time difference for the spotlight abstraction-based approach is not very large as the task-set sizes are increased. For example, comparing the EDF runs for task-set input with sizes 6 and 7, the execution time difference exponential is 36488 ms (69549 ms–3066 ms) for the no-abstraction experiments while it is a mere 4 ms (195 ms–191 ms) for the abstraction based experiments. This observation is supported by the difference in the number of transitions as the task-set sizes are increased. That is, for the EDF runs with task-set input of sizes 6 and 7, the difference in task-set sizes is 28141 (36935–8794) for the standard non-abstraction-based approach while for the abstraction-based approach, each run, with either 6 or 7 tasks has a maximum of 1366 transitions (i.e. 683 × 2). This also shows that the spotlight abstraction algorithm, which manages and prepares the abstract queues for the model checker, does not present any unbearable run-time overhead for the model checking process. However, it improves the performance of the tool.

Table 2 displays the results of the experiments where we compared spotlight abstraction-based TVMC tool to the TIMESTOOL and UPPAAL-RTLIB. In the table, the abbreviations EBA, SCL, and N/A means Exception-St9 Bad Allocation, Server Connection Lost, and Not Applicable, respectively. For all experiments a spotlight size of $k = 4$ was used. Therefore, the number of tasks per iteration used in the experiments is 4. The maximum number of tasks in the spotlight iteration is thus 4 plus 1 abstract task summarizing the shade. The choice of 4 tasks per iteration, rather than 5 or 6 tasks, allows for a quick and guaranteed execution of each spotlight per iteration.

The results demonstrate that for smaller task-sets TVMC executes the schedulability analysis within hundreds of milliseconds for all the considered scheduling policies. For these task-sets TIMESTOOL and RTLIB also run the schedulability analysis in milliseconds, where RTLib is generally the fastest approach. However, when the total number of tasks is greater than 10, RTLib runs out of memory. In experiments with task-sets sizes greater than 9, TIMESTOOL reported a *Server Connection Lost* (SCL) error for EDF queues. TIMESTOOL was ran on a standalone computer, not online in a distributed system environment. For the FIFO counterparts, with task-sets sizes greater than 7, the TIMESTOOL reported heap space exhaustion (*Exception-St9 Bad Allocation*) (EBA). Not Applicable (N/A) means that the results were not computed because the tools did not scale up to support larger task-sets. Our tool was still capable to produce definite schedulability results for larger task-sets due to the spotlight abstraction approach that is iterative and keeps the number of tasks that are considered at the same time small.

6   Conclusions

We presented the features and components of the iterative model checking tool, TVMC, that applies spotlight abstraction to perform the schedulability analysis for real-time task queues. With a supporting example, the technical details of the verification approach were explained. The empirical results showed that TVMC can analyse schedulability within hundreds of milliseconds for both FIFO and EDF task-sets. Thus, it can compete with the well-established TIMESTOOL and RTLIB. Of the three compared approaches RTLib is the fastest for analysing smaller task sets. However, for experiments with larger task-sets, TIMESTOOL and RTLIB reported a server connection loss or a bad memory allocation exception, whereas TVMC was still able to produce a definite schedulability result. This shows that the iterative spotlight abstraction is a promising technique for reducing the complexity of schedulability analysis. It enables keeping the number of tasks that the model checker has to consider at the same time small, and thus, also succeeds when larger task-sets are analysed.

The results presented did not explore larger task-sets because the established tools TIMESTOOL and Uppaal that are compared with TVMC do not support larger task-sets. Due to its iterative nature, the TVMC approach is scalable for larger task-sets [Nxumalo et al., 2021]. Currently, the challenge with real-time system models is that there are no publicly available benchmarks which can be used to determine the applicability of our approach to larger task-sets. Further evaluation will be explored to determine the effectiveness of our approach for larger task-sets.

Our plans for future work include incorporating pre-emptive task scheduling for dynamic and priority schedulers, which is one of the major challenges in model checking schedulability properties. This can be implemented by using the binary-search inspired technique [Foughali and Hladik, 2020] to model dynamic schedulers. For future work, the performance of the tool over a wider range of task-set sizes, different types of tasks, more scheduling policies, under different hardware or operating system configurations will be explored extensively.

References

Ahn, S.J., Hwang, D., Kang, M., Choi, J.: Hierarchical system schedulability analysis framework using UPPAAL. IEICE Trans. Inf. Syst. **99-D**(8), 2172–2176 (2016)

lur, R., Dill, D.L.: A Theory of Timed Automata. Theor. Comput. Sci. **126**(2), 183–235 (1994). https://doi.org/10.1016/0304-3975(94)90010-8

Amnell, T., Fersman, E., Mokrushin, L., Pettersson, P., Yi, W.: TIMES: a tool for schedulability analysis and code generation of real-time systems. In: Formal Modeling and Analysis of Timed Systems: First International Workshop, FORMATS 2003, Marseille, France, 6–7 September 2003. Revised Papers, pp. 60–72 (2003)

Bengtsson, J., Yi, W.: Timed automata: semantics, algorithms and tools. In: Desel, J., Reisig, W., Rozenberg, G. (eds.) ACPN 2003. LNCS, vol. 3098, pp. 87–124. Springer, Heidelberg (2004). https://doi.org/10.1007/978-3-540-27755-2_3

Bertout, A., Forget, J., Olejnik, R.: Minimizing a real-time task set through task clustering. In: Jan, M., Hedia, B.B., Goossens, J., Maiza, C. (eds.) 22nd International Conference on Real-Time Networks and Systems, RTNS '14, Versaille, France, 8–10 October 2014, p. 23. ACM (2014)

Brandenburg, B.B., Gul, M.: Global scheduling not required: simple, near-optimal multiprocessor real-time scheduling with semi-partitioned reservations. In: RTSS, pp. 99–110. IEEE Computer Society (2016)

Chen, Z., Lei, H., Yang, M.-L., Liao, Y.: SET-MRTS: an empirical experiment tool for real-time scheduling and synchronization. J. Electorn. Sci. Technol. **20**, 100149 (2022)

David, A., Rasmussen, J., Larsen, K., Skou, A.: Model-based framework for schedulability analysis using uppaal 4.1, pp. 93–119 (2009)

Fersman, E., Pettersson, P., Yi, W.: Timed automata with asynchronous processes: schedulability and decidability. In: Katoen, J.-P., Stevens, P. (eds.) TACAS 2002. LNCS, vol. 2280, pp. 67–82. Springer, Heidelberg (2002). https://doi.org/10.1007/3-540-46002-0_6

Foughali, M., Hladik, P.: Bridging the gap between formal verification and schedulability analysis: the case of robotics. J. Syst. Archit. **111**, 101817 (2020)

Larsen, K.G., Pettersson, P., Yi, W.: UPPAAL in a nutshell. Int. J. Softw. Tools Technol. Transf. **1**(1–2), 134–152 (1997)

Lu, Q., Madsen, M., Milata, M., Ravn, S., Fahrenberg, U., Larsen, K.G.: Reachability analysis for timed automata using max-plus algebra. J. Log. Algebraic Methods Program. **81**(3), 298–313 (2012)

Mikučionis, M., et al.: Schedulability analysis using uppaal: herschel-planck case study. In: Margaria, T., Steffen, B. (eds.) ISoLA 2010. LNCS, vol. 6416, pp. 175–190. Springer, Heidelberg (2010). https://doi.org/10.1007/978-3-642-16561-0_21

Nxumalo, M., Timm, N., Gruner, S.: Spotlight abstraction in model checking real-time task schedulability. In: Laarman, A., Sokolova, A. (eds.) SPIN 2021. LNCS, vol. 12864, pp. 63–80. Springer, Cham (2021). https://doi.org/10.1007/978-3-030-84629-9_4

Schrieb, J., Wehrheim, H., Wonisch, D.: Three-valued spotlight abstractions. In: FM 2009: Formal Methods, Second World Congress, Eindhoven, The Netherlands, 2–6 November 2009. Proceedings, pp. 106–122 (2009)

Shan, L., Graf, S., Quinton, S.: RTLib: a library of timed automata for modeling real-time systems. Research report, Grenoble 1 UGA - Université Grenoble Alpe; INRIA Grenoble - Rhone-Alpes (2016)

Singhoff, F., Legrand, J., Nana, L., Marcé, L.: Cheddar: a flexible real time scheduling framework. In: SIGAda, pp. 1–8. ACM (2004)

Stallings, W.: Operating Systems - Internals and Design Principles, 7th ed. Pitman, New Jersey (2011)

Timm, N.: Three-valued abstraction and heuristic-guided refinement for verifying concurrent systems. PhD thesis, University of Paderborn (2013)

Parsing Semi-structured Languages:
A Crochet Pattern to Diagram Translation

Lisa van Staden and Lynette van Zijl[(✉)]

Stellenbosch University, Stellenbosch, South Africa
{lvs,lvzijl}@sun.ac.za

Abstract. Parsers for semi-structured natural languages must be able to parse both structured and free text. The common approach for these parsers is to make use of natural language processing to parse the free text sections. This paper investigates the semi-structured natural language found in crochet patterns. We show that the natural language found in crochet patterns is restrictive enough for typical multi-phase methods used in compilers to parse these patterns. To measure the success of the pattern parsing, we translate patterns to crochet diagrams. Two different parsers are implemented. The first parser creates a uniform, structured representation of the crochet pattern. We define a formal language for this representation, that can be applied to most crochet patterns. The second parser translates the formal language to a crochet diagram. This approach proves to be successful for a wide range of different patterns.

Keywords: semi-structured language · parsing · crochet pattern translators

1 Introduction

A semi-structured natural language is a language that contains formal elements, but these elements can be separated by arbitrary natural language text[1].

Examples of semi-structured languages can usually be found in written text where a specified template is followed. For example, when writing requirements and specifications documents, it is usually expected that one adheres to such a template. Yet, these documents also include natural language. Crochet and knitting patterns consist of common keywords and there are well-known conventions used when writing these patterns, but these patterns also contain some natural language.

This paper will specifically consider crochet patterns and diagrams. Figure 1 shows an example of a text pattern and its corresponding diagram.

Crochet patterns consist of conventionally used keywords that indicate the type of stitch or action to be performed. In Fig. 1, there are many occurrences of

---

[1] Compilers make use of different phases, including lexical analysis, syntactic analysis, semantic analysis and code generation [1].

© The Author(s), under exclusive license to Springer Nature Switzerland AG 2023
A. Gerber and M. Coetzee (Eds.): SAICSIT 2023, CCIS 1878, pp. 61–77, 2023.
https://doi.org/10.1007/978-3-031-39652-6_5

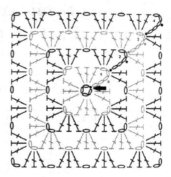

Traditional Granny Square

Square is worked in 4 colors (A,B,C,D)

With A, ch 4 and join with ss to form ring.

Round 1 (RS): With A, ch 5 (counts as 1 dc and 2-ch sp), (3 dc in ring, ch 2) 3 times, 2 dc in ring, join with ss to third ch of starting ch 5. Fasten off A.

Round 2: With B, join with ss to any 2-ch corner sp, ch 5, 3 dc in same corner sp, *ch 1, (3 dc, ch 2, 3 dc) in next ch-2 corner sp; rep from * twice more, ch 1, 2 dc in same corner sp as ch 5 at beg of round, join with ss to third ch of starting ch 5. Fasten off B.

Round 3: With C, join with ss in any 2-ch corner sp, ch 5, 3 dc in same corner sp, *ch 1, 3 dc in next ch-1 sp, ch 1, (3 dc, ch 2, 3 dc) in next 2-ch corner sp; rep from * twice more, ch 1, 3 dc in next ch-1 sp, ch 1, 2 dc in same sp as ch 5 at beg of round, join with ss to third ch of starting ch 5. Fasten off C.

Round 4: With D, join in any 2-ch corner sp, ch 5, 3 dc in same corner sp, *(ch 1, 3 dc in next ch-1 sp) twice, ch 1, (3dc, ch 2, 3 dc) in next 2-ch corner sp; rep from * twice more, (ch 1, 3dc in next ch-1 sp) twice, ch 1, 2 dc in same sp as ch 5 at beg of round, join with ss to third ch of starting ch 5. Fasten off.

Fig. 1. Basic granny square pattern (left) and diagram (right) [10]

keywords like `ch`, `ss` and `dc`. These keywords are abbreviations for `chain, slip stitch` and `double crochet`, respectively. These patterns are usually written in the format of a list of rounds or rows[2], where each row keyword is followed by the row number and then a list of stitch instructions [3]. For example, in Fig. 1, one finds the word `Round` followed by a number and then a list of instructions.

Similarly, crochet diagrams follow a convention. Specific symbols indicate certain stitch types [10]. Figure 2 shows an example of a double crochet (dc) stitch symbol. The use of this symbol can be observed in Fig. 1. The location of these symbols on the diagram correlate to the location of the stitch in the finished crochet project. Hence, one can regard crochet diagrams as a language with formal structure.

Fig. 2. Crochet stitch symbols: chain stitch, single crochet, double crochet, 6-shell double crochet [10]

Comparing a text pattern to the diagram of the same crochet project, it is observed that the stitch abbreviations found in a certain row, correlate to a stitch symbol in that same row in the diagram. As an example, the stitches used in the first round of the crochet pattern seen in Fig. 1, have corresponding symbols in the inner light grey round of the corresponding diagram. Furthermore, the crochet pattern also indicates the parent stitch[3] of each stitch. Figure 3 shows examples of parent stitches.

---

[2] In this paper, the words, `rows` and `rounds` will be used interchangeably. Usually `rows` are used in patterns to be completed row by row and `rounds` are used in patterns to be completed in a circular fashion.

[3] A parent stitch refers to the stitch that is being stitched into.

Fig. 3. Ring parent stitch (left) and double crochet parent stitch (right)

Therefore, by extracting the stitches and their parent stitches in each row, one should be able to calculate the estimated coordinates for each stitch by using geometry and the conventional size and gradient of each symbol, corresponding to that stitch.

The objective of this paper is to find a method to translate the pattern to the diagram. This method should be able to convert a semi-structured text-based language to a structured visual representation.

To extract the stitch information from a crochet pattern, it is necessary to parse the pattern. The standard approach to parse a semi-structured language is to make use of natural language processing. However, the natural language found in crochet patterns is restricted. We will show that it is sufficient to only extract the keywords and a few important words that provide context, to be able to parse the semi-structured language found in crochet patterns.

The method used to translate the text pattern to the diagram will make use of two parsers. One parser will transpile[4] the semi-structured natural language to a self-defined formal text language. The second parser will transpile the self-defined formal text language to the diagram.

Based upon the assumption that the language found in crochet patterns is restrictive enough, this project will show that it is possible to successfully translate crochet patterns to crochet diagrams, using typical multi-phase compiler methods.

2 Related Work

2.1 Translating Semi-structured Natural Language

Usually, the scope of the natural language found in requirements and specifications documents is restricted. Most of the studies concerning the parsing of semi-structured natural language have focused on these types of documents [2,4,5,8]. These studies usually rely on using a combination of different types of parsers. There are two types of parsers to consider. One type is formal language parsers, which are designed to parse rigidly defined syntax efficiently. Another type of parser is a natural language parser, which is good at interpreting free text. Therefore, combining these two types of parsers produces a parser with characteristics of both [6].

Iwama et al. [5] propose a method for constructing a parser for industrial software specifications containing formal and natural language descriptions that

---

[4] A transpiler is a type of compiler that compiles a language that is on a certain abstract level to another language that on the same abstract level [7].

make use of parser combinators. This method consists of writing natural language processing functions and applying them to certain parts of the text.

Osborne et al. [8] show how to remove ambiguities from a controlled language, resulting in a mapping from a semi-structured natural language to a less ambiguous semi-structured natural language. This approach uses natural language processing techniques to produce different parses for ambiguous constructions and choosing the parse branches that are most probable. By training the system with a large set of constructions, the probabilities for unseen constructions can be determined.

Ishihara et al. [4] show a method to translate natural language specifications of communication protocols into algebraic specifications; that is, a translation from a semi-structured natural language into a formal language. Natural language processing and the properties of the target formal language is used to determine the state of the information that has been parsed. Implicit information in the natural language can then be determined by evaluating the current state of the program when parsing the next set of input.

The semi-structured natural language in crochet patterns is typically more structured than the language in requirements and specifications documents. Furthermore, many of the terms used in crochet patterns are abbreviations that are only used in crochet patterns. This means that using natural language processing on the patterns might not be useful or advantageous.

2.2   Crochet Pattern Parsing

To our knowledge, the only other attempt at compiling crochet patterns into diagrams is a Ruby project named Christel [11]. This project consists of a grammar that can be used to write a formal language version of crochet patterns, which can then be rendered to diagrams. Circular crochet patterns are also catered for. However, there are many limitations present in the grammar. The grammar only allows four types of stitches: chain, single crochet, slip stitch and magic ring. The parent stitches are not specified, which means that the combinations of using stitches in each row are limited to one stitch per parent (see Fig. 4 for examples of Christel input).

```
10 ch
10 ch , 4 sc
4 sc in ring , slst
```

Fig. 4. Christel example inputs

Christel cannot be used to parse semi-structured text crochet patterns, as the crochet patterns must be manually rewritten into the formal language.

3   Analysis of Crochet Patterns

For the purpose of this work, we consider traditional crochet patterns that are worked in rounds or rows. Crochet patterns can be written according to British or American conventions[5]. This paper assumes American terminology in all the patterns considered.

To illustrate some of the issues that could occur, Fig. 5 shows a crochet pattern for a hat and a throw. In both cases, each round is a description of a sequence of different stitches interspersed with numerical values, short unstructured text phrases (such as "around each" and "join with") and other keywords[6].

Round 2: Ch 1 loosely, 2 fpdc around beginning
dc-2 (first fpdc), 2 fpdc around each
remaining dc; join with slip st in
first fpdc—14 (16) fpdc.
Round 3: Ch 1 loosely, 2 fpdc around each fpdc
around; join with slip st in first
fpdc—28 (32) fpdc.

Round 2: Ch 3, 2 dc in same st, ch 1, skip next st,
*3 dc in next st, ch 1, skip next st;
repeat from * around, slip st in top of
beginning ch-3 – 24 dc and 8 ch-1 spaces.
Fasten off.

Fig. 5. Hat crochet pattern (top) and throw pattern (bottom)

In Fig. 5, the throw pattern at the bottom has a round that starts with three chains, followed by two double crochet stitches. The number of chains is indicated by the keyword ch followed by a 3, but the number of double crochet stitches (dc) is indicated by first having a 2 that is then followed by the keyword. If the integer that describes the number of stitches can precede or follow the keyword, how does one know which integer is associated with which keyword? In the above example, the distinction can be made by the comma that separates the terms.

The use of the asterisk is also important. The aim of the asterisk to indicate the beginning of a set of instructions that should be repeated.

Crochet is based on stitching into previous stitches, usually from the previous round or row. These previous stitches are known as the parent stitch of the current stitch. In the pattern, the parent stitch is usually indicated by keywords

---

[5] The difference between American and British crochet patterns lie in the terms used for certain stitches. For example, where American patterns use single crochet (sc) or double crochet (dc), British patterns would use double crochet or treble crochet (tr), respectively.

[6] The stitch table at http://www.cs.sun.ac.za/~lvzijl/CrochetSymbols gives a full list of stitches used in our parser.

like in, next and first, which follows after the current stitch. The specific keyword for the parent stitch is not always used in the pattern. The parent stitch is sometimes just referred to as a stitch (in Fig. 5 this is indicated by the keyword st). In other cases, the presence of the parent stitch is only implied, as for example by sc in next.

To create a diagram from a crochet pattern, the stitches used in each row must be extracted. The parents of these stitches must also be extracted, so that the location can be determined. Certain words and characters can be relied on to determine the relation between stitches and to separate stitches from parent stitches.

4   Implementation

4.1   Crogram

To translate the semi-structured natural language found in a crochet pattern to a formal language, we defined a formal language called Crogram. The EBNF for Crogram can be seen in Fig. 10. Note that Crogram is LL(1).

It is important that the formal language indicates what the relative positions of all the stitches are, so that the coordinates can easily be determined by the formal language parser. Crogram defines a language that consists of different rows, where each row contains a list of stitches. For all stitches (except chains) the parent stitch is indicated with indices.

To avoid having a long Crogram text, where each stitch with its parent is written out, Crogram allows repeat rules, operators, and lists and groups of stitches.

In the case that multiple stitches will have the same parent stitch, the stitches can be written as a list on the left of the "->"-symbol. For example, in Fig. 6, the single crochet stitch (SC) is stitched twice into the stitch at index 2 of row 1.

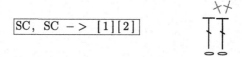

Fig. 6. Crogram example of a list of stitches and a diagram representation.

In the case that one stitch has multiple parent stitches, one can make use of the "&"-operator. For example, in Fig. 7, the single crochet stitch (SC) has three parents in row 1 at indices 1, 2 and 3.

```
SC -> [1][&:1, 2, 3]
# alternatively:
SC -> [1][&:1:3]
```

Fig. 7. Crogram example of "&"-operator and a diagram representation

In the case that one wants to stitch one or multiple stitches into subsequent parent stitches, one can make use of the "|"-operator. For example, in Fig. 8, there are three single crochet stitches (SC) with parent stitches in row 1 with indices 1, 2 and 3, respectively.

```
SC -> [1][|:1, 2, 3]
# alternatively:
SC -> [1][|:1:3]
```

Fig. 8. Crogram example of "|"-operator and a diagram representation

In the case that one wants to stitch a repeated pattern of stitches into subsequent parent stitches, one can make use of the "/"-operator. For example, in Fig. 9, two double crochet stitches (DC) and then one double crochet stitch are stitched in turn into parent stitches in row 2 from indices 1 to 18.

```
(DC, DC), DC -> [2][/:1:18]
```

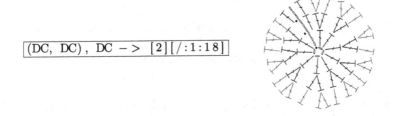

Fig. 9. Crogram example of "/"-operator and a diagram representation

Larger examples are given in the next section.

4.2 Semi-structured Natural Language to Formal Language

As discussed in Sect. 2.1, the common approach to parse semi-structured natural language, is to make use of natural language processing. However, unlike in requirements and specifications documents, the natural language in crochet patterns has a small scope. This paper assumes that the scope is small enough that it is possible to parse the semi-structured natural language by following typical multi-phase compiler methods (with some exceptions).

$\langle pattern \rangle$ ::= $\langle id \rangle$ $\langle body \rangle$

$\langle body \rangle$ ::= $\{\langle index \rangle$ $\langle row \rangle\}$

$\langle row \rangle$ ::= '{' { ($\langle crochet\ chain \rangle$
           | $\langle crochet\ stitch \rangle$) {';' ($\langle crochet\ chain \rangle$
           | $\langle crochet\ stitch \rangle$)} '}'

$\langle crochet\ chain \rangle$ ::= 'CH' [$\langle repeat \rangle$]

$\langle crochet\ stitch \rangle$ ::= ($\langle stitch \rangle$
           | $\langle group \rangle$) {',' ($\langle stitch \rangle$
           | $\langle group \rangle$)} '->' $\langle index \rangle$ [$\langle index \rangle$] [$\langle repeat \rangle$]

$\langle repeat \rangle$ ::= '*' $\langle number \rangle$

$\langle group \rangle$ ::= '(' $\langle stitch \rangle$ {',' ($\langle chain \rangle$
           | $\langle stitch \rangle$)} ')'

$\langle index \rangle$ ::= '[' [$\langle operator \rangle$ ':'] $\langle number \rangle$ [(':' $\langle number \rangle$)
           | {',' $\langle number \rangle$}] ']'

$\langle operator \rangle$ ::= '&'
           | '|'
           | '/'

$\langle stitch \rangle$ ::= ? A stitch abbreviation ?

$\langle id \rangle$ ::= $\langle alphabetic\ character \rangle$ {($\langle alphabetic\ character \rangle$
           | $\langle number \rangle$)}

$\langle comment \rangle$ ::= '#' ? any printable characters on the same line?

Fig. 10. Crogram EBNF

Lexical Analysis. The lexical analysis phase tokenises all the significant words. There are 24 different tokens. STITCH is one of these tokens and it can have 37 different values (the parser can recognise 37 different types of stitches).

The stitches can be abbreviated differently in different crochet patterns. For example, the slip stitch can be abbreviated as slst, sl st or slip st. A synonym table of possible lexemes is kept to match tokens.

The token lexemes are not necessarily separated by white space. For example, sl st should result in the <STITCH, SLST> token and ch4 should result in two different tokens, namely, <CHAIN, CH> and <NUMBER, 4>. Therefore, the returned tokens are the longest matching lexemes in the text and the start of a NUMBER token is necessarily after white space.

Ordinal words, for example first and second, return number tokens.

Where compilers usually produce a syntax error when unrecognised text occurs, this compiler will ignore the text. After the pattern has been tokenised,

	Ch 4, join with slip st in first ch to form ring.
Round 1 (right side):	Ch 3, 9 dc in ring, join with slip st in top of beginning ch-3 – 10 dc.
Round 2:	Ch 3, dc in same st as joining slip st, 2 dc in each dc around, join with slip st in top of beginning ch-3 – 20 dc.
Round 3:	Ch 3, dc in same st as joining slip st, dc in next dc, * 2 dc in next dc, dc in next dc; repeat from * around, join with slip st in top of beginning ch-3 – 30 dc

Fig. 11. Extract from a crochet pattern (hat)

the tokens are filtered to reduce redundancy. For example, empty brackets or two separators following each other are removed.

Syntactic Analysis. The syntactic analysis phase constructs a parse tree of the tokens. The rules that must be extracted from the tokens are shown in Fig. 14. Not all of the tokens will form part of the parse tree. Some of the tokens are only used to indicate when to start or end a new rule. For example, the SEPARATOR token can indicate the end of a <stitch action> rule and the IN token can indicate the start of a <location> rule. Figure 13 shows the parse tree of the tokens in row 1 of Fig. 11.

Semantic Analysis and Code Generation. The semantic analysis and code generation phases are executed simultaneously. At the end of each <row> rule construction in the parse tree, a row table is updated with the stitches, and their parent indices, of that row. The index of the current parent stitch is updated as new stitches or skip actions are added (a caveat of this is that it is not possible to parse patterns where stitches have parent stitches that are before the parent of the most recent stitch in the row).

There are certain types of tokens that are expected to appear in each rule and they are extracted when the rule is parsed. For example, the <stitch action> rule must contain one or more STITCH tokens, an optional NUMBER token to indicate the number of stitches required, and a <location rule>.

When a <stitch action> rule is analysed, the parent of the stitch(es) must be determined from the <location> rule. When parsing the <location> rule, the parser determines if the following types of tokens are present:

- EACH: Indicates that the stitch should be stitched into every described stitch of the row
- STITCH: Describes the stitch type of the parent stitch.
- NUMBER: Any integer
- PLACE: Words like next or last (Fig. 15).

```
{[0]} {
        CH * 4;
        SLST -> [0][0]
    }

{[1]} {
        CH3 -> [0][0];
        DC -> [0] * 9;
        SLST -> [1][0]
    }

{[2]} {
        CH3 -> [1][0];
        DC -> [1][0];
        DC, DC -> [1][$\mid$:1:9];
        SLST -> [2][0]
    }

{[3]} {
        CH3 -> [2][0];
        DC, (DC, DC) -> [2][/:1:20]
    }
```

<CHAIN, CH> <NUMBER, 4> SEPARATOR <STITCH, SLST>
IN <NUMBER, 1> <CHAIN, CH> FORM <STITCH, RING>
SEPARATOR
ROW <NUMBER, 1> COLON <CHAIN, CH> <NUMBER, 3>
SEPARATOR <NUMBER, 9> <STITCH, DC> IN
<STITCH, RING>
SEPARATOR <STITCH, SLST> IN OF
<NUMBER, 1> <CHAIN, CH3>

Fig. 12. Part of the hat pattern written in Crogram, and the respective tokens

The NUMBER token can either have ordinal meaning (since ordinal words were replaced with NUMBER tokens) or it can describe in how many of the parent stitch, the stitch should be repeated. The distinction is made by the presence of the PLACE token. Since the PLACE token indicates position, it is assumed that if there is a NUMBER token, it describes the number of repetitions. If there is no PLACE token, the NUMBER token is assumed to indicate the position. Figure 15 shows the difference between a NUMBER token with countable meaning versus ordinal meaning.

In the case where it is unknown how many times to repeat the child actions of a <repeat> rule, a look-ahead is performed before each repeating set of actions. If the look-ahead determines that there are not enough valid parent stitches left in the same row, the repetition stops.

In the case that the <location> rule refers to the last stitch of the row, a look-ahead is also performed to find the last stitch.

When the parsing has completed, the Crogram text is written.

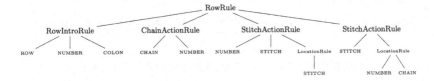

Fig. 13. Parse tree for row 1 of the hat crochet pattern

⟨*body*⟩   ::= {⟨*row*⟩}

⟨*row*⟩   ::= [⟨*row introduction*⟩] ⟨*stitch action*⟩ ⟨*separator*⟩
                  | ⟨*chain action*⟩ ⟨*separator*⟩
                  | ⟨*repeat*⟩
                  | ⟨*skip action*⟩ ⟨*separator*⟩}

⟨*row intro*⟩   ::= ⟨*row*⟩ ⟨*number*⟩ ⟨*colon*⟩

⟨*stitch action*⟩ ::= ? at least one stitch, maybe a number ? ⟨*in*⟩ ⟨*location*⟩

⟨*crochet action*⟩ ::= ⟨*chain*⟩ [⟨*number*⟩]

⟨*repeat*⟩   ::= ('*'
                  | ⟨*times*⟩ ⟨*number*⟩)) { ⟨*stitch action*⟩
                  | ⟨*chain action*⟩
                  | ⟨*skip action*⟩ }
                    ? something like, '**repeat from ***' ? ⟨*location*⟩

⟨*skip action*⟩   ::= ⟨*skip*⟩ [⟨*location*⟩]

⟨*location*⟩   ::= ? something like, '**next stitch**' ?
                  | ⟨*across*⟩

Fig. 14. The context-free-like rules expected in a pattern

4.3 Formal Language to Diagram

ANTLR4 [9] was used to generate a parser for Crogram. Stitches are added to
a graph structure. As the stitches are added, their coordinates are calculated
based upon the indices of their parent stitches and the type of pattern (round
or square). If there are multiple stitches in one parent stitch, these stitches are
evenly spaced at a specific angle. Since the coordinates and angle of a stitch
is only dependent on the location of the parent stitch and not the real-world
tension of the yarn, the shape of diagrams will either be round or square. Once
the parsing is completed, the symbols corresponding to each stitch are plotted.

<STITCH, SC> IN <PLACE, NEXT> <NUMBER, 2> <STITCH, DC>

<STITCH, SC> IN <NUMBER, 1> <STITCH, DC>

Fig. 15. Example of NUMBER with countable meaning (top) and ordinal meaning (bottom)

5   Results

Different styles (from different authors) of patterns are considered; including patterns that are to be stitched in the round as opposed to row by row.

We want to show that all of the following types of patterns can be parsed:

– Contains multiple rows/rounds
– Contains multiple types of stitches
– Contains multiple stitches in a single parent
– Contains skip actions
– Contains repeat rules

5.1   Semi-structured Natural Language to Crogram

There were a few issues encountered when parsing the patterns.

Patterns often have rows with similar stitches; to make the pattern text shorter, patterns have text that indicate that certain rows should be repeated or that the stitches that follow the row keyword must be applied to more than one row. For example, Fig. 16 shows an extract from a pattern that indicates that from row 4 to row 9, rows 2 and 3 must be repeated. Our current parser can only parse single rows and also cannot parse row repetitions.

Rows 4 - 9: Repeat Rows 2 and 3 three times.

Fig. 16. Row repetition example

Sometimes the parent stitch can be described with phrases like "...the center of...". Phrases like these can have valuable meaning, but it will not be tokenised by the parser. A parent stitch can also be described with phrases like "ch-5 space". This type of phrase describes multiple stitches as one group and would return the following tokens: CHAIN, NUMBER and GENERAL, where it should have returned only one token. Figure 17 shows a pattern extract that includes a combination of these two phrases and the Crogram result.

Note that on line 5, where the single crochet stitch (SC) is stitched into the ch-7 space the first time, the parent of this single crochet stitch is only one

> Row 3: Ch 1 (does not count as a st), turn, sc in first dc,
> shell in next sc, **sc in center of next ch-7 space,**
> shell in next sc; repeat from * across, sc in last dc.

```
1  [3]  {
2          CH1 -> [2][121];
3          SC -> [2][121];
4          DC6SHELL -> [2][117];
5          SC -> [2][116];
6          DC6SHELL -> [2][109];
7          SC -> [2][108];
8          DC6SHELL -> [2][101];
                  .
                  .
                  .
```

Fig. 17. Example of "center of next ... space" in table mat doily pattern and Crogram result

stitch after the previous stitch (on line 4). It is supposed to be four stitches after the previous stitch (the centre of seven chains would be the fourth chain). The reason for this error is that the phrase was parsed as the equivalent to "sc in next ch" and the rest of the phrase was ignored. Figure 18 shows an altered version of Fig. 17 that produces the expected result.

> Row 3: Ch 1 (does not count as a st), turn, sc in first dc,
> shell in next sc, **skip next 3 ch, sc in next ch,**
> shell in next sc; repeat from * across, sc in last dc.

```
1  [3]  {
2          CH1 -> [2][121];
3          SC -> [2][121];
4          DC6SHELL -> [2][117];
5          SC -> [2][113];
6          DC6SHELL -> [2][109];
7          SC -> [2][105];
8          DC6SHELL -> [2][101];
                  .
                  .
                  .
```

Fig. 18. Altered table mat doily pattern and Crogram result

Stitches from specific rounds must strictly be written after their **round** keyword. Figure 19 shows an example where different stitches belong to different rounds in the diagram (the stitches at the first bullet point should be in their own round), but they are written after the same **round** keyword.

Round 1:
- **CH4 and join with SS to form ring**
- CH3 (counts as first DC)
- 2 DC into ring
- Repeat 3 times:
  - CH3
  - 3 DC into ring
- CH3
- Join with SS to top of CH3.

- **CH4 and join with SS to form ring**

Round 1:
- CH3 (counts as first DC)
- 2 DC into ring

Fig. 19. Extract from granny square pattern (top) and the altered version (bottom)

The parser can only parse a parent stitch of a stitch if the `<location>` rule comes after the stitch. Figure 20 shows an extract of a pattern for which the parser cannot build a parse tree, because the location description "In the corner space" comes before the stitches. The parser is also not able to analyse "corner space" as a parent ("corner space", in this case, refers to the space of a corner created by four chain stitches).

Round 2:
- CH4 (counts as DC+CH1 here and through-out pattern)
- Skip next DC
- DC in next DC
- **In the corner space: 2DC, CH3, 2DC**

Round 2:
- CH4 (counts as DC+CH1 here and through-out pattern)
- Skip next DC
- DC in next DC
- **2DC in next CH, CH3, skip next CH, 2DC in next CH**

Fig. 20. Extract from granny square pattern (top) and altered version (bottom)

This parser does not make use of the operators in Crogram to shorten the output. Although this does not make a difference to the performance of the Crogram parser, it does make the Crogram output less readable to the user.

5.2   Crogram to Diagram

We give a few examples of the output diagrams generated from the Crogram input.

Figure 21 shows the original diagram of the table mat doily from Sect. 4.2 (see Fig. 17 and Fig. 18), as well as the output diagram generated by our project. This is an example of a row by row crochet pattern.

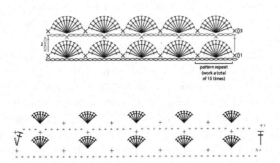

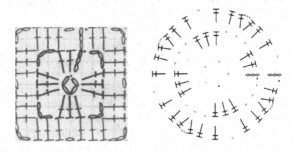

Fig. 21. Original diagram of table mat doily, and the generated output

Note that both the shell stitch symbol and the single crochet stitch symbol differ slightly. The shell stitch in the original pattern was tokenised as a DC6SHELL stitch by the parser. The designer of this pattern uses a different single crochet symbol than our parser. Also note that the stitches at the ends are angled differently than in the original diagram; the behaviour of our parser is to always set stitches at a specific angle if they share a parent stitch.

Another result is a granny square, shown in Fig. 22.

Fig. 22. Granny square diagram

Note that the shape of the diagram is round and not square as seen in the original diagram drawn by the author. The reason for this is that our parser places stitches at an angle that is the same as their parent stitches. Also, the angles of the stitches are not always correct, but all the stitches are placed correctly relative to the other stitches.

6   Conclusion and Future Work

There are improvements that can be made to both parsers. The semi-structured natural language parser can be expanded to recognise more words. There are many different types of crochet stitches and more could be added to be recognised by the parser. Some of the more complex phrases that describe the parent stitch (as discussed in Sect. 5.1) can be made parsable. One area to consider is to change the Crogram grammer to an LL(*) grammar, to cover more possibilities.

The writing of the Crogram output can include the use of operators to improve the readability.

The drawing of the diagram can be improved. It is worth investigating if the diagram can be drawn with TikZ. It will be an interesting problem to draw the symbols at coordinates and angles that mimic the real-world tension in the yarn.

The semi-structured natural language parser interprets the tokens rule by rule and the Crogram parser interprets line by line. Therefore, it should be possible to adjust the project to compile crochet patterns in real-time; as a user is typing the pattern text, the diagram should be drawn.

The success of this project implies that the same principle can be applied to other semi-structured natural languages, like knitting patterns or pseudocode.

References

1. Bornat, R.: Understanding and Writing Compilers: A Do-it-Yourself Guide. MacMillan (1990)
2. Deeptimahanti, D., Sanyal, R.: Semi-automatic generation of UML models from natural language requirements. In: Proceedings of the 4th India Software Engineering Conference, ISEC 2011, pp. 165–174. ACM, New York (2011)
3. Edelstein, M., Peleg, H., Itzhaky, S., Ben-Chen, M.: Amigo: computational design of amigurumi crochet patterns. In: Proceedings of the 7th Annual ACM Symposium on Computational Fabrication, pp. 1–11 (2022)
4. Ishihara, Y., Seki, H., Kasami, T.: A translation method from natural language specifications into formal specifications using contextual dependencies. In: Proceedings of the IEEE International Symposium on Requirements Engineering, pp. 232–239 (1993)
5. Iwama, F., Nakamura, T., Takeuchi, H.: Constructing a parser for industrial software specifications containing formal and natural language description. In: 34th International Conference on Software Engineering (ICSE), pp. 1012–1021 (2012)
6. Iwama, F., Nakamura, T., Takeuchi, H.: Parser combinators for parsing semi-structured texts. Comput. Softw. **29**, 4258–4277 (2012)
7. Kulkarni, R., Chavan, A., Hardikar, A.: Transpiler and its advantages. Int. J. Comput. Sci. Inf. Technol. **6**(2), 1629–1631 (2015)
8. Osborne, M., MacNish, C.K.: Processing natural language software requirement specifications. In: Proceedings of the Second International Conference on Requirements Engineering, pp. 229–236 (1996)
9. Parr, T.J., Quong, R.W.: ANTLR: a predicated-LL(k) parser generator. Softw.: Pract. Experience **25**(7), 789–810 (1995)

10. Seitz, K., Rein, P., Lincke, J., Hirschfeld, R.: Digital crochet: toward a visual language for pattern description. In: Proceedings of the 2022 ACM SIGPLAN International Symposium on New Ideas, New Paradigms, and Reflections on Programming and Software, pp. 48–62 (2022)

11. Wolfsteller, F.: Christel. https://github.com/fwolfst/christel. Accessed 18 May 2023

Information Systems Track

A Review of Knowledge Sharing Challenges within E-government Projects: A Perspective of the Ipe Knowledge Sharing Model

Katazo N. Amunkete[✉] and Lisa F. Seymour

Department of Information Systems, University of Cape Town, Cape Town, South Africa
kamunkete@gmail.com, lisa.seymour@uct.ac.za

Abstract. Knowledge sharing is a complex activity. It is an activity that has been highlighted to be challenging among team members working on different projects. These projects include software development projects. Studies have developed literature reviews to highlight knowledge sharing challenges existing within different types of software development projects but there is currently no review that looks at the challenges in the context of e-government projects. A review would assist with identifying whether knowledge sharing challenges within e-government projects have been extensively explored through empirical studies and have emerged from both developed and developing contexts. Team members working on e-government projects work in an environment with different bureaucratic processes and knowledge sharing challenges in these projects would differ from those of software development projects in the private sector. A systematic literature review was conducted for the paper and analysis of the literature was guided by a model that highlights factors that influence knowledge sharing among individuals. The analysis contributes to an understanding of the current state of literature on knowledge sharing challenges within e-government projects and identifies possible gaps that exist in the literature in line with the model proposed for the analysis.

Keywords: Knowledge sharing · E-government projects · Ipe knowledge sharing model

1 Introduction

Knowledge is a critical resource to organisations [1]. It is comprised of experiences, interpretations and reflections of those experiences and the contexts in which the experiences take place [2]. To reap greater benefits from knowledge, effective knowledge sharing among an organisation's employees is encouraged [3]. Knowledge sharing entails an exchange of knowledge between individuals and includes team members sharing knowledge among one another. This knowledge can be in the form of giving advice on how to accomplish tasks and sharing work related experiences that can help with solving problems [4]. The sharing of knowledge results in diverse experiences and new sets of knowledge [5], thus leading to the formation of new and innovative ideas.

© The Author(s), under exclusive license to Springer Nature Switzerland AG 2023
A. Gerber and M. Coetzee (Eds.): SAICSIT 2023, CCIS 1878, pp. 81–96, 2023.
https://doi.org/10.1007/978-3-031-39652-6_6

Knowledge sharing can assist with retaining knowledge within a project [6]. This is especially important in projects with a high turnover among team members. High turnover is evident among software development projects [7] and the projects experience challenges with knowledge sharing [8]. In the absence of effective knowledge sharing, the departure of team members from a software development project can lead to knowledge loss within the project [9]. Project operations can be disrupted as the departing team members were involved with different aspects of the project [10]. Although studies have reported on knowledge sharing challenges within software development project teams [8, 11, 12], less attention has been paid to knowledge sharing within software development project teams in the government sector.

In the government sector, software development projects are usually initiated to develop e-government systems. E-government primarily has to do with the government delivering services to its clients, the citizens, using the internet and different information technologies [13]. The goals of e-government include the delivery of improved government services to citizens and improved access to information that pertains to government services and essential public announcements [14]. Effective knowledge sharing among team members working on e-government projects can lead to more innovative systems for the benefit of citizens and can ensure that in the event of project members departing a project, their knowledge is not lost to the project. As stated earlier, the departure of team members from a project can hamper and disrupt project operations.

Project teams working on e-government projects work in an environment with knowledge sharing barriers that include bureaucratic processes, internal politics, and organisational inertia [15, 16] which can introduce a myriad of knowledge sharing challenges. The government sector experiences high levels of staff turnover [17], even more specifically within its Information Communication Technology (ICT) workforce [18].

The objective of this paper is to contribute to an understanding of the current gaps in literature on knowledge sharing challenges within e-government projects. There is a need for a comprehensive overview that looks at the challenges holistically to highlight gaps in the literature addressing knowledge sharing challenges within team members working on the projects. Understanding knowledge sharing challenges within e-government projects would assist with designing and developing solutions that can mitigate the challenges and improve knowledge sharing among team members working on the projects. To achieve the objective of the paper, a systematic literature review was conducted and the papers found were analysed using the lens of a knowledge sharing model by [19]. In this paper the authors will refer to the model as the Ipe 2003 knowledge sharing model.

The rest of the paper will be structured as follows. In Sect. 2, the tenets of the Ipe 2003 knowledge sharing model will be discussed. The discussion in Sect. 3 will be centred around the systematic literature review approach followed for the study. An analysis of the literature will be provided in Sect. 4 and the paper will end with a conclusion in Sect. 5.

2 The Ipe 2003 Knowledge Sharing Model

Different factors lead to knowledge sharing challenges. The Ipe 2003 knowledge sharing model proposes four factors that influence knowledge sharing among individuals in an organisation. The four factors that make up the model are: (1) the nature of the knowledge to be shared, (2) motivation to engage in knowledge sharing activities, (3) the opportunities available to engage in knowledge sharing, and (4) the culture and sub-cultures of an organisation. The factors and their interrelations are presented in Fig. 1.

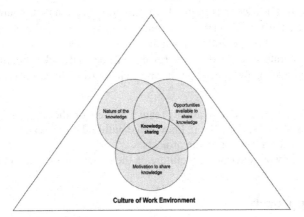

Fig. 1. A model for knowledge sharing between individuals in organisations (Adapted from [19])

Fig. 1 can be summarised as follows [19, 20]: The nature of the knowledge to be shared may exist in different formats and this affects how the knowledge can be effectively shared. Knowledge exists in either a tacit or an explicit format [21]. Explicit knowledge is documented and is the type of knowledge that we find in formats such as books and manuals [22]. Tacit knowledge is made up of the skills, experiences, and competencies that people have and is embedded in their minds [23]. Compared to explicit knowledge, tacit knowledge is harder to detect, articulate and share with others [24]. The value that is attributed to the knowledge equally influences whether individuals would be willing to share that knowledge and with whom they will be willing to share it. The value of the knowledge can be at a personal level, such as any rewards that attached to sharing or at an organizational level, such as sharing to meet organisational objectives [25].

Motivation to share knowledge depends on whether an individual has a strong personal motivation to share their knowledge. Motivation can be influenced by both internal and external factors, such as perceived power and rewards available for sharing respectively [20].

Within organisations, there exists formal and informal opportunities for knowledge sharing. Formal opportunities include training programmes and are referred to as purposive learning channels, while informal opportunities include personal relationships and social networks, which are referred to as relational learning channels [19]. Purposive learning channels are more explicit and structured as opposed to relational learning channels and the nature of knowledge shared within these channels can differ.

The culture of a work environment influences the nature of knowledge shared or to be shared, the motivation to share, and the opportunities available to share knowledge [19]. The culture of the work environment is also referred to as organisational culture.

Organisational culture are the common values, beliefs, and assumptions that members of the organisation hold [26]. An organisation's work environment culture can inhibit or promote knowledge sharing among employees and determines how receptive employees are to sharing their tacit knowledge [27, 28]. Different sub-cultures that can be present in an organisation, such as those present in a department or project, can add further complexity to how knowledge is shared between individuals in that organisation [19].

In this study, the model serves as a lens for analysing the literature used in the study. As aligned to the Ipe 2003 knowledge sharing model and the objective of the paper, existing literature selected for the review will be analysed to highlight how they address the phenomenon of knowledge sharing challenges within e-government projects in aspect of:

1. motivation to share knowledge among team members on the projects.
2. opportunities available for sharing knowledge within the projects.
3. nature of knowledge shared on the projects.
4. the influence of work environment culture on the knowledge sharing practices within the projects.

3 Study Approach

E-government is a phenomenon that is predominantly researched within the field of information systems. Different types of literature reviews have been proposed for information systems stand-alone literature reviews and examples of these include systematic reviews, meta-analysis, narrative and descriptive reviews [29, 30]. For this study, a systematic literature review was conducted. Systematic literature reviews are conducted for different reasons, which include summarising, describing, and identifying knowledge gaps within a specific domain or phenomenon of interest [31–33]. This aligns well with the objective of this study, which is to contribute to an understanding of the current gaps in literature on knowledge sharing challenges within e-government projects. The types of gaps identified in literature depend on the focus and objectives of the literature review being conducted. These gaps can be in terms of things such as the types of knowledge contributions present in the literature focus of interest, philosophical underpinnings informing the studies of interest, and others [34].

In a paper synthesising literature on literature review guidelines for information systems [35] it was found that the guidelines usually comprise the following 5 stages: (1) defining a protocol, (2) searching for literature, (3) selecting papers for review and (4) analysing, synthesising and interpreting the papers, and (5) writing up the review. This is in line with a paper [29] which analyses literature on guidelines for systematic literature reviews in information systems research. The stages identified are: (1) determining focus of review and planning appropriate course of action, (2) literature search, (3) articles selection, (4) analysis and interpretation, and (5) presenting results. The stages have been used to conduct the systematic literature review in this paper. The first stage which deals with defining the protocol entails setting out the primary goal of the review and drafting the study's objectives that will serve to guide the review [36, 37]. The objective of this paper is defined in Section 1. The first stage also sets out how the review will be carried out and what the other 4 stages will entail. What stages 2 to 5 entail and how they were applied in this study will be the focus of Sections 3.1, 3.2, 3.3 and 3.4.

3.1 Searching for Literature

Searching for literature involves the processes of acquiring and selecting relevant literature for the analysis [38]. In the literature search stage, it is necessary to define the databases that were used for the searches and the search terms that were used [35].

To find relevant literature for this review, searches were conducted on the following databases: Emerald, Google Scholar, ProQuest, ScienceDirect, Scopus, Taylor & Francis, Web of Science, and Wiley Online Library. The databases were selected, as they return results from a wide range of journals, including those in the information systems domain. The Association for Computing Machinery (ACM) and JSTOR databases were also selected for the review, but searches done on the databases did not yield positive returns. JSTOR did not return any results, while ACM returned thousands of results which were difficult to filter and included results such as author profiles and grey literature. Interestingly, some of the other databases such as Google Scholar returned results of papers that were linked to ACM.

To find literature centred around knowledge sharing challenges within e-government projects. Different combinations of the following search terms were used on the databases: *"knowledge sharing" OR "knowledge transfer" AND (e-government OR egovernment OR government OR e-governance)*. Although some authors, such as [39] argue that the terms "knowledge sharing" and "knowledge transfer" mean different things, the terms have often used interchangeably in some studies [39, 40] and thus both were used to find literature for this paper. The terms e-government and e-governance have also been used interchangeably in various studies [41, 42], to mitigate the omission of relevant articles from the review the same was applied in this study. Only studies written in English were consulted and no time span constraints were applied to the searches. The term egovernment was also used as some authors do not include the dash within the term while others do. When searching with the term containing the dash, some databases would return both results containing either e-government or egovernment, but this was not the case for all the databases as some would only return results containing e-government. Another term used in place of the terms e-government or egovernment was government, to ensure that articles that do not mention the terms explicitly but use terms such as "digital government" were also returned. The searches carried out were limited to finding the terms within the titles, abstracts and keywords of the results returned. Some databases such as Google Scholar only allow to limit searches to titles but not to abstracts, while databases such as ScienceDirect only give an option to simultaneously search titles, abstracts, and keywords without an option to choose only one of the 3 parameters. Other databases such as ProQuest provide an option to return only results that have been peer-reviewed, while some do not. These varieties in search selections, restrictions and filtering options resulted in varied returns from the different databases, with some databases returning hundreds of results while others returning less than 50. Fig. 2 provides an overview of the results returned from each database. A total of 973 papers were returned from the databases.

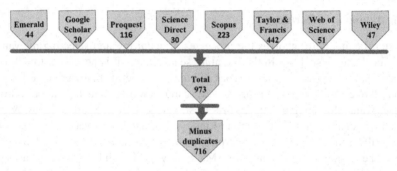

Fig. 2. Results returned from the databases.

Reviewing the results returned was done following the sequence of databases as presented earlier. Duplicate results were found in the databases, and these were noted. A total of 257 papers were duplicates.

3.2 Selecting Articles for the Review

Selecting the articles to be used in a review first involves setting inclusion and exclusion criteria [29] and secondly reviewing the introductions and conclusions of the papers that have passed the first review [31]. The inclusion criteria used in this study were: (1) generally papers mentioning knowledge sharing challenges in the context of e-government projects published in any year and (2) papers whose titles or abstracts referred to knowledge sharing and to e-government projects or the other terms used interchangeably with the two. The exclusion criteria were: (1) papers not written in English, (2) grey literature and (3) papers whose titles or abstracts did not refer to concepts related to knowledge sharing and e-government projects.

Applying the inclusion and exclusion criteria resulted in 18 papers being selected. While, reviewing the introductions and conclusions of the 18 papers resulted in 6 papers that were relevant to the objective of this study. The papers are highlighted in Table 1. The studies are mapped and classified according to the tenets of the Ipe 2003 knowledge sharing model. The table highlights what types of studies they are, whether they are empirical or literature-based, the tenets of the Ipe 2003 knowledge sharing model that the studies address, and whether they have been carried out in developed or developing country contexts. Classifying countries according to the categories of developing or developed country was done according to the United Nations country classification [43].

Table 1. Papers on knowledge sharing within e-government projects mapped against Tenets of Ipe 2003 knowledge sharing model.

Study	Type of Study (Empirical (EM) or Literature Review (LR))	Context (Developed or Developing)	Nature of the knowledge	Motivation	Opportunities	Culture
Context matters: enablers and barriers to knowledge sharing in Australian public sector ICT projects [51]	EM (Qualitative)	Australia (Developed)		✓	✓	✓
The effect of organizational social factors on employee performance and the mediating role of knowledge sharing: focus on e-government utilization in Mongolia [44]	EM (Quantitative - Positivist)	Mongolia (Developing)				✓
Exploring stakeholders' expectations of the benefits and barriers of e-government knowledge sharing [45]	EM (Quantitative - Positivist)	United States of America (Developed)				✓
Exploration and Exploitation: Knowledge Sharing in Digital Government Projects [52]	EM (Grounded Theory Methodology)	Switzerland and the United States (Developed)				✓
Organizational Factors Affecting Knowledge Sharing Capabilities in E-government: An Empirical Study [53]	EM (Quantitative - Positivist)	The Republic of Korea (Developing)				✓
A Knowledge Management System for E-government Projects and Actors [54]	EM (Design)	Italy (Developed)			✓	

The titles of some of the excluded papers met the inclusion criteria but reading through their abstracts, the purposes for which the papers were written did not align to the objective of the review carried out for this paper. For interest's sake, a few examples of such papers are "Research collaboration and knowledge sharing in e-governance: Temporal analysis of co-author network". The title of the paper appeared relevant but the purpose of the paper was to introduce a procedure for identifying temporal evolution and growth of co-author research collaborations in the domain of research on e-governance [46]. The papers "Knowledge access, creation and transfer in e-government portals" and "E-government portals: a knowledge management study" also appeared relevant, but both were concerned with examining knowledge management mechanisms within e-government portals in select countries and the flow of knowledge from e-government portals to intended users [47, 48]. Two other studies that appeared relevant from the titles were "Enabling Knowledge Sharing within e-Government Back-Office Through Ontological Engineering" and "Exploring the determinants of cross-boundary information sharing in the public sector: An e-Government case study in Taiwan", which were concerned with creating interoperability between systems and the seamless sharing of knowledge between e-government systems as opposed to the sharing of individuals among team members working on e-government projects [49, 50].

The six papers presented in Table 1 were analysed for this review. Papers found during the search that did not meet the inclusion criteria for the review but generally spoke to either knowledge sharing challenges within software development projects or to issues of knowledge sharing within the government sector in general, assisted with developing a critical analysis of the six papers and with elaborating on the gaps present in the literature.

3.3 Analysing and Interpreting the Literature

The analysis and interpretation stage involves selecting a method for analysis. Different methods are available for analysis, with examples being grounded theory analysis, meta-analysis techniques, qualitative analysis and critical discourse analysis [35]. Following the Ipe 2003 knowledge sharing model, discussed in Sect. 2, the literature selected was analysed qualitatively using a deductive approach.

3.4 Writing up the Results

Stage 5, which is the writing up stage, entails how the review will be structured and the form that a paper will take [35]. The write up should be structured in a way that details why the review was carried out, how it was carried out and what the results of the review are [31]. Why the review in this paper was carried out is detailed in Sects. 1 and 2. How it was carried out is detailed in Sect. 3 and the results of the review are presented in Sect. 4.

4 Discussion and Analysis

This section starts with an overview of the six papers that have been selected and then moves on to summarising the papers. That only six studies relevant to the objective of this study were found indicates the lack of literature on the phenomenon of knowledge sharing challenges within e-government projects. Interestingly all the papers were empirical studies, originating from both developed and developing country contexts. Three of the studies were of a quantitative nature, one qualitative, one grounded-theory and the other a design study. Although the studies were carried out in varied contexts and employed different methods, there is still a need for more studies exploring the phenomenon. The papers selected for the review are now summarized.

A paper that was very much related to the phenomenon of interest in this study is the paper by Karagoz et al. [51] that extending a theory related to knowledge sharing barriers. The authors confirmed that the theory did not apply to software development projects in the public sector. Although the paper was focused on extending a theory, the authors did deal with aspects on knowledge sharing challenges within e-government projects.

The second paper [44] provides relevant considerations for developing a work environment culture in the government sector that can contribute to the effective implementation of e-government projects, it does address some challenges with the influence of the work environment culture but not specific to team members working on e-government projects.

The third paper [45] focused on the barrier and benefits of e-government knowledge sharing expected by different stakeholders at the initiation of inter-organisational e-government projects. It touches on how the stakeholders' expectations are influenced by the culture of the work environment, more so in an environment where stakeholders originate from orgaisations with differing cultures.

The fourth paper [52] builds a theory on knowledge sharing processes within the conception and implementation stages of e-government projects, more specifically, it was written to "advance theory on the interdependencies between the introduction of ICTs and formal and informal organizational structures by closely examining two coordination mechanisms that coexist in DGPs [Digital Government Projects]: hierarchies and social networks" [52, para. 5]. In contrast, the fifth paper [53] contributed to an understanding of how organisational structure, culture, and information technology influence knowledge sharing capabilities in e-government projects.

The final paper [54] presented the design of a web-based knowledge management system for sharing knowledge within e-government projects. Any challenges that might have been faced in making use of the web-based opportunity were not the objectives of their study and were not elaborated on.

Next, we will look at the studies in relation to addressing the tenets of the Ipe 2003 knowledge sharing model. For the discussion, the tenets of the model will be referred to as: Tenet 1 - nature of knowledge shared, Tenet 2 - motivation for sharing knowledge, Tenet 3 - opportunities available for sharing knowledge and Tenet 4 - the influence of work environment culture on knowledge sharing. None of the studies addressed knowledge sharing challenges related to Tenet 1, while only one study did not address challenges related to Tenet 4. The fifth study [51] addressed knowledge sharing challenges related to Tenets 2, 3 and 4. Four studies [44, 45, 52, 53] addressed knowledge sharing challenges related to Tenet 4. The next section will focus on discussing the results from the tenets of the Ipe 2003 knowledge sharing model. The discussion will incorporate papers that generally speak to either knowledge sharing challenges within software development projects or within the government sector in general.

4.1 Motivation to Share Knowledge on E-government Projects

The motivation for sharing knowledge is directly linked to the voluntary willingness of individuals to share their knowledge [55]. This perspective of willingness makes knowledge sharing a difficult activity to deal with within project teams. Individuals drive whether there will be any knowledge shared [56]. Knowledge sharing is better facilitated when employees are intrinsically motivated to share their knowledge [23].

Different factors have been attributed as contributing factors to employees' unwillingness to share knowledge. Some of these factors are a lack of clarity on what is expected in terms of knowledge sharing, poor collaboration among team members, fear of losing power, uncertainty whether what one knows will be perceived as being correct and a fear of being misunderstood [57]. A lack of rewards for sharing and mistrust or low levels of trust among team members are also factors that impede the willingness to share one's knowledge [44]. Surveying the concept of knowledge sharing within software development projects in South Africa, team members might be unwilling to share without some form of reward [58]. Others view the knowledge that they possess as an asset that they would like to protect from others [59] and thus avoid sharing it.

A lack of motivation to share knowledge among government employees would render any opportunities availed to share knowledge futile [60]. Motivation and willingness to share knowledge are tightly tied to an individual and more research is required to understand from the perspective of team members working on e-government projects, what would lead them to voluntarily share their knowledge. Most team members working on e-government projects operate in an environment that is characteristic of being resource-constrained and the idea of rewards for sharing, especially those of a monetary kind might not fit in well with some of the contexts. However, the first paper highlighted in Table 1 [51] surveyed project managers on e-government projects in Australia and found that rewards and trust among team members where great motivating factors for knowledge sharing within the projects.

4.2 The Nature of Knowledge Shared on E-government Projects

Although study [54] provided an example of an opportunity used in sharing knowledge within e-government projects, the study did not touch on the nature of the knowledge shared on the platform presented. Relying on literature pointing to knowledge sharing within software development projects [61], both tacit and explicit knowledge are shared on projects. The willingness to share tacit knowledge is more challenging than the willingness to share explicit knowledge [62]. Tacit knowledge is difficult to measure and articulate and it is difficult to know what a person knows, as this knowledge is embedded within them. Given differences between tacit and explicit knowledge, different challenges would be present with their sharing within e-government projects.

4.3 Opportunities for Sharing Knowledge on E-government Projects

Opportunities for sharing knowledge can be both formal and informal and can either be ICT or non-ICT based. The study by Morici et al. [54] presents an opportunity to share knowledge among team members working on an e-government project. This is the only literature found that was directly linked to an opportunity that enabled knowledge sharing within an e-government project. The opportunity is presented through a web-based knowledge management system. The system worked on different levels of authorisation to enable different views for users depending on their roles on a project. Overall, there is a lack of studies that address what opportunities are available for sharing knowledge within software development projects and what challenges these opportunities present. Generally, in the government sector, intranets are used for sharing knowledge and their use in the context has not been effective in furthering knowledge sharing aspirations in the context [56].

4.4 The Influence of Work Environment Culture on Knowledge Sharing Practices within E-government Projects

A bureaucratic culture is viewed as a common characteristic of government institutions [63, 64]. "Generic features of the bureaucratic culture are: management style is relatively authoritarian, a high degree of control, top-down communication, individuals search for stability, limited initiatives, and centralized decision making" [28] (p. 3). This bureaucratic nature results in rigid rules and regulations [57], which impede on knowledge sharing behaviour. There is no consensus on whether bureaucracy inhibits or promotes knowledge sharing as different study results have contradicted this [51]. Other factors of the work environment culture of the government that can inhibit knowledge sharing within the context are central decision-making, a high level of confidentiality, budget constraints and restrictions, security concerns, and a culture of secrecy [15, 52, 65]. Generally, a bureaucratic work environment leads to the hoarding of knowledge as hoarding knowledge is seen as a way of maintaining the environment's valuable resource [17]. A well formulated strategy for rewarding employees that effectively share their knowledge and building a culture of trust in the government can contribute to improving knowledge sharing among government employees [44].

4.5 Implications of Poor Knowledge Sharing within E-Government Projects

Due to outcomes in the government sector being hard to measure as opposed to those in the private sector, the idea of effective knowledge sharing is not critically engaged within the government sector [57]. Ineffective knowledge sharing within e-government projects can hamper public service delivery [66]. Firstly, this can be due to citizen-centric systems developed from the projects, not being completed on time due to knowledge loss being experienced because of team members departing a project. Ineffective knowledge sharing coupled with high staff turnover on software development projects can impact the timely completion of a project [7]. Secondly, knowledge sharing leads to the generation of innovative ideas [56] and ineffective knowledge sharing can stifle innovation within e-government projects, leading to a lack of innovative e-government systems [67]. Overall, adopting e-government projects is faced with challenges such as a lack of technologies and required infrastructure to advance the projects, inadequate legal frameworks and behavioral issues [63]. These challenges can have direct effects on the knowledge sharing practices within e-government projects and affect how effectively team members are sharing knowledge.

5 Conclusion

This paper looked at literature addressing the phenomenon of knowledge sharing challenges within e-government projects from the lens of the Ipe 2003 knowledge sharing model. From the lens of the model mentioned, it is evident that most literature closely related to the phenomenon has touched on the influence of the culture of the government work environment on knowledge sharing within the context. Generally, there is a lack of literature addressing the phenomenon. Most studies on knowledge sharing challenges within different types of software development projects have been from the private sector.

E-government projects like other different kinds of projects comprise different activities from the initiation to the completion phases of a project. These phases and activities would present a diverse range of knowledge sharing challenges in addition to those generally applicable to the government as an institution or sector. The culture of the work environment in which e-government projects find themselves would also present additional challenges to those found within other types of software development projects. Table 1 highlights that the phenomenon under study in this review has not been explored in different contexts, such as in African governments, which may be resource-constrained and might divulge further challenges of interest.

This study has several limitations. The first limitation is that only literature in English was consulted, and the authors acknowledge that there might be other relevant studies written in other languages. Also, although care was taken in the search process, relevant studies might have been missed by the authors. Lastly, due to the scarcity of literature on the phenomenon of interest, the study largely relied on literature in the domain of knowledge sharing challenges within different types of software development projects and within the government sector in general to make a case for the need of effective knowledge sharing within e-government projects.

Research is required that explores the diverse knowledge sharing challenges on e-government projects from the other three tenets of the Ipe 2003 knowledge sharing model. A gap exists in understanding the whats, whys, hows and challenges of the motivation to share knowledge among team members working on e-government projects, the types of knowledge shared on the projects and the opportunities available to share knowledge on the projects. Research could be advanced through qualitative studies that could provide rich descriptions of the phenomenon.

References

1. Grant, R.M.: Knowledge-based view. In: Wiley Encyclopedia of Management, pp. 1–2 (2015)
2. Yee, Y.M., Tan, C.L., Thurasamy, R.: Back to basics: building a knowledge management system. Strategic Direct. **35**(2), 1–3 (2019)
3. Alamil, H., et al.: Drivers for sharing knowledge in the Kingdom of Saudi Arabia construction industry: an empirical study. In: Proceedings of the 2019 3rd International Conference on Information System and Data Mining. Association for Computing Machinery, New York (2019)
4. Adam, N.A.: Employees' innovative work behavior and change management phases in government institutions: the mediating role of knowledge sharing. Adm. Sci. **12**(1), 28–28 (2022)
5. Lartey, P.Y., et al.: Knowledge management issues in India: a public sector perspective. Int. J. Public Adm. **44**(3), 215–230 (2021)
6. Mosala-Bryant, N.N., Hoskins, R.G.: Motivational theory and knowledge sharing in the public service. SA J. Inf. Manage. **19**(1) (2017)
7. Ma, L., Zhang, X., Ding, X.: Enterprise social media usage and knowledge hiding: a motivation theory perspective. J. Knowl. Manage. **24**(9), 2149–2169 (2020)
8. Akgün, A.E., et al.: Knowledge sharing barriers in software development teams: a multiple case study in Turkey. Kybernetes **46**(4), 603–620 (2017)
9. Robillard, M.P.: Turnover-induced knowledge loss in practice. In: ESEC/FSE 2021 - Proceedings of the 29th ACM Joint Meeting European Software Engineering Conference and Symposium on the Foundations of Software Engineering, vol. 11, pp. 1292–1302 (2021)
10. Naidoo, R.: Role stress and turnover intentions among information technology personnel in South Africa: the role of supervisor support. SA J. Hum. Resour. Manage. **16** (2018)
11. Khoza, L.T. and A.B. Pretorius, Factors negatively influencing knowledge sharing in software development. SA Journal of Information Management, 2017. **19**(1).
12. Zahedi, M., Shahin, M., Ali Babar, M.: A systematic review of knowledge sharing challenges and practices in global software development. Int. J. Inf. Manage. **36**(6), 995–1019 (2016)
13. MacLean, D., Titah, R.: A systematic literature review of empirical research on the impacts of e-government: a public value perspective. Public Adm. Rev. **82**(1), 23–38 (2022)
14. Chang, C.-H., Almaghalsah, H.: Usability evaluation of e-government websites: a case study from Taiwan. Int. J. Data Netw. Sci. **4**(2), 127–138 (2020)
15. Ashok, M., et al.: How to counter organisational inertia to enable knowledge management practices adoption in public sector organisations. J. Knowl. Manage. **25**(9), 2245–2273 (2021)
16. Manaf, H.A., et al.: Differences in personality and the sharing of managerial tacit knowledge: an empirical analysis of public sector managers in Malaysia. J. Knowl. Manage. **24**(5), 1177–1199 (2020)
17. Dewah, P., Mutula, S.M.: Knowledge retention strategies in public sector organizations. Inf. Dev. **32**(3), 362–376 (2014)
18. Palvia, P., et al.: The World IT Project. World Scientific-Now Publishers Series in Business. World Scientific/NOW Publishers (2020)
19. Ipe, M.: Knowledge sharing in organizations: a conceptual framework. Hum. Resour. Dev. Rev. **2**(4), 337–359 (2003)
20. Nguyen, T.-M., Siri, N.S., Malik, A.: Multilevel influences on individual knowledge sharing behaviours: the moderating effects of knowledge sharing opportunity and collectivism. J. Knowl. Manage. **26**(1), 70–87 (2022)
21. Acharya, A., Mishra, B.: Exploring the relationship between organizational structure and knowledge retention: a study of the Indian infrastructure consulting sector. J. Knowl. Manage. **21**(4), 961–985 (2017)

22. Lei, H., Gui, L., Le, P.B.: Linking transformational leadership and frugal innovation: the mediating role of tacit and explicit knowledge sharing. J. Knowl. Manage. **25**(7), 1832–1852 (2021)
23. Thomas, A., Gupta, V.: The role of motivation theories in knowledge sharing: an integrative theoretical reviews and future research agenda. Kybernetes **51**(1), 116–140 (2022)
24. Rashid, M., Clarke, P.M., O'Connor, R.V.: A systematic examination of knowledge loss in open source software projects. Int. J. Inf. Manage. **46**, 104–123 (2019)
25. Chen, C.-A., Hsieh, C.-W.: Knowledge sharing motivation in the public sector: the role of public service motivation. Int. Rev. Adm. Sci. **81**(4), 812–832 (2015)
26. Oufkir, L., Kassou, I.: Measuring knowledge management project performance. In: Rocha, Á., Adeli, H., Reis, L.P., Costanzo, S. (eds.) WorldCIST'18 2018. AISC, vol. 745, pp. 72–81. Springer, Cham (2018). https://doi.org/10.1007/978-3-319-77703-0_7
27. Levallet, N., Chan, Y.E.: Organizational knowledge retention and knowledge loss. J. Knowl. Manage. **23**(1), 176–199 (2019)
28. Hendryadi, et al.: Bureaucratic culture, empowering leadership, affective commitment, and knowledge sharing behavior in Indonesian government public services. Cogent Bus. Manage. **6**(1) (2019)
29. Bai, Z., et al.: Conducting systematic literature reviews in information systems: an analysis of guidelines. Issues Inf. Syst. **20**(3), 83–93 (2019)
30. Templier, M., Paré, G.: Transparency in literature reviews: an assessment of reporting practices across review types and genres in top IS journals. Eur. J. Inf. Syst. **27**(5), 503–550 (2017)
31. Okoli, C.: A guide to conducting a standalone systematic literature review. Commun. Assoc. Inf. Syst. **37**(1), 43–43 (2015)
32. Khan, M.A., et al.: Software defect prediction using artificial neural networks: a systematic literature review. Sci. Program. **2022**, 1–10 (2022)
33. Boell, S.K., Cecez-Kecmanovic, D.: On being 'systematic' in literature reviews in IS. J. Inf. Technol. **30**(2), 161–173 (2015)
34. Boell, S.K., Cecez-Kecmanovic, D.: A hermeneutic approach for conducting literature reviews and literature searches. Commun. Assoc. Inf. Syst. **34** (2014)
35. Oosterwyk, G., Brown, I., Geeling, S.: A synthesis of literature review guidelines from information systems journals. In: Proceedings of 4th International Conference on the Internet, Cyber Security and Information Systems, vol. 12. Kalpa Publications in Computing (2019)
36. Silveira, P., et al.: Security analysis of digitized substations: a systematic review of GOOSE messages. Internet Things **22** (2023)
37. Cicchetti, A., Ciccozzi, F., Pierantonio, A.: Multi-view approaches for software and system modelling: a systematic literature review. Softw. Syst. Model. **18**(6), 3207–3233 (2019). https://doi.org/10.1007/s10270-018-00713-w
38. Sturm, B., Sunyaev, A.: Design principles for systematic search systems: a holistic synthesis of a rigorous multi-cycle design science research journey. Bus. Inf. Syst. Eng. **61**(1), 91–111 (2018). https://doi.org/10.1007/s12599-018-0569-6
39. Tangaraja, G., et al.: Knowledge sharing is knowledge transfer: a misconception in the literature. J. Knowl. Manage. **20**(4), 653–670 (2016)
40. Hamid, N.A.A., Salim, J.: A conceptual framework of knowledge transfer in Malaysia e-government IT outsourcing: an integration with transactive memory system (TMS). Int. J. Comput. Sci. Issues (IJCSI) **8**(5), 51–64 (2011)
41. Lee-Geiller, S., Lee, T.: Using government websites to enhance democratic E-governance: a conceptual model for evaluation. Govern. Inf. Q. **36**(2), 208–225 (2019)
42. Umbach, G., Tkalec, I.: Evaluating e-governance through e-government: practices and challenges of assessing the digitalisation of public governmental services. Eval. Program. Plann. **93**, 102118 (2022)

43. United Nations, Statistical Annex - Country Classifications (2022)
44. Park, M.J., Dulambazar, T., Rho, J.J.: The effect of organizational social factors on employee performance and the mediating role of knowledge sharing: focus on e-government utilization in Mongolia. Inf. Dev. **31**(1), 53–68 (2015)
45. Zhang, J., Dawes, S.S., Sarkis, J.: Exploring stakeholders' expectations of the benefits and barriers of e-government knowledge sharing. J. Enterp. Inf. Manage. **18**(5), 548–567 (2005)
46. Bindu, N., Sankar, C.P., Kumar, K.S.: Research collaboration and knowledge sharing in e-governance. Transf. Govern.: People Process Policy **13**(1), 2–33 (2019)
47. Behzadi, H., Isfandyari-Moghaddam, A., Sanji, M.: E-government portals: a knowledge management study. Electron. Libr. **30**(1), 89–102 (2012)
48. Goh, D.H.L., et al.: Knowledge access, creation and transfer in e-government portals. Online Inf. Rev. **32**(3), 348–369 (2008)
49. Brusa, G., Caliusco, M.L., Chiotti, O.: Enabling knowledge sharing within e-government back-office through ontological engineering. J. Theor. Appl. Electron. Commer. Res. **2**(1), 33–48 (2007)
50. Yang, T.-M., Wu, Y.-J.: Exploring the determinants of cross-boundary information sharing in the public sector: an e-Government case study in Taiwan. J. Inf. Sci. **40**(5), 649–668 (2014)
51. Karagoz, Y., Whiteside, N., Korthaus, A.: Context matters: enablers and barriers to knowledge sharing in Australian public sector ICT projects. J. Knowl. Manage. **24**(8), 1921–1941 (2020)
52. Binz-Scharf, M.C.: Exploration and exploitation: knowledge sharing in digital government projects. In: Proceedings of the 2004 Annual National Conference on Digital Government Research. Digital Government Society of North America (2004)
53. Kim, S., Lee, H.: Organizational factors affecting knowledge sharing capabilities in e-government: an empirical study. In: Knowledge Management in Electronic Government, pp. 281–293 (2004)
54. Morici, R., Nunziata, E., Sciarra, G.: A Knowledge Management system for e-government projects and actors. In: Wimmer, M.A. (ed.) KMGov 2003. Lecture Notes in Computer Science, vol. 2645, pp. 304–309. Springer, Heidelberg (2003). https://doi.org/10.1007/3-540-44836-5_32
55. Matlala, M.E., Maphoto, A.R.: Prospects for, and challenges of, knowledge sharing in the South African public sector: a literature review. In: The Social Sciences International Research Conference (SSIRC) 2022 (2022)
56. Osupile, K., Makambe, U.: The nexus between organisational culture and knowledge sharing in a government department in Botswana. Int. J. Public Sect. Manage. **34**(2), 118–136 (2021)
57. Al-Ajmi, Z., Al-Busaidi, K.A.: Mitigating knowledge-sharing risks among ICT knowledge workers in the government sector. VINE J. Inf. Knowl. Manage. Syst. (2022)
58. Khoza, L.T., Bwalya, K.J.: An insider's perspective of knowledge sharing in software development projects. J. Inf. Knowl. Manage. **20**(03), 2150030–2150030 (2021)
59. Fernandes, A.A.R.: The effect of organization culture and technology on motivation, knowledge asset and knowledge management. Int. J. Law Manage. **60**(5), 1087–1096 (2018)
60. Ncoyini, S., Cilliers, L.: An evaluation of knowledge sharing in South African local government. In: International Conference on Information Resources Management (CONF-IRM 2016 Proceedings). Association for Information Systems AIS Electronic Library (AISeL) (2016)
61. Mtsweni, E.S., Mavetera, N.: Individual barriers of tacit knowledge sharing within information system development projects. In: Proceedings of the First International Conference on Data Science, E-Learning and Information Systems, New York, NY, USA. ACM (2018)
62. Quratulain, A., et al.: Knowledge sharing and social dilemma in bureaucratic organizations: evidence from public sector in Pakistan. Cogent Bus. Manage. **6**(1) (2019)
63. Abu-Shanab, E., Shehabat, I.: The influence of knowledge management practices on e-government success. Transf. Govern.: People Process Policy **12**(3/4), 286–308 (2018)

64. Hassan, I.S., Hamid, Z.A., Omar, A.: Knowledge Sharing Intention, Attitudes and Workplace Emotions at a Bank in Malaysia. In: European Conference on Knowledge Management, pp. 497–505. Academic Conferences International Limited, Kidmore End (2019)
65. Deverell, A.C., Burnett, S.: Need-to-know cultures: an investigation into intra-organisational and extra-organisational knowledge sharing cultures in local government in the UK. Knowl. Process Manage. 19(3), 131–141 (2012)
66. Dikotla, M.A.: Knowledge sharing in selected municipalities of Limpopo Province. South Afr. J. Libr. Inf. Sci. 85(01), 1–11 (2019)
67. Manoharan, A.P., Ingrams, A.: Conceptualizing E-government from local government perspectives. State Local Govern. Rev. 50(1), 56–66 (2018)

Synthesis of a Governance Framework for Blockchain Technology: A Meta-synthesis

Aldo Damon(ID) and Sumarie Roodt(✉)(ID)

Department of Information Systems, University of Cape Town, Rondebosch, Cape Town 7700,
South Africa
{DMNALD001,Sumarie.Roodt}@myuct.ac.za

Abstract. The governance of blockchain (BC) technology is a topic of continuing study, and a multidisciplinary perspective on blockchain governance is essential for building a formal governance framework for this emerging technology. While there may be some misconceptions surrounding the topic of blockchain governance, it is worth noting that blockchain technology itself has garnered increasing attention from both academic and business communities worldwide. Blockchain stakeholders cannot work or make rational decisions optimally without enough insight into the governance of blockchains. The element that organisations and end-users must consider in their decisions, is the element of regulation for the blockchain technology or network, which regulators and developers still need to grasp this concept. There is a pressing need for meta-synthesis concerning blockchain governance to address the limitations of individual studies, generate new insights and understandings, identify gaps in the existing research, and keep up with the latest developments in this rapidly evolving field. This Meta-synthesis study intends to provide a systematic literature review to evaluate the current Information Systems (IS) literature in search of evidence of governance concerns and frameworks within the blockchain technology environment. In this research, literature shall be used to inform the development and proposition of the synthesized integrated blockchain governance framework model so that there is a common frame of reference for researchers and assists practitioners and business managers of companies in conducting more organised analyses of blockchain governance. As the issue was completely addressed throughout the five-stage assessment, the remaining 30 publications were coded using Nvivo software, 42 codes were created. Each author contributed to summarising and categorising the resultant codes (axial coding). The innovative blockchain governance framework proposes four perspectives: Open-Source System (OSS) Governance Phases, Open-Source System (OSS) Life Cycle Stages, blockchain governance framework dimensions and layers and the Technology-Organisation-Environment (TOE) framework model. It is one of the first research papers in the information systems field to make use of a meta-synthesis approach to consolidate the existing qualitative research and to systematically come up with a blockchain governance framework.

© The Author(s), under exclusive license to Springer Nature Switzerland AG 2023
A. Gerber and M. Coetzee (Eds.): SAICSIT 2023, CCIS 1878, pp. 97–116, 2023.
https://doi.org/10.1007/978-3-031-39652-6_7

1 Introduction

Blockchain technology, which was first introduced in Nakamoto's seminal paper in 2008, has now become a general-purpose technology used in various applications where a 'trust' problem is observed in a system of transactions [1]. Governments and other public sector entities are increasingly adopting blockchain technology, with over two hundred use cases worldwide. Blockchain technology offers registry immutability, transparency, transaction traceability, and security based on cryptographic techniques, among other features. Although blockchain presents advantages such as significant future efficiency improvements and cost-saving potentials, businesses face challenges when implementing new technologies such as blockchain [2, 3]. The question of how to advance goals that may appear to be in direct opposition to one another often arises, and concerns about the future of the business can hinder progress in the present [4]. Businesses like the insurance industry for example are among the late technological adopters in the supply chain, but the adoption of blockchain technology is becoming essential in various industries [5]. However, blockchain networks are vast and complicated for business management to make decisions, which is why a governance perspective is necessary [6, 7]. Stakeholders must deploy blockchain projects properly or make reasonable decisions by exploring and understanding blockchain legislation, regulations, and infrastructure needs. Blockchain governance is sometimes misunderstood, and it is crucial for businesses interested in blockchain development or adoption to have a thorough understanding of the governance concerns that may arise [8]. This paper explores Distributed Ledger Technology (DLT) governance from an academic perspective using meta-synthesis, which is a valuable research methodology for addressing the limitations of individual studies and providing a more comprehensive and integrated understanding of the subject.

The Structure of this meta-synthesis paper begins with an overview of the blockchain foundation to provide readers with a foundation of knowledge about the technology before diving into the governance problem statement. The research purpose and objectives are then presented before the methodology, which includes framing of the review exercise and phases of the review exercise. The paper then delves into governance and control definition, followed by an exploration of governance challenges, and insights into Open-Source Systems (OSS) governance theories. The applicability of OSS governance theories to blockchain technology projects and blockchain governance is then discussed, leading to a more focused examination of blockchain governance, and its conceptual framework, dimensions, and layers from other studies. The paper then returns to the problem statement and proposes an integrated theoretical framework in the form of TOE model by combining other qualitative research results. Thereafter, the paper discusses the results and implications of the study and concludes with a summary, lessons learnt, limitations, and future research.

2 Blockchain Foundation

Blockchain technology has garnered significant attention in both societal and technological media outlets due to its potential to revolutionize digital transactions, data storage, sensitive information management, and identity. By exhibiting key characteristics like decentralization, transparency, data security, automation through smart contracts and interoperability [9, 10]. These characteristics position blockchain to transform numerous sectors and has been likened to the impact of the internet on information and the internal combustion engine on the automobile industry [11].

There are three main types of blockchain networks: decentralized, centralized, and distributed. Decentralized blockchain networks, such as Bitcoin and Ethereum, are characterized by their open and trusting nature, where anyone can participate [9]. In contrast, centralized blockchain networks are designed for a specific group of trusted participants and are often used for sharing sensitive data or streamlining internal processes [12]. Finally, distributed blockchain networks offer a hybrid between public and private networks, where a group of organizations form a decentralized network with the benefits of both public and private networks [13].

As seen in Fig. 1 it provides a visual of each type of blockchain network which offers unique advantages and disadvantages, and the choice of network depends on the specific needs and requirements of the application. As such, understanding the different types of blockchain networks and their characteristics is crucial for choosing the appropriate network for a given application.

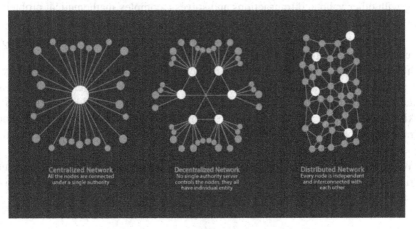

Fig. 1. Main types of blockchain networks [9]

2.1 Blockchain Made Simple

Blockchain technology is a decentralized and secure system that provides an automated mechanism of trust without a central authority [14]. The design of the database methodology used to document and preserve data records in a decentralized ledger makes the ledger irreversible, traceable, and resistant to change [15]. Transactions in a blockchain are kept in the data component of a block, and each subsequent blockchains data from preceding blocks, making them highly resistant to change and secured by cryptography [16].

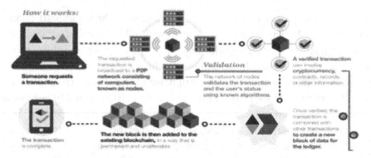

Fig. 2. Visual explainer of blockchain technology by pwc [17]

Based on Fig. 2 in order to initiate a transaction on a blockchain, Individual A creates a digital signature with a private key, the amount of cryptocurrency to send, and Individual B's public key. Individual A broadcasts the transaction to the network, and nodes on the network validate the transaction by verifying Individual A's digital signature and confirming the availability of sufficient cryptocurrency in the digital wallet [18]. Once the transaction is validated, a miner on the network includes it in a block along with other validated transactions and solves a complex mathematical problem to add the block to the blockchain, earning cryptocurrency as a reward [18].

Blockchain technology has evolved from its original purpose of cryptocurrency to encompass various applications in contracts, commerce, finance, and markets [9, 19]. With the advent of Blockchain 2.0, smart contracts have emerged as an alternative to cash transactions, expanding the scope of blockchain beyond currency transfers and digital payments [9]. Furthermore, Blockchain 3.0 offers even broader applications in banking, capital markets, trading, and economic activities, including the development of smart cities that utilize blockchain and smart contracts for intelligent administration, connectivity, energy management, and economics [20].

While blockchain technology brings numerous advantages, it does not guarantee interaction between parties or provide retribution [14]. Nevertheless, its decentralized and secure nature has contributed to its popularity across various applications.

3 Blockchain Technology in Organisations

3.1 Problem Statement

Blockchain technology has extensive applications in various types of organizations, impacting business management in multiple ways. It offers secure and transparent data storage and sharing, automated business processes, new business models, and the creation of digital assets. However, its implementation requires businesses to reevaluate existing models, invest in technology and infrastructure, and develop new skills [8]. Blockchain also influences specific areas of business management, including supply chain, finance, and human resources [8]. To leverage its potential, business managers must understand its impact and devise strategies accordingly.

Nevertheless, the exploitation and impact of blockchain technology pose challenges and risks for businesses. The lack of regulatory frameworks and standards complicates compliance and legal navigation, potentially resulting in legal and financial repercussions. Moreover, the energy consumption associated with blockchain transactions presents a significant barrier to adoption, leading to high operational costs and environmental concerns. For instance, the insurance industry can benefit from blockchain by facilitating efficient information flow, automation, fraud prevention, and audit trails, ultimately enhancing customer service and profitability [21]. However, recent findings expose limitations in the system that hinder broad adoption of blockchain technology [11]. Issues such as the lack of structures to establish stakeholder accountability, ambiguity in acceptance/rejection rules, and the absence of corrective mechanisms within the blockchain environment hinder its mass adoption. The absence of robust governance stands as the primary obstacle, irrespective of academic debates surrounding the advantages and disadvantages of blockchain [22].

4   Purpose for the Study

4.1   Blockchain Governance Problem Statement

As Beck et al. [23] emphasised, Blockchain governance has not been investigated. On the basis of a lack of analysis and understanding, this study determined that there are insufficient tools and resources accessible to better comprehend Blockchain governance. This gap persists, despite the fact that ecosystem actors would benefit from a full grasp of Blockchain governance. In the same way that corporations and end users must take governance into consideration when selecting a Blockchain product or platform, regulators and developers must also comprehend this element [24].

Hsieh et al. [25] said that a deeper understanding of blockchain governance is required, but Ziolkowski [26] claimed that "little is known about what and how crucial decisions are made and enforced in blockchain networks." Despite its significance, Finck [24] believes that blockchain governance is mainly unexplored territory. For this purpose, this study shall investigate the business management viewpoint on the aforementioned issues of researchers. Consequently, this leads to the study's issue statement:

With growing concerns about Blockchain governance, it is unclear how business management should control Blockchain implementation projects.

Blockchain technology presents notable security challenges concerning transaction integrity and confidentiality. These challenges encompass vulnerabilities in cryptographic algorithms and risks associated with the management of private keys [27]. Furthermore, decentralized blockchain networks are susceptible to various consensus attacks, including the 51% attack, double spending attack, Sybil attack, eclipse attack, and Denial of Service (DoS) attack, which jeopardize the security of blockchain transactions [27, 28]. To mitigate these concerns, the adoption of robust cryptographic algorithms, secure key management practices, and resilient consensus protocols is imperative [29]. Additionally, continual monitoring, vulnerability assessments, and proactive defence mechanisms are crucial for timely threat detection and response [29]. By implementing these measures, the security of blockchain transactions can be reinforced, fostering trust in the widespread adoption of blockchain technology across industries.

4.2 Research Purpose and Objective

The purpose of this research is to advance the current understanding of blockchain governance by investigating the various dimensions and themes relevant to the effective governance of blockchain technology, specifically within the organizational context. This study aims to fill the existing knowledge gap on this subject and provide valuable insights that could inform and enhance the development of blockchain governance frameworks and policies.

By reporting on themes that encapsulate the primary characteristics and layers of blockchain governance from the perspective of company management in an understandable way, this research seeks to investigate the knowledge on the issue of blockchain governance and aid companies in conducting more organised analyses of blockchain governance [30].

5   Research Methodology

5.1 Research Philosophy

The word research philosophy refers to the creation and nature of knowledge [30]. This study will start by exploring the fundamental concepts of ontology and epistemology, which are two important principles in philosophy.

Ontology. The ontological position examines knowledge and existence, determining if something exists [31]. It distinguishes between subjectivism and objectivism, where objectivists believe in objectively gathering information, while subjectivists emphasize knowledge from individual perspectives [30]. This study adopts an ontological perspective that focuses on the subjective reality of participants, specifically examining the perspectives of organizational group members. Considering the complexity and distinct nature of organizations within market contexts, relevant data is collected to understand the participants' reality [30].

Epistemology. Epistemology, as explained by Burrell and Morgan [32], deals with how we learn, identify trustworthy information, and share knowledge. Levers [33] discusses knowledge utilization and its characteristics. Researchers can choose between positivism and interpretivism, with interpretivism emphasizing social constructs in revealing reality [30]. This research aligns with an interpretative perspective, recognizing knowledge and reality as social products inseparable from social actors [34].

5.2 Methodology

This exploratory study used the meta-synthesis research approach. By combining and comparing the results or metaphors of several qualitative investigations, meta-synthesis may be utilised to generate interpretative translations, ground narratives, and theories [35]. The method is based on an interpretative strategy and seeks to "rigorously combine qualitative research results" in order to provide transferable information. The authors of this study choose to do a qualitative research synthesis meta-synthesis [36].

Qualitative research synthesis has emerged as a valuable method to analyse and extract evidence-based practices from current studies [38]. It originated from the criticism faced by qualitative research methods [35]. The growth of qualitative research synthesis can be divided into four phases, with meta-synthesis being the fourth and most widely used strategy for combining study results. Qualitative meta-synthesis consists of three components: it is a qualitative research strategy that synthesizes qualitative research, it involves the systematic integration and comparison of primary results across individual qualitative investigations on a specific issue, and it employs reciprocal translation to translate research from one field to another. Meta-synthesis provides a comprehensive understanding of phenomena, contributes to theory development, and supports evidence-based practice [38–45]. Reciprocal translation, also known as conceptual translation, is a method for analysing and bridging research frameworks from different fields [37]. The Quality Assessment Framework (QAF) employs reciprocal translation to analyse consistency and gaps in research conceptual frameworks [37].

5.3 Meta-synthesis

The research technique of "meta-synthesis" involves synthesising and contrasting the results or metaphors of several qualitative investigations to develop interpretative translations, underpinning narratives, or conceptual frameworks [35].

Framing the Review Exercise. Similar to other research strategies, the qualitative meta-synthesis is guided by a well-formulated research question. To realise the aims and objectives of this study, several research questions have been specified [30]. The research is structured around the main research question (RQ).

- RQ: what areas should be considered when needing to Govern Blockchain technology within an organisation?

   The qualitative meta-synthesis is used to answer the research topic, which is themed [30]. The primary research topic has been broken down into a series of subsidiary ones with the purpose of improving the study's organisation (SQ).

- SQ: To what degree are other industries using Blockchain technology?
- SQ: What concepts and structures does the governance of blockchains encompass?
- SQ: Why does Blockchain technology have to be regulated in organisations?
- SQ: What are the perceptions of the stakeholders regarding blockchain governance?
- SQ: How does the synthesized blockchain governance framework influence business managers' comprehension of blockchain governance?

Phases of the Review Exercise. The primary goals of the review were to ensure variety in the selection of papers, broad representation in the inclusion decisions, impartiality in the evaluation of research, authenticity in the analysis of studies, and clarity in the synthesis of findings are all summarised in the below Fig. 3 which shows that the review exercise consisted of five phases. The study's scope was determined by identifying and refining relevant themes, resulting in four main themes. These themes were further divided into sub-themes. Two of the main themes focused on the core concepts of the topic, namely "Blockchain governance" and "Blockchain technology." The other two themes explored the interconnections between these concepts, specifically "Governance challenges for technology adoption" and "Governance of opensource systems".

1. *Locating papers.* First, A comprehensive electronic database search was conducted using databases like IEEE Xplore, Elsevier, Academic Search Premier, ScienceDirect, Scopus, EconLit, and Dissertations and Theses AandI. Specific search strings related to topics such as blockchain governance, cryptocurrency governance, distributed ledger governance, and open-source software governance were used to identify relevant articles.

2. *Deciding what to include.* This study employed meta-synthesis, which allows for the integration of various techniques [42]. It included a wide range of paper types and methodological approaches, ranging from novels to unpublished theses. Selection criteria were based on logic and good judgement, focusing on works published between 2014 and 2022, excluding related theories, and prioritizing full-text availability. Relevance was ensured through the assessment of titles and abstracts, while consistency and accessibility were maintained by including only English sources. The comprehensive coverage of the subject was achieved by incorporating diverse paper types such as books, journal articles, conference papers, standards, patterns, theses, and reports. Different types of studies were also considered to enhance the understanding of the research landscape. In summary, the selected literature represents a diverse collection of materials contributing to this meta-synthesis.

3. *Appraisal of studies.* This study addressed the gap in strategies for assessing study quality in the integration of qualitative research findings [60]. It emphasized the importance of not overlooking significant research, rather than prioritizing inclusiveness over research quality [46]. To ensure the reliability of the chosen literature, the study implemented rigorous selection criteria. High-quality, relevant, and informative sources were included, while works outside the study scope and materials of questionable quality were excluded. Redundant or repetitive information was also excluded to prioritize novel insights, particularly in new studies. The systematic evaluation of content and structure was facilitated using Ngwenyama's Ten Basic Claims framework [47]. As a result of these exclusion criteria, the selected literature is robust, relevant, and aligned with the research objectives.

4. *Analysis.* Since the relationships across studies might be mutual, complementary, or contradictory, avoiding the trap of attempting to force a match for the sake of displaying uniformity in order to protect the authenticity of the results. All the chosen papers were carefully read in order to extract salient information from which the researcher could compile and develop overarching themes and concepts. Then, according to

Sherwood [46], they were "juxtaposed to find homogeneity to indicate discordance and dissonance.".

5. *Synthesis.* For this qualitative data synthesis, a meta-synthesis technique will be used, supported by the philosophical stance that one's beliefs and perceptions influence their knowledge of reality. Systematically and exhaustively, data are classified and organised into descriptive themes, from which new, higher-order themes are produced, providing additional insights beyond those offered by the source studies themselves [48].

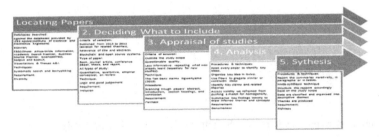

Fig. 3. Summary of the five phases of the review exercise.

5.4 Description of Sample

As the topic was thoroughly covered during the course of the five-stage review process, the remaining 30 publications were analysed and coded with the use of Nvivo software [49]. Following the coding criteria provided by Wolfswinkel et al. [49], a total of 42 codes were generated. The resultant set of codes was then summarised and organised into categories (axial coding) using input from each of the authors. In the end, this study narrowed these down to 18 distinct groups that would serve as placeholders for the various components of the framework that would be provided below. By using selective coding, the researcher was able to identify five overarching categories that captured the essence of the many sources of friction. For this reason, the procedure is shown in Fig. 4.

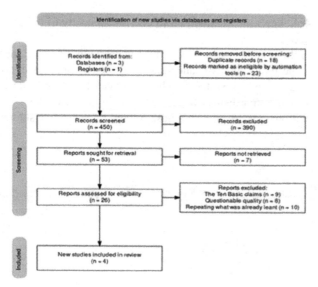

Fig. 4. Preferred Reporting Items for Systematic Review and Meta-Analysis using PRISMA Model flowchart.

6 Results and Discussion

As mentioned previously, the study adopts a subjective and interpretive stance along with a meta-synthesis methodology. It systematically presents the review findings by summarizing the literature on blockchain technology, governance characteristics, challenges, and decentralized frameworks. The TOE framework is qualitatively analysed and evaluated for its potential contribution to bridging the literature gap. A conceptual framework and integrated solutions are proposed to address the research objectives. The research aims to investigate blockchain governance knowledge, assisting companies in conducting organized analyses [30].

Comparative analysis of existing studies on blockchain governance reveals key themes and the necessity for meta-synthesis. Research has focused on governance models, mechanisms, regulatory frameworks, stakeholder engagement, scalability, and performance considerations. Consensus mechanisms like proof-of-work (PoW), proof-of-stake (PoS), and delegated proof-of-stake (DPoS), as well as governance mechanisms such as voting systems and dispute resolution processes, have been explored [50]. Stakeholder involvement and incentive alignment, involving developers, users, miners, investors, and regulators, have been examined. Scalability and performance challenges have been addressed through techniques like sharing and off-chain solutions [9].

While existing studies provide valuable insights, meta-synthesis is required to achieve a comprehensive understanding of blockchain governance. It integrates fragmented knowledge, bridges gaps, and generates new insights. By synthesizing findings from multiple studies, it advances theories and practices in blockchain governance. Meta-synthesis offers a holistic perspective, capturing the complex interactions among technical, legal, economic, and socio-political factors, thereby enhancing our overall understanding. The tabulation table in Fig. 5 presents a comprehensive list of selected articles imported into NVivo 12, along with the keywords used for coding, and facilitating data analysis [51].

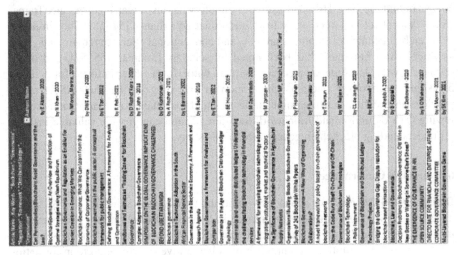

Fig. 5. Tabulate of Articles

6.1 Governance Definition

Governance has several meanings in many contexts, including politics, IT, and business. Social science articles split governance into markets, hierarchies, and networks [52]. Governance is the process of integrating organisational and economic activity via decision rights, incentives, and responsibility [23].

6.2 Governance Challenges

The use of blockchain technology has led to the emergence of decentralised organisational structures, as businesses experiment with new ways of managing economic activity. However, the governance of blockchain technology has been a topic of debate, with the lack of proper regulation being a major challenge. This paper highlights the need for alternate governance systems to enable asynchronous work practices, and how the open-source community has developed an open-source governance framework to address this need. The paper draws parallels between blockchain development projects and conventional open-source projects, with multiple large public blockchains being produced and distributed as free and open-source software. The paper suggests that the literature on open-source software development can provide valuable insights for understanding blockchain governance. Ultimately, it is important for businesses to address the issue of governance to fully utilise the potential of blockchain technology [53–58].

Some see blockchain as a governance tool but forget it must be regulated for its effective implementation. The discussion is rooted in transaction costs theory, which explores the impact of effective governance on economic production within businesses [53]. To meet the demands of modern business structures, researchers have explored decentralised organisational structures, such as project-based firms [53] and disposable enterprises [55], which have led to more adaptable organisational forms that can control output [53, 55]. The open-source community has also created governance frameworks that reflect this trend away from traditional governance [57, 58]. The similarity between blockchain development projects and conventional open-source projects, such as Bitcoin and Ethereum, has been noted by scholars Lindman [55–57], and open-source software development has been found to outperform other platforms for building blockchain technology solutions [56]. Lindman [57] suggests that the OSS literature provides an excellent starting point for discussing blockchain governance, and the following OSS definition and framework literature section can provide valuable insights for understanding blockchain governance in this study.

6.3   In OSS Governance

Defining OSS Governance. Two viewpoints are used to assess the aim of OSS governance. One possibility is to see governance as a means of resolving the OSS development coordination dilemma. The second viewpoint is to consider OSS management as a reaction to the institutional component of collaborative activity and group formation [59].

Conceptual Framework for OSS Governance. In recent years, open-source initiatives have emerged as a potential alternative to traditional hierarchical organizational structures. Scholars have proposed various governance frameworks to describe the evolution of these projects. One such framework is the life cycle stages theory of OSS, which proposes four governance phases de facto governance, designing governance, implementing governance, and stabilizing governance. According to Lattemann and Stieglitz [60], each phase is associated with a different set of governance tools and community dynamics. Similarly, de Laat [58] identifies three stages of governance within OSS communities spontaneous, internal, and external. In this stage, innovation and productivity are often achieved without formal governance structures, while internal governance tools are developed during the growth phase. The external governance stage focuses on the institutionalization of OSS communities. The study by Lattemann and Stieglitz [60] and de Laat [58] provides valuable insights into the governance of open-source initiatives, which can be useful for understanding the governance of blockchain development projects, as highlighted by Lindman [57].

This text outlines the governance phases of open-source software (OSS) initiatives. Scholars have proposed various frameworks for understanding the evolution of OSS governance, such as the life cycle stages theory and governance phases theory. Lattemann and Stieglitz [60] identify four related governance phases: de facto governance, designing governance, implementing governance, and stabilizing governance. Each phase is associated with different approaches to governance, such as founder objectives, democratic procedures, and transparency measures. Meanwhile, de Laat [58] proposes a three-stage model of OSS governance, starting with spontaneous governance, followed by internal governance characterized by the development of governance tools, and ending with external governance focused on the institutionalization of OSS communities. These frameworks provide a starting point for understanding the governance of blockchain technology, as open-source governance frameworks are also utilized in blockchain development projects [56, 57]. By examining the similarities and differences between OSS and blockchain governance, this paper aims to contribute to a better understanding of how to effectively regulate blockchain technology.

Applicability of OSS Governance Theories to Blockchain Technology Projects and Governance. Garagol and Nilsson [61] utilized de Laat's six-dimensional governance framework to investigate the presence of these processes in Ethereum as a blockchain project. The study found that Ethereum embodies the first five elements of OSS governance, while the sixth dimension of autocracy vs. democracy was unclear, with no identifiable leadership. Additionally, the authors proposed a seventh factor, which is initiative-based development.

7 Blockchain Governance

In recent years, there has been a shift in the focus of academic literature on blockchain governance. While some scholars have emphasized blockchain as a governance instrument, others have highlighted the importance of blockchain governance [62]. For the purposes of this literature study, the latter perspective will be the focus. Blockchain governance can be classified into several types, including governance that is dictated by the nature of the system and governance that is driven by a cohesive vision backed up by appropriate stakeholder choices, strategic planning, and execution [11]. Ultimately, governance in the context of blockchain involves controlling, integrating, and monitoring the system, as well as monitoring performance and deviation circumstances [11, 62].

While governance takes different forms depending on the context, in the context of blockchain governance, scholars have failed to reach a consensus on its definition [62]. However, scholars have identified two distinct functions that governance serves in the context of blockchain. One function involves governance by infrastructure, which refers to regulations related to the source code of the blockchain's technical system. These regulations can be limiting decision-making in terms of enforcement and are often referred to as on-chain regulations in the IT sector. The second function of blockchain governance involves governance by rules, which can be endogenous or exogenous. Endogenous rules are those that are derived from the internal reference community, while exogenous rules are derived from an external reference community [17].

While on-chain regulations offer several advantages, such as replicating the transaction database and providing incentives to miners, some scholars caution against embracing an entirely on-chain rule system. They argue that human nature can affect ostensibly automated processes, as seen in the case of a typographical error that cost an institution millions of dollars [63]. Additionally, the DAO case in June 2016 demonstrated the potential risks of on-chain governance, as an attacker was able to exploit smart contracts to launch an assault [22]. Thus, while on-chain governance has its benefits, it is essential to carefully consider the risks and limitations of this approach in the context of blockchain governance.

8   Conceptual Framework for Blockchain Governance

8.1   The Blockchain Governance Framework: Conceptual Framework

Blockchain Governance Dimensions. Scholars have categorised government into many dimensions. Pelt et al. [8] say blockchain governance concerns are the major governance challenges for blockchains. Pelt et al. [8] suggest starting with a synthesis matrix. A synthesis matrix helps organise thoughts and synthesise relevant sources [8]. To establish the BG framework, Pelt et al. [8] created a synthesis matrix using literature analyses. Granularity is not regarded at that time. In this approach, both software release selection and decision-making methods are governance ideas [8].

The dimensions synthesis matrix comprises 122 rows and columns after identifying governance principles [8]. The synthesis matrix handles these concerns. The methods used identified 15 governance concept clusters [8]. Pelt et al. [8] labelled each cluster. They highlight governance traits. After that, they chose the BG framework's Dimensions: Roles, Incentives, membership, communication, and decision-making.

Blockchain Governance Layers. The BG architecture requires a set of blockchain governance layers as the second building piece. Using analytical levels or layers is considered as a way to break down governance into more manageable components. This technique differentiates between governance layers using Carter, [64] tiered framework. Separates governance into three levels: off-chain community layer, off-chain development layer, and on-chain protocol layer.

Combining Governance Dimensions and Layers. An initial collection of governance concepts is created throughout the governance dimension identification process. Pelt et al., [8] proceed to merge the governance features and layers. This approach uncovers two exceptions. First, the edge is regarded to represent the dimension of formation and context. Second, the framework's questions are based on blockchain governance themes from the researchers' findings.

8.2   Theoretical Framework

The TOE Framework. The purpose of this paper is to explore the application of the Technology-Organization-Environment (TOE) framework to evaluate the governance dimensions and layers of blockchain in organisations. The TOE framework was initially introduced by Tornatzky and Fleischer [65] to evaluate technology adoption and service innovation within organizations. It assesses an organization's technological innovation via three organizational aspects: the technological framework, organizational factors, and the external environment. Several researchers have used the TOE model to evaluate software uptake and operational technology utilization [66, 67].

The TOE framework has been applied to study the characteristics and fundamental operational procedures of organizational departments [68]. The type, size, and sector of organizations impact the adoption of new technologies, requiring unique data processing techniques per department [69]. Organizational research on IT deployment is done to assess the organization's current position on new technologies, and the TOE framework has been employed to evaluate such positions. The results were centred on the company's supply chain, but the rest may be applied to the entire organization [65].

The TOE framework has limitations, and other literary frameworks such as the technology Admission Model (TAM) and Planted Competency Theory (TPB) have also been recognized [70]. These frameworks emphasize users and their comprehension of technology usability. However, the TOE structure best fits this research purpose, as innovation adoption is framed by organizational decision-making according to Tornatzky and Fleischer [65]. The TOE framework links three qualitative components, including cultural and industrial variety, and is considered a well-developed and systematic theoretical lens through which technology adoption may be analysed [67, 71].

Therefore, the proposed study will adopt the TOE framework to evaluate the governance dimensions and layers of blockchain, using the OSS phases, Lifecycle, and BC governance dimensions and layers as moderators [72]. This proposed conceptual framework in Fig. 6 will investigate the major considerations that should be taken into account when considering blockchain governance for business managers, as blockchain governance and governance viewpoints vary based on the users and technology. The conceptual framework of the study will comprise multi-stages before the final perceived blockchain governance problems stage, and the state will be made up of the technology, organization, and environment structure to establish the business environment affected, which is adapted from Tornatzky et al. [65], as well as the four governance phases and stages that represent a sense of time, proposed by Niknejad, Hussin and Amiri [73].

To adopt/evaluate a blockchain governance framework for businesses in South Africa, the TOE and OSS Governance framework will help investigate the major considerations that should be taken into account when considering Blockchain Governance.

OSS Governance Phases				
	De Facto	Design	Implement	Stabilize
Technological	Blockchain Governance Framework Dimensions and Layers			
Organisational				
Environmental				
	Introduction	Growth	Maturity	Decline/Revive
OSS Life Cycle Stages				

Fig. 6. Theoretical Framework for Blockchain Governance

9 Conclusion

In this article, the researcher addressed the governance decisions required to design a blockchain-based system in organizations and examined how contextual factors in the public sector influence the available choices in blockchain governance. To answer these questions, the researcher developed a novel conceptual framework for analysing blockchain governance in the public sector, based on the TOE framework for organizational applicability, the OSS phases, the Lifecycle, and public management concepts and theories. The proposed framework suggests that blockchain governance in the public sector is moderated by design decisions concerning infrastructure and application architecture, interoperability, decision-making mechanism, incentive mechanism, consensus mechanism, organization, accountability, and control of governance.

Our contribution to the literature is twofold. First, despite the widespread interest in blockchain in the public sector and the challenges concerning governance, academic production in the field of public administration on the topic has been conspicuously absent. To address this gap, the researcher used a meta-synthesis approach to consolidate existing qualitative research and investigate how blockchain-based systems can be governed in light of the knowledge base in public administration literature. Second, the conceptualization of governance in blockchain literature is fragmented, and a more cohesive framework is needed to systematically consolidate and analyse the implications of governance decisions in the design of blockchain-based systems. The proposed framework provides a common frame of reference for researchers and assists companies in conducting more organized analyses of blockchain governance, which can be applied in other sectoral areas as well.

The analysis has several key takeaways for system designers and decision-makers interested in applying blockchain-based solutions in public management. First, policy-makers and system designers need to reflect on the interlinkages between governance levels and assess the implications of choices at one level to other levels of governance. Second, institutional factors, such as cost-benefit calculations, norms and values, path dependency concerning technological infrastructure, and regulatory framework, may play a determinant role in governance choices. Therefore, it is important to consider these institutional factors while designing a blockchain-based system in manual industries such as health, insurance, and education.

9.1 Limitation

This article's literature review of blockchain governance in organizations is not without limitations. One of the limitations is that not all potential papers were included in the sample due to the diversity in blockchain applications and the high interest resulting in hundreds of articles published mainly in the last three years from the time of writing. Additionally, the study tried to limit the sample strictly to the scope of the review because the topic involves various concepts from both governance and blockchain, which may have led to the exclusion of some satisfactory papers. However, the researchers were confident they saturated the topic because there was a repetition of what had already been lent. While this literature review may not be sufficient on its own to make a case for blockchain governance in organizations, it gives the background and a point to understand the topic while inspiring further empirical investigations.

9.2 Future Research

In conclusion, this paper identifies two areas of future work that could improve the proposed Blockchain Governance (BG) framework. The first is empirical validation, which is necessary to confirm the exploratory findings of the current study. The validation research could be done using various methods such as technical action research, surveys, interviews and focus groups. The feedback obtained from these methods could be used to refine the BG framework incrementally. The second area of future work is to define what entails good blockchain governance, which could be context-specific and highlight different quality properties such as transparency, efficiency, and balance of power. The proposed BG framework could be extended to connect with a direct value judgement or used for performance analysis. By exploring these areas of research, this study can further refine and improve the BG framework and provide valuable insights into blockchain governance.

References

1. Nakamoto, S.: Bitcoin: a peer-to-peer electronic cash system (2008)
2. Ostern, N., Rosemann, M., Moormann, J.: Determining the idiosyncrasy of blockchain: an affordances perspective (2020)
3. Abbatemarco, N., De Rossi, L.M., Gaur, A., Salviotti, G.: Beyond a blockchain paradox: how intermediaries can leverage a disintermediation technology (2020)
4. Dodd, D., Favaro, K.: Managing the right tension. Harv. Bus. Rev. **84**(62–74), 160 (2006)
5. Pauline, A.-K.: Blockchain, a catalyst for new approaches in insurance (2017)
6. Stringham, E.P.: Private governance. Private Governance (2015). https://doi.org/10.1093/acp rof:oso/9780199365166.001.0001
7. Salter, A.W.: Space debris: a law and economics analysis of the orbital commons. SSRN Electron. J. (2018). https://doi.org/10.2139/ssrn.3191395
8. van Pelt, R., Jansen, S., Baars, D., Overbeek, S.: Defining blockchain governance: a framework for analysis and comparison. Inf. Syst. Manag. **38**, 1–21 (2020). https://doi.org/10.1080/105 80530.2020.1720046
9. Mazzorana-Kremer, F., Swan, M.: Blockchain Blueprint for a New Economy. O'Reilly Media, Inc., Sebastopol. - References - Scientific Research Publishing (2015, 2019)
10. Wust, K., Gervais, A.: Do you need a blockchain? In: 2018 Crypto Valley Conference on Blockchain Technology (CVCBT) (2018). https://doi.org/10.1109/cvcbt.2018.00011
11. John, T., Pam, M.: Complex adaptive blockchain governance. In: MATEC Web of Conferences, vol. 223, p. 1010 (2018). https://doi.org/10.1051/matecconf/201822301010
12. Böhme, R., Christin, N., Edelman, B., Moore, T.: Bitcoin: economics, technology, and governance. J. Econ. Perspect. **29**, 213–238 (2015). https://doi.org/10.1257/jep.29.2.213
13. Crosby, M., Weerakkody, N., Pattanayak, P., et al.: BlockChain technology: beyond bitcoin. Int. J. Inf. Manage. **50**, 302–309 (2016). https://doi.org/10.1016/j.ijinfomgt.2019.08.012
14. Grima, S., Spiteri, J., Romanova, I.: The challenges for regulation and control in an environment of rapid technological innovations. AIDA Eur. Res. Ser. Insur. Law Regul. **4**, 83–98 (2019). https://doi.org/10.1007/978-3-030-27386-6_4
15. Ababa, A.: Blockchain technology in Africa (2017)
16. Golosova, J., Romanovs, A.: The Advantages and disadvantages of the blockchain technology (2018)
17. PwC: Making sense of bitcoin and blockchain (2013)
18. D'Aliessi, M.: How does the blockchain work? (2019)
19. Scott, B., Loonam, J., Kumar, V.: Exploring the rise of blockchain technology: towards distributed collaborative organizations. Strateg. Chang. **26**, 423–428 (2017). https://doi.org/10.1002/jsc.2142
20. Efanov, D., Roschin, P.: The all-pervasiveness of the blockchain technology (2018)
21. Johnson, G.: Gary Johnson Receives G. Duffield Smith Outstanding Publication Award (2017)

22. Zachariadis, M., Hileman, G., Scott, S.V.: Governance and control in distributed ledgers: understanding the challenges facing blockchain technology in financial services. Inf. Organ. **29**, 105–117 (2019). https://doi.org/10.1016/j.infoandorg.2019.03.001
23. Beck, R., Müller-Bloch, C., King, J.L.: Governance in the blockchain economy: a framework and research agenda. J. Assoc. Inf. Syst. **19**, 1020–1034 (2018). https://doi.org/10.17705/1jais.00518
24. Lyons, T., Courcelas, L., Timsit, K.: Thematic report 1 blockchain for government and public services a thematic report prepared by the European union blockchain observatory & forum blockchain for government and public services an initiative of the (2018)
25. Hsieh, Y.-Y., Vergne, J.-P., Wang, S.: The Internal and external governance of blockchain-based organizations: evidence from cryptocurrencies (2017)
26. Ziolkowski, R., Parangi, G., Miscione, G., Schwabe, G.: Examining gentle rivalry: decision-making in blockchain systems (2019)
27. Kalodner, H., Carlsten, M., Ellenbogen, P., et al.: An empirical study of Namecoin and lessons for decentralized namespace design (2015)
28. Rizun, P., Wilmer, E., Miller, A.: Block n roll: efficient 51% attacks against cryptocurrencies. In: Proceedings of the 2021 ACM SIGSAC Conference on Computer and Communications Security (2021)
29. Yu, G., Wang, X., Yu, K., et al.: Survey: sharding in blockchains. IEEE Access **8**, 14155–14181 (2020). https://doi.org/10.1109/access.2020.2965147
30. Saunders, M., Lewis, P., Thornhill, A.: Research Methods for Business Students, 8th edn. Pearson (2019)
31. Furlong, P., Marsh, D.: A skin not a sweater: ontology and epistemology in political science. Theory Methods Polit. Sci. 184–211 (2010). https://doi.org/10.1007/978-0-230-36664-0_10
32. Burrell, G., Morgan, G.: Sociological Paradigms and Organisational Analysis. Routledge, London (2017)
33. Levers, M.-J.D.: Philosophical paradigms, grounded theory, and perspectives on emergence. SAGE Open **3**, 1–6 (2013). https://doi.org/10.1177/2158244013517243
34. Pawlikowski, P., Rico, N., Sell, S.: Positivism: a concept analysis. Int. J. Nurs. Clin. Pract. **5** (2018). https://doi.org/10.15344/2394-4978/2018/284
35. Sandelowski, M., Docherty, S., Emden, C.: Qualitative metasynthesis: issues and techniques. Res Nurs. Health **20**, 365–371 (1997). https://doi.org/10.1002/(sici)1098-240x(199708)20:4%3c365::aid-nur9%3e3.0.co;2-e
36. Major, C.H., Savin-Baden, M.: An Introduction to Qualitative Research Synthesis. Routledge, London (2012)
37. Pope, C., Mays, N.: Qualitative research: Reaching the parts other methods cannot reach: an introduction to qualitative methods in health and health services research. BMJ **311**, 42–45 (1995). https://doi.org/10.1136/bmj.311.6996.42
38. Ludvigsen, M.S., Hall, E.O.C., Meyer, G., et al.: Using Sandelowski and Barroso's meta-synthesis method in advancing qualitative evidence. Qual. Health Res. **26**, 320–329 (2015). https://doi.org/10.1177/1049732315576493
39. Finfgeld, D.L.: Metasynthesis: the state of the art—so far. Qual. Health Res. **13**, 893–904 (2003). https://doi.org/10.1177/1049732303253462
40. Zimmer, L.: Qualitative meta-synthesis: a question of dialoguing with texts. J. Adv. Nurs. **53**, 311–318 (2006). https://doi.org/10.1111/j.1365-2648.2006.03721.x
41. Hoon, C.: Meta-synthesis of qualitative case studies. Organ. Res. Methods **16**, 522–556 (2013). https://doi.org/10.1177/1094428113484969
42. Walsh, D., Downe, S.: Meta-synthesis method for qualitative research: a literature review. J. Adv. Nurs. **50**, 204–211 (2005). https://doi.org/10.1111/j.1365-2648.2005.03380.x

43. Yahyapour, S., Shamizanjani, M., Mosakhani, M.: A conceptual breakdown structure for knowledge management benefits using meta-synthesis method. J. Knowl. Manag. **19**, 1295–1309 (2015). https://doi.org/10.1108/jkm-05-2015-0166

44. Nye, E., Melendez-Torres, G.J., Bonell, C.: Origins, methods and advances in qualitative meta-synthesis. Rev. Educ. **4**, 57–79 (2016). https://doi.org/10.1002/rev3.3065

45. Annells, M.: Guest editorial: a qualitative quandary: alternative representations and meta-synthesis. J. Clin. Nurs. **14**, 535–536 (2005). https://doi.org/10.1111/j.1365-2702.2005.011 97.x

46. Sherwood, G.D.: Meta-synthesis of qualitative analyses of caring: defining a therapeutic model of nursing. Adv. Pract. Nurs. Q. **3**, 32–42 (1997)

47. Ngwenyama, O.: The ten basic claims of information systems research: an approach to interrogating validity claims in scientific argumentation. SSRN Electron. J. (2019). https://doi.org/10.2139/ssrn.3446798

48. Egerton, T., Diamond, L., Buchbinder, R., et al.: Barriers and enablers in primary care clinicians' management of osteoarthritis: protocol for a systematic review and qualitative evidence synthesis. BMJ Open **6**, e011618 (2016). https://doi.org/10.1136/bmjopen-2016-011618

49. Wolfswinkel, J.F., Furtmueller, E., Wilderom, C.P.M.: Using grounded theory as a method for rigorously reviewing literature. Eur. J. Inf. Syst. **22**, 45–55 (2013). https://doi.org/10.1057/ejis.2011.51

50. Jansen, C., De Vries, J.: Blockchain governance: a framework proposal. In: 51st Hawaii International Conference on System Sciences (2018)

51. Fereday, J., Muir-Cochrane, E., Dip, G., Ed, A.: demonstrating rigor using thematic analysis: a hybrid approach of inductive and deductive coding and theme development. Int. J. Qual. Methods (2006)

52. Chhotray, V., Stoker, G.: Governance Theory and Practice. Palgrave Macmillan UK (2009)

53. Sydow, J., Lindkvist, L., DeFillippi, R.: Project-based organizations, embeddedness and repositories of knowledge: editorial. Organ. Stud. **25**, 1475–1489 (2004). https://doi.org/10.1177/0170840604048162

54. Bakker, K.: Privatizing Water. Cornell University Press, Ithaca (2010)

55. Porru, S., Pinna, A., Marchesi, M., Tonelli, R.: Blockchain-oriented software engineering: challenges and new directions, pp. 169–171 (2017)

56. Bian, Y., Mu, W., Zhao, J.L.: Online Leadership for open source project success: evidence from the GitHub blockchain projects. In: PACIS 2018 Proceedings (2018)

57. Nyman, L., Lindman, J.: Code forking, governance, and sustainability in open source software. Technol. Innov. Manage. Rev. **3** (2013)

58. de Laat, P.B.: Governance of open source software: state of the art. J. Manage. Govern. **11**, 165–177 (2007). https://doi.org/10.1007/s10997-007-9022-9

59. Markus, M.L.: The governance of free/open source software projects: monolithic, multidimensional, or configurational? J. Manage. Govern. **11**, 151–163 (2007). https://doi.org/10.1007/s10997-007-9021-x

60. Lattemann, C., Stieglitz, S.: Framework for governance in open source communities. In: Proceedings of the 38th Annual Hawaii International Conference on System Sciences (2005). https://doi.org/10.1109/hicss.2005.278

61. Nilsson, O., Garagol, D.: Public blockchain communities a study on how governance mechanisms are expressed within blockchain communities. gupea.ub.gu.se (2018)

62. Katina, P.F., Keating, C.B., Sisti, J.A., Gheorghe, A.V.: Blockchain governance. Int. J. Crit. Infrastruct. **15**, 121 (2019). https://doi.org/10.1504/ijcis.2019.098835

63. Crepaldi, M.: Why blockchains need the law. In: Proceedings of the Seventeenth International Conference on Artificial Intelligence and Law - ICAIL 2019 (2019). https://doi.org/10.1145/3322640.3328780

64. Carter, N.: An overview of governance in blockchains (2018)
65. Tornatzky, L.G., Klein, K.J.: Innovation characteristics and innovation adoption-implementation: a meta-analysis of findings. IEEE Trans. Eng. Manage. EM **29**, 28–45 (1982). https://doi.org/10.1109/tem.1982.6447463
66. Gangwar, H., Date, H., Ramaswamy, R.: Understanding determinants of cloud computing adoption using an integrated TAM-TOE model. J. Enterp. Inf. Manag. **28**, 107–130 (2015). https://doi.org/10.1108/jeim-08-2013-0065
67. Pudjianto, B.W., Hangjung, Z.: Factors affecting E-government assimilation in developing countries. SSRN Electron. J. (2009). https://doi.org/10.2139/ssrn.1553651
68. Parker, C.M., Castleman, T.: Small firm e-business adoption: a critical analysis of theory. J. Enterp. Inf. Manag. **22**, 167–182 (2009). https://doi.org/10.1108/17410390910932812
69. Molla, A., Licker, P.S.: eCommerce adoption in developing countries: a model and instrument. Inf. Manage. **42**, 877–899 (2005). https://doi.org/10.1016/j.im.2004.09.002
70. Leeson, P.T.: Anarchy unbound (2014). https://doi.org/10.1017/cbo9781139198813
71. Oliveira, T., Martins, M.F.: Understanding e-business adoption across industries in European countries. Ind. Manag. Data Syst. **110**, 1337–1354 (2010). https://doi.org/10.1108/026355 71011087428
72. Borgman, H.P., Bahli, B., Heier, H., Schewski, F.: Cloudrise: exploring cloud computing adoption and governance with the TOE framework. In: 2013 46th Hawaii International Conference on System Sciences (2013). https://doi.org/10.1109/hicss.2013.132
73. Niknejad, N., Hussin, A.R.C., Amiri, I.S.: Literature review of service-oriented architecture (SOA) adoption researches and the related significant factors. In: Niknejad, N., Hussin, A.R.C., Amiri, I.S. (eds.) The Impact of Service Oriented Architecture Adoption on Organizations. SpringerBriefs in Electrical and Computer Engineering, pp. 9–41. Springer, Cham (2019). https://doi.org/10.1007/978-3-030-12100-6_2

Factors Influencing the Use of Parental Control Software (PCS) Used by Parents in South Africa

Morné de Bruyn and Tendani Thabela-Chimboza[(✉)] [iD]

Department of Information Systems Cape Town, The University of Cape Town, Cape Town, South Africa
mdb@wam.co.za, tendani.chimboza@uct.ac.za

Abstract. Parental Control Software (PCS) is central to parenting in the digital world. PCS applications allow parents to monitor screen time and restrict their children's online activities. The influx of new technology and easily accessible online content prompted many parents to use PCS. As informed by the Protection Motivation Theory (PMT), we investigated the factors influencing parents' use of PCS in South Africa. Semi-structured interviews were conducted with 15 parents. The total number of children observed was 32 between the ages of 6–18. The study found that using PCS is influenced by the need to safeguard children from mental and physical health challenges, cyber risks, and behavioral challenges associated with inappropriate content. Most significantly, parents in South Africa use PCS to cope with the fears related to children's use of technology that can expose them to many cyber risks. The study revealed that the PCS used in South Africa is limited to the device's operating systems, for example, Google Family Link. While parents' technological skills significantly influenced the choices of PCS, the lack of awareness of other PCS technologies with better monitoring tools was overwhelming.

Keywords: Parental Control Software · Screen time · Digital Parenting · Cyber risks

1 Introduction

Parental Control Software (PCS) includes all tools and mechanisms parents use to monitor screen time and restrict online activities [1, 2]. The use of PCS became essential during COVID-19 lockdowns when individual family members, including children, spent more time on their mobile devices [3]. Parents used mobile devices as digital pacifiers to cope with work-from-home pressures during this period. South African telecommunication companies provide cheaper plans that enable households to access the internet [4]. At least 95% of South African children have internet access from home or school [5]. However, while online, children are unaware of the risks [6].

An earlier study about online activities by children shows that parents often do not monitor the content their children are watching [7]. The same survey also revealed that 70% of children between the ages of 9–17 in South Africa access the internet

© The Author(s), under exclusive license to Springer Nature Switzerland AG 2023
A. Gerber and M. Coetzee (Eds.): SAICSIT 2023, CCIS 1878, pp. 117–135, 2023.
https://doi.org/10.1007/978-3-031-39652-6_8

without consent from their parents [2]. The South African children's mobile device and internet access monitoring activities are complicated because one in two children are more technically skilled than their parents [1].

PCS is at the heart of protecting children from harmful online content [1]. Today's children find themselves in a world where they are readily exposed to technology and digital media [3]. This exposure, coupled with the widespread availability of mobile devices, has provided children with growth opportunities while increasing their exposure to many cyber risks [8]. PCS may assist parents in managing the risks associated with mobile device use, but the use of such applications is low [3]. Like most parents worldwide, parents in South Africa find themselves as gatekeepers in this digital landscape.

Protecting children from harmful online content and associated cyber risks while allowing access to digital media to enrich their lives is a delicate balancing act [4]. The study highlights parents' various considerations when using PCS to monitor and control their children's mobile device usage. This study asked the question;

What factors influence parents' usage of parental control software in South Africa?

2 Literature Review

2.1 Children's Access to Online Content and the Use of PCS

Online content has many advantages for early child development [2]. For this reason, many parents make efforts to purchase mobile devices for their children to access a plethora of child-friendly and educational content. However, if not mediated, online content may introduce many challenges that warrant using PCS [9].

Parental control in the context of children's access to online content can be conceptualized in three categories [10];

- monitoring – parents' passive surveillance of their children's online activities. An example is checking what children are watching on their mobile devices but not constantly or consistently with the assumption that they can self-regulate.
- mediation – conversations between parents and children about online activities. This may include a discussion about the dangers of prolonged screen time.
- restrictions – introducing and implementing rules and limitations regarding children's online activities. For example, time restrictions on YouTube Kids.

PCS tools have features for content filtering, website restrictions, screen time restriction, download controls, location tracking, and social media monitoring [10]. Noteworthy, most parents gravitate towards PCS for screen time restrictions, content filtering, and website restrictions [3, 11, 12].

The earliest study regarding PCS in South Africa was conducted in 2011 by scholars who observed the severity of risks associated with "potentially dangerous mobile media content" for adolescents [13, p. 227]. This study was conducted against the adoption of the instant messenger called MXIT, which allowed young people to converse with people across the country, including strangers [13]. The same study suggested that PCS could assist parents in protecting their children from dangerous mobile media content such as adult-rated media, explicit media, and gambling [13]. To protect children from harmful content through PCS, the literature suggests that parents must know the available tools, cost, and usability [13, 14].

Parents have inherently negative biases regarding their children and internet usage [15]. This negative bias and the reported adverse effects of mobile devices on children concern parents, but mobile devices have become instilled in everyday life and cannot be dismissed [16]. Parents in developed countries have conceptualized mobile device screen time as a reward or leisure time for their children to commit to modern socialization [3, 14]. In South Korea, PCS was viewed as the cornerstone of reducing smartphone addiction for children [17]. In the United States of America (USA), a survey of 330 parents revealed that the perceived usefulness of a PCS influences parents' adoption [14]. In this context, parents were found to be aware of potential threat of prolonged screen time on adolescents' self-esteem, academic performance, and physical health [14]. Similar to [13], parents in the USA were concerned about "sexually explicit, violent or politically objectionable material," which can influence problematic behavior from children [14, p. 225].

Using PCS benefits or protects children and safeguards parents' mental well-being [9]. Unmonitored screen time and content for children may result in problematic behavior that course stress on their parents. The various TikTok challenges that teenagers participate in, which often leave them injured or dead, have caused immense stress on parents [18]. Table 1 presents the top five Tik Tok life-threatening challenges that teenagers participated in 2021 as identified by Cyber Purify[1].

Table 1. Top five TikTok life-threatening challenges in 2021

Challenge	Description
Skull breaker challenge	Three people jump to break their skulls, resulting in severe head pain
Coronavirus linking challenge	Young people worldwide licked surfaces in public areas to show they are not scared of the virus
Silhouette Challenge	Young people took silhouette footage and shared them on Tik Tok which resulted in exposing their bodies online without consent
The corncob challenge	This challenge encouraged teenagers to eat corn plugged into a turning drill that injured them in their oral cavity
Color-changing eye challenge	This Tik Tok challenge influenced teenagers to use chlorine-based chemicals to change the color of their eyes which can result in loss of vision

---

[1] Cyber Purify is an organization based in America that advocates for child online protection rights. https://cyberpurify.com/knowledge/

Privacy issues continue influencing parents' need to protect their children from pervasive cyber predators [12]. In many cases where children have fallen prey to cybercriminals, parents constantly blame themselves for negligence [9, 17]. The current study contributes to knowledge about decisions made by parents in the Global South regarding monitoring mobile devices and children's online activities. We initiated the study based on the idea that children are vulnerable technology users and unaware of the inherent dangers. Furthermore, children in South Africa reside in a context where nation-states are lagging in designing online safety strategies for protecting children [19, 20].

3   Theoretical Framework

Protection Motivation Theory (PMT), as described by Rogers in 1975, theorizes why users protect themselves from potential risks. As shown in Fig. 1, the PMT framework consists of three primary constructs: threat appraisal, ownership appraisal, and coping appraisal. Initially, the threat appraisal acknowledges the possibility of risk, and where risk is perceived, the severity of that risk is then determined [21].

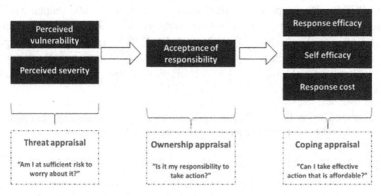

Fig. 1. Protection Motivation Theory

PMT explains why technology may be adopted to safeguard users from perceived threats. Studies about protecting children's rights in the context of mobile device usage have also employed PMT as a central theory [14]. To determine factors that influence parents' decision to use PCS, we particularize the three constructs of PMT:

- **Threat appraisal**: This construct involves the identification of a threat and vulnerability associated with the use of technology. The current study was initiated on the idea that children's use of mobile devices may present threats [8, 22]. The severity of these threats and vulnerabilities are ascertained by parents who often passively observe their children's online activities. The combined threat detection and severity determine if the threat should be addressed.
- **Ownership appraisal:** This construct is concerned with identifying the actor who accepts responsibility for controlling and supervising children's use of mobile devices. Responsibility is not necessarily limited to only parents but can be taken by social media creators, game creators, and children.

- **Coping appraisal:** This construct explains the decision-making factors taken by the responsible actor to mitigate the associated risks. The responsible actor identified in the ownership appraisal determines if they can address the threat efficiently and affordably.

4 Research Design

The study was conducted in South Africa where most children have access to connected mobile devices at home and school [5, 7]. The unique aspect of South African children and mobile devices is that they are constantly reported to fall prey to cyber predators and exposed to inappropriate content that influences problematic behavior (e.g., cyberbullying or self-harm) [20, 23]. Therefore, South Africa, as a research context for PCS usage, has the potential to produce grounds for motivating parents to seek technological solutions that can harmonize their children's online activities.

The study followed qualitative interpretivism research principles. An interpretive paradigm offered an in-depth understanding of South Africa's contextual factors implicated in parents' decisions to use PCS. Moreover, qualitative and interpretive approach to a socio-technical phenomenon, precisely the narrative that emerges from the subject, provides profound insight that can influence the direction of future research in a similar context [24, 25].

4.1 Data Collection and Analysis

Data was collected through 15 semi-structured interviews conducted between June and August 2022. Figure 2 shows the research instrument derived from the PMT framework [26].

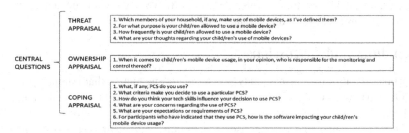

Fig. 2. Interview instrument categorized according to PMT theoretical framework

The primary locations for data collection were Limpopo province and Western Cape. These two locations were based on the assumption that the manifestation of PCS use may differ between rural and urban areas [27]. We used purposive sampling [28] to identify 15 Interviewees with children between the ages of 6–18 in South Africa. The total number of children observed was 32. The South African Child Care Act No. 74 of 1983 defines a child as any person between 0 and 18 years [29]. The number of 15 interviews was solely based on saturation, where the answers sounded the same [30].

The majority of the parents' interviews had pre-teens, and they were married. Moreover, most parents resided in urban areas. This was solely because they were solicited online and could do interviews on Teams. Table 2 shows the demographics of the research participants.

NVIVO is a Computer Assisted Qualitative Data Analysis Software (CAQDAS) that was used to code the interviews [31]. The six principle of thematic analysis were used to code and develop insightful findings regarding the factors that influence parental use of PCS in South Africa [32]. To interpret the interviews, we coded all statements as P1-P15. Thematic analysis was useful in pattern making that allowed us to leverage emerging themes concerning aspect of PCS usage by parent in South Africa.

4.2 Ethical Considerations

Some ethical considerations while collecting data included obtaining ethical clearance and a consent letter from the University of Cape Town to be used for soliciting research participants. Researchers needed to ascertain the participants considering the sensitive aspect of collecting data about children's technological behaviours [33].

4.3 Study Limitations

The time limitation due to strict deadlines affected the quantity of data available for analysis. Logistic limitations due to the location of potential interviewees was overcome by performing interviews via video conferencing. This research was also limited by the number of participants available and willing to provide details of their experiences. The interviews performed were predominantly on participants aged between 37 and 47, even though the age of the parents was not specified as a criterion. This may have been exasperated by the snowball effect of referrals. Parents from a younger or older age demographic may present different viewpoints. During data collection an analysis processes, we established that we missed the opportunity to compare the factors for PCS use between parents in rural and urban locations.

5 Findings and Discussions

The primary goal of the current study was to determine factors that influence parents in South Africa to use PCS. We employed PMT because it has been traditionally employed in information systems studies that sought to explain risk mitigation behaviour [26, 34]. The study found that parents use PCS to cope with their fear and mitigate the risks associated with unmonitored online activities by children. These risks emanate from lack of awareness of risky behaviour on online platforms. Proponents of PMT suggest that people are motivated by protective behaviours to mitigate the risks associated with perceived threat. In is this context, fear is the primary motivation for behaving in a particular manner [35]. These motivational factors are threat appraisal (perceived vulnerability and perceived severity), ownership appraisal (accepting responsibility), and coping appraisal (response efficacy, self-efficacy, and response cost). Figure 3 illustrates the themes that emerged from the three primary constructs of PMT regarding factors that influence parents' use of PCS in South Africa. These factors are discussed in subsequent sections.

Table 2. Demographics of the research participants

Participant code	Age	Gender	Current education level	Residence type	Household composition	Gender and age
P1	37	Female	Matric Certificate	Urban	Married with two children	Boy 10 Girl 6
P2	47	Male	Bachelor's Degree	Urban	Married with two children	Boy 17 Girl 10
P3	39	Female	Master's Degree	Urban	Married with two children	Girl 10 Girl 7
P4	40	Female	Qualified Chattered Accountant	Rural	Married with four children	Boy 18 Boy 16 Boy 8 Boy 6
P5	42	Male	Matric Certificate	Urban	Married with two children	Boy 17 Boy 9
P6	43	Female	Bachelor's Degree	Urban	Divorced with one child	Girl 15
P7	47	Male	Postgraduate Diploma	Urban	Married with one child	Girl 11
P8	46	Female	National Higher Diploma	Urban	Married with two children	Girl 14 Boy 11
P9	42	Male	Matric Certificate	Urban	Married with two children	Girl 13 Boy 10
P10	31	Female	TVET N4	Rural	Single with two children	Girl 9 Boy 11
P11	44	Female	Matric Certificate	Urban	Married with two children	Girl 12 Girl 9
P12	45	Male	Matric Certificate	Urban	Married with two children	Girl 12 Boy 10
P13	41	Male	Matric Certificate	Urban	Married with two children	Boy 15 Boy 12
P14	41	Female	Matric Certificate	Urban	Married with three children	Boy 17 Girl 14 Boy 13
P15	38	Feale	A-level	Urban	Married with three children	Boy 11 Girl 8 Boy 6

Threat appraisal	Perceived vulnerability	Frequency and reason for device usage
		Exposure to inappropriate content
	Perceived severity	~~Cyberbullying and revenge porn~~ ~~Hyperconectivity and adction~~ ~~Mental and physical health threat~~ ~~Technoference~~
Ownership appraisal	Accepting responsibility	Child autonomy
		Ethical development of PCS
		Government responsibility for relevant policy frameworks
Coping appraisal	Response efficacy	Cyber risk awareness
	self-efficacy	parental digiital literacy
	Response cost	PCS cost

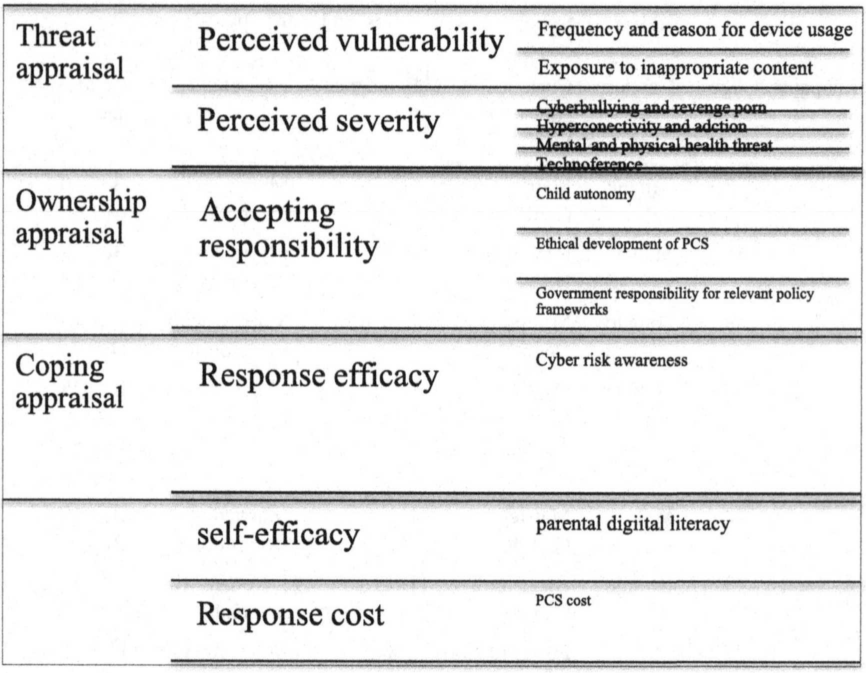

Fig. 3. Factors influencing PCS use by parents.

5.1 Threat Appraisal

Perceived Vulnerability
Several studies show that perceived vulnerabilities are the starting point of navigating how social actors determine protective behaviors [36]. Vulnerabilities provide an idea of the threats children can face through their mobile devices. Below is the discussion about specific vulnerability factors. In the current study, themes that emerged regarding perceived vulnerabilities were frequency and reasons for device use and exposure to inappropriate content.

Frequency and Reason for Device Usage
The frequency and reason for mobile device usage were viewed as factors influencing PCS use. Data shows that, if unmonitored, children can easily spend the whole day on their mobile devices. In the sample of 15 parents, most children owned a mobile device, while very few used their parents' devices. In addition to Google Classroom, the most used platforms were WhatsApp, TikTok, YouTube Kids, and games such as Minecraft, Roblox, and FIFA, respectively. Globally, studies show children spend between three to four hours on mobile devices [37]. The reason for usage ranges from playing games, and entertainment to educational support. The majority of the parents mentioned that teenagers tend to spend more time on their mobile devices swiping from one social media network (typically Tik Tok and YouTube shorts) to the next. Children who are in high school are the ones who frequently use mobile devices to access their educational materials.

"My 6-year-old uses it predominantly for entertainment. They will play. They will use the phone for Roblox, and whatever other games they play there as well" [P15].

I have a 18 year old who if he's done with matric [high school work] stuff would rather play FIFA or roam around Tik Tok and not watch Netflix on the home TV [P4].

Noteworthy, 95% of the interviewed parents mentioned that they bought their children with the aim of supporting their educational activities, and not entertainment.

"It is educational as for my daughter's and my son's school, they actually use tablets for learning it's one of the few schools that do that. But they use it for education and entertainment" [P3].

Frequency of mobile device use was different for the children from the selected data collection locations. Parents in urban areas observed that their children spend more time on their phones because there is little play time given the residential set up in the cities which is very individualistic.

"Sometimes I feel sorry for my children. For my cousin who is in the rural areas, her children play outside more than sitting in the house with phones. Sometimes when I visit home I am embarrassed because the boys just want to play Minecraft while the other are running around" [P 15].

Statements above allude to the idea that most parents give their children mobile devices solely for educational purposes. This is because most Covid-19 lockdowns, schools continued to share materials online for homework purposes [38]. Despite the good intention of the parents, it became apparent during the analysis that children will always find ways to visit other sites that have nothing to do with education.

Exposure to Inappropriate Content

Parents were concerned that unmonitored video streaming might expose children to inappropriate content that cannot be unseen. Studies have shown that age-inappropriate content may affect children's emotions and behaviour [39]. P1 voiced this concern by saying: *"so I do worry about him going on, watching porn or weird stuff like that."* Advertising and music videos were identified as the primary sources of inappropriate content that children can be exposed to, primarily through TikTok and YouTube. Children's curious minds allow them to ask or view anything. Once they view questionable behaviors on these videos, they search on Google. This was the case with the daughter of P10:

"my daughter when she was about seven or eight google searched girls kissing girls...I crapped my pants because why would she be looking at that,".

There are evidence based studies that have attributed problematic sexual behaviours from adults to early exposure to sexual content [40]. Accepting this threat increase the likelihood of parents to seek approaches to monitor their children's mobile device usage behaviours.

Perceived Severity Prompting PCS Usage by Parents

Once parents have recognized the vulnerabilities associated with children's mobile device usage, they determine the severity of the threat. The study established that cyberbullying and revenge porn, hyperconnectivity and addiction, technoference, and mental and physical health risks were sources of perceived severity that influenced parents to use PCS. While cyberbullying, hyperconnectivity and addiction are dominant cyber risks in the context of children mobile device use[6, 20, 22, 41], Technoference has not been studied sufficiently [42, 43].

Mental and Physical Health Threat

Realization of possible mental and physical health threat influenced parents to use PCS. From the parents with teenagers, cyberbullying was the primary vulnerability identified. Parents acknowledged that prolonged screen time and exposure to social media increase the likelihood for children to experience cyberbullying. This finding is consistent with [44] who found a correlation between internet use by children and mental health challenges. Children use platforms such as WhatsApp to send threatening messages to each other. Most of the times, parents may not find out because the children are warned not to be on WhatsApp. The addictive nature of mobile devices and children's inability to self-regulate their usage often have a psychological impact. P4 laments a change in his sons' moods when spending too much time on their mobile devices.

> *"It changes their moods, it makes them snappy, it makes them miserable...but yes basically we've noticed that both the boys are very moody if they spend too much time, regardless of if it's PlayStation, YouTube or just mobile games on the mobile device or on the laptop."*

Most parents observed that children compete in terms of possessions or body features. Most of this competition takes place on social media. Therefore, exposure to social media platforms introduces some level of self-awareness where if a child realizes that they lack something, for example expensive phones may trigger depression. A more serious concern was raised by P1 when voicing that *"the red flags like if they are mentioning something about wanting to kill themselves or depression vibes"*.

This concern was repeated by P5, who said, *"where it's suicide trends or a suicide group, that kind of thing, that obviously plays on my mind when they figure out that they will not get what they want"*.

For the teenagers who are on social media such as Facebook, parents observed that not receiving *'Likes'* can be a trigger for feeling lonely not liked by peers.

> *"If you're not getting likes I mean you hear the horror stories of kids that are going into depression and doing horrible things because they're not getting likes and people are not, and it's the negative stuff you know?" [P11].*

Essentially, a social media post that does not attract likes triggers depressive behaviors for teenagers who go through adolescent seeking validation and a sense of belonging from their peers [45, 46].

Sitting for long hours hold and staring at the phone at proximity resulted in numerous physical challenges. Parents reported that their children complained about their necks and painful palms. One participant expressed his concern regarding mobile device usage and physical ailments by expressing that:

"kids come in and say... but my arm is sore, my shoulder is sore, my neck is sore, my back and I'm like well you've been sitting all awkwardly the whole time with the phone, ten centimetres away from your face, I'm not surprised that you know, it hurts when you make a fist or your, straightening your arm hurts" [P7].

Children exposed to excessive screen time develop sleeping problem early. The concern regarding the quality of sleep of children was referenced by two participants, with P8 stating that *"their eyes are more tired; they don't have a good night's rest";* and P5 who noted that *"we have those discussions because she has trouble sleeping".*

Cyberbullying and Revenge Porn
Most cyberbullying activities were seen to be taking place in the schooling environment. This was despite various campaigns and efforts from government level to curb cyberbullying from schools [46]. Cyberbullying was observed to be the most severe risk because it is sometimes difficult to confirm from children [20].

"...cyberbullying is a major thing." [P15]

"My son had someone come over for a sleepover, and the other friend said you are stealing my best friend, and he was sending all these messages about what he is going to do to him." [P8].

As an emerging source of cyberbullying in high schools, most parents mentioned that they have seen children experiencing mobile victimisation through revenge porn. Revenge porn is an image-based sexual abuse where the perpetrator shares unconsented sexual images of the victim [47].

"Revenge porn, if they have a boyfriend and they are sharing things with their boyfriend and stuff like that. They boyfriend starts blackmailing them with the picture. Sadly, our girls are still not aware that they should not share naked pictures or allow anyone to take them" [P2].

The South African Film and publications Amendment Act No 11 of 2019, provides that revenge porn is a punishable crime [48]. Perpetrators can pay a fine to the tune of R300 000 ($16,563.97 USD) or serve 4 years in prison [48]. Despite the presence of this policy in South Africa, revenge porn is a reality and it largely affects female [42].

Hyperconnectivity and Addiction
Addiction to mobile device usage is a consequence of hyperconnectivity [49]. Hyperconnectivity is associated with overexposure to screens, especially to online content or games on mobile devices [50]. Hyperconnectivity has been blamed for children's lack of outdoor playtime [51]. Children's use of mobile devices and their connection to an online environment that is constantly providing an onslaught of information can overwhelm their senses and limit their ability to decompress [2]. The study found that as more exciting content become ubiquitous, children find it difficult to disassociate with their device which result into addictive tendencies [41]. Moreover, the exciting content stimulates

children's fear of missing out (FOMO) which plays an integral role in development of internet addiction as shown by [6].

> *"I recognise though that the need to be online all the time does not allow you to switch off, so your brain actually is constantly wired... So we talk about that, your brain is always switched on, it's always processing information" [P5].*

> *"The tablet is kind of playing in the background, but she is not watching it, she is playing other stuff" [P1].*

> *"You cannot be bored for five minutes before you're looking for your phone and those are all addictions"[P7].*

In the context of the current study, hyperconnectivity and addiction was viewed as the primary disadvantage of giving children mobile devices; P6 mentioned that *"the disadvantages is I think they can get sucked in, it is addictive, like it is for all of us, I know myself. So, too much time spent, not finding time for other things. I think that is a very big disadvantage"*. As shown by P6, while parents are concerned about this behaviour, they equally acknowledge that they have also developed some addiction to their mobile devices.

Technoference

Technoference refers to the interference in social relationship between children and parents resulting from mobile devices use [42]. P6 indicated that *"nowadays the guys... have conversations with each other, sitting next to each other on the phone"*. P1 concurred that "when they get together, they are actually more on their devices". P10 believes that *"I think they have become a little bit more anti-social."* While Technoference is evident between children and their peers, P3 readily admits that adults are also guilty given that they do not actively call the children out when they are constantly on their: that *"I think maybe it hinders them a little bit in how they engage with others, but I think that, that is also the same for adults"*.

5.2 Ownership Appraisal

Ownership appraisal is associated with taking responsibility to mitigate the identified risks. Although parents accepted their role in shaping negative behaviours around children's mobile device use, they felt that there were not enough efforts from the government to increase awareness of the cyber risks and harmful aspects of mobile device usage. Therefore, the themes that emerged in the ownership appraisal construct were parents' admission to giving children mobile device, child autonomy, and government responsibility for relevant policy frameworks.

Parent Acceptance of Responsibility

Aspects of responsibility are manifested in three ways. Firstly, to a certain extent, parents used PCS with the believe that their children would have autonomy to self-regulate [10]. Secondly, some parents believed that developers of PCS would apply digital ethics that are specifically suited for protecting children from harmful content [52]. Thirdly, some parents place the responsibility of protecting children on the government that should develop and implement relevant policies.

Child Autonomy

The participants described the notion of allowing a child to control and decide for themselves and thereby shape their own lives [53]. Child autonomy is based on parents' belief that the children will self-regulate and will be aware of the danger of not controlling themselves with their devices. Furthermore, child autonomy was associated with the trust between parents in children regarding the right thing to do in context of mobile device use. Many children were allowed to control the usage of their devices themselves, as voiced by P7:

> *"we have got much trust for our kids...I do not like to look through what is happening on the phone...we have got a fairly open relationship, I think because I am here quite a lot of the time sitting in the space, so, we have got a lot of trust, saying it loud, and hopefully, that trust will not be disrespected or abused in any way."*

P8 expanded on this viewpoint by stating, *"you also realise that your kids, when you give them that responsibility or give them an education is that that they also have got to take some responsibility of what they do with mobile devices."* P1 describes that *"before it gets to that point where I actually need to turn it off while they are watching, they just put it off themselves and they will bring it and say okay, they are done."* The concept of trust within the theme of child autonomy was described by P3 in the following statement:

> *"I generally...I leave it to the girls to...to self-regulate, I think is the best way to put it. Within reason. And the girls are aware of that now so they do not share any information online. And that is where trust comes in."*

Ethical Development of PCS

An overwhelming number of participants acknowledged that they were responsible for the children's mobile device usage. However, other parents mentioned that they trust that the developers of the devices they use would ensure that they had features for protecting the children with P10 adamantly voicing his opinion that:

> *"I use the Google family link that I downloaded onto my iPhone. I believe that they can never allow us to use tools that are unethical or do not deliver what the developers in the software updates promise".*

Government Responsibility to Develop Relevant Policies

Few parents felt that the government was showing very little effort in increasing awareness of the dangers of mobile devices for children. This speaks to the aspects of government policies and strategies regarding online safety for children. One of the participants echoed that they felt that the current privacy laws to not really protect the children. For example, for parents in rural areas, they observed that the government schools were not doing anything regarding this subject matter; *"I know that my children are aware of the problem with the internet because they go to the school in town. This is not the case for my brother's children who attend the school in our village"* [P10].

5.3 Coping Appraisal

Coping appraisal refers to the mechanisms that parents put in place to mitigate the risks. A major coping appraisal for parents was using a restrictive approach were parents took their mobile device completely or use a PCS that restrict screen time [54]. Therefore, the study identified these associations among the coping appraisal sub-constructs: response efficacy (increasing cyber risk awareness at home), self-efficacy (parental digital literacy), and response cost (the cost of PCS).

Response Efficacy
Increasing cyber risk awareness at home
Most participants stated that educating children on the dangers of mobile device usage and the internet was important. However, there seems to be a consensus that it should be the responsibility of the school to raise awareness. P10 strongly proposed that *"education is where we start with children. Not monitoring software, but there is proper education, from a parental side or from a teaching side and cyber security awareness should be taught at every school."* Literature also suggest that risk awareness should be the responsibility of the parents who purchase the device [1]. Thus, while showing how they device works, the parent must also teach their children risks that are associated with each platform.

Self-efficacy
Parents' Digital Literacy
Parents' digital literacy was the primary driver of PCS use. There were few parents that mentioned that they installed PCS such as Bark because they knew how to operate it. However, most parents used the PCS which came as a setting in the phone or the operating system of the phone. Participants understand mobile devices/internet as technology, and their ability to implement mechanisms to monitor and control their children's mobile devices play an essential role.

> *"I mean, I will not say my tech skills are on point. But I think yes, it does. Because if you are not tech savvy, you are sort of not clued up. I personally, believe that it is a limitation. So constantly trying to at least understand what is out there, what is happening, what is new, what is relevant. So being tech savvy also means that you are constantly looking at educating yourself and understanding what is out there and learning how to at least harness whatever is available there to the best of your ability. And so that you are sort of able to use it, so that it mutually benefits yourself, as well as your kids"*[P7].

Technological skill levels indicated by participants varied from proficient with P4 stating that *"for me I mean, I fully understand software and how things work and that's what I do for a living so, I wouldn't have any problems installing and finding an application to do the necessary"*.

Response Cost
Cost of PCS Influence Parents' Usage
The response cost pertains to the actual monetary cost of implementing control & monitoring mechanisms but also the effect such implementation has on the relationship

between parent and child. Most parents admitted that they use PCS because there is not much cost implications for using them. This is because the parents' used PCS that came with the operation systems of their phones rather than buying PCS applications from IOS or Google play. Ultimately, the psychological cost of not monitoring children's mobile device activities was considered a high risk and a stressful behaviour by parents; *"without the Google Family link, I contently worried about what my 12 year old girl was doing on TikTok" [P11].*

6 Conclusion and Future Studies

The study began by posing the question of - What factors influence the use of PCS by parents in South Africa? To answer the research question, we interviewed 15 parents through the lens of PMT theory. Unmonitored screen time and content is a growing challenge for parents in South Africa. Factors that influence parents to use PCS are entrenched in the need to monitor and regulate children's mobile device usage and access to online content. Parents use PCS to cope with the perceived fear of mental and physical health, and cyber risks associated with unmonitored screen time and online content. Prolonged screen time affects children's sleep and may cause body pains. Exposure to harmful online content and unhealthy use of social media networks were reported to increase the likelihood of cyberbullying and depressive behaviour among teenagers. Similar to the South Korean context, protecting children from hyperconnectivity and addiction was also a key determinant for using PCS in South Africa.

While they take responsibility for purchasing mobile devices for their children, data suggests that parents in South Africa are not aware of potential cyber risks that can emerge from giving children autonomy to self-regulate the use of mobile device and access to online content. There was a great consensus among parents that children are more technically skilled than their parents, and in many cases, this enable children to by-pass the monitoring, restrictive and mediation mechanisms that are employed by parents.

Parents in South Africa are choosing to use PCS to avoid the effects on parent-children's relationships that comes from excessive screen time. Technoference emerged as a challenge for parents who were struggling to have quality time with their children.

Future studies around areas of mobile device use by children in South Africa should investigate contextual factors that makes the case unique. For example, the researchers could employ quantitative methods to determine the awareness of the availability of the PCS tools. Part of this survey could also identify specific tools that are used beyond those that are embedded in the mobile device operating systems. Another qualitative inquiry could be a comparison of PCS use in urban and rural South Africa. There are different PCS tools for different ages; a scholar may investigate the efficacy of these tools on various age groups. Finally, there is a need to investigate the PCS along with digital parenting approaches (mediation, restrictive, and monitoring) as highlighted in [55, 56].

References

1. Akter, M., Godfrey, A.J., Kropczynski, J., Lipford, H.R., Wisniewski, P.J.: From parental control to joint family oversight: can parents and teens manage mobile online safety and privacy as equals? In: Proceedings of the ACM on Human-Computer Interaction, Association for Computing Machinery (2022). https://doi.org/10.1145/3512904
2. Hosokawa, R., Katsura, T.: Association between mobile technology use and child adjustment in early elementary school age. PLoS ONE 13(7), e0199959 (2018). https://doi.org/10.1371/journal.pone.0199959
3. Toombs, E., et al.: Increased screen time for children and youth during the COVID-19 pandemic. Ontario COVID-19 Science Advisory Table (2022). https://doi.org/10.47326/ocsat.2022.03.59.1.0
4. Chassiakos, Y.R., Radesky, J., Christakis, D., Moreno, M.A., Cross, C.: Children and adolescents and digital media. Pediatrics, 138(5), e20162593–e20162593 (2016). https://doi.org/10.1542/peds.2016-2593
5. UNICEF, "One third of children in South Africa at risk of online violence, exploitation and abuse," UNICEF Press Centre, Pretoria, 08 Feb 2022. https://www.unicef.org/southafrica/press-releases/one-third-children-south-africa-risk-online-violence-exploitation-and-abuse. Accessed 10 Apr 2023
6. Anastasya, Y.A., Hadiah, C.M., Amalia, I., Suzanna, E.: Correlation between fear of missing out and internet addiction in students. Int. J. Islam. Educ. Psychol. 3(1), 35–43 (2022). https://doi.org/10.18196/ijiep.v3i1.14038
7. Phyfer, J., Burton, P., Leoschut, L.: South African Kids Online: Barriers, opportunities & risks. UNICEF, Pretoria (2016)
8. Siibak, A., Mascheroni, G.: Children's data and privacy in the digital age. Hans-Bredow-Institut, Hamburg (2021).https://doi.org/10.21241/ssoar/76251
9. Bertrandias, L., Bernard, Y., Elgaaied-Gambier, L.: How using parental control software can enhance parents' well-being: the role of product features on parental efficacy and stress. J. Interact. Mark. 58(2–3), 280–300 (2023). https://doi.org/10.1177/10949968221144270
10. Wisniewski, P., Ghosh, A.K., Xu, H., Rosson, M.B., Carroll, J.M.: Parental control vs. teen self-regulation: is there a middle ground for mobile online safety? In: Proceedings of the 2017 ACM Conference on Computer Supported Cooperative Work and Social Computing, Portland Oregon, pp. 51–69. ACM, USA (2017). https://doi.org/10.1145/2998181.2998352
11. Farrington, K.: Best 7 Parental Control Apps of 2023. VeryWellFamily, 26 Feb 2023. https://www.verywellfamily.com/best-parental-control-apps-4779963. Accessed 11 Apr 2023
12. Ali, S., Elgharabawy, M., Duchaussoy, Q., Mannan, M., Youssef, A.: Betrayed by the guardian: security and privacy risks of parental control solutions. In: Annual Computer Security Applications Conference, Austin, pp. 69–83. ACM, USA (2020). https://doi.org/10.1145/3427228.3427287
13. Marais, J., Van Niekerk, J., Von Solms, R.: Mobile parental control: South African youth at risk. In: 2011 6th International Conference on Pervasive Computing and Applications, Port Elizabeth, South Africa: IEEE, pp. 227–232 (2011). https://doi.org/10.1109/ICPCA.2011.6106509
14. Stewart, K., Brodowsky, G., Sciglimpaglia, D.: Parental supervision and control of adolescents' problematic internet use: understanding and predicting adoption of parental control software. Young Consum. 23(2), 213–232 (2022). https://doi.org/10.1108/YC-04-2021-1307
15. Ghosh, A.K., Badillo-Urquiola, K., Guha, S., Laviola, J.J., Wisniewski, P.J.: Safety vs. surveillance: What children have to say about mobile apps for parental control. In: Conference on Human Factors in Computing Systems - Proceedings, Association for Computing Machinery (2018). https://doi.org/10.1145/3173574.3173698

16. Odgers, C.L., Jensen, M.R.: Annual research review: adolescent mental health in the digital age: facts, fears, and future directions. J. Child Psychol. Psychiatry **61**(3), 336–348 (2020). https://doi.org/10.1111/JCPP.13190
17. Lee, E.J., Ogbolu, Y.: Does parental control work with smartphone addiction?: A cross-sectional study of children in South Korea. J. Addict. Nurs. **29**(2), 128–138 (2018). https://doi.org/10.1097/JAN.0000000000000222
18. Bonifazi, G., Cecchini, S., Corradini, E., Giuliani, L., Ursino, D., Virgili, L.: Investigating community evolutions in TikTok dangerous and non-dangerous challenges. J. Inf. Sci.(2022). https://doi.org/10.1177/01655515221116519/ASSET/IMAGES/LARGE/10. 1177_01655515221116519-FIG8.JPEG
19. Wang, G., Zhao, J., Van Kleek, M., Shadbolt, N.: Protection or punishment? Relating the design space of parental control apps and perceptions about them to support parenting for online safety. In:Proceedings of the ACM Human-Computer Interaction, vol. 5, no. CSCW2 (2021). https://doi.org/10.1145/3476084
20. Paruk, M.E., Nassen, R.: Cyberbullying perpetration and victimisation amongst adolescent psychiatric patients at lentegeur hospital, South Africa. South Afr. J. Psychiatry **28** (2022). https://doi.org/10.4102/sajpsychiatry.v28i0.1755
21. Herath, T., Rao, H.R.: Protection motivation and deterrence: a framework for security policy compliance in organisations. Eur. J. Inf. Syst. **18**(2), 106–125 (2009)
22. Baldry, A.C., Sorrentino, A., Farrington, D.P.: Cyberbullying and cybervictimization versus parental supervision, monitoring and control of adolescents' online activities. Child. Youth Serv. Rev. **96**, 302–307 (2019). https://doi.org/10.1016/J.CHILDYOUTH.2018.11.058
23. Mpholo, A.: Cyberbullying: SA has 4th highest global death rate among teens | Roodepoort Record. Roodepoort Record, Johannesburg, p. 1, 15 April 2021
24. Cecez-Kecmanovic, D., Kennan, M.A.: The methodological landscape: information systems and knowledge management. Res. Methods Inf. Syst. Contexts, no. February 2015, pp. 113–138 (2013)
25. Beard, K.L.: The role of social context in the production of scientific knowledge (2015). https://trace.tennessee.edu/utk_chanhonoproj/1852
26. Oakley, M., Himmelweit, S.M., Leinster, P., Casado, M.R.: Protection motivation theory: a proposed theoretical extension and moving beyond rationality—the case of flooding. Water **12**(7), 1848 (2020). https://doi.org/10.3390/W12071848
27. Lembani, R., Gunter, A., Breines, M., Dalu, M.T.B.: The same course, different access: the digital divide between urban and rural distance education students in South Africa. J. Geogr. High. Educ. **44**(1), 70–84 (2020). https://doi.org/10.1080/03098265.2019.1694876
28. Etikan, I.: Comparison of convenience sampling and purposive sampling. Am. J. Theor. Appl. Stat. **5**(1), 1 (2016). https://doi.org/10.11648/j.ajtas.20160501.11
29. Child Care Act 74 of 1983 (2007)
30. Alshenqeeti, H.: Interviewing as a data collection method: a critical review. Engl. Linguist. Res. **3**(1), 39–45 (2014). https://doi.org/10.5430/elr.v3n1p39
31. Leech, N.L., Onwuegbuzie, A.J.: Beyond constant comparison qualitative data analysis: using NVivo. Sch. Psychol. Q. **26**(1), 70–84 (2011). https://doi.org/10.1037/a0022711
32. Braun, V., Clarke, V.: Thematic analysis: handbook of research methods in health social sciences. In: Thematic analysis: Handbook of Research Methods in Health Social Sciences, pp. 843–860 (2019)
33. Bahn, S., Weatherill, P.: Qualitative social research: a risky business when it comes to collecting 'sensitive' data. Qual. Res. **13**(1), 19–35 (2012). https://doi.org/10.1177/146879411 2439016
34. Vance, A., Siponen, M., Pahnila, S.: Motivating IS security compliance: insights from habit and protection motivation theory. Inf. Manage. **49**(3–4), 190–198 (2012). https://doi.org/10. 1016/j.im.2012.04.002

35. Maddux, J.E., Rogers, R.W.: Protection motivation and self-efficacy: a revised theory of fear appeals and attitude change. J. Exp. Soc. Psychol. **19**(5), 469–479 (1983). https://doi.org/10.1016/0022-1031(83)90023-9
36. Chenoweth, T., Minch, R., Gattiker, T.: Application of protection motivation theory to adoption of protective technologies. In: 2009 42nd Hawaii International Conference on System Sciences, pp. 1–10 (2009). https://doi.org/10.1109/HICSS.2009.74
37. Radesky, J.S., et al.: Young Children's use of smartphones and tablets. Pediatrics **146**(1), e20193518 (2020). https://doi.org/10.1542/peds.2019-3518
38. Koran, N., Berkmen, B., Adalıer, A.: Mobile technology usage in early childhood: pre-COVID-19 and the national lockdown period in North Cyprus. Educ. Inf. Technol. **27**, 1–26 (2021). https://doi.org/10.1007/s10639-021-10658-1
39. Kennedy, A.M., Jones, K., Williams, J.: Children as vulnerable consumers in online environments. J. Consum. Aff. **53**(4), 1478–1506 (2019). https://doi.org/10.1111/joca.12253
40. Lin, W.-H., Liu, C.-H., Yi, C.-C.: Exposure to sexually explicit media in early adolescence is related to risky sexual behavior in emerging adulthood. PLoS ONE **15**(4), e0230242 (2020). https://doi.org/10.1371/journal.pone.0230242
41. Mustafaoğlu, R., Zirek, E., Yasacı, Z., Özdinçler, A.R.: The negative effects of digital technology usage on children's development and health. Addicta Turk. J. Addict. **5**(2) (2018). https://doi.org/10.15805/addicta.2018.5.2.0051
42. McDaniel, B.T., Radesky, J.S.: Technoference: longitudinal associations between parent technology use, parenting stress, and child behavior problems. Pediatr. Res. **84**(2), 210–218 (2018). https://doi.org/10.1038/s41390-018-0052-6
43. Stockdale, L.A., Coyne, S.M., Padilla-Walker, L.M.: Parent and child technoference and socioemotional behavioral outcomes: a nationally representative study of 10- to 20-year-old adolescents. Comput. Hum. Behav. **88**, 219–226 (2018). https://doi.org/10.1016/J.CHB.2018.06.034
44. Chang, F.-C., et al.: Children's use of mobile devices, smartphone addiction and parental mediation in Taiwan. Comput. Hum. Behav. **93**(April 2018), 25–32 (2019). https://doi.org/10.1016/j.chb.2018.11.048
45. Cino, D., Mascheroni, G., Wartella, E.: 'The kids hate it, but we love it!': parents' reviews of circle. Media Commun. **8**(4), 208–217 (2020). https://doi.org/10.17645/mac.v8i4.3247
46. Shallen, L.: "Towards a Digital Tool for Monitoring and Reporting Mobile Victimisation among South African school.," PhD, University Of Cape Town, Cape Twon (2020). https://open.uct.ac.za/bitstream/handle/11427/31691/thesis_com_2019_lusinga_shallen.pdf?sequence=1
47. Gámez-Guadix, M., Mateos-Pérez, E., Wachs, S., Wright, M., Martínez, J., Íncera, D.: Assessing image-based sexual abuse: measurement, prevalence, and temporal stability of sextortion and nonconsensual sexting ('revenge porn') among adolescents. J. Adolesc. **94**(5), 789–799 (2022). https://doi.org/10.1002/jad.12064
48. Mbude, P.: Revenge porn is illegal in SA, culprits could face a R300 000 fine and 4 years in prison - here's how other countries compare. News24, Johannedburg, p. 1, 16 July 2020
49. Pedrouzo, S.B., Krynski, L.: Hyperconnected: children and adolescents on social media. The TikTok phenomenon. Arch. Argent. Pediatr. **121**(4) (2023). https://doi.org/10.5546/aap.2022-02674.eng
50. Carras, M.C., Van Rooij, A.J., Van de Mheen, D., Musci, R., Xue, Q.-L., Mendelson, T.: Video gaming in a hyperconnected world: a cross-sectional study of heavy gaming, problematic gaming symptoms, and online socializing in adolescents. Comput. Hum. Behav., **68**, 472–479 (2017). https://doi.org/10.1016/j.chb.2016.11.060
51. Papadakis, S., Kalogiannakis, M., Zaranis, N.: Educational apps from the android google play for Greek preschoolers: a systematic review. Comput. Educ. **116**, 139–160 (2018). https://doi.org/10.1016/J.COMPEDU.2017.09.007

52. Chandra, K., Singh, N.K., Gounder, S., Verma, R., Mudliar, S.S.: The unethical practices on social media. IOSR J. Humanit. Soc. Sci. IOSR-JHSS **22**(7), 46–54 (2017). https://doi.org/10.9790/0837-2207064654

53. Mühlbacher, S., Sutterlüty, F.: The principle of child autonomy: a rationale for the normative agenda of childhood studies, Global Stud. Child. **9**(3), 249–260 (2019). https://doi.org/10.1177/2043610619860999

54. Lee, S.J.: Parental restrictive mediation of children's internet use: effective for what and for whom? New Media Soc. **15**(4), 466–481 (2013). https://doi.org/10.1177/1461444812452412

55. Livingstone, S., Blum-Ross, A., Zhang, D.: What do parents think, and do, about their children's online privacy? Parent. Digit. Future: Surv. Rep. **3** (2018). www.parenting.digital

56. Işıkoğlu, N., Erol, A., Atan, A., Aytekin, S.: A qualitative case study about overuse of digital play at home. Curr. Psychol. **42**(3), 1676–1686 (2021). https://doi.org/10.1007/s12144-021-01442-y

Towards a Taxonomy of Technological Innovations in Higher Education

Thandeka Dlamini[1]([⊠]) and Aurona Gerber[2]

[1] Department of Informatics, University of Pretoria, Pretoria, South Africa
thandeka.dlamini@tuks.co.za
[2] Centre for AI Research, Pretoria and Department of Computer Science, CAIR, University of the Western Cape, Cape Town, South Africa
agerber@uwc.ac.za

Abstract. The process of innovation within Higher Education is complex and is limited by internal structural hinderances, lack of knowledge on various technological innovations and their use. Academics in this field have suggested that the limitation stems from lack of comprehension of the fundamental characteristics of the different innovations. The study aims to build towards addressing this problem through the development of a taxonomy to provide distinguishing characteristics of the various innovations available. To develop the taxonomy, the taxonomy development method by Nickerson, Varshney and Muntermann [1] was adopted. A systematic literature review was conducted to discover the dimensions for the conceptual-to-empirical approach and an empirical analysis on a sample of innovations that are said to have a disruptive potential was done to discover additional dimensions. The resulting taxonomy has seven different dimensions with two to three characteristics in each. The findings yielded different categorization of innovations according to disruptive, sustaining or efficiency innovation. The taxonomy should be of value for any scholar interested in innovation in Higher Education.

Keywords: Disruptive Innovation · Taxonomy · Higher Education Innovation

1 Introduction

Although universities have historically provided higher-quality education than other post-secondary institutions [2], modern institutions are currently faced with competition from the global environment [3, 4]. HEIs find themselves at the brink of being abruptly disrupted by new entrants in the post-secondary education sector [5]. This includes competition from other institutions as well as technology developments with visible disruptive threats to traditional pedagogies and brick-and-mortar campuses as a whole [3]. Authors like Sharples [6] and Horváth [7] have predicted that Disruptive Technologies (DT)s are yet to drastically impact HEIs. Authors such as Blin and Munro [8] and Meyer [9] disagree and argue that DTs will supplement rather than replace conventional teaching methods. The question remains as to how long current models will remain viable.

© The Author(s), under exclusive license to Springer Nature Switzerland AG 2023
A. Gerber and M. Coetzee (Eds.): SAICSIT 2023, CCIS 1878, pp. 136–148, 2023.
https://doi.org/10.1007/978-3-031-39652-6_9

HEIs. Like many organizations. Are inclined to adopt the use of the terms "disruptive technology" or "disruptive innovation" to suggest a high esteem for transformation and innovation, however, there is often a mismatch between strategy and actual practice [10]. A study by Flavin and Quintero [11] found that from studying 44 UK HEIs, the term *"Disruptive Innovation/Technology"* was applied liberally in the strategic documents but for these institutions, being innovative implied that management would pursue innovations that would "enhance, augment, support or improve" the functions of HE, of which Flavin and Quintero [11] and Flavin and Quintero [10] interpret it to mean improving existing practices rather than displacing or transforming them.

One other challenge is that DTs are not so easy to identify and there is a wide variety in innovative technologies. Organizations are finding it difficult to discern between new technologies that are disruptive and those that are not. Determining whether the innovation is disruptive or sustaining is one of the crucial aspects in finding and adopting DTs [12]. Although the phrase *disruptive technology* is frequently used, the underlying principles are still generally misunderstood [13]. One of the most common mistakes by scholars and individuals in general is that of mislabeling any breakthrough technology as a "Disruptive Technology", the term has become a "catchphrase" that is promulgated haphazardly without much regard for its theoretical foundations [14, 15]. However, some researchers contend that this difficulty stems from Christensen's inability to give comprehensive criteria for DT identification and categorization [14, 16]. Some criteria tend to be neglected or ignored while distinguishing DTs, resulting in incorrect identification of the innovation [17]. Regardless of how often the notion is utilized, researchers and managers still have a limited understanding of what a DT is [18]. The ambiguous description of a DT becomes deceptive in and of itself [19], which is exacerbated by the lack of defined characteristics [17]. It is apparent that more effort has to be made in clarifying the theory's fundamental ideas and to apply them accurately in order to eliminate any ambiguity.

The study aims to clearly distinguish between the various technological innovation types described in the Theory of Disruptive Innovation (TDI) by categorizing them in accordance with their derived dimensions and characteristics in order to address the identification problem of potential disruptive innovations in HE. Using the taxonomy development method recommended by Nickerson, Varshney and Muntermann [1] for taxonomy development in the Information Systems (IS) discipline, a taxonomy is the tool of choice for classification in order to create a more thorough method of differentiating between the plethora of innovations available in and around HEIs. The taxonomy will give insight into the similarities and differences that exist in the various innovations used within the HE context, therefore also revealing underlying patterns that may not be visible by studying a single instantiation [20, 21]. It is crucial for any institution aiming to effectively explore technological innovations to study and understand their characteristics so as to effectively align the correct innovation to the institution's strategic objectives. The taxonomy will be evaluated against technological innovations that are used in the fulfilment of HE functions, this will provide empirical cases for further identification of dimensions and their characteristics. This study will be beneficial to scholars in education that intend on implementing technological innovations in HEI for the purposes of either being a disruptor in their field or for the general betterment of HE functions.

The research questions that will be addressed in this study are as follows:

1. *What are the characteristics of disruptive, sustaining and efficiency innovations?*
2. *How can technological innovations used in higher education functions be classified in terms of their characteristics?*

This paper commences with Sect. 2 that provides an overview of the literature on the theory of disruptive innovation, technology in Higher Education and finally the taxonomy development process by Nickerson, Varshney and Muntermann [1]. The research method for this study is described in Sect. 3, the results and creation of the taxonomy in Sect. 4, and the proposed taxonomy is presented in Sect. 5, followed by a conclusion of the study in Sect. 6.

2 Background

2.1 Theory of Disruptive Innovation

The concept of a Disruptive Technology (DT) was first introduced in an article - Disruptive Technologies: Catching the Wave authored by Bower and Christensen [12] the authors demonstrate how established companies are overthrown by new entrant organizations that take advantage of new/ existing technologies. This notion was later preceded by a standalone theory known as the theory of disruptive innovation (TDI), which suggests that owing to poor performance of a DT, mainstream customers shy away from adopting the technology, and that results in incumbents reluctance to invest in the technology [12]. While incumbents fail to perceive the value brought on by the technological innovation, they instead respond by investing resources into incremental improvements [22] to their existing products, of which end up being too hefty for their customer base [23].

In The Innovator's solution: Creating and Sustaining Successful Growth, Christensen made formidable strides to add more context to the theory by replacing the word "Technology" with "Innovation". According to Flavin [24], Christensen and Raynor [25] sought to clarify that disruption is not a result of a technology's intrinsic qualities, but rather of an ongoing practice [9]. Over the years the TDI has been extended and applied across various industries and different contexts. Some of the popular instances of disruption include Kodak being disrupted by digital photography innovation [26], the fall of Blockbuster due to an innovative DVD subscription model introduced by Netflix [27], which later changed to a video streaming subscription service. The two primary categories of technological innovations identified by Christensen in the TDI are disruptive and sustaining innovations [12, 28, 29]. Later years saw the introduction of efficiency innovations [30]. Although never studied extensively, efficiency innovations improve an organization's performance by reducing resources, either by eliminating components that produce a product and substituting them with less expensive alternatives, or by reducing other resources such as labor and even going to the extent of outsourcing resources [30, 31].However, just like other theories, it has received its fair share of criticism, some constructive [14, 18, 32]. In his work, Christensen [33] claimed that DTs are often less complex, more affordable, and more reliable [25], and repeatedly reiterates this notion throughout his prominent work [29, 33, 34]. However, these suggestions do not represent legitimate qualities; rather, they just outline the value gained from adoption of the innovation [14, 18, 35, 36].

2.2 Technology in Higher Education Functions

Higher education institutions are key contributors to overall regional and global development [37], economic growth and the global society [38]. This is achieved through the main functions in HEIs are: Teaching, Research and Service [39, 40]. While all HEIs are the primary distributors of knowledge through teaching activities, universities specifically are mostly responsible for dissemination of new knowledge through research dissemination [41, 42]. Overall, HEIs strive to create a combination of teaching and research outputs, as these two functions account for the majority of academic undertaking [43, 44].

In order to improve both the internal procedures of course delivery and the provision of quality education, HEIs leverage the use of technology to enable flexibility in learning [45, 46]. With regards to research and publishing, HEIs are collaborating on strategies to make published resources available to students and worldwide audiences; the open access publication paradigm enables easy access and dissemination of research outputs [47]. The Provision of services such as counselling sessions can be given for personal as well as academic purposes, to ensure that students enroll into the appropriate courses that match their individual competencies [48, 49]. With the advancements in technology, institutions have outsourced social media platforms as a means to ensure that these services are easily accessible to students [48].

With a diverse use of technological innovations in HE, these technologies have been implemented as more of a support aid for traditional instruction rather than a mechanism to transform the education landscape and reinvent pedagogy [9, 50]. Marshall [51] claims that transformation in HEIs is unlikely to occur since HE cultures, and current resources severely impede innovation. HEIs find themselves at the brink of being disrupted by new entrants in the post-secondary education sector [5].

2.3 Taxonomy Development

A taxonomy is a classification tool used for developing a better understanding and analysis of complex objects in a specific domain of interest [52]. Terms like "typology," "classification system," or "framework" are frequently used synonymously with it According to McKnight and Chervany [53], they afford the ability to identify relationships, similarities and differences between concepts and aid in deriving order in muddled findings in a domain of interest [1, 54].

Taxonomy development within the Information Systems field has seen significant growth over the last decade, scholars like Nickerson, Varshney and Muntermann [1] have contributed to the standardization of taxonomies by proposing a logical approach that directs researchers in taxonomy development within a particular domain and prohibits reliance on ad hoc or intuitive development which is how some taxonomies have been deduced in the past [54, 55]. Applying a systematic procedure to taxonomy creation serves as a tool for eliminating chances of inconsistencies and incorrect interpretations of the objects being studied [55]. The approach to taxonomy development by Nickerson, Varshney and Muntermann [1] is based on Design Science principles and the resulting taxonomy is regarded as an artifact which is one of the contributions that can come out of a design science research [1, 56]. Various researchers in IS and other social science fields have adopted Nickerson, Varshney and Muntermann [1]'s method for taxonomy development, a few examples are taxonomies on: *digital platforms* [57], *Business model patterns* [58], *Mobile finance applications* [59] and *IOT enabled business models* [60] to mention a few. Oberländer, Lösser and Rau [52] reported that there has been a 20% increase in taxonomy developments within the IS domain, since the introduction of this method.

The approach by Nickerson, Varshney and Muntermann [1] suggests that a taxonomy is composed of a set of varying dimensions and characteristics, where the dimensions consist of mutually exclusive and collectively exhaustive characteristics. These two restrictions imply that each object cannot have more than one of the same characteristics within each dimension. The taxonomy's overarching theme, the *Meta-characteristic* is initially established at the start of the development process and is based on the taxonomy's intended usage and purpose. The authors recommend that since the approach is iterative, there should be a stated set of conditions that the taxonomy must satisfy in order to terminate.

The following step is to recognize the taxonomy's ending conditions. These have been classified into two categories: subjective and objective conditions. Nickerson, Varshney and Muntermann [1] provide an extensive list of the process terminating conditions. In their research, Smuts, Winter, Gerber and van der Merwe [20] summarize the conditions into themes that describe the ending conditions for a more comprehensive list. The subjective conditions are given as; Concise, robust, comprehensive, extendible, explanatory [1] and the objective conditions are; Uniqueness, completion and comprehensive object sampling and identification [20]. The next step in the process is to determine the approach to be used in the taxonomy development, this stage allows the process to be iterative. The approach can either be *empirical-to-conceptual* or *conceptual-to-empirical*, and the iterations provide for the flexibility to switch between the two approaches until the ending conditions are satisfied. The empirical-to-conceptual approach begins with a study of empirical cases, from which dimensions are derived by inductively categorizing the instances' characteristics. While the Conceptual-to-empirical works deductively, by conceptualizing additional dimensions on characteristics that may have been missed from the previous iterations.

3   Research Method

As suggested in Nickerson, Varshney and Muntermann [1], the taxonomy development begins with defining the meta-characteristic which will be the guide for all other characteristics to follow and the ending conditions to determine when the process will terminate. The meta-characteristic for this study is the development of a classification scheme for technological innovations used in higher education functions, the ending conditions adopted were the subjective and objective conditions taken from Nickerson, Varshney and Muntermann [1]. Since the following phase in the taxonomy development is to decide on the approach to be used, the process of constructing this taxonomy began with a conceptual-to-empirical approach in the first iteration. Given the abundance of literature on the TDI, an SLR was performed to discover dimensions that might be conceptually derived. The SLR followed the guidelines for conducting an SLR as provided by Kitchenham [61], which suggest beginning with formulating research questions, which were given in Sect. 1 above.

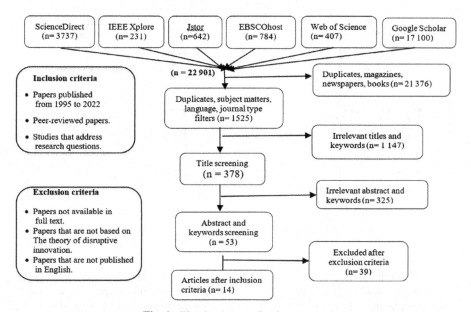

Fig. 1. The document selection process

To acquire relevant literature sources a search string was derived and inserted in six electronic databases, namely, (ScienceDirect, IEEE Xplore, Jstor, EBSCOhost, Web of Science, Google Scholar. To make the search string more specific in acquiring relevant results, the string was designed to find sources on the characteristics of the mentioned innovations. The search string was given as: *"characteristics"* AND (*"disruptive technolog*"* OR *"disruptive innovat*"*). All databases' constraints were considered while creating the search phrase; for instance, Science Direct does not permit the use of wildcard characters, therefore, the terms "technology" and "innovation" were used in their place. The data selection process engaged in to acquire relevant sources as well as the inclusion and exclusion criteria is depicted in Fig. 1. Filters for language, subject matter, and journal type were applied, the inclusion and exclusion criteria were applied only 14 articles met the requirements in the inclusion criteria. The data extraction provided 10 potential dimensions that were obtained directly from the 14 selected studies in the first iteration. Further analysis was undertaken to extract a persuasive list of dimensions; thematic analysis permitted the formation of themes that represent the data's common meaning and enabled the identification of a more appropriate list of dimensions [62]. The potential dimensions were examined in order to derive more appropriate dimensions. In order to combine related dimensions into a single meaning, duplicates of the potential dimensions were synthesized using the TDI concepts found in the literature review. For example, the dimensions *Market, Target market* and *Process* were aggregated to Market Entry, it represents the market served by the innovation. The results gave rise to five dimensions for this iteration. Figure 2 displays the first iteration, which yielded seven dimensions.

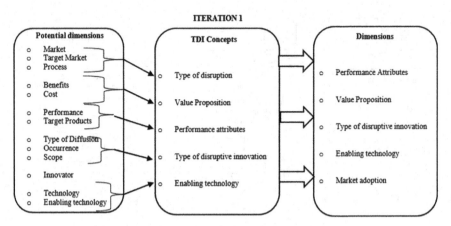

Fig. 2. First iteration of the conceptual-to-empirical approach

For the empirical-to-conceptual iterations, a subset of objects within the domain of interest are studied to further discover dimensions and subsequent characteristics to be added to the taxonomy [63], in this case existing technological innovations. An unpublished dissertation study conducted by Dlamini and Gerber [64] provide a list of innovations found to potentially be used in HE and also possess a disruptive potential to HE functions. In the second iteration, the innovations were studied to derive more dimensions, this formed part of the empirical-to-conceptual iterations, which gave rise to the applied strategy. Further scrutinization ensued, the third iteration entailed the elimination of the performance attributes because it was difficult to determine the values of that particular dimension when applied to the sample of technological innovations as they required the progression of the performance attributes to be assessed over a lengthy period of time. The fourth and final dimensions involved the inspection of the value proposition which was then separated into three different dimensions with varying characteristics, namely, *cost, ease of use* and *convenience*.

4   Results

The above method yielded seven different dimensions which have different mutually exclusive characteristics. The characteristics were derived from those of disruptive innovations as they are the ones that have been studied widely. Not much work has been focused on the others especially [10].

Type of Disruptive Innovation: The type of disruptive innovation refers to the different innovative applications that result in the innovation. It can either be a *product, service* or *business model* [65]. This dimension is reinforced by the notion made by Christensen and Raynor [66] that a DI can be a product, service, or business model innovation.. Wang, Qureshi, Guo and Zhang [67] refers to it as the scope as it represents the parameter in which a DI can be defined within. While other academics refer to the service characteristic as a process [36, 68].

Market Adoption: When an innovation is launched, the adoption is most likely very low, owing to the fact that it is mostly adopted by consumers in a niche market, these are made up of consumers regarded as the low end of an established market and new consumers in a new emerging market that stem from previous non consumption [69, 70]. A study by Thomond and Lettice [65] found that a positive relationship exists between adoption and the performance dimension of an innovation, implying that when performance improves so does the adoption of the innovation, therefore improving the overall performance of the innovation [65]. The market adoption dimension is therefore made up of three characteristics: *low end, new market* and *mainstream market.*

Enabling Technology: A DI must have a technology integrated in it to be considered a disruptive technology [67, 71, 72]. Liu, Liu, Chen and Mboga [73] added that "Technology innovation is the source of disruptive innovation" and continued to say that "without technological change, disruptive innovation is like water without a source." (p:6). The technology itself does not have to be new, according to Wang, Qureshi, Guo and Zhang [67], Therefore, the characteristics for this dimension Re either the innovation is the enabler, or it is enabled by another technology (*enabled* or *enabler*).

Applied Strategy: This dimension addresses how the innovation has been applied in HE, a study by Flavin [24] investigated this phenomenon in order to establish how the strategy is informed by an innovation. When assessing the examples of innovation and their application, the researchers found that three variations could be found and each of those relates to the different innovations given by Christensen, Bartman and Bever [30]. The findings coincide with Flavin and Quintero [11] in that the innovations that were applied to transform the institutions can be regarded as disruptive, those that were set up to improve or enhance existing innovations are sustaining and finally those that reduce the cost of resources are efficiency innovations. Therefore, the three characteristics are *Transform, improve existing functions* and *reduce costs.*

Affordability: The dimension was identified as being the cost of the innovation, Christensen in his work has maintained that a DI is less expensive and when compared to a sustaining innovation [29, 74]. The characteristics of this dimension are *Cost effective* and *expensive.*

Ease-of-Use: It has been noted that DIs are simple as compared to preceding innovations, meaning that they are not complicated to a point where they are difficult to use [75]. The characteristics identified for this dimension are *simple* and *complicated.*

Convenience: It is crucial to recognize that convenience may be a complex quality to describe, which is why the definitions supplied by Yale and Venkatesh [76] and Farquhar and Rowley [77] will be employed for this study; The convenience of a product is the benefit it delivers to a consumer in terms of saving time and effort. *Convenient* and *inconvenient* are the characteristics that fall under this dimension.

5 Proposed Taxonomy

The purpose of this study was to develop a taxonomy of technological innovations in higher education by categorization of their dimensions and related characteristics. Figure 3 illustrates the proposed taxonomy applied on a sample of innovations identified to be implemented in HE functions [64]. The illustrations revealed the categorizations according to the type of technological innovation and the variants that exist from each. The important finding is the strategy applied, it determines purpose and how the innovation will be implemented within an institution [11], the rest of the dimensions are consistent with Christensen's definition of DI characteristics. The taxonomy yielded different categorizations of innovations as per the dimensions and characteristics given. Although an increase in the sample size may have produced slightly different results. For example, an institution that wants to be disruptive can identify that the innovation can

Technology	Category	Type of innovation	Market adoption	Enabling technology	Cost	Ease of use	Convenience	Applied Strategy
Competency Based Education		Model	Low end	Enabled	Cost effective	Simple	Convenient	Transform
Distance Education	Disruptive	Model	New market	Enabled	Cost effective	Simple	Convenient	Transform
MOOCs		Service	New market	Enabled	Cost effective	Simple	Convenient	Transform
Online learning		Service	Low end	Enabled	Cost effective	Simple	Convenient	Transform
Metaverse		Product	Low end	Enabled	Expensive	Complicated	Convenient	Improve existing function
Internet of things		Product	Low end	Enabler	Expensive	Complicated	Convenient	Improve existing function
3D printing		Product	Low end	Enabled	Expensive	Complicated	Convenient	Improve existing function
AI tools	Sustaining	Product	Low end	Enabled	Cost effective	Simple	Convenient	Improve existing function
Gamification		Product	Low end	Enabled	Cost effective	Simple	Convenient	Improve existing function
Mixed reality tools (AR & VR)		Product	Low end	Enabled	Expensive	Complicated	Convenient	Improve existing function
Blockchain		Service	Low end	Enabler	Expensive	Complicated	Inconvenient	Improve existing function
Digital academic libraries	Efficiency	Service	Mainstream	Enabled	Expensive	Simple	Convenient	Reduce resources
Cloud computing		Service	Low end	Enabled	Expensive	Complicated	Convenient	Reduce resources

Fig. 3. Proposed taxonomy of technological innovations in higher education

be either a service, model or even a product which can create an entirely new market for the institution or at first be attractive to the underserved users. It must be cost effective, simple and convenient to the target market and must be applied to be transformative to the institution and not just exist to support functions and reduce costs to the institution.

6 Conclusion

This report's contribution is the classification of technological innovations within the context of higher education into a taxonomy to support an approach to identify different technological innovations. By adopting the suggested approach for taxonomy development by Nickerson, Varshney and Muntermann [1], this study followed an accepted method within IS for taxonomy development. The taxonomy depicts seven dimensions for identifying technological innovations in HE, of which each possessed two to three unique characteristics. The study's limitations include the sample of innovations used, and potentially a bigger sample might enhance the results. The limited studies on efficiency innovations hinders the full exploration of the innovations' characteristics, which may have affected the results of the study. To bring more diversity to future studies, we recommend further specialized investigations of the characteristics of efficiency innovations as limited research exists on these categories of innovations. Further research might also include application of the proposed taxonomy in different domains.

References

1. Nickerson, R.C., Varshney, U., Muntermann, J.: A method for taxonomy development and its application in information systems. Eur. J. Inf. Syst. **22**, 336–359 (2013)
2. Conole, G.G.: MOOCs as disruptive technologies: strategies for enhancing the learner experience and quality of MOOCs. Revista de Educación a Distancia (RED) (2013)
3. Bancilhon, J.-M., Kennedy, I.: How can e-commerce be applied to a traditional, noncommercial environment such as a university? (2002)
4. Flavin, M.: Disruptive Technology Enhanced Learning: The Use and Misuse of Digital Technologies in Higher Education. Springer, Heidelberg (2017). https://doi.org/10.1057/978-1-137-57284-4
5. Archer, W., Garrison, R., Anderson, T.: Adopting disruptive technologies in traditional universities: Continuing education as an incubator for innovation. Canadian J. Univ. Continuing Educ. **25** (1999)
6. Sharples, M.: Disruptive devices: mobile technology for conversational learning. Int. J. Continuing Eng. Educ. Life Long Learn. **12**, 504–520 (2002)
7. Horváth, I.: Disruptive technologies in higher education. In: 2016 7th IEEE International Conference on Cognitive Infocommunications (CogInfoCom), pp. 000347–000352. IEEE (2016)
8. Blin, F., Munro, M.: Why hasn't technology disrupted academics' teaching practices? Understanding resistance to change through the lens of activity theory. Comput. Educ. **50**, 475–490 (2008)
9. Meyer, K.: The role of disruptive technology in the future of higher education. Educause Q. **33** (2010)
10. Flavin, M., Quintero, V.: An international study of technology enhanced learning-related strategies from the perspective of disruptive innovation. Interact. Technol. Smart Educ. **17**, 475–488 (2020)

11. Flavin, M., Quintero, V.: UK higher education institutions' technology-enhanced learning strategies from the perspective of disruptive innovation. Res. Learn. Technol. **26** (2018)
12. Bower, J.L., Christensen, C.M.: Disruptive technologies: catching the wave (1995)
13. Christensen, C.M.: The ongoing process of building a theory of disruption. J. Prod. Innov. Manag. **23**, 39–55 (2006)
14. Danneels, E.: Disruptive technology reconsidered: a critique and research agenda. J. Prod. Innov. Manag. **21**, 246–258 (2004)
15. Rose, E.: On reflection: disrupting "disruptive technology" in higher education. Educ. Technol. Mag. Managers Change Educ. **54**, 56–57 (2014)
16. Hopster, J.: What are socially disruptive technologies? Technol. Soc. **67**, 101750 (2021)
17. Martínez-Vergara, S.J., Valls-Pasola, J.: Clarifying the disruptive innovation puzzle: a critical review. Eur. J. Innov, Manag. **24**, 893–918 (2020)
18. Markides, C.: Disruptive innovation: In need of better theory. J. Prod. Innov. Manag. **23**, 19–25 (2006)
19. Sood, A., Tellis, G.J.: Demystifying disruption: a new model for understanding and predicting disruptive technologies. Mark. Sci. **30**, 339–354 (2011)
20. Smuts, H., Winter, R., Gerber, A., van der Merwe, A.: "Designing" Design Science Research–A Taxonomy for Supporting Study Design Decisions. In: Drechsler, A., Gerber, A., Hevner, A. (eds.) The Transdisciplinary Reach of Design Science Research, vol. 13229, pp. 483–495. Springer, Heidelberg (2022). https://doi.org/10.1007/978-3-031-06516-3_36
21. Krug, S., Nickerson, R., Campidelli, H.: A preliminary taxonomy for software failure impact (2012)
22. Nickerson, R., Muntermann, J., Varshney, U., Isaac, H.: Taxonomy development in information systems: Developing a taxonomy of mobile applications. In: European Conference in Information Systems (2009)
23. King, A.A., Baatartogtokh, B.: How useful is the theory of disruptive innovation? MIT Sloan Manag. Rev. **57**, 77 (2015)
24. Flavin, M.: Home and away: the use of institutional and non-institutional technologies to support learning and teaching. Interact. Learn. Environ. **24**, 1665–1673 (2016)
25. Christensen, C., Raynor, M.: The Innovator's Solution: Creating and Sustaining Successful Growth. Harvard Business Review Press, Harvard (2003)
26. Lucas, H.C., Goh, J.M.: Disruptive technology: how Kodak missed the digital photography revolution. J. Strateg. Inf. Syst. **18**, 46–55 (2009)
27. Chopra, S., Veeraiyan, M.: Movie rental business: Blockbuster, Netflix, and Redbox. Kellogg School of Management Cases (2017)
28. Christensen, C., Raynor, M.E., McDonald, R.: Disruptive Innovation. Harvard Business Review (2013)
29. Christensen, C.M., McDonald, R., Altman, E.J., Palmer, J.E.: Disruptive innovation: an intellectual history and directions for future research. J. Manage. Stud. **55**, 1043–1078 (2018)
30. Christensen, C.M., Bartman, T., Bever, D.V.: The hard truth about business model innovation (2016)
31. Denning, S.: Christensen updates disruption theory. Strateg. Leadersh. **44**, 10–16 (2016)
32. Danneels, E.: Dialogue on the Effects of Disruptive Technology on Firms and Industries, vol. 23, pp. 2–4. Wiley Online Library (2006)
33. Christensen, C.M.: The Innovator's Dilemma: When New Technologies Cause Great Firms to Fail. Harvard Business School Press, Boston (1997)
34. Christensen, C.M., Eyring, H.J.: The Innovative University: Changing the DNA of Higher Education from the Inside Out. Wiley, Hoboken (2011)
35. Dan, Y., Chieh, H.C.: A reflective review of disruptive innovation theory. In: PICMET'08–2008 Portland International Conference on Management of Engineering & Technology, pp. 402–414. IEEE (2008)

36. Govindarajan, V., Kopalle, P.K.: The usefulness of measuring disruptiveness of innovations ex post in making ex ante predictions. J. Prod. Innov. Manag. **23**, 12–18 (2006)
37. Arbo, P., Benneworth, P.: Understanding the regional contribution of higher education institutions: a literature review (2007)
38. Castells, M.: The role of Universities in Development, the Economy and Society. Transcript of a lecture given by Manuel Castells at the University of the Western Cape (2009)
39. Xing, B., Marwala, T.: Implications of the fourth industrial age for higher education. The_Thinker__Issue_73__Third_Quarter_2017 (2017)
40. BucĂŢA, G.: Reflections on the role of higher education institutions in introducing emerging technologies into the educational process in the face of the pandemic challenge COVID-19. Revista Academiei Fortelor Terestre **26**, 363–371 (2021)
41. Muresan, M., Gogu, E.: Tertiary education's role in research and innovation. Procedia Soc. Behav. Sci. **46**, 3681–3688 (2012)
42. Xiaohua, T.: Research on higher education human resource department's knowledge management of teachers in the era of big data. In: 2020 International Conference on Big Data and Informatization Education (ICBDIE), pp. 83–86. IEEE (2020)
43. Altbach, P.G.: The complex roles of universities in the period of globalization. (2008)
44. Cloete, N., Bailey, T., Pillay, P.: Universities and Economic Development in Africa. African Minds (2011)
45. Castro Benavides, L.M., Tamayo Arias, J.A., Arango Serna, M.D., Branch Bedoya, J.W., Burgos, D.: Digital transformation in higher education institutions: a systematic literature review. Sensors **20**, 3291 (2020)
46. Limani, Y., Hajrizi, E., Stapleton, L., Retkoceri, M.: Digital transformation readiness in higher education institutions (HEI): the case of Kosovo. IFAC-PapersOnLine **52**, 52–57 (2019)
47. Weller, M., Anderson, T.: Digital resilience in higher education. Eur. J. Open Dist. E-Learn. **16**, 53 (2013)
48. Anderson, T., McGreal, R.: Disruptive pedagogies and technologies in universities. J. Educ. Technol. Soc. **15** (2012)
49. Grubb, W.N.: The Roles of Tertiary Colleges and Institutes: Trade-offs in Restructuring Postsecondary Education. World Bank, Washington, DC (2003)
50. Flavin, M.: Disruptive technologies in higher education. Res. Learn. Technol. **20** (2012)
51. Marshall, S.: Change, technology and higher education: are universities capable of organisational change? Aust. J. Educ. Technol. **26** (2010)
52. Oberländer, A.M., Lösser, B., Rau, D.: Taxonomy research in information systems: a systematic assessment (2019)
53. McKnight, D.H., Chervany, N.L.: What trust means in e-commerce customer relationships: an interdisciplinary conceptual typology. Int. J. Electron. Commer. **6**, 35–59 (2001)
54. Bailey, K.: Typologies and taxonomies in social science. Typologies and taxonomies, pp. 1–16 (1994)
55. Nickerson, R.C., Muntermann, J., Varshney, U.: Taxonomy development in information systems: a literature survey and problem statement (2010)
56. Hevner, A.R., March, S.T., Park, J., Ram, S.: Design science in information systems research. MIS Q. **28**, 75–105 (2004)
57. Blaschke, M., Haki, K., Aier, S., Winter, R.: Taxonomy of digital platforms: a platform architecture perspective (2019)
58. Weking, J., Hein, A., Böhm, M., Krcmar, H.: A hierarchical taxonomy of business model patterns. Electron. Mark. **30**(3), 447–468 (2018). https://doi.org/10.1007/s12525-018-0322-5
59. Torno, A., Werth, O., Nickerson, R.C., Breitner, M.H., Muntermann, J.: More than mobile banking-a taxonomy-based analysis of mobile personal finance applications. In: PACIS, p. 179 (2021)

60. Woroch, R., Strobel, G.: Understanding value creation in digital companies-a taxonomy of IoT enabled business models. In: ECIS (2021)
61. Kitchenham, B.: Procedures for performing systematic reviews. Keele, UK, Keele University **33**, 1–26 (2004)
62. Braun, V., Clarke, V.: Thematic analysis. American Psychological Association (2012)
63. Remane, G., Nickerson, R., Hanelt, A., Tesch, J.F., Kolbe, L.M.: A taxonomy of carsharing business models (2016)
64. Dlamini, T., Gerber, A.: Investigating the impact of disruptive technologies on higher education functions. Informatics, p. 158. University of Pretora (2023)
65. Thomond, P., Lettice, F.: Disruptive innovation explored. In: Cranfield University, Cranfield, England. Presented at: 9th IPSE International Conference on Concurrent Engineering: Research and Applications (CE2002), pp. 17–28 (2022)
66. Christensen, C., Raynor, M.: The Innovator's Solution: Creating and Sustaining Successful Growth. Harvard Business Review Press, Harvard (2013)
67. Wang, C., Qureshi, I., Guo, F., Zhang, Q.: Corporate social responsibility and disruptive innovation: the moderating effects of environmental turbulence. J. Bus. Res. **139**, 1435–1450 (2022)
68. Mahto, R.V., Belousova, O., Ahluwalia, S.: Abundance – a new window on how disruptive innovation occurs. Technol. Forecast. Soc. Chang. **155**, 119064 (2020)
69. Si, S., Chen, H.: A literature review of disruptive innovation: what it is, how it works and where it goes. J. Eng. Tech. Manage. **56**, 101568 (2020)
70. Barahona, J.C., Elizondo, A.M.: The disruptive innovation theory applied to national implementations of e-procurement. Electron. J. e-Gov. **10**, 107–119 (2012)
71. Petzold, N., Landinez, L., Baaken, T.: Disruptive innovation from a process view: a systematic literature review. Creativity Innov. Manag. **28**, 157–174 (2019)
72. Montgomery, N., Squires, G., Syed, I.: Disruptive potential of real estate crowdfunding in the real estate project finance industry. Prop. Manag. **36**, 597–619 (2018)
73. Liu, W., Liu, R.-H., Chen, H., Mboga, J.: Perspectives on disruptive technology and innovation: exploring conflicts, characteristics in emerging economies. Int. J. Conflict Manag. **31**, 313–331 (2020)
74. Christensen, C.M., Horn, M.B., Caldera, L., Soares, L.: Disrupting college: how disruptive innovation can deliver quality and affordability to postsecondary education. Innosight Institute (2011)
75. Christensen, C.M.: The Innovator's Dilemma: When New Technologies Cause Great Firms to Fail. Harvard Business Review Press, Harvard (2013)
76. Yale, L., Venkatesh, A.: Toward the construct of convenience in consumer research. ACR North American Advances (1986)
77. Farquhar, J.D., Rowley, J.: Convenience: a services perspective. Mark. Theory **9**, 425–438 (2009)

A Conceptual Model of Agility in Information Systems

Theresa Lillie[1]([⊠]) [ID], Sunet Eybers[2] [ID], and Aurona Gerber[3,4] [ID]

[1] Department of Informatics, University of Pretoria, Pretoria, South Africa
tessa.lillie@wol.co.za
[2] University of South Africa, Science Campus, Florida, Johannesburg, South Africa
[3] Department of Computer Science, University of the Western Cape, Cape Town, South Africa
[4] Centre for Artificial Intelligence Research, CAIR, Pretoria, South Africa

Abstract. Due to rapid, unexpected changes in business environments, agility in organizations has become crucial. Agility requires that information technology (IT) enables organizational capabilities for sensing and responding timeously and effectively to threats and opportunities. Over the past few decades management, strategy, and Information Systems (IS) literature adopted a view of agility as a synergy between sensing and responding capabilities. However, there is currently limited research on what exactly constitutes agility within organizations and, furthermore, how agile capabilities and a culture of agility actualizes in teams and practices within an organization. Even though software development practitioners adopted agile software development approaches to deliver more value to the business in less time through short, prioritized iterations, understanding what it means to "be agile" in the larger sociotechnical organizational contexts remains elusive. This study aims to address the requirement for an improved, more unified understanding of agility within sociotechnical contexts. The study adopted a systematic literature review (SLR) of the characteristics of agility in IS literature as its approach. From the characteristics of agility extracted from the SLR, a conceptual model of agility within sociotechnical organizational contexts is proposed as the primary contribution of this research. The model should be of value to scholars and practitioners interested in organizational agility.

Keywords: Agile · Sociotechnical · Organizational Agility · Agility Features · Dynamic Capabilities

1 Introduction

Hypercompetition, unpredictable disruption and turbulence cause uncertainty in the business environment, and organizations must manage such uncertainty. Successfully managing uncertainty is a key feature of organizational agility [1]. Despite this apparent demand for agility, there is limited documented research on agility within organizations, including a lack of consensus on what it means to be an "agile organization" [2, 3]. Approaches and methods for achieving organizational agility seem equally intangible

© The Author(s), under exclusive license to Springer Nature Switzerland AG 2023
A. Gerber and M. Coetzee (Eds.): SAICSIT 2023, CCIS 1878, pp. 149–164, 2023.
https://doi.org/10.1007/978-3-031-39652-6_10

[1–5]. Thus far, scientific research has focused primarily on the features of agile organizations, with limited studies on how organizations can develop and embed agile capabilities enabling them to thrive in continuously changing environments [3]. However, to enable organizational agility, IT agility is required [6–9]. Even though a substantial body of scientific knowledge about agility is documented in IS literature [6, 10], there remains a limited understanding of what agility in sociotechnical contexts is. This study aims to identify the characteristics of agility in IS by conducting an SLR and then developing a conceptual model of agility in IS.

2 Agility and Its Requirement in Information Systems

Due to rapid, unexpected changes in business environments, agility in organizations has become crucial. However, there is currently limited research on what constitutes agility in organizations and how agile capabilities and a culture of agility actualizes in organizational teams and practices or sociotechnical contexts [2, 3, 11]. This study aimed to contribute to an improved, more unified understanding of agility within sociotechnical contexts by answering the research question: *What are the characteristics of agility in IS?*

2.1 Agility in Organizations

Over the past few decades management, strategy, and IS literature adopted a congruent view of agility as a synergy between sensing and responding capabilities [6–8, 12, 13]. Additionally, researchers often use the terms "flexibility" and "agility" interchangeably and synonymously [1, 11]. Teece, Peteraf and Leih [1, p. 17] define "agility" as "the capacity of an organization to efficiently and effectively redeploy/redirect its resources to value creating and value protecting (and capturing) higher-yield activities as internal and external circumstances warrant", however, this definition is not explored further. New technologies combined with smart management may enable organizations to achieve more with fewer resources. However, the trade-off between short-term cost saving and long-term deterioration in capability must be balanced [14].

Van Oosterhout, Waarts and van Hillegersberg [15, p. 132] suggest that the goal of agility is to cope with change in a highly dynamic business environment, and offer the following definition: "[b]usiness agility is the ability to swiftly and easily change businesses and business processes beyond the normal level of flexibility to effectively manage unpredictable external and internal changes". However, it is acknowledged that agility is costly to realize and maintain, is not required in all organizational situations, and, in some cases, can be detrimental to the organization's success [1, 11]. Responsiveness should be stimulated by changes in the organization's environment instead of driving excessive transformation without stimulus [3].

For sustainable and effective management in increasingly volatile business environments, agility should be incorporated as an overarching principle, guiding strategic and operational activities [3]. Furthermore, agility-enhancing capabilities should be developed and integrated continuously to manifest agility as a performance-enhancing paradigm [3], enabling the business to create change and respond to change effectively

[16]. Currently, approaches and methods for achieving organizational agility remain intangible [1, 2, 4, 5, 11].

According to Kappelman and Zachman [17, p. 15], organizations will be more likely to succeed and thrive over the next few generations of the Information Age if they are able to "do more with less, faster, while traditional boundaries blur, and the rules of engagement change". Such enterprises will comprise people who are effective and efficient communicators, quickly establishing a shared vision to construct their infrastructures and processes, thereby being responsive, adaptable, integrated, interoperable, secure, efficient, effective, lean, and agile [17].

2.2   The Requirement for Agility in Information Systems

A substantial body of knowledge exists in IS literature related to Agile software development approaches and methods [16, 18–21]. It has been over two decades since the Manifesto for Agile Software Development was published by Beck *et al.* [22], providing organizations' software development teams with values and principles for Agile software development approaches that practitioners have since widely adopted. Agile software development approaches are intended for small teams to deliver more value to the business in less time through short prioritized iterations [23]. However, what it means to "be agile", specifically within the larger sociotechnical contexts of an organization, remains elusive [18].

Sidky [4] defines organizational agility as a culture founded in the principles and values of Agile that is supported by the organization's leadership, strategy, structure, processes and people, and manifested through adoption by people and embedment in organizational habits. Denning [24] explains that large-scale Agile frameworks, such as the Scaled Agile Framework (SAFe), often fail as they attempt to "align" Agile teams with corporate goals, such as increasing the stock price and meeting quarterly targets, whereas Agile practices focus on delivering value for their customers in short iterations. This discrepancy results in constant friction between the enterprise and the Agile team levels in the organization [24].

Tallon *et al.* [6] identified four broad categories for antecedents of IT-enabled agility in organizations: technological, behavioral, organizational or structural, and environmental. As a technological enabler, IT facilitates agility at the process level, for example, supplier agility, operations agility and partnering agility [7]. IT agility could have knock-on effects, for example, where technology is improved to increase production but results in overloading the logistical process that supplies the products to the customer [6]. Data operations platforms and data streaming capabilities are structural enablers of organizational agility. However, often batching, transformation, and integration processes are prerequisites to making the information available to decision-makers, and thus the timeliness and richness of the source data are potentially lost [6].

Strategic planning and managerial foresight are crucial in benefiting from the behavioral enablers of agility due to IT investment risks [13, 25]. Managers should promote calculated risk-taking [6] and consider the cost, timing, availability, accuracy and accessibility of the information needed for sensing, deciding and acting in response to opportunities and threats in the environment [26].

Tallon and Pinsonneault [13] found that alignment between IT and business strategy enabled organizational agility in turbulent organizational environments provided the IT was flexible, for example, flexible IT infrastructure that is scalable and adaptable to changes in the environment. However, Chakravarty, Grewal and Sambamurthy [9] found that even though IT competencies enable organizational agility, the positive effects of IT competencies diminished as the rate of change in the organizational environment increased. In the highly-competitive business environment where digital markets are converging, enterprises are required to combine organizational with IS agility, thus taking a more integrative view of the organization and its IS [10].

In conclusion, to an ever-increasing degree, organizations depend on IT agility to respond timeously and effectively to unforeseen threats and opportunities in the environment [6]. However, agility is an abstract concept, and the scientific perspectives and theoretical constructs for organizational agility are diverse in their content and structure in IS literature [1–4, 13, 27, 28]. Furthermore, there is no consistent definition of agility in organizational sociotechnical contexts [2, 29]. An SLR of the characteristics of agility in IS aimed to address the requirement for an improved, more unified understanding of agility.

3   Method: A Systematic Literature Review of Agility in Information Systems

The systematic literature search and review of agility in IS was directly shaped by the keyword "agile". Okoli [30] proposes guidelines, that were adopted in this study, for conducting the SLR: (1) identify the purpose of the SLR, (2) define the SLR protocol, (3) define the inclusion and exclusion rules, (4) conduct the literature searches, (5) extract the data, (6) appraise the quality of the found articles, (7) synthesize the literature, and (8) write the review.

Scopus was selected as the research database for its inclusion of peer-reviewed literature from top-rated IS journals, advanced search options, and comprehensive export capabilities. The search terms for "agile" or "agility" produced an overwhelming number of articles that needed to be assessed for accuracy and relevance. To balance relevance and accuracy, articles from the IS "Basket of Eight" journals [31] were preferred for their quality, and articles by the main authors of agility in IS were included. Abstracts, titles and keywords from the found articles were manually assessed to identify the relevance to the research question. Additionally, the references of particularly relevant works were scanned for seminal and additional articles and proceedings, and used for backward literature searches [32], including those in other disciplines, such as strategic management and decision sciences. The SLR process used is presented in Fig. 1.

4   Data Theming, Coding and Analysis

A first-principles approach was adopted to make sense of the multiple descriptions and levels of agility found in the literature, identifying those traits and qualities that co-exist with the achievement of agility in real-world sociotechnical organizational contexts.

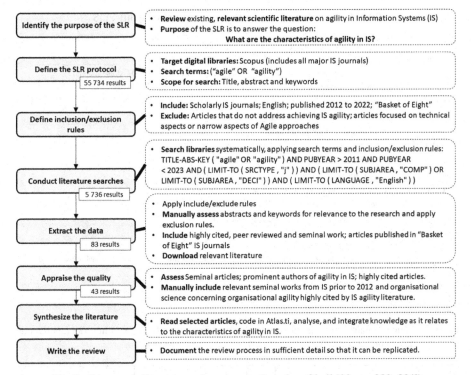

Fig. 1. Systematic literature review process (based on Okoli [30, pp. 883–884])

The characteristics of agility identified in the literature were considered from three perspectives that served as overarching units of analysis: capabilities that are required to "achieve agility", what "achieved agility" looks like, and the nature of the contexts applicable to "achieving agility". The 43 found articles were coded and analyzed using the qualitative research tool Atlas.ti, applying the thematic analysis method. Thematic analysis is a qualitative data coding and analysis method for systematically identifying and organizing themes, representing patterns of meaning across a data set [33]. Word and word-part regular expression searches, including synonyms, were used in Atlas.ti to identify agility characteristics in the IS literature and apply inductive coding, as shown in Table 1.

The concept-centric approach proposed by Webster and Watson [32] was adopted to synthesize the literature. The concept matrix, including the emphases on the concepts in the literature based on document and code co-occurrence analysis in Atlas.ti, is presented in Table 2. For brevity, only the top 10 articles with the highest overall number of occurrences of the agility characteristics are included here.

Table 1. Inductive coding of the characteristics of agility in IS

Codes for agility characteristics	Regular expression search terms used
Competence	competenleffectivelexpertlknowledge creationlknowledge managementlknowledge sharllearnlspeciali
Flexibility	flexibladaptlreconfigur
Leanness	leannesslleanlcostlefficientlwastelwastage
Responsiveness	responsivelrespondlrespondinglproactivelreact
Reusability	reusabladoptlrepeatablroutinlstandardi
Scalability	scalablscaling
Speed	speedlfastlquicklrapidlswiftltimeousltimellvelocity
Coordinating	coordinatl planlalignlshared understandlcollaboratlstandardi
Integrating	integratlcombinelcombinationlincorporat
Learning	learnlknowledge creatlknowledge managelknowledge sharlunderstand
Sensing	senselsensinglenvironmental changelopportunitlthreat
Decision-making	decisionldecideldeciding
Complex	complexldifficultlenvironmental changelinstabilitylinterdependenlturbulenluncertainlunexpectedlunforeseenlunpredictablunstablelvolatillwicked problem
Complicated	complicatedlexpertlspecialilstabililstable

Table 2. Concept matrix of characteristics of agility in IS literature (including document/code co-occurrences and emphases)

Arti-cles	Coordinating	Sensing	Competence	Integrating	Complex	Responsiveness	Speed	Learning	Reusability	Flexibility	Decision-making	Leanness	Complicated	Scalability
To-tals:[1]	1762	1560	1346	1251	1247	1130	1103	1083	1066	831	800	484	295	172
1. [34]	92	94	41	189	24	120	20	43	31	21	8	10	15	0
2. [26]	43	127	45	44	100	32	102	26	19	16	77	2	2	0
3. [35]	96	174	39	52	22	110	42	37	11	12	11	2	3	1
4. [36]	58	89	32	190	24	80	18	34	16	28	8	13	13	1
5. [6]	72	116	43	19	44	59	41	30	15	39	47	17	9	1
6. [37]	312	23	29	12	26	19	14	32	29	6	15	14	7	0
7. [11]	20	35	31	31	76	66	49	31	8	24	21	36	8	2
8. [38]	57	37	29	17	38	32	59	32	15	34	51	12	3	0
9. [39]	63	52	42	36	27	22	42	18	16	22	34	13	19	2
10. [27]	29	17	27	60	11	13	17	76	77	16	35	2	13	2
… 43.	…	…	…	…	…	…	…	…	…	…	…	…	…	…

5   Synthesis of Findings

The data analysis indicated a strong emphasis on the capabilities of coordinating, sensing, integrating and learning, and less of an emphasis on decision-making. The agile features of competence, responsiveness, speed, reusability and flexibility were prominent, and leanness and scalability were less significant. Complex contexts were more strongly associated with agility than complicated contexts. Dynamic capabilities were used as a theoretical lens or discussed in multiple studies indicating the sense-respond focus in achieving organizational agility, which demands IT agility. The context relevant to organizational and IT agility was frequently described in terms of complexity, such as uncertainty and turbulence.

Based on capabilities that are required to "achieve agility", what "achieved agility" looks like, and the nature of the contexts relevant to "achieving agility", overarching themes were created to categorize and synthesize the characteristics of agility in IS literature: (1) **dynamic capabilities** govern organizational activities [1, 7], (2) **agility features** are action qualifiers that enable agility by manifesting the features in the actions [10], and (3) the **sociotechnical contexts** associated with agility in IS are complex and complicated, for example, the contingency perspective of Park, El Sawy and Fiss [26] and the unstable equilibrium perspective of Fischer and Baskerville [40].

5.1   Dynamic Capabilities Associated with Agility in Information Systems

Sensing and acting (learning, integrating, coordinating) capabilities govern actions that support agility when reconfiguring organizational resources in response to turbulent, high-speed environments [41, 42]. Therefore, dynamic capabilities are required to achieve agility in IS. Some authors view organizational agility as a higher-order dynamic capability [7, 11, 43, 44]. Table 3 presents dynamic capabilities associated with agility in IS.

5.2   Features Associated with Agility in Information Systems

The features of agility in IS manifest in the actions and interactions of people and technology in the sociotechnical contexts of IS [10]. Table 4 presents features of agility identified from the IS literature.

5.3   Sociotechnical Contexts Associated with Agility in Information Systems

Large organizations' high-speed, unpredictable environments involve many unexpected, unclear events, increased complexity due to high levels of interdependence amongst sociotechnical components, many new questions, fewer rules and knowledge, and the emergence of new processes [26]. Crick and Chew [50] propose a perspective of an organization as a complex and complicated sociotechnical system that has interdependent finer-grain sociotechnical components of routines and individuals' and technologies' agencies. Park, El Sawy and Fiss [26] found that the larger an organization, the higher the complexity and interdependencies in the sense-decide-act process, presenting

Table 3. Dynamic capabilities associated with agility in IS

Dynamic capability	Association with agility in IS
Sensing	Sensing and responding are components of organizational agility that are both enabled by IT [7]. Knowledge-oriented IT supports sensing, and process-oriented IT enables responding [8]. Sensing to respond includes scanning the environment [42, 45]. Scanning identifies opportunities and threats, contributing to agility because it informs, facilitates and speeds up the ensuing processes [46]
Decision-making	Decision-making agility is a core requirement for achieving IT agility, it requires sensing and precedes acting [26]. IT governance enhances IT strategic agility when decision rights and the relevant knowledge to make those decisions are colocated [47]. Leveraging data analytics for improved decision-making with consequential agility is often practised in organizations. However, agility outcomes are dependent on the fit between data analytics tools, tasks, users, business processes and the data itself [43]
Learning	Turbulence in the organizational environment increases uncertainty and requires organizations to process new information more rapidly to sustain the enterprise's competitive advantage [48]. In fast-changing, dynamic organizational environments, top managers experience high levels of uncertainty and have an increased need for information and the capability to process it [49]. Processes in organizations change through the organizational learning loop, whereby learning occurs through performing and embedding practices and routines involving social and technological agents, which might not always align with managerial intentions [50]
Coordinating	Creating shared, corporate-sponsored IT platforms for sufficiently predictable processes that are standardized across business units enables quick deployment, enhancing agility for the business unit [51]. Standardization supports inter-team coordination and enhances team performance [52]. Formal alignment of IT and business strategy can impair organizational agility due to inertia stemming from an unwillingness to deviate from the strategy, even when rapid environmental changes demand adaptation. However, social alignment between IT executives and business stakeholders positively influences coordination and organizational agility because their shared understanding enables swift responses to environmental changes as adaptations can be coordinated between business units and flexible, improvisational IT functions [37]

(continued)

Table 3. (*continued*)

Dynamic capability	Association with agility in IS
Integrating	Integration capability enables an organization's two primary agile capabilities of sensing and responding [34]. Shorter development iterations in Agile teams enable the team to integrate new knowledge from discussing the releases with changing requirements based on user feedback [28]. Integrating systems enables flexibility and responsiveness by enabling a seamless exchange of information [53]

managers with challenges in sharing information and coordinating tasks, thus there is variability in organizations' paths to achieving agility. Uncertainty and volatility present complexity where new dynamic capabilities and organizational patterns can emerge, whereas existing capabilities and patterns can evolve in more stable contexts [58].

Complex Sociotechnical Contexts: Removing all sources of uncertainty in the organizational environment is seldom possible, and enterprises must build new capabilities to cope with ongoing uncertainty [48]. Chen *et al.* [49] found that the higher the level of complexity in the environment, the greater the influence of IT capability on business process agility because complexity demands more agility from processes to sustain the organization's survival. Proficiency in dynamic capabilities fosters the agility required to manage deep uncertainty by enabling managers to make improved decisions resulting in effective asset orchestration and integration [1]. Fischer and Baskerville [40] emphasize that dealing with complexity requires diversity and flexibility.

Complicated Sociotechnical Contexts: Park, El Sawy and Fiss [26] explain that the high-speed, predictable environments of large organizations involve high levels of interdependence amongst sociotechnical components resulting in some complexity. However, well-understood events, clearly defined questions, applicable rules and knowledge, and routines provide some control and stability to managers and experts.

Sensing, Decision-Making and Acting in Complex and Complicated Sociotechnical Contexts: When strategizing for agility, Galliers [12, p. 3] states that "information itself may usefully be perceived as a medium through which alignment might take place, with necessary information being provided 'top-down' in support of the business strategy and 'bottom-up' in terms of learning from on-the-ground realities associated with the use made and impact of existing systems and platforms". Thus, agility in IS enables agile IS from the bottom up, whereas agile IS can be strategized and governed from the top downward.

Park, El Sawy and Fiss [26] suggest that IT can support organizational agility by supporting the three strategic tasks of sensing, decision-making and acting (reconfiguring organizational resources to adjust to rapid changes and uncertainty in the organizational environment). The sense-respond framework proposed by Park, El Sawy and Fiss [26] acknowledges the complex dynamics of IT agility and provides a holistic, top-down

Table 4. Features associated with agility in IS

Feature	Association with agility in IS
Competence	Adaptable functional competencies form part of an organization's capability to respond to change [45]. IT competence and a firm's innovation capacity enable organizational agility [25]. IT expertise, knowledge, and learning from change build IT competencies [16]. IT competencies, in turn, facilitate the firm's ability to sense and seize opportunities in rapidly changing business environments, enabling the organization's strategic agility [9]. An IT function with superior capability can execute IT projects faster and cost-effectively, enabling the organization to respond effectively to market opportunities [54]
Responsiveness	Organizational structures must constantly respond to changes in the competitive environment and regulatory compliance requirements [20]. The speed of response must match the nature of the changes in the environment instead of responding reactively [16]. Agility implies the organization's ability to sense and respond to opportunities and threats [34, 35]
Speed	Pure speed should not be used to measure agility because sometimes a slower suitable response to change is better than a rushed, unsuitable response [16]. Conboy [16, p. 337] defines speed that is effective for achieving agility as the organization's ability "to rapidly or inherently, create change, or to proactively or reactively embrace change through its internal components and relationships with its environment". The effective use of data analytics contributes to speed in decision-making which, in turn, improves the organization's speed in responding to opportunities and threats in the environment [43]. Speed is required in change management processes that can quickly identify and differentiate key strategic IT assets from those no longer generating value for the business [55]. Speed is strongly influenced by reuse [56]
Reusability	Using existing IT capabilities to solve new business problems enhances organizational agility [51]. Established ready-for-use agile processes provide an organization with quick access to resources enabling a rapid and flexible response [7]. Standardization enhances organizational resource utilisation and positively influences teams' coordination, thereby improving team agility [52]. By implementing a reusable, flexible IT platform, an organization can enable its operational agility and reduce costs [39]. Reuse strongly influences speed through repeatability [56]

(*continued*)

Table 4. (*continued*)

Feature	Association with agility in IS
Flexibility	Reconfigurable assemblages of skills, processes, decision rules and structures provide managers with flexible IT solutions and services for responding to environmental changes [46]. Flexibility implies that IT infrastructure, such as network bandwidth, memory, storage, and processor capacity, can scale as demand increases [6]. Flexible IT can enable dynamic IT and business strategy alignment, enhancing process agility [13]. Flexibility characterizes the readiness and propensity to adapt to ever-changing situations, enabling responses to threats and opportunities while acting under time constraints [10]. Large-scale adoption of agility frameworks is increasingly popular in organizations but often lacks flexibility at scale, presenting coordination and communication challenges [4]
Leanness	Agility should not be pursued irrespective of its cost because "change is costly and achieving agility often involves sacrificing efficiency" [1, p. 13]. Leanness is the "contribution to perceived customer value through economy, quality, and simplicity" [16, p. 339]. Simplicity is an essential agile principle related to efficiency and is "the art of maximising the amount of work not done" [18, p. 126]. However, striving for simplicity and leanness should not inhibit the ability to respond to change [22]. Lean Agile approaches aim to reduce resource wastage, including time and effort [19]
Scalability	Scaled agility can be initiated at the strategic, middle management or individual "agile advocate" level, shifting the organization away from working in functional silos towards more interdisciplinary, cross-functional ways of working [57]. However, scaling up teams in the organization for improved agility presents challenges as transparency amongst stakeholders decreases accordingly [19] and having more agile teams does not imply that more agility will be achieved [4]. The scalability of IT infrastructure supports flexibility [6]

perspective of the agility-building process with the three primary strategic tasks of sensing, decision-making, and acting, thereby explaining the process of seizing events and making decisions that enable actions.

5.4 A Conceptual Model of Agility in Information Systems

Due to the increasing volatility in the external environment of organizations, there is an increased requirement for agility that enables businesses to respond to change swiftly and effectively [3, 7, 13, 59, 60]. Teams and individuals are under pressure to adapt and evolve continuously to cope with environmental volatility [1]. Dynamic capabilities have been applied reliably as a theoretical lens in IS research on IT and organizational agility [6] and, as found in this SLR of agility in IS, seem highly relevant to IS research on agility.

This study adopted the sense-respond process proposed by Park, El Sawy and Fiss [26] to position the characteristics of agility in IS within an agility-building process.

Figure 2 presents the conceptual model of agility in IS that was developed through the SLR of agility in IS.

Three overarching categories characterizing IS agility were found in the literature: **dynamic capabilities** of agile IS, the nature of **sociotechnical contexts** relevant to agile IS, and the **features** of agile IS. Park, El Sawy and Fiss [26] emphasize decision-making as a distinct element of organizational agility and combine an information-processing view of organizations with dynamic capabilities to build an understanding of the dynamics between IT agility, organizational agility and the organizational environment.

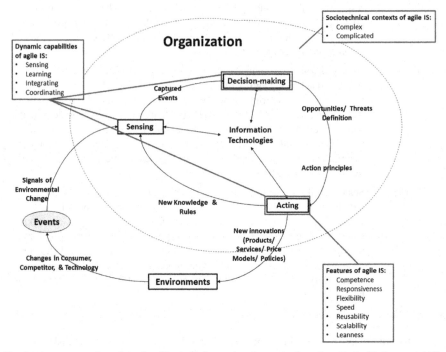

Fig. 2. A conceptual model of agility in Information Systems (based on Park, El Sawy and Fiss [26, p. 653])

6   Conclusion

The primary contribution of this research to IS and practitioner knowledge is a conceptual model of agility in IS, which was developed using the characteristics of agility that were identified through an SLR. Interrelationships amongst the characteristics of agility were found in the IS literature, for example, between speed and reusability [7, 56], learning and competence [16, 47, 50], scalability and flexibility [6, 39], reusability and coordination [52], and flexibility and complexity [26, 40]. Future research can investigate the dynamics between the proposed conceptual model's components. Limitations of the study include potential researcher's bias in identifying words, synonyms and word parts related to agility and its characteristics in the SLR.

Scholars and practitioners can use the conceptual model of agility in IS when studying agility in sociotechnical contexts. Future research could refine the process to further clarify the definition and implications of agility in IS and organizations in general, as well as potentially extend the conceptual model of agility to support the achievement of agility in organizations. The proposed model was not tested and should, therefore, be seen as a work-in-progress. Future studies can address this limitation by applying the model to qualitative case studies, thereby testing its components and relationships.

References

1. Teece, D.J., Peteraf, M., Leih, S.: Dynamic capabilities and organizational agility: risk, uncertainty, and strategy in the innovation economy. Calif. Manage. Rev. **58**(4), 13–35 (2016). https://doi.org/10.1525/cmr.2016.58.4.13
2. Wendler, R.: Dimensions of organizational agility in the software and IT service industry – insights from an empirical investigation. Commun. Assoc. Inf. Syst. **39**(1), 439–482 (2016). https://doi.org/10.17705/1CAIS.03921
3. Appelbaum, S.H., Calla, R., Desautels, D., Hasan, L.: The challenges of organizational agility (part 1). Ind. Commer. Train. **49**(1), 6–14 (2017). https://doi.org/10.1108/ICT-05-2016-0027
4. Sidky, A.: A transformation approach for scaling and sustaining agility at an enterprise level: a culture-led agile transformation approach. In: Organizational Culture and Behavior: Concepts, Methodologies, Tools, and Applications, vol. 1–4, pp. 172–195. IGI Global (2017)
5. Sanchez, L.M., Nagi, R.: A review of agile manufacturing systems. Int. J. Prod. Res. **39**(16), 3561–3600 (2001)
6. Tallon, P.P., Queiroz, M., Coltman, T., Sharma, R.: Information technology and the search for organizational agility: a systematic review with future research possibilities. J. Strateg. Inf. Syst. **28**(2), 218–237 (2019). https://doi.org/10.1016/j.jsis.2018.12.002
7. Sambamurthy, V., Bharadwaj, A., Grover, V.: Shaping agility through digital options: reconceptualizing the role of information technology in contemporary firms. MIS Q. **27**(2), 237–263 (2003). https://doi.org/10.2307/30036530
8. Overby, E., Bharadwaj, A., Sambamurthy, V.: Enterprise agility and the enabling role of information technology. Eur. J. Inf. Syst. **15**(2), 120–131 (2006). https://doi.org/10.1057/palgrave.ejis.3000600
9. Chakravarty, A., Grewal, R., Sambamurthy, V.: Information technology competencies, organizational agility, and firm performance: enabling and facilitating roles. Inf. Syst. Res. **24**(4), 976–997 (2013). https://doi.org/10.1287/isre.2013.0500
10. Salmela, H., Baiyere, A., Tapanainen, T., Galliers, R.D.: Digital agility: conceptualizing agility for the digital era. J. Assoc. Inf. Syst. **23**(5), 1080–1101 (2022). https://doi.org/10.17705/1jais.00767
11. Walter, A.-T.: Organizational agility: ill-defined and somewhat confusing? A systematic literature review and conceptualization. Manage. Rev. Q. **71**(2), 343–391 (2021)
12. Galliers, R.D.: Strategizing for agility: confronting information systems inflexibility in dynamic environments. In: Donnellan, B., Larsen, T.J., Levine, L., DeGross, J.I. (eds.) TDIT 2006. IIFIP, vol. 206, pp. 361–362. Springer, Boston, MA (2006). https://doi.org/10.1007/0-387-34410-1_23
13. Tallon, P.P., Pinsonneault, A.: Competing perspectives on the link between strategic information technology alignment and organizational agility: insights from a mediation model. MIS Q. **35**(2), 463–486 (2011)

14. Bolman, L.G., Deal, T.E.: Reframing Organizations: Artistry, Choice, and Leadership, 6th edn. John Wiley & Sons Inc, Hoboken, NJ, USA (2017)
15. van Oosterhout, M., Waarts, E., van Hillegersberg, J.: Change factors requiring agility and implications for IT. Eur. J. Inf. Syst. 15(2), 132–145 (2006). https://doi.org/10.1057/palgrave.ejis.3000601
16. Conboy, K.: Agility from first principles: reconstructing the concept of agility in information systems development. Inf. Syst. Res. 20(3), 329–354 (2009). https://doi.org/10.1287/isre.1090.0236
17. Kappelman, L.A., Zachman, J.A.: The enterprise and its architecture: ontology & challenges. J. Comput. Inf. Syst. 53(4), 87–95 (2013). https://doi.org/10.1080/08874417.2013.11645654
18. Baham, C., Hirschheim, R.: Issues, challenges, and a proposed theoretical core of agile software development research. Inf. Syst. J. 32(1), 103–129 (2022). https://doi.org/10.1111/isj.12336
19. Edison, H., Wang, X., Conboy, K.: Comparing methods for large-scale agile software development: a systematic literature review. IEEE Trans. Softw. Eng. 48(8), 2709–2731 (2022). https://doi.org/10.1109/TSE.2021.3069039
20. Conboy, K., Carroll, N.: Implementing large-scale agile frameworks: challenges and recommendations. IEEE Softw. 36(2), 44–50 (2019). https://doi.org/10.1109/MS.2018.2884865
21. Sidky, A., Arthur, J., Bohner, S.: A disciplined approach to adopting agile practices: the agile adoption framework. Innov. Syst. Softw. Eng. 3(3), 203–216 (2007). https://doi.org/10.1007/s11334-007-0026-z
22. Beck, K., Martin, R.C., Cockburn, A., Fowler, M., Highsmith, J.: Manifesto for Agile Software Development (2001). https://agilemanifesto.org/. Accessed 23 Feb 2022
23. Boehm, B., Turner, R.: Balancing Agility and Discipline: A Guide for the Perplexed. Addison-Wesley, Boston (2004)
24. Denning, S.: How to make the whole organization 'Agile.' Strateg. Leadersh. 44(4), 10–17 (2016). https://doi.org/10.1108/SL-06-2016-0043
25. Ravichandran, T.: Exploring the relationships between IT competence, innovation capacity and organizational agility. J. Strateg. Inf. Syst. 27(1), 22–42 (2018). https://doi.org/10.1016/j.jsis.2017.07.002
26. Park, Y., El Sawy, O.A., Fiss, P.C.: The role of business intelligence and communication technologies in organizational agility: a configurational approach. J. Assoc. Inf. Syst. 18(9), 648–686 (2017). https://doi.org/10.17705/1jais.00001
27. Knabke, T., Olbrich, S.: Building novel capabilities to enable business intelligence agility: results from a quantitative study. IseB 16(3), 493–546 (2017). https://doi.org/10.1007/s10257-017-0361-z
28. Werder, K., Maedche, A.: Explaining the emergence of team agility: a complex adaptive systems perspective. Inf. Technol. People 31(3), 819–844 (2018). https://doi.org/10.1108/ITP-04-2017-0125
29. Wendler, R.: The structure of agility from different perspectives. In: 2013 Federated Conference on Computer Science and Information Systems (FedCSIS), pp. 1177–1184 (2013)
30. Okoli, C.: A guide to conducting a standalone systematic literature review. Commun. Assoc. Inf. Syst. 37(1), 879–910 (2015). https://doi.org/10.17705/1CAIS.03743
31. Association for Information Systems: "Senior Scholars' Basket of Journals," (2023). https://aisnet.org/page/SeniorScholarBasket. Accessed 26 Jan 2023
32. Webster, J., Watson, R.T.: Analyzing the past to prepare for the future: writing a literature review. MIS Q. 26(2), xiii–xxiii (2002)
33. Braun, V., Clarke, V.: Thematic analysis. In: APA Handbook of Research Methods in Psychology, Vol 2: Research Designs: Quantitative, Qualitative, Neuropsychological, and Biological. American Psychological Association, Washington, vol. 2, pp. 57–71 (2012)

34. Nazir, S., Pinsonneault, A.: Relating agility and electronic integration: the role of knowledge and process coordination mechanisms. J. Strateg. Inf. Syst. **30**(2), 101654 (2021). https://doi.org/10.1016/j.jsis.2021.101654

35. Roberts, N., Grover, V.: Leveraging information technology infrastructure to facilitate a firm's customer agility and competitive activity: an empirical investigation. J. Manage. Inf. Syst. **28**(4), 231–269 (2012). https://doi.org/10.2753/MIS0742-1222280409

36. Nazir, S., Pinsonneault, A.: IT and firm agility: an electronic integration perspective. J. Assoc. Inf. Syst. **13**(3), 150–171 (2012)

37. Liang, H., Wang, N., Xue, Y., Ge, S.: Unraveling the alignment paradox: How does business-IT alignment shape organizational agility? Inf. Syst. Res. **28**(4), 863–879 (2017). https://doi.org/10.1287/isre.2017.0711

38. Barlette, Y., Baillette, P.: Big data analytics in turbulent contexts: towards organizational change for enhanced agility. Prod. Plan. Control **33**(2–3), 105–122 (2022). https://doi.org/10.1080/09537287.2020.1810755

39. Richardson, S., Kettinger, W.J., Banks, M.S., Quintana, Y.: IT and agility in the social enterprise: a case study of St Jude Children's Research Hospital's 'Cure4Kids' IT-platform for international outreach. J. Assoc. Inf. Syst. **15**(1), 1–32 (2014). https://doi.org/10.17705/1jais.00351

40. Fischer, L.H., Baskerville, R.: Explaining sociotechnical change: an unstable equilibrium perspective. Eur. J. Inf. Syst. **00**(00), 1–19 (2022). https://doi.org/10.1080/0960085X.2021.2023669

41. Teece, D.J.: The foundations of enterprise performance: dynamic and ordinary capabilities in an (economic) theory of firms. Acad. Manage. Perspect. **28**(4), 328–352 (2014). https://doi.org/10.5465/amp.2013.0116

42. Pavlou, P.A., El Sawy, O.A.: Understanding the elusive black box of dynamic capabilities. Decis. Sci. **42**(1), 239–273 (2011). https://doi.org/10.1111/j.1540-5915.2010.00287.x

43. Ghasemaghaei, M., Hassanein, K., Turel, O.: Increasing firm agility through the use of data analytics: the role of fit. Decis. Support Syst. **101**, 95–105 (2017). https://doi.org/10.1016/j.dss.2017.06.004

44. Lee, O.-K., Sambamurthy, V., Lim, K.H., Wei, K.K.: How does IT ambidexterity impact organizational agility? Inf. Syst. Res. **26**(2), 398–417 (2015). https://doi.org/10.1287/isre.2015.0577

45. Teece, D.J., Pisano, G., Shuen, A.: Dynamic capabilities and strategic management. Strateg. Manag. J. **18**(7), 509–533 (1997). 10.1002/(Sici)1097-0266(199708)18:7<509::Aid-Smj882>3.0.Co;2-Z

46. Karimi-Alaghehband, F., Rivard, S.: Information technology outsourcing and architecture dynamic capabilities as enablers of organizational agility. J. Info. Technol. **34**(2), 129–159 (2019)

47. Tiwana, A., Kim, S.K.: Discriminating IT governance. Inf. Syst. Res. **26**(4), 656–674 (2015). https://doi.org/10.1287/isre.2015.0591

48. Ashrafi, A., Ravasan, A. Z., Trkman, P., and Afshari S.: The role of business analytics capabilities in bolstering firms' agility and performance. Int. J. Inf. Manage. **47**, 1–15 (2019). http://doi.org/10.1016/j.ijinfomgt.2018.12.005

49. Chen, Y., Wang, Y., Nevo, S., Jin, J., Wang, L., Chow, W.S.: IT capability and organizational performance: the roles of business process agility and environmental factors. Eur. J. Inf. Syst. **23**(3), 326–342 (2014). https://doi.org/10.1057/ejis.2013.4

50. Crick, C., Chew, E.K.: Microfoundations of organizational agility: a socio-technical perspective. Commun. Assoc. Inf. Syst. **46**, 273–295 (2020). https://doi.org/10.17705/1CAIS.04612

51. Queiroz, M., Tallon, P.P., Coltman, T., Sharma, R.: Conditional paths to business unit agility: corporate IT platforms and the moderating role of business unit IT autonomy. Eur. J. Inf. Syst. **00**(00), 1–20 (2022). https://doi.org/10.1080/0960085X.2022.2039564

52. Kwak, C., Lee, J., Lee, H.: Do teams need both hands? An analysis of team process ambidexterity and the enabling role of information technology. Int. J. Inf. Manage. **51**, 102038 (2020). https://doi.org/10.1016/j.ijinfomgt.2019.11.006

53. Huang, P.Y., Niu, B., Pan, S.L.: Platform-based customer agility: an integrated framework of information management structure, capability, and culture. Int. J. Inf. Manage. **59,** 102346 (2021). https://doi.org/10.1016/j.ijinfomgt.2021.102346

54. Lowry, P.B., Wilson, D.: Creating agile organizations through IT: the influence of internal IT service perceptions on IT service quality and IT agility. J. Strateg. Inf. Syst. **25**(3), 211–226 (2016). https://doi.org/10.1016/j.jsis.2016.05.002

55. Queiroz, M., Tallon, P.P., Sharma, R., Coltman, T.: The role of IT application orchestration capability in improving agility and performance. J. Strateg. Inf. Syst. **27**(1), 4–21 (2018). https://doi.org/10.1016/j.jsis.2017.10.002

56. Martini, A., Pareto, L., Bosch, J.: Enablers and inhibitors for speed with reuse. In: Proceedings of the 16th International Software Product Line Conference, vol. 1, pp. 116–125 (2012). https://doi.org/10.1145/2362536.2362554

57. Limaj, E., Bernroider, E.W.N.: A taxonomy of scaling agility. J. Strateg. Inf. Syst. **31**(3), 101721 (2022). https://doi.org/10.1016/j.jsis.2022.101721

58. Eisenhardt, K., Martin, J.: Dynamic capabilities: what are they? Strateg. Manage. J. **21**(10–11), 1105–1121 (2000). https://doi.org/10.1002/1097-0266(200010/11)21:10/11%3c1105::AID-SMJ133%3e3.0.CO;2-E

59. Orgeldinger, J.: The implementation of Basel committee BCBS 239: short analysis of the new rules for data management. J. Cent. Bank. Theory Pract. **7**(3), 57–72 (2018). https://doi.org/10.2478/jcbtp-2018-0023

60. Brown, S.L., Eisenhardt, K.M.: The art of continuous change: linking complexity theory and time-paced evolution in relentlessly shifting organizations. Adm. Sci. Q. **42**(1), 1–34 (1997). https://doi.org/10.2307/2393807

A Framework for Information Security Risk Management from an Interoperability Perspective

Heinke Lubbe[(⊠)] [iD] and Rudi Serfontein [iD]

School of Computer Science and Information Systems, North-West University, 11 Hoffman Street, Potchefstroom, South Africa
lubbeheinke7@gmail.com

Abstract. The fundamental idea behind the modern networked economy revolves around strategic business partnerships. As a result, interoperable systems are of utmost importance as it allows businesses to exchange technical business information across organizations to meet the demand at the lowest possible cost. This paper addresses the problem of implementing adequate risk management in interoperable environments since the number of potential threats increases with the number of communicating entities. In other words, the goal is to propose a theoretical framework that can be applied in both the analysis and design phases of interoperable systems. The framework proposed in this study builds on the ATHENA and ECOLEAD interoperability frameworks, and combines them with crucial information security features to produce the novel framework.

Keywords: Interoperability · Information Security Risk Management · Framework development

1 Introduction

The current, and perhaps leading, business paradigms are focused on strategic business partnerships [1]. This is the fundamental idea behind the modern networked economy. The effect thereof can be seen in the growing complexities in markets as numerous nations shift their focus to international trading. The reason behind this phenomenon is that, in most scenarios, a traditional business cannot satisfy all its customer's needs. As a result, leading businesses tend to form value networks with several partners where interoperable systems are of utmost importance [2]. Interoperable systems, within the context of this paper, refers to the ability of multiple heterogeneous computer systems to work together and grant reciprocal access to each other's resources and functionalities [3].

Interoperable systems therefore allow organizations to exchange technical business information across organizations to meet the demand at the lowest possible cost. Thus, interoperable enterprise information systems play a crucial role in succeeding in this collaborative, yet competitive, environment. Although enterprises attempted to accommodate interoperability by changing their organizational structures [4], this has a direct

© The Author(s), under exclusive license to Springer Nature Switzerland AG 2023
A. Gerber and M. Coetzee (Eds.): SAICSIT 2023, CCIS 1878, pp. 165–179, 2023.
https://doi.org/10.1007/978-3-031-39652-6_11

impact on the effectiveness of their existing risk management frameworks. Risk management, in this context, refers to the ability of an organization to adopt information security strategies that will mitigate the risks presented by the threat landscape [5].

Existing literature emphasizes how numerous enterprises attempted to incorporate interoperability by changing their existing structures [4]. Some of these changes lean towards technical technological changes as technology allows for quick access to information across corporate boundaries. This is often thought of as an advantage as information is among the assets with the most value to organizations [6]. However, this presents several difficult research problems regarding privacy, information security, and trust. As explained by Jacobs, et al. [7], the number of potential threats increases with the number of communicating entities. Thus, several questions need to be answered before collaborating partners engage in an interoperable environment where information is shared, regardless of where the partners are located geographically. Numerous organizations approached this crisis by integrating several unique products to increase their security [8]. However, these products remain ineffective since they could not communicate with other platforms, and thus they are not able to receive vital data from complementary systems [8].

Despite the rise of interoperability, the question remains of how many papers investigated information security frameworks within the interoperable domain. Based on search results conducted on 14 June 2023, only 6030 of the papers that were published since 2010, and are accessible via Google Scholar, include the key words "information security" and "risk management framework". The number drops to 1070 after adding the key words "interoperability" and "business". The search was further refined to exclude papers with the keywords "healthcare", "smart grid", "cloud", and "clinical". Publications with these key words were excluded specifically because the focus of this paper is strictly on business interoperability. This search returned 204 results. Papers from the pre-print site arxiv.org were also excluded to ensure high value results, which returned 200 results. The results drop to 47 when only considering papers newer than 2020. None of these papers analysed interoperability frameworks in addition to information security frameworks, indicating a lack of recent research within this field. This may also indicate that limited research has gone into information security within the context of interoperability [9]. In addition to the limited research, the interoperable model poses a new set of challenges when attempting to apply an existing information security framework in the domain of interoperability [6].

In this paper two interoperability frameworks are analysed and the underpinning general interoperability framework is presented. Information security frameworks that can be applied within an interoperable context are then also considered, and the risk management approaches are extracted. The paper concludes by presenting a novel information security risk management framework that has also addresses interoperability.

2   Interoperability Frameworks Review

The importance of business interoperability has become increasingly apparent in today's interconnected and dynamic business environment. With the rise of digital technology and global supply chains, businesses need to be able to collaborate and communicate effectively with each other to achieve common goals. In response to this need, several research projects have emerged to provide frameworks for improving business interoperability. According to [10], ATHENA, ECOLEAD, and COIN are the three research initiatives that have attained business interoperability. As such, these frameworks were taken into consideration since the focus of this paper is specifically on business interoperability. In terms of scope and flexibility, ATHENA and ECOLEAD are considerably more flexible than COIN. ATHENA and ECOLEAD also do not require specific proprietary protocols. This makes ATHENA and ECOLEAD more compatible with systems when compared with COIN. However, COIN is comparable to ECOLEAD in other business interoperability criteria, such as integration capabilities, scalability, adaptability, and risk and security considerations. Taking this into consideration, this paper will focus on ATHENA and ECOLEAD.

Research projects such as ATHENA and ECOLEAD are some of the first projects to address Business Interoperability [10]. These frameworks encapsulate both Capability Maturity Model Integration (CMMI) as well as Government Interoperability Maturity Matrix (GIMM) models. The fundamental distinction between these two is that the first emphasizes the dyadic communication between two firms that entail business interoperability, whilst the latter focuses on the organization and maturing of Information Systems and Software [10]. Both of these frameworks are discussed followed by a consideration of their features and commonalities.

2.1 ATHENA

The (Advanced Technologies for interoperability of Heterogeneous Enterprise Networks and their Applications) ATHENA Interoperability Framework takes a comprehensive approach towards a multidisciplinary and model-driven solution method to address problems related to interoperability [11]. The comprehensive approach to interoperability is achieved by building upon Interoperability Development for Enterprise Applications and Software (IDEAS) as introduced by [12]. The IDEAS Interoperability Framework was designed for capturing and linking this data from multiple perspectives [11]. The three parts of the ATHENA Interoperability Framework (AIF) are [11]:

- **Conceptual integration:** This part places the focus on languages, metamodels, concepts, and modeling relationships in conceptual integration. It provides a modeling base that can be used to systematize numerous aspects of interoperability.
- **Applicative integration:** This part is concerned with techniques, standards, and models of domains.
- **Technical integration:** This part provides information and communication technology platforms and tools for creating and using business software and application systems.

ATHENA excels in two criteria's [11]. The first is that ATHENA provides an approach to interoperability that is generic and extensible. The second is that the three research areas' findings (enterprise modelling.

which define interoperability requirements and supports solution implementation, and platforms which provide implementation frameworks, and ontology to identify interoperability semantics in the enterprise) have been successfully incorporated into the conceptual framework. Thus, ATHENA concentrates on business processes as well as IT problems including information, application, and platform interoperability to create a comprehensive set of research solutions that are backed up by in-depth business and economic research. It is for this reason that frameworks such as The Federated Interoperability Framework still incorporate principles and enablers as defined by the AIF [13].

2.2   ECOLEAD

ECOLEAD was initiated to lay the groundwork for an advanced network-based and collaborative industry society by developing the requisite solid foundations and processes [14]. A collaborative network (CN) is made up of several entities (such as companies) that are mostly independent and geographically dispersed. Despite this, these entities work together to attain more shared aims. The core premise of ECOLEAD is that significant growth in the materialization of networked collaborative business ecosystems necessitates a holistic strategy [14]. As a result, ECOLEAD focuses on three key and interconnected emphasis areas, which are called the pillars of ECOLEAD. These pillars, which are Virtual Organizations (VO) Breeding Environments, Dynamic Virtual Organizations, and Professional Virtual Communities are considered the foundation for vibrant and long-term networked businesses. This is show in Fig. 1.

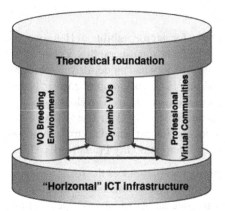

Fig. 1. Focus areas of ECOLEAD [14]

The three pillars uphold the theoretical basis which seeks to support in the emergence of Collaborative Networks as a recognized scientific discipline. The pillars can be defined as follow:

- **VO Breeding Environments:** This can be described as a group of companies and their supporting institutions that hold the ability and desire to interact with one another over the long term.
- **Dynamic Virtual Organizations:** Provisional partnerships of businesses that join forces to exchange resources to respond better to business opportunities.

- **Professional Virtual Communities:** Virtual communities are social structures made up of networks of individuals who facilitate their connections via the use of technology.

These pillars not only uphold a theoretical basis, but also build upon a horizontal ICT infrastructure which enhances collaboration between networked organisations. The ICT infrastructure achieve this by establishing easy to use collaborative behaviours in networked organisations. Thus, when compared to ATHENA, the ECOLEAD initiative takes a more comprehensive approach when it comes to both temporary as well as long-term organizations, and networks of both businesses and individuals. As a result, ECOLEAD produces a novel foundation for advanced collaborative networked businesses [14]. This differs from ATHENA in that ATHENA excels in research solutions for business processes as well as IT problems such as information, application, and platform interoperability. Nonetheless, ECOLEAD is still being used to establish collaborative networks for Living Labs (LLs) [13]. The following section extracts and analyses some of the concepts underpinning both the ATHENA and ECOLEAD framework.

2.3 The Interoperability Framework

From ATHENA and ECOLEAD, it can be observed that the general structure of underpinning interoperable framework consists of three dimensions namely barriers, enterprise levels, and interoperability approaches. [15] combines these three dimensions into a singular model, which is shown in Fig. 2. This is referred to as the Chen model in this paper.

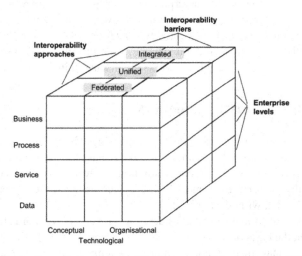

Fig. 2. General dimensions of the interoperability framework [15]

Barriers can be divided into three categories. The first interoperability barriers are conceptual, which are incompatibilities caused by the disparities in semantic and syntactic information to be transmitted between entities. These issues relate to the programming level in addition to modeling with a high level of abstraction. In other words, this barrier relates to the ability of entities in a heterogeneous system to be able to understand each other [16]. The second type of interoperability barriers are technological. These are incompatibilities that are caused by incompatible information technologies (such as platforms, infrastructure, and architecture) being used by interoperable systems and are related to computer-based standards. The last interoperability barriers are organizational. Organizational barriers are closely related to defining authority, and responsibility, and also incompatibilities including the organizational structures. As such, this barrier determines productivity within the enterprise.

These interoperability barriers can occur at several levels of the enterprise [15]. Data interoperability is the lowest layer on which interoperability barriers can form. Data interoperability refers to the capacity to locate and exchange data from a variety of sources, which may be stored on various machines with dissimilar operating systems, and hardware, as well as database management systems. The next is services interoperability. This enterprise level is focused on discovering, composing, and integrating several applications cohesively. The term "service" encompasses not just computer-based applications, but also networked corporations and company functions as well. The third level is process interoperability. The primary goal of process interoperability is to ensure diverse processes operate in unity. In a networked organization, it's also essential to map out how to integrate two companies' internal processes to establish a unified process. The last layer is business interoperability. Business interoperability denotes working homogeneously at the organizational and corporate levels, despite differences in decision-making, work techniques, regulations, company culture, and commercial tactics. This allows for business to be conducted across firms.

This third dimension of the underpinning interoperable framework provides for the classification of enterprise interoperability knowledge and solutions based on the methods for reducing various interoperability barriers.

With these discussion on interoperable frameworks, information security frameworks should also be considered. These frameworks are discussed in the next section.

3 Information Security Frameworks

A framework based on corporate architecture is introduced by the enterprise information security architecture (EISA). The framework acts as a base for the selection of a portfolio of the top enterprise application security solutions as well as risk management. As a result, the Intelligent Service-Oriented EISA, as well as the Agile Governance Model (AGM) Based Model, will be examined.

The AGM-Based Model can be considered a synthesis of standards and theoretical models [16]. On the basis of Service-Oriented Architecture (SOA) principles and information security management standards, it provides a macro-level governance structure. The abstract meta-level governance structure is used as a foundation upon which a governance structure embodies pertinent roles established along with responsibilities that are related to organizational levels. Given this governance structure, seven spheres of governance are divided into horizontal and vertical facets. The spheres serve as meta-categories for various governance bodies that may be assigned to various organizational locations. Areas where these spheres overlap, both horizontally and vertically, manifest the need for appropriate communication linkages. The SOA Security Governance structure is built underneath by adding AGM with information security-related aspects which contributes to the obligations and roles of security governance activities [17].

It is clear from the aforementioned literature at hand that this architecture does not facilitate technological compatibility. Given the following facts, this approach implicitly allows organizational and semantic interoperability:

- The model's long-term ambitions;
- Adding "communications and operation management" to this model's real-time layer; and
- The model's view of the roles and duties in information security.

Intelligent Service-Oriented EISA, in contrast to the AGM model, takes a comprehensive approach to the problem, but it also has a technical viewpoint. Both risk control activities and information security are incorporated into the design of the service-oriented intelligent enterprise information security architecture which embodies numerous enterprise information technology techniques in distinguishable layers [18]. The "Integration and Intelligent Layer" of this architecture specifically addresses the issue of "inter-application" and "inter-process" communications [16]. The three interoperability components of technical, organizational, and semantic interoperability are thus expressly supported by this model. This is advantageous as systems can understand each other regardless of the computer-based standards implemented. In other words, maximal productivity can be achieved within the enterprise.

In terms of implementing an adequate risk management strategy, it was noted that the Agile Governance Model incorporates standards like ISO/IEC 17799 to specify the obligations and roles of security governance activities in operations in intricate organizational structures while the Intelligent Service-Oriented EISA implemented standards from the ISO/IEC 27000 series within its Information security management system. One of these standards for risk management is ISO/IEC 27005. During this risk management framework, before conducting a risk assessment, the established context is assessed. The risk treatment is finally implemented if there is sufficient information to identify the necessary steps to reduce the risks to a manageable level. If the data is insufficient, another cycle is carried out using a modified context. This provides a more resilient approach as a consequence.

Other risk management frameworks include EBIOS, which is divided into a cycle of five phases [19]. Phase 1 focuses on context analysis in terms of the reliance on the information system for global business processes. Phases 2 and 3 of the security threat analysis and needs analysis are carried out in a clear dichotomy, resulting in an objective understanding of their opposing natures. Phases 4 and 5 results in an objective risk diagnosis when this dispute has been resolved by traceable reasoning.

Lastly, NIST SP 800-30 is also analysed in terms of an interoperability perspective. The three primary stages of risk evaluation, mitigation, and assessment make up the complete risk management process of NIST SP 800-30 [20]. To be able to identify preventative and risk-reducing remedies, the risk assessment procedure evaluates probable hazards along with their effects. The process of risk mitigation involves prioritizing the identified risks and putting in place and maintaining sufficient preventive actions. Following the execution of the countermeasure, a continuous evaluation procedure establishes whether the risk has been reduced to an adequate level or whether more controls are necessary [21].

The following section extracts the key risk management attributes from the discussed information security frameworks and combines them to produce a novel risk management framework that can be applied in interoperable environments.

4 Novel Framework

This section presents a framework that is built on the general structure underpinning interoperable frameworks, such as ATHENA [11] and ECOLEAD [14]. The framework also incorporates crucial information security features from the identified information security frameworks to produce the novel framework that can be applied in both the analysis and design phases of interoperable systems. In other words, a novel information security framework, with regards to risk management and interoperability, is presented in this section. The framework consists of six phases, similar to EBOIS [22], but structured similar to ISO/IEC 27005 [23].

An empirical research methodology was therefore utilized in aggregation with the design science research paradigm to provide the framework with a well-founded practical knowledge [24]. This approach made it possible to follow NIST SP 800-64 as a guideline to construct the novel framework. [25] states that NIST SP 800-64 enhances the development of Risk Management Framework as it offers a sample roadmap for incorporating assurance and security functionality into the life cycle. Integrating the methodology into the development of the framework allows for early detection and remediation of security flaws and issues with systems. It also contributes to the understanding of potential engineering difficulties. Furthermore, the life cycle also leverages security tools and practices to identify shared security services and consequently improve the security posture of the framework. Lastly, improved framework integration and interoperability that would be challenging to achieve if security is taken into account independently at different framework levels [25].

The phases are strategically structured to allow practitioners to compare the outcomes of each phase with that of a different framework, or reuse data from other approaches during the developed risk management lifecycle. This overcomes the conceptual, technological, and organizational barriers of interoperability. Figure 3 provides an overview of the structure of the novel framework.

Phase one initiates the evaluation process by determining the scope and context of the business process that will be investigated. The scope can consist out of the business's functions, objectives, contractual or legal requirements, and information security policy. This is similar to the focus point of ATHENA [11]. The scope is followed by identifying participants in the collaborative network as outlined by ECOLEAD [14], business and auxiliary assets, feared events, and the baseline for security. Phase one is therefore very similar to phase one of ISO/IEC 27005 [23] and EBIOS [22].

Phase two consists of several tasks that involve calculating the impact of potential threat actors on a qualitative and quantitative scale. As such, this phase involves the establishment of risk evaluation criteria, impact criteria, and risk acceptance criteria.

The first subtask for phase two involves the identification of critical stakeholders that orbit around the business process and contribute to the successful execution of the business process. A stakeholder is considered critical when it can contribute to an attack vector which in turn could lead to a feared event. Examples of stakeholders include suppliers and courier services. Subtask two identifies threats related to the identified stakeholders that could manifest the feared events identified in phase one. It is critical to gather precise information regarding the threats, which stakeholders they might exploit, the impact of the enterprise resources on the threats, and their possible motives. The identified threat actors are then assessed according to risk evaluation criteria similar to ISO/IEC 27005 [23]. Threat actors that are more severe than others are then selected and further evaluated by means of creating a digital threat mapping of the ecosystem. A well-informed threat actor will likely follow the path of least effort. In other words, attack the stakeholder that appears to be the weakest. As such, the creation of digital threat mapping is followed by outlining the sequence of events that a threat might follow in order for the threat actor to reach its target. These strategic scenarios are then assessed in terms of their likelihood and severity. The evaluation performed during this phase considers the security baseline of the investigated object and the ecosystem's degree of vulnerability, in addition to the resources and motives that are thought to be the source of the risk.

Phase three is concerned with risk treatment. The enterprise needs to establish a risk treatment in order to reduce the identified risks. This may include risk sharing, risk avoidance, risk retention, and risk modification to name but a few [26]. This could contribute to a reduction in the intrinsic threat level experienced by critical stakeholders.

After risk treatment, the residual risk needs to be reviewed and approved by the appropriate managers in phase four. The company must decide on how to handle the examined residual risk. As a result, the organization lists acceptable risks along with a rationale for any risks that do not adhere to its standard risk acceptance criteria.

Phase five states that the stakeholders and the accountable parties must be informed of information security threats. Phase five can therefore form part of a company's policy. Information security risk communication could help the success of risk management, convey risk assessment findings, aid in decision-making, raise awareness, etc. The organization needs to create a risk communication plan for both regular operations and emergency scenarios. Of importance is that the risk communication plan adheres conceptual, applicative, and technical integration as outlined by ATHENA [11]. An ongoing understanding of the organization's information security risk management process and outcomes should be the result of all of this [26].

During the last phase of the framework, companies are expected to perform constant monitoring and review in order to ensure that the risk assessment, the risk management strategies, and their implementation remain relevant and appropriate to the circumstances.

The effectiveness of the framework is tested in the following section by applying the framework to an artificial environment. This is due to time limitations as effectively testing the framework should be done on interoperable environments over a larger timespan.

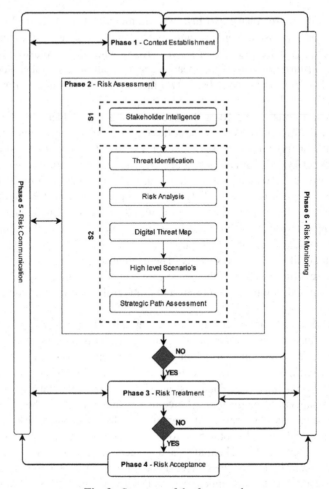

Fig. 3. Structure of the framework

5 Illustrative Example

The framework is evaluated using a clothing manufacturing company as a distinguishable scenario. This specific scenario confronts the framework with a collaborative network where strategic business partnerships form. Interoperability is important in this scenario as they allow business partners to meet the demand at the lowest possible cost. The interoperable system consists of a clothing manufacturer that specializes in custom embroidered and printed clothes for schools. The company sources its material from a factory overseas, but does all of the stitching in-house. For printing the company does all of the designs itself, but makes use of a partner company to handle the actual printing. The company makes use of courier services to distribute the manufactured clothes to wholesale distributors and clothes retailers. Apart from this, the clothing manufacturing company makes use of a cloud service provider to host the web applications where clients can place orders. This illustrates the importance of incorporating a similar approach to ECOLEAD into the framework as the environment consists out of both temporary and long-term organizations. This is illustrated in Fig. 4.

The framework initiates the evaluation process by determining the scope. This scenario exclusively focusses on the identification and manufacturing of clothes. As such, both business and its supporting assets associated with this business process are identified along with the feared event associated with the business assets should they get compromised. Phase one is therefore highly dependent on the organizations ability to accurately identify all business and auxiliary assets. The correct identification of business and auxiliary allows management to easily determine the severity of the feared events based on the implications that the feared event holds, such as a leaking knowledge of how the enterprise manufacture clothes could have a financial impact. When assessing the severity of feared events, the impact thereof should be considered from several perspectives. This includes an indirect, direct, external, and internal perspective. It's recommended to use an already existing scale, or use a severity scale similar to EBIOS if the enterprise do not have a scale. Phase one ends by establishing a security baseline, thereby supporting governance.

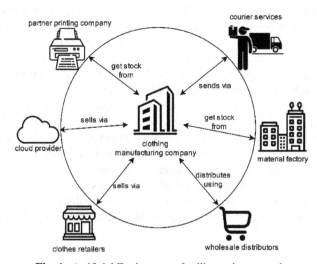

Fig. 4. Artificial Environment for illustrative example

The evaluation using the framework then continues by identifying each of the enterprises' stakeholders and the threats that the stakeholders might introduce. This order of steps differs from EBIOS to intensify the focus of the framework on stakeholder-related risks when compared to other frameworks. Though adequate to consider only the enterprises' stakeholders, one could expand the duration and depth of the framework by considering the stakeholder of the enterprises' stakeholders. This differs slightly from the EBIOS approach in that EBIOS first identifies threats and then assigns the threats to stakeholders. Nonetheless, having thorough insights to what threats a stakeholder might introduce proved to be one of the major limitations to this step.

Following the flow of tasks, the framework then analyses the stakeholders quantitatively and the threats qualitatively. In this regard the framework is very subjective. The results obtained from the stakeholder analysis are then used to construct a digital threat map. The results obtained from the threat analysis are then used to identify more severe threats among all the threats identified and then construct high-level scenarios. For example, a hacktivist might try to take advantage of unsecure communication channels in order to stop the production line. This simplifies the risk treatment phase as it provides a clearer overview of what components of the ecosystem an attacker will likely exploit in order to make the feared events a realization.

The identified threats are then considered in phase three by implementing countermeasures. The clothing manufacturing company needs to establish a risk treatment in order to contribute to a reduction in the intrinsic threat level experienced by critical stakeholders. Phase three provide limited guidance in this regard. Risk treatment may include risk sharing, risk avoidance, risk retention, and risk modification such as incorporating multi-factor authentication (MFA) or modifying their security policies and procedures.

Once the necessary countermeasures have been identified and implemented, the enterprise needed to assess the risk presented by each attack path again to determine its residential risk. Should the residential risk be low enough as determined by the company, the enterprise can continue to the next phase. However, if the residential risk is too high, then the enterprise needs to return to the previous phase. The process of determining acceptableness of residential risk is subjective, which might limit the success rate of this framework.

After this, the framework requires the clothes manufacturer to inform stakeholders and the accountable parties of the information security threats identified. This allows the framework to improve the success of risk management, convey risk assessment findings, aid in decision-making, and raise awareness. The framework also provides the opportunity for an organization to create a risk communication plan for both regular operations and emergency scenarios. The framework, however, does not provide detailed guidance on how to develop the risk communication plan.

During the last phase of the framework, the clothes manufacturer is expected to perform constant monitoring and review in order to ensure that the risk assessment, the risk management strategies, and their implementation remain relevant and appropriate to the circumstances.

6   Conclusion

In this paper it is emphasized how the leading business paradigms are focused on strategic business partnerships. Existing literature highlights how numerous enterprises attempted to incorporate interoperability by changing their existing structures. Despite the rise of interoperability, little research has gone into information security within the domain of interoperability. During this paper two interoperable frameworks, namely ATHENA and ECOLEAD, are analyzed. The Chen model combines some of the concepts underpinning both frameworks into a singular model that consists of three dimensions. Along with these discussion on interoperable frameworks, information security frameworks are also considered. In this regard, the Intelligent Service-Oriented EISA, as well as the

AGM Based Model is analyzed. Some of the key risk management attributes from the discussed information security frameworks are identified and combined to produce a novel risk management framework that can be applied in interoperable environments. The framework consists out of six phases that are strategically structured to allow practitioners to compare the outcomes of each phase with that of a different framework, or reuse data from other approaches during the developed risk management lifecycle. The framework is then demonstrated within an artificial environment where the effects of variables beyond the scope of the study could be minimized. The framework allows for high levels of interoperability since the functional components can be addressed by the components of other frameworks in a similar manner. In essence, this means that interoperability can be attained at different levels of the interoperable model. The framework offers a reliable structure, but some phases require a high level of subjectivity. Furthermore, it imposes a certain approach to risk calculation.

In conclusion, this paper makes a contribution by illustrating how interoperable frameworks, as well as information security frameworks, can be used to develop a novel framework that allows for information security to be considered within interoperable systems. The paper synthesizes and combines key concepts to propose a novel risk management framework that also addresses interoperability. This contribution expands the understanding of how information security can be effectively integrated into interoperable environments. Methodologically, the paper made use of the NIST SP 800–64 and design science research principles as guidance. Due to time constraints, an illustrative example is used to demonstrate the usability of the framework in principle.

For future work, the framework can be improved by making it less subjective. This would eliminate single points of failure whereby a field expert might assign a low threat level to a high-severity threat. The framework can also be improved to take threats that reside outside the technological scope, such as natural disasters, into consideration. Lastly, the framework could be applied in a real-world interoperable system to identify weaknesses and potential areas for improvement.

References

1. Islam, A., Wahab, S.A.: The intervention of strategic innovation practices in between regulations and sustainable business growth: a holistic perspective for Malaysian SMEs. World J. Entrepr. Manage. Sustain. Dev. **17**(3), 396–421 (2021)
2. Mazak, A., Huemer, C.: A standards framework for value networks in the context of Industry 4.0. In: 2015 IEEE International Conference on Industrial Engineering and Engineering Management (IEEM), pp. 1342–1346. IEEE (2015)
3. Chen, D., Doumeingts, G., Vernadat, F.: Architectures for enterprise integration and interoperability: Past, present and future. Comput. Ind. **59**(7), 647–659 (2008)
4. Gong, Y., Janssen, M.: Roles and capabilities of enterprise architecture in big data analytics technology adoption and implementation. J. Theor. Appl. Electron. Commer. Res. **16**(1), 37–51 (2021)
5. Sawant, P., Kpmg, I.: Holistic approach to information security risk management. Inter. J. Eng. Res. Tech. **9**(7), 42–44 (2020)
6. Rantos, K., Spyros, A., Papanikolaou, A., Kritsas, A., Ilioudis, C., Katos, V.: Interoperability challenges in the cybersecurity information sharing ecosystem. Computers **9**(1), 18 (2020)

7. Jacobs N., et al.: Analysis of system and interoperability impact from securing communications for distributed energy resources. In: 2019 IEEE Power and Energy Conference at Illinois (PECI), pp. 1–8. IEEE (2019)
8. Crumpler, W.D., Lewis, J.A.: Cybersecurity and the Problem of Interoperability (2020)
9. van Veenstra, A.F., Ramilli, M.: Exploring information security issues in public sector inter-organizational collaboration. In: Janssen, M., Scholl, H.J., Wimmer, M.A., Tan, Y.-H. (eds.) EGOV 2011. LNCS, vol. 6846, pp. 355–366. Springer, Heidelberg (2011). https://doi.org/10.1007/978-3-642-22878-0_30
10. Zutshi, A., Grilo, A., Jardim-Goncalves, R.: The business interoperability quotient measurement model. Comput. Ind. 63(5), 389–404 (2012)
11. Berre, A.-J., et al.: The ATHENA interoperability framework. In: Gonçalves, R.J., Müller, J.P., Mertins, K., Zelm, M. (eds.) Enterprise Interoperability II. Springer, London, pp. 569–580 (2007). https://doi.org/10.1007/978-1-84628-858-6_62
12. Chen, D., Doumeingts, G.: European initiatives to develop interoperability of enterprise applications—basic concepts, framework and roadmap. Annu. Rev. Control. 27(2), 153–162 (2003)
13. Tchoffa, D., Figay, N., Ghodous, P., Panetto, H., El Mhamedi, A.: Alignment of the product lifecycle management federated interoperability framework with internet of things and virtual manufacturing. Comput. Ind. 130, 103466 (2021)
14. Camarinha-Matos, L.M., Afsarmanesh, H., Ollus, M.: ECOLEAD: a holistic approach to creation and management of dynamic virtual organizations. In: Camarinha-Matos, L.M., Afsarmanesh, H., Ortiz, A. (eds.) Collaborative Networks and Their Breeding Environments. PRO-VE 2005. IFIP — The International Federation for Information Processing, vol. 186, pp. 3–16. Springer, Boston (2005). https://doi.org/10.1007/0-387-29360-4_1
15. Zamiri, M., Sarraipa, J., Goncalves, R.J.: A reference model for interoperable living labs towards establishing productive networks. In: Archimède, B., Ducq, Y., Young, B., Karray, H. (eds.) Enterprise Interoperability IX. I-ESA 2020. Proceedings of the I-ESA Conferences, vol. 10, pp. 183–199. Springer, Cham (2023). https://doi.org/10.1007/978-3-030-90387-9_16
16. Chen, D.: Enterprise interoperability framework. In: EMOI-INTEROP (2006)
17. Shariati, M., Bahmani, F., Shams, F.: Enterprise information security, a review of architectures and frameworks from interoperability perspective. Procedia Comput. Sci. 3, 537–543 (2011)
18. Korhonen, J.J., Yildiz, M., Mykkänen, J.: Governance of information security elements in service-oriented enterprise architecture. In: 2009 10th International Symposium on Pervasive Systems, Algorithms, and Networks, pp. 768–773. IEEE (2009)
19. Sun, J., Chen, Y.: Intelligent enterprise information security architecture based on service oriented architecture. In: 2008 International Seminar on Future Information Technology and Management Engineering, pp. 196–200. IEEE (2008)
20. Bajan, P.M., et al.: Illustration of cybersecurity and safety co-engineering using EBIOS RM and IEC 61508. In: 32nd European Safety and Reliability Conference (ESREL 2022) (2022)
21. Stoneburner, G., Goguen, A., Feringa, A.: Risk management guide for information technology systems. NIST Spec. Publ. 800(30), 800–830 (2002)
22. Ekelhart, A., Fenz, S., Neubauer, T.: Aurum: a framework for information security risk management. In: 2009 42nd Hawaii International Conference on System Sciences, pp. 1–10. IEEE (2009)
23. Desroches, V.: Gérer ses risques numériques avec EBIOS Risk Manager. In: Congrès Lambda Mu 22 «Les risques au cœur des transitions»(e-congrès)-22e Congrès de Maîtrise des Risques et de Sûreté de Fonctionnement, Institut pour la Maîtrise des Risques (2020)
24. Fahrurozi, M., Tarigan, S.A., Tanjung, M.A., Mutijarsa, K.: The use of ISO/IEC 27005: 2018 for strengthening information security management (a case study at data and information Center of Ministry of Defence). In: 2020 12th International Conference on Information Technology and Electrical Engineering (ICITEE), pp. 86–91. IEEE (2020)

25. Weber, S.: Design science research: Paradigm or approach? (2010)
26. Radack S.: The system development life cycle (sdlc). National Institute of Standards and Technology (2009)
27. Jones, A.: A framework for the management of information security risks. BT Technol. J. **25**(1), 30–36 (2007)

Virtuality's Influence on Performing Information Systems Development

Phillip Mangiza and Irwin Brown$^{(\boxtimes)}$ (iD)

Department of Information Systems, University of Cape Town, Cape Town, South Africa
Mngphi019@myuct.ac.za, irwin.brown@uct.ac.za

Abstract. Virtual ways of working such as work-from-home, remote-work and telecommuting have traditionally been implemented by organizations usually to a few employees for specific projects. The transitioning of organizations from a co-located environment to a fully virtual context induced by the COVID-19 pandemic had effects on the process of performing Information Systems Development (ISD). This study employed a single case study of a medium-sized software organization with one hundred and thirty employees that had transitioned to a virtual environment. Data was collected through seventeen interviews and from relevant documents. A literature-derived Systems Development as Performing (sd-as-p) framework was modified and updated with subthemes that emerged from the thematic analysis of case data. The enactment of virtuality was found to influence the following processes of performing ISD, namely (1) leading; (2) communicating; (3) collaborating; (4) knowing; (5) developing with agility; (6) dealing with challenges; (7) trusting; and (8) assessing achievements.

Keywords: Virtuality · Virtual Teams · Remote Work · Fully Remote Mode · Remote First · Work-From Home · Information Systems Development · Software Development · Software Engineering

1 Introduction

Tijunaitis et al. [40] define virtuality as "the movement of physical or in-person processes to online platforms or tools which mimic or replace traditional processes". Some of the factors which influence the rise of virtual working include globalization, changes in business environment and improvements in information and communication technologies (ICTs) [1]. The COVID-19 pandemic forced most countries to adopt social distancing measures that restricted the movement and activities of people in their territories thereby necessitating organizations to operate virtually [31]. Virtual teams have limited face-to-face contact and work interdependently by utilizing digital communication technologies to achieve common goals [11]. Virtuality is mostly practiced by virtual project teams and partly by a few individuals from co-located teams but not in a more continuous way [20]. Virtual teams operate across several boundaries which can be highlighted by coordinates of time, place, and organization [43]. Some organizations create and structure virtual teams deliberately based on the availability and skills of resources [2]. Saraiva

© The Author(s), under exclusive license to Springer Nature Switzerland AG 2023
A. Gerber and M. Coetzee (Eds.): SAICSIT 2023, CCIS 1878, pp. 180–199, 2023.
https://doi.org/10.1007/978-3-031-39652-6_12

et al. [33] define remote work as "a form of virtual work performed virtually outside the conventional workplace where collaboration happens through computer-based technology". Technological advancement has led to the global emergence of business models and organizational strategies [35]. One such business model that is increasing post the COVID-19 pandemic is the concept of the fully remote mode (FRM) of work [32]. Elkordy [12] describes a fully remote company as a company that operates without a co-located physical office but allows employees to work from anywhere including their homes, co-working spaces, and coffee shops. According to Saura et al. [35] telework did not get much attention in academic studies before the outbreak of the COVID-19 pandemic. Rapid technological advancement and the outbreak of the COVID-19 pandemic fuelled the increase of virtual working including in the Information Technology (IT) industry.

The performing of Information Systems Development (ISD) has recently been conceptualized as a process involving (1) the execution of ISD activities by individuals when constructing information systems solutions (the doing of ISD), and (2) the assessment of ISD achievements (the done) [16]. ISD is strongly linked to other business development functions within an organization [17] which work effectively and efficiently in a co-located environment. The development of software requires daily collaboration between software developers and other stakeholders from other business functions [10, 3]. Virtuality in ISD has been extensively explored in academic research, however, these studies place focus on a narrow context of well-organized virtual teams created for specific temporary project tasks. They do not address the influence of virtuality on the process of performing ISD in a broader context of an organization operating in a fully remote mode [20]. This study investigates virtuality's influence on the process of performing of ISD within a fully remote organizational context and in so doing answers the following research question: *"How does virtuality influence the processes of performing ISD in organizations operating within a fully remote context?"*.

The following section provides the conceptual grounding of the study, followed by the research methodology in Sect. 3. The study results will be presented in Sect. 4, followed by discussion of the research findings in Sect. 5. Section 6 concludes the paper with the study's key contributions and limitations.

2 Conceptual Background

ISD involves collaboration between information systems (IS) personnel such as product or project managers, researchers, UX designers, systems analysts, testers, systems developers, and users [45]. Numerous and complex tasks that are necessary in the creation of software products are tied together [10]. According to the principles of agile software development, the main measure of progress in software development is working software [5]. Geeling et al. [16] highlight that the "the doing" of ISD involves processes of leading, enacting agency ("adaptations to technology or the way it is used to align with organizational or professional culture") and dealing with challenges. "The done" includes the process of assessing achievements. Processes of performing ISD identified in literature (inclusive of [16]) encompass leading, communicating, collaborating, trusting, knowing, dealing with challenges, developing with agility, assessing achievements and the enactment of virtuality. These processes and their associated challenges in a virtual context are summarized in Table 1.

Table 1. Summary of the processes of performing ISD and virtuality challenges.

Processes of Performing ISD	Definition	Challenges of Virtuality
Leading	"The behavior and actions of leaders that shape the perceptions and feelings of followers" [16]. Leading involves defining and communicating the team's vision and aligning staff to support the vision [31]. Leaders support their team members and cultivate a healthy environment for team cohesion and remove barriers that impact their team's productivity [15]	• Supporting team tasks, emotional needs of virtual teams and leading dispersed teams is challenging [13] • Relationships among face-to-face teams grow organically but in cases of virtual teams, managers have to proactively guide relationship building processes [27] • Poor communication; absence of team cohesion, the loss of team control and failure in project coordination [8]
Communicating	A multimodal process involving both nonverbal and verbal components comprising of facial expression, gaze, gesture, and body attitude [22]. Synchronous and asynchronous communication is vital to team functioning whether the team is co-located or virtual [30]	• The unavailability of face-to-face interactions of team members negatively affects engagement of team members on collaborative efforts [23] • Inadequate communication and misinterpretation of information [48]
Collaborating	Involves synchronous and asynchronous interactions and tasks to accomplish common goals [30]. ISD requires daily collaboration among various stakeholders [5]. Collaborative technological tools enable ISD teams to conduct their tasks [30]	• Virtual collaborative sessions are not as impactful as face-to-face interactions [29] • Collaboration on projects become difficult to manage virtually when the team grows [30]
Trusting	An environment of trust is crucial in software development teams [14]. Trust comes from visible actions demonstrated by team members facilitating goal attainment of the team [41]. Virtual working on ISD projects requires high levels of trust among team members [41, 48]. Trust impacts leadership [27], and is also built by knowledge transfer, knowledge sharing and knowledge exchange [4]	• Virtuality makes it difficult for team members to observe each other in informal interactions and also non-verbal communications are lost in technological-based communications [30] • The development of trust and team cohesion is difficult in virtual teams [24] • Lack of trust among virtual team members [38]

(continued)

Table 1. (*continued*)

Processes of Performing ISD	Definition	Challenges of Virtuality
Knowing	ISD is a team effort that requires software developers rely on each other's abilities and knowledge [5, 48]. Knowledge sharing is a key component that can be used by virtual teams to build trust [19] and improve team performance [21]. Improvement in knowledge sharing within virtual teams can be fostered by the use of online platforms and repositories [18]. Characteristics of individuals pertaining to knowledge, skills, and abilities (KSAs) should be considered and addressed in a virtual context to ensure individuals will not become bottlenecks for work outcomes [42]	• Face-to-face environments include learning by observing; face-to-face team building exercises are hard to implement virtually when performing ISD [30]
Dealing with challenges	Includes taking actions to prevent or remove impediments when performing ISD [16]	• Challenges in virtual teams include technology resources, trust, communication, dealing with uncertainty of roles caused by multiple participation of members on various virtual teams, leading, factors such as geographic distance, social, cultural, technical, experiential differences, emotional factors, and conflicts [41, 30, 11, 26]
Developing with agility	ISD is a complex undertaking that requires cooperation between developers and other stakeholders such as users, clients, and other business functions [47]. In agile software development, talent, commitment, and professionalism are critical for success [39]. ISD involves early and continuous delivery of valuable software; frequent software delivery; change of requirements; daily collaboration between business, people, and software developers; provision of the right environment, support, and trust to software developers; face to face communication; self-organization of teams [5, 14, 47]. Agile software development increases performance and productivity in self organizing teams [25]	• The virtual context makes it difficult for daily collaboration between business, people, and software developers; provision of the right environment, support, and trust within software development teams; face to face communication; and self-organization of software development teams [30, 13]
Assessing achievements	Involves "the assessment of the outcomes of ISD work and the criteria used to make the assessment" [16]. The primary measure of progress in software development is working software [3, 39, 5, 14]. ISD output quality is measured through an agreed-upon definition of done [37]	• Ensuring data quality conformance and maintenance is difficult in a virtual environment [30]

(*continued*)

Table 1. (*continued*)

Processes of Performing ISD	Definition	Challenges of Virtuality
Enacting virtuality	The use of and reliance on technology-based tools for communication and collaboration and infrastructure such as hardware, software, internet connectivity and cloud computing platforms when performing ISD [12, 7, 30]	• Failure or unavailability of technological tools and infrastructure will affect team's performance [30] • Lack of technical know-how on the utilization of online tools impacts individual's performance [36]

The processes of performing ISD identified in Table 1 resulted in the modification of the theory of Systems Development as Performing (sd-as-p) by Geeling et al. [16]. The modified sd-as-p theory in Fig. 1 below was then used as a conceptual model to guide data collection in this study.

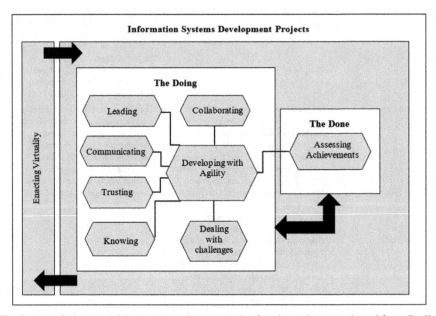

Fig. 1. Modified theory of Systems Development as Performing (sd-as-p) (adapted from Geeling et al. [16]).

3 Research Methodology

A single case study was selected as appropriate to address the research question as a case study is "an empirical inquiry that investigates a contemporary phenomenon within its real-life context, especially when the boundaries between phenomenon and context are not clearly evident" [46]. The organization chosen as case was a software development house that had transitioned from a co-located context to a virtual context (fully remote). The organization was of medium size containing one hundred and thirty employees dispersed across multiple locations including South Africa, Mexico, Kenya, United Kingdom, Peru, Thailand, Uganda, and Germany. Ethics in research approval to undertake the study was granted by the institution from which the study was conducted, with permission obtained from the management of the case organization. The participants from the key business divisions were purposively selected [34] and interviewed. They were selected based on their roles and the key business divisions they work in. In total seventeen participants were interviewed as in Table 2 below.

Table 2. Participants' profiles and business divisions.

Participant	Organizational Role	Business Division
TT	Software Developer and Team Lead	Technology
RP	Software Delivery Manager	Technology
TH	Scrum Master	Technology
KCM	Data Quality Assurance Specialist	Data Production
TKM	Junior Software Developer	Technology
LR	Country manager, Mexico	Business Development
NN	Scrum Master and Line Manager	Technology
TM	Head of Software Engineering	Technology
JP	Head of Data Production	Data Production
CL	Head of Research	Product, Research
IS	Lead Product Manager	Product
SJN	Product Manager	Product
SM	QA Automation Specialist	Product, Technology
RK	Operations Manager	Product, Operations
CW	Head of Data Processing	Data Production
JS	Senior Software Engineer	Technology
EK	Head of Data Engineering	Data Engineering
RWG	Remote working guide	All Divisions
CVD	Company values document	All Divisions

In addition to interview data, secondary data in the form of a remote working guide (RWG) and the company values document (CVD) were collected from the case and were treated as participants in the data analysis process as shown in Table 2 above. These secondary data sources were also utilized in the validation process of this study [34]. A research protocol comprising of semi structured open-ended questions derived from the processes of performing ISD model in Fig. 1 was developed and utilized during the data collection process. Rich and detailed qualitative data [9] was collected from the seventeen participants using interviews. The duration of the interviews ranged from between thirty minutes to an hour per interview and were conducted virtually and recorded using Microsoft Teams.

Data analysis was conducted by following a step-by-step thematic analysis guide as prescribed by Braun & Clarke [6] comprising of six phases explained in Table 3 below. Thematic analysis involves the identification of patterns and themes within qualitative data [28]. An inductive research approach [34] was adopted in this study, this approach allowed the identification of emerging themes, subthemes, and the modification of the sd-as-p model based on the data collected from participants' interviews and company documents.

Table 3. Thematic Analysis Stages (Adapted from Braun & Clarke [6]).

Phase	Description	Explanation
1. Familiarizing with data	"Transcribing data (if necessary), reading and re-reading the data, noting down initial ideas"	• The initial transcription of the interviews was done automatically using the transcription functionality of Microsoft Teams • Transcription files were downloaded from Microsoft Teams as a Microsoft Word document and uploaded to NVivo 12 software for cleaning, editing, and error checking • The recorded video files were played back during this process for the purpose of finding and rectifying errors. This process of reading, re-reading, and listening to the recorded data files allowed the researcher to familiarize with the data and to check the transcription for accuracy • Initial ideas and nodes were noted and recorded in NVivo 12 software
2. Generating initial codes	"Coding interesting features of the data in a systematic fashion across the entire data set, collating data relevant to each code"	• Data features from the data files (interviews and secondary documents) were systematically coded in NVivo 12 software into relevant nodes • The initial nodes in this phase were guided by the research interview protocol questions and data was initially coded around these questions • Emerging nodes from data extracts were also created and relevant data from the files was coded accordingly
3. Searching for themes	"Collating codes into potential themes, gathering all data relevant to each potential theme"	• After all data was collated and coded into the nodes, a long list of nodes and sub nodes was generated • The related nodes were analyzed, combined, and sorted into potential themes

(continued)

Table 3. (*continued*)

Phase	Description	Explanation
4. Reviewing themes	"Checking if the themes work in relation to the coded extracts (Level 1) and the entire data set (Level 2), generating a thematic 'map' of the analysis"	• Initial themes identified in phase 3 were further reviewed and refined by merging related themes, removal of the initial themes that did not have enough supporting data, and creation of new themes and sub themes • Cycles of checking and re-checking of themes against each other and back to the data files with the aim of attaining a level of internal coherence, consistence, and distinctiveness [6] were done
5. Defining and naming themes	"Ongoing analysis to refine the specifics of each theme, and the overall story the analysis tells, generating clear definitions and names for each theme"	• Further refinement of themes was conducted by removing candidate themes that were not relevant, or did not have enough supporting data • Unrelated themes were separated and related themes were combined and renamed • NVivo 12 software [44] and whiteboards were utilized for better visualization and sense making • As coding is an ongoing organic process [6], further coding was done with careful consideration of themes that were relevant and of interest to this study
6. Producing the report	"The final opportunity for analysis. Selection of vivid, compelling extract examples, final analysis of selected extracts, relating back of the analysis to the research question and literature, producing a scholarly report of the analysis"	• Data extracts that easily identified examples of themes and subthemes were embedded within the narrative of the research and reported in Sect. 4 of this paper

4   Findings

The below section will discuss the themes and subthemes that emerged from the data analysis pertaining to the processes of performing ISD virtually. Table 4 shows the themes and subthemes derived from NVivo 12 analysis.

Table 4. Themes and emerging subthemes.

Theme	Sub-themes
Leading	• Clarifying goals and objectives • Adapting leadership styles • Providing leadership support
Communicating	• Asynchronous and synchronous communication • Overcommunication
Collaborating	• Cross-functional collaboration • Engagement and participation • Administrative overheads
Trusting	• Relationship building • Honouring commitments • Active involvement
Knowing	• Knowledge gathering • Knowledge sharing • Knowledge utilization
Dealing with challenges	• Strengthening social fabric • Prioritising employee wellness
Developing with agility	• Championing early and continuous software delivery • Encouraging self-organization • Providing a conducive environment
Assessing achievements	• Quality assurance • Progress tracking • Celebrating outcomes
Enacting Virtuality	• Virtual culture • Technology infrastructure • Online productivity tools

4.1 Leading

Three main subthemes emerged from the analysis of the case data under leading, viz clarifying goals and objectives, adapting leadership styles, providing leadership support.

Clarifying Goals and Objectives: ISD workers and leaders in fully virtual businesses must spend more time and effort communicating and clarifying the expected outcomes [23, 31]:

> *"Spend more time clarifying objectives and direction. Communication is often harder over text. Double-check that you've understood deliverables correctly, align with your team and/or line manager on what success looks like." (RWG)*

Adapting Leadership Styles: Virtual leaders, therefore, ought to adapt their leadership approach by encouraging shared or upward leadership styles for the success of ISD:

> *"I do adapt my leadership style to the person and to the context that I'm speaking to and the relationship I have with that person, which is of course impacted by virtuality." (RK)*

"I think that another aspect that changes is, you're kind of changing your scope of leadership to a smaller team space... it feels like it's easier to focus on few individuals." (JS)

Providing Leadership Support: Provision of leadership support in a virtual setting is one of the most critical responsibilities of ISD leaders. It emerged that leadership support needed by virtual team includes ensuring leadership availability and motivating the team:

"For me as a team lead, in my Slack like as soon as I see a red badge or something like unread notification to me it's like high priority, so I have to jump on it. ... I can't be holding somebody else up... I know I have a lot of things on my plate as well, but I really try to be responsive on Slack." (TT)

"Probably one of our biggest challenges with leadership is maintaining morale in the absence of social interaction." (IS)

4.2 Communicating

The communication theme covers asynchronous and synchronous communication, and overcommunication. Communication plays an integral part in performing ISD in a virtual context, one participant stated that:

"I do feel that compared to in the past, more time is spent communicating than it was when we were not virtual." (IS).

Asynchronous and Synchronous Communication: Communication is a multimodal process involving both nonverbal and verbal components [22]. Synchronous and asynchronous ways of communicating are used when performing ISD virtually. Asynchronous communication increases when working virtually:

"The communication I have is synchronous... a lot of regular calls with a lot of people, one on ones and team ceremonies, team calls... Then work asynchronously...I send them a question and they respond whenever they have time." (EK)

"a lot of meetings that would have happened in a face-to-face conversation they've been happening in sort of asynchronously." (TKM)

Overcommunication: Virtuality removes teams from organic information flows that a co-located environment provides resulting in the need to communicate more when operating virtually:

"I think the first thing when it comes to virtuality is you need to be as clear as possible, so a lot of times you will need to overcommunicate." (RP)

"we've also had to shuffle, to a much more asynchronous way of communicating. So overcommunication is important...." (RK)

4.3 Collaborating

Collaborating while performing ISD comprises of cross functional collaboration, engagement and participation, and administration overheads.

Cross Functional Collaboration: Virtuality increases cross-functional collaboration between ISD teams and other business functions thus ensuring successful ISD delivery and quality outcomes:

> "...the idea of cross functional collaboration was always there, it's not new, but I think there's a heightened awareness because we're now doing remote work and it's not optional for most people. What used to happen before is that you'd have your marketing, your product, your research teams, and things they were doing was siloed... Now we are all more immersed in each other's worlds than we were before, ... we really are walking in stride with design, walking in stride with product research..." (TM)

> "there's also collaboration from the team externally... I worked with the Scrum Master to create rituals within the team, so we have a planning session, we have an open-door session every day." (CL)

Engagement and Participation: Lack of visibility of non-verbal cues are part of the challenges faced in performing ISD virtually. Collaborative tools are key in facilitating virtual engagement and participation:

> "My developers on my team they're more likely to have these Zoom calls to discuss something or do a code review or pair together." (EK)

> "I found that a lot of collaboration is much more visual which works a lot better for me because we have tools like Miro, it makes it a lot easier to represent like workflows and collaborate in real time on how information flows and that kind of thing in a visual way" (SJN)

Administrative Overheads: Collaborating in a virtual context adds administrative overheads such as those pertaining to checking availabilities on people's calendars when setting up meetings or collaborative sessions:

> "When you have to set up those meetings to collaborate with those people. It involves a lot of admin before you can actually get to the actual things that you want to talk to." (KCM)

> "I think in all senses it makes collaboration a little bit more difficult because it's more time consuming to set up meetings with someone and to organize time together." (JS)

4.4 Trusting

Subthemes that emerged from relating to trust when performing ISD included relationship-building, honouring commitments, and active involvement.

Relationship-Building: Virtuality influences the process of building relationships thereby affecting trust as trust is strongly linked to team relationships and a key component of ISD. Trust-building takes longer in a virtual context and sometimes there is a false perception of the availability of trust in a virtual context when in fact it is not there:

> *"Virtuality slows down the process of building trust ..." (NN)*

> *"Trust is built overtime and you will only go so far with me as far as you trust me and that takes time and I think the one thing with the virtual world is we think that trust is there when it isn't, we think that vulnerability is there when it isn't because we see into people's homes, and we assume that because we have that we can suddenly be at a trust level that we're not." (CL)*

Honouring Commitments: In addition to relationship-building, honouring commitments when performing ISD is important in fostering and earning trust when working in a virtual environment. Trust in a virtual context is built and fostered by timely delivery of agreed goals:

> *"There's this movement away from basing your trust on someone's presence, and it becomes much more outputs based ... it's rather about the outputs and are they achieving the goals that are necessary and within a reasonable timeline of expectation... If you're not seeing the results of somebody's work, it's difficult to start trusting them in a remote setting, I think." (JP)*

> *"I think the work as well with the guys do speak for themselves, you know, because it can feel like you can get away with a lot of stuff but when it comes to delivering and you are not delivering, that's very evident. I guess trust is earned." (SM)*

Active Involvement: Virtuality increases the need for software developers to be actively involved in ISD activities such as brainstorming sessions and contributing to software development events such as pull requests, for them to gain trust from their peers:

> *"...there's quite a few people that joined in the office for like two weeks and then they had to move virtually... it wasn't as easy as the people that already had settled relationships, they had to prove with PRs (Pull Request), they had to prove in sessions with their teams that they are there, they had to make a positive contribution and being responsive so this is a very big point that I saw within the engineering spaces...." (RP)*

4.5 Knowing

The findings on the influence of virtuality on the process of knowing when Performing ISD virtually pertain to knowledge gathering, sharing and utilization.

Knowledge Gathering: Virtuality significantly improved knowledge gathering. Asynchronous ways of working forced all teams to improve knowledge documentation thus enhancing the process of ISD:

> *"...because we are remote first, we are forced to document a lot of things. Knowledge base is quite big at this company, but everything is so well documented on Notion, our meetings have Google Docs attached to and it's quite elaborate."* *(NN)*

Knowledge Sharing: Sudden creativity and innovation when performing ISD virtually is affected by virtuality's influence on knowledge sharing. Knowledge sharing in a virtual context is more structured and formal:

> *"You can't just overhear somebody and say oh, they're doing something cool, I'm going to listen to them."* *(IS)*

> *"We don't have these moments of sudden creativity or accidental creativity because we're not bumping into each other at a water cooler, you know..."* *(CL)*

Knowledge Utilization: Challenges in knowledge utilization when performing ISD virtually include, difficulty in discovering gathered information or data, lack of time to adequately analyse data and make use of it, and ensuring the data is up to date for correct utilization:

> *"I would put utilization underneath 50% ... utilization is poor, but the knowledge-base is there and the hunger for knowledge is there. It's just because we're trying to be all-inclusive and be in all our meetings and we just don't have the time to ingest and output as a normal developer..."* *(TH)*

> *"I think discoverability of information can be hard... I don't really know a lot of the time where to find some information because I feel like there's so much information that I don't know where to ..."* *(IS)*

> *"Also, that documentation is not always up to date, and that's also just another major struggle like are we giving people the right things to read...."* *(RK)*

4.6 Dealing with Challenges

The identified ways of dealing with ISD challenges in a virtual environment include measures such as adding human social connections, and prioritising employee wellness.

Adding Human Social Connections: The process of performing ISD requires teamwork and social fabric is essential when dealing with challenges:

> *"Information systems development is a team sport... the social fabric underpins the team dynamic in the sense that when people have a sense of camaraderie, they*

see themselves as humans first, friends first, then colleagues later. It does kind of create a harmony and a way of dealing with challenges in a way that we are a collective, we as a collective need to succeed" (TM)

Prioritising Employee Wellness: Challenges relating to employee wellness encountered when performing ISD virtually are of physical and psychological nature such as fatigue, and developer burn-out:

"...people are already struggling with the cognitive load and the workload..." (RP)

"There's a strong sense of meeting fatigue. I think that with agile development there's a lot of ceremonies, you know, you have stand-ups, you have retros, you have planning, you have backlog grooming, so you have all these ceremonies and I hear a lot from people like oh, do I really need to be there? I've been in like so many hours of meetings already today. Online meetings are more tiring as you have to concentrate a lot more to hear what people are saying." (IS)

4.7 Developing with Agility

The research findings pertaining to developing with agility in a virtual context comprise of championing early and continuous development, encouraging self- organization and providing a conducive environment.

Championing Early and Continuous Development: Virtuality cuts down software delivery times. Faster delivery times are due to factors such as cross-team collaboration, and faster adoption of productivity tools:

"I think when I look at our company a year or two ago, we were shipping at a slower pace than we are today... I think the combination of heightened cross-functional collaboration, fewer distractions might be leading to us being able to ship faster [...] there's probably been faster adoption now of agile tools than there was previously because we now don't have the benefit of having a physical stand up at 9:00 AM in the morning where we all stand around the board with our coffee and talk about what you did the day before and what you're going to do now. So, there's been an increased adoption of digital tools for Agile workflows..." (TM)

Encouraging Self-organization: Virtuality encourages self-organization in teams and individuals. Decision-making largely shifts from being driven by leaders; a tendency usually found in co-located environments to being made by the ISD teams:

"So, we'll have a cycle zero or a first point of contact with the team members in the team, our product owners or managers at Scrum Masters, our stakeholders, and the first question be there is what do we want out of this? Are we boxing to a time frame? Or are we boxing to outcomes? And part of Agile it used to be one thing we've got a time box to achieve this outcome. Now it's no longer up to us to decide. It's up to team members to decide when is that outcome going to be delivered." (TH)

"I take ownership and I support ownership in others. I will never knowingly let my team down." (CVD)

Providing a Conducive Environment: Successful ISD in a virtual context requires an environment of trust, accountability, and the right people:

"You want to foster a culture of trust and accountability because those are the things that are going to ensure that work will still happen. If you don't have trust and accountability, then how are you going to prevent people waking up, picking up work items on Azure DevOps and then slacking off the rest of the day on Netflix, because now there are no safeguards." (TM)

"Virtuality allows you to have people from a broader geographic area so there is more of that type of talent that you're looking for that's available." (JS)

4.8 Assessing Achievements

Subthemes that emerged pertaining to assessing achievements included ensuring quality output, tracking ISD progress, and celebrating achievements.

Quality Assurance: Ensuring quality conformance and maintenance is difficult in a virtual environment as user experiences can be incorrectly curated or moderated by the user and in some cases quality checks such as context can be omitted thereby providing incorrect data to the ISD process and consequently resulting in incorrect ISD outcomes:

"We need to work harder to ensure we maintain the data quality and the conformance to the standards that we set ourselves." (CW)

"We get to be in people's homes every single time we talked to them, whereas before you might have seen them in a workshop space ..., but on the other hand, it's quite difficult to really understand what's going on because they can moderate that experience, they can curate an experience for you, so what's been a challenge is how much of the experiences curated." (CL)

Progress Tracking: There are improvements in the tracking process due to enhanced visibility and measurement features in technological tools because of virtuality:

"...in most of our development situations, we have some form of tracking tools, and we always have for the past I think ten years used some form of tools to track tasks, how we manage our progress, the burn down of work, things like that. All of these has been tracked through a tool. Now it's just been massively improved on, so it's easier to read, it's easier to manage." (TH)

Celebrating Outcomes: ISD outcomes are celebrated virtually using emojis and text messages. Without those celebrations, team motivation and cohesion get affected resulting in poor team performance:

"I would say this is probably one of our major downfall. In an old era, we used to celebrate things. Everything used to be celebrated in a very big way. 'Hey everyone, we launched in Lima. Let's go have a big party... now everybody sends

an emoji, that is it, so we've lost the whole celebrating our victories to a degree. We've also in our losses, we also just add a tear icon, add a sad face. Oh, that's so sad, moving on. We've lost the point of making sure we have the big highs, and the low lows and making sure we embrace them." (TH)

4.9 Enacting Virtuality

Research findings under the enactment of virtuality consist of virtual culture, technological infrastructure, and online productivity tools.

Virtual Culture: Virtuality has a strong effect on company culture. Virtuality takes away natural in-person social elements that are crucial in building organizational culture. A virtual culture must be deliberately developed throughout the business. This culture includes implementation of virtual social interactions or fun activities and adapting to new technologies and ways of working:

"Building a remote culture is very different to building an in-office culture. Some examples could be like having a drink on the rooftop Friday afternoon ...or seeing someone is visibly upset and going up to them and saying, 'let's talk about this', these are all things built into the culture and if you think of company culture as this is the way we do things around here, how you would do things remotely and how you would do things in an office are vastly different." (RK)

Technological Infrastructure: Technological infrastructure is integral for any virtual work including ISD. Without the technological infrastructure such as reliable internet connectivity, computer hardware and reliable electricity supply, performing ISD in a virtual context is not possible:

"...I've personally had it where my internet died, my hotspot didn't work, I could do nothing... so it becomes more costly if you lose people during a call and having key players have internet problems." (RP)

"...the hardware also got a long way to come... I've got a decent laptop, a dev spec laptop, it's 8 gigabytes of RAM, it's pretty good but it struggles with Miro board" (IS)

Online Productivity Tools: Performing ISD virtuality necessitates the use of online productivity tools viz, 1) Communication tools such as Slack, Zoom, Google Workspace, Notion, WhatsApp, Signal, Facebook, and Twitter; 2) Collaboration tools such as Miro whiteboard, Gather, and Google Jamboard; 3) Project Management tools such as ClickUp, Azure DevOps, and Jira; and 4) Knowledge repository tools such as Notion, Google Docs and Google Drive:

"...mostly Slack is the number one, then Zoom for face calls, we all use ClickUp a lot which is project management tool" (EK)

"...we probably have six or seven communication apps, you know, we have Facebook, WhatsApp, Twitter, Signal because you just don't know how people will want to reach out to you and being available to them is the biggest thing." (CL)

"... when we collaborate in real time, things like Miro Board, Google Jamboard are on the right track...we need shared workspaces like that." (IS)

5 Discussion

The research findings in Sect. 4 provided a basis for the modification of the initial sd-as-p model shown in Fig. 1, to an updated sd-as-p model shown in Fig. 2 below.

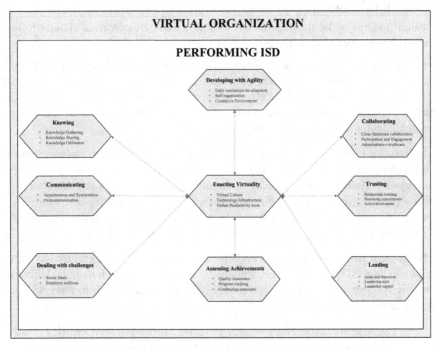

Fig. 2. Updated Systems Development as Performing (sd-as-p) model.

The analysis of empirical case data provides more detail and clarity concerning the processes of performing ISD in a virtual context. There is coherence between literature studies and this study's findings pertaining to the main processes of performing ISD. Additionally, the case data revealed how enacting virtuality is central to the processes of performing ISD in fully remote organizations. The initial model in Fig. 1 was therefore reframed as shown in Fig. 2. The relationships between the processes of performing ISD are mediated by the enactment of virtuality (technological tools and infrastructure such as software, hardware, and internet connectivity). Without the enactment of virtuality all other processes of performing ISD cannot be carried out [12, 29, 11]. The utilization of technology tools enable real time progress tracking and quality checks when performing ISD virtually hence the process of assessing achievements ("the done") was grouped together with other processes ("the doing") in the updated sd-as-p model above.

6 Conclusion

The study revealed the main processes of performing ISD that are influenced by virtuality viz leading, communicating, collaborating, trusting, knowing, dealing with challenges, developing with agility, assessing achievements, and enacting virtuality. There was coherence between literature findings and the findings of this study pertaining to the influence of virtuality on these main processes of performing ISD. Additionally, several sub-themes emerged during the thematic data analysis.

The findings in this study have both theoretical and practical significance. On the theoretical contribution, the revised sd-as-p model can be used to understand how the processes of performing ISD are influenced by virtuality. The practical contribution is that ISD organizations and teams already operating in virtual contexts can utilize some of the study's findings to streamline their processes, and co-located businesses wishing to transition to the full remote business mode can utilize this study's findings to assist with the transition.

Due to factors such as the time constraints and difficulties in finding ISD organizations that had transitioned to fully virtual mode during the pandemic, a single case was investigated. As more companies are now shifting to fully virtual ways of working, the study provides an opportunity for in-depth investigations and analysis on the revised sd-as-p theoretical model by use of multiple case studies. Future studies can further investigate relationships between processes of performing ISD when operating in a virtual context. The updated model could be further investigated and analyzed especially relating to the subthemes and whether the subthemes can constitute main themes on their own or whether more themes and subthemes can be added to the model. Furthermore, more research can be conducted in larger organizations.

References

1. Abarca, V.M.G., Palos-Sanchez, P.R., Rus-Arias, E.: Working in virtual teams: a systematic literature review and a bibliometric analysis. IEEE Access **8**, 168923–168940 (2020)
2. Adewole, K.F.: Lived experiences of project leaders who successfully managed projects while working with virtual teams (Publication No. 2020. 27829130) [Doctoral dissertation, Capella University]. ProQuest Dissertations Publishing (2020)
3. Alsaqqa, S., Sawalha, S., Abdel-Nabi, H.: Agile software development: methodologies and trends. Int. J. Interact. Mob. Technol. (IJIM) **14**(11), 246 (2020)
4. Alsharo, M., Gregg, D., Ramirez, R.: Virtual team effectiveness: the role of knowledge sharing and trust. Inf. Manage. **54**(4), 479–490 (2017)
5. Beck, K., et al.: Manifesto for agile software development. Agile Alliance (2001). http://agilemanifesto.org/
6. Braun, V., Clarke, V.: Using thematic analysis in psychology. Qual. Res. Psychol. **3**(2), 77–101 (2006)
7. Bundhun, K., Sungkur, R.K.: Developing a framework to overcome communication challenges in agile distributed teams–Case study of a Mauritian-based IT service delivery centre. Glob. Transit. Proc. **2**(2), 315–322 (2021)
8. Castellano, S., Chandavimol, K., Khelladi, I., Orhan, M.A.: Impact of self-leadership and shared leadership on the performance of virtual R&D teams. J. Bus. Res. **128**, 578–586 (2021)

9. Castillo-Montoya, M.: Preparing for interview research: the interview protocol refinement framework. Qual. Rep. **21**(5), 811–831 (2016)
10. Collignon, S.E., Nazir, S., Surendra, N.C.: Agile systems development: privacy theoretical lens to challenge the full information disclosure paradigm. Inf. Manage. **59**(6), 103679 (2022)
11. Dulebohn, J.H., Hoch, J.E.: Virtual teams in organizations. Hum. Resour. Manag. Rev. **27**(4), 569–694 (2017)
12. Elkordy, M.E.: Starting and managing a fully remote business. HR Future **2022**(2), 10–11 (2022)
13. Ford, R.C., Piccolo, R.F., Ford, L.R.: Strategies for building effective virtual teams: trust is key. Bus. Horiz. **60**(1), 25–34 (2017)
14. Fowler, M., Highsmith, J.: The agile manifesto. Softw. Dev. **9**(8), 28–35 (2001)
15. Gallego, J.S., Ortiz-Marcos, I., Ruiz, J.R.: Main challenges during project planning when working with virtual teams. Technol. Forecast. Soc. Chang. **162**, 120353 (2021)
16. Geeling, S., Brown, I., Weimann, P.: Performing IS development: culture's emergent influence. In: ICIS Conference 2019, Munich, Germany (2019)
17. Guinan, P.J., Parise, S., Langowitz, N.: Creating an innovative digital project team: levers to enable digital transformation. Bus. Horiz. **62**(6), 717–727 (2019)
18. Harris, W.J.: Technology adoption by global virtual teams: Developing a cohesive approach. SAM Adv. Manag. J. **83**(1), 4 (2018)
19. Hao, Q., Yang, W., Shi, Y.: Characterizing the relationship between conscientiousness and knowledge sharing behavior in virtual teams: an interactionist approach. Comput. Hum. Behav. **91**, 42–51 (2019)
20. Hoegl, M., Muethel, M.: Enabling shared leadership in virtual project teams: a practitioners' guide. Proj. Manag. J. **47**(1), 7–12 (2016)
21. Hung, S.W., Cheng, M.J., Hou, C.E., Chen, N.R.: Inclusion in global virtual teams: exploring non-spatial proximity and knowledge sharing on innovation. J. Bus. Res. **128**, 599–610 (2021)
22. Jarvenpaa, S.L., Keating, E.: When do good communication models fail in global virtual teams? Organ. Dyn. **50**(1), 100843 (2021)
23. Kirkman, B.L., Stoverink, A.C.: Building resilient virtual teams. Organ. Dyn. **50**(1), 100825 (2021)
24. Kozlowski, S.W., Chao, G.T., Van Fossen, J.: Leading virtual teams. Organ. Dyn. **50**(1), 100842 (2021)
25. Kumar, G., Bhatia, P.K.: Impact of agile methodology on software development process. Int. J. Comput. Technol. Electron. Eng. (IJCTEE) **2**(4), 46–50 (2012)
26. Levasseur, R.E.: People skills: leading virtual teams—a change management perspective. Interfaces **42**(2), 213–216 (2012)
27. Liao, C.: Leadership in virtual teams: a multilevel perspective. Hum. Resour. Manag. Rev. **27**(4), 648–659 (2017)
28. Maguire, M., Delahunt, B.: Doing a thematic analysis: a practical, step-by-step guide for learning and teaching scholars. All Ireland J. High. Educ. **9**(3) (2017)
29. Meluso, J., Johnson, S., Bagrow, J.: Making virtual teams work: redesigning virtual collaboration for the future. SocArXiv, pp. 1–14 (2017)
30. Morrison-Smith, S., Ruiz, J.: Challenges and barriers in virtual teams: a literature review. SN Appl. Sci. **2**(6), 1–33 (2020). https://doi.org/10.1007/s42452-020-2801-5
31. Newman, S.A., Ford, R.C.: Five steps to leading your team in the virtual COVID-19 workplace. Organ. Dyn. **50**(1), 100802 (2021)
32. Pashchenko, D.: Fully remote software development due to covid factor: results of industry research (2020). Int. J. Softw. Sci. Comput. Intell. (IJSSCI) **13**(3), 64–70 (2021)
33. Saraiva, C., São Mamede, H., Silveira, M.C., Nunes, M.: Transforming physical enterprise into a remote organization: transformation impact: digital tools, processes and people. In:

2021 16th Iberian Conference on Information Systems and Technologies (CISTI), pp. 1–5. IEEE (2021)

34. Saunders, M., Lewis, P., Thornhill, A.: Research Methods for Business Students. Prentice Hall, Harlow (2016)
35. Saura, J.R., Ribeiro-Soriano, D., Saldaña, P.Z.: Exploring the challenges of remote work on Twitter users' sentiments: from digital technology development to a post-pandemic era. J. Bus. Res. **142**, 242–254 (2022)
36. Schulze, J., Krumm, S.: The "virtual team player" a review and initial model of knowledge, skills, abilities, and other characteristics for virtual collaboration. Organ. Psychol. Rev. **7**(1), 66–95 (2017)
37. Schwaber, K., Sutherland, J.: The scrum guide. Scrum Alliance **21**(19), 1 (2011)
38. Shameem, M., Kumar, C., Chandra, B.: Challenges of management in the operation of virtual software development teams: a systematic literature review. In: 2017 4th International Conference on Advanced Computing and Communication Systems (ICACCS), pp. 1–8. IEEE (2017)
39. Tam, C., da Costa Moura, E.J., Oliveira, T., Varajão, J.: The factors influencing the success of on-going agile software development projects. Int. J. Proj. Manage. **38**(3), 165–176 (2020)
40. Tijunaitis, K., Jeske, D., Shultz, K.S.: Virtuality at work and social media use among dispersed workers. Employee Relat.: Int. J. (2019)
41. Tyagi, S., Sibal, R., Suri, B.: Empirically developed framework for building trust in distributed agile teams. Inf. Softw. Technol. **145**, 106828 (2022)
42. Wang, Y., Haggerty, N.: Individual virtual competence and its influence on work outcomes. J. Manag. Inf. Syst. **27**(4), 299–334 (2011)
43. Weimann, P., Pollock, M., Scott, E., Brown, I.: Enhancing team performance through tool use: how critical technology-related issues influence the performance of virtual project teams. IEEE Trans. Prof. Commun. **56**(4), 332–353 (2013)
44. Wong, L.P.: Data analysis in qualitative research: a brief guide to using NVivo. Malay. Family Phys.: Off. J. Acad. Family Phys. Malay. **3**(1), 14 (2008)
45. Yang, H.L., Tang, J.H.: Team structure and team performance in IS development: a social network perspective. Inf. Manage. **41**(3), 335–349 (2004)
46. Yin, R.K.: Case Study Research: Design and Methods, 2nd edn. Sage, Thousand Oaks (1994)
47. Zaitsev, A., Gal, U., Tan, B.: Coordination artifacts in agile software development. Inf. Organ. **30**(2), 100288 (2020)
48. Zuofa, T., Ochieng, E.G.: Working separately but together: appraising virtual project team challenges. Team Perform. Manage.: Int. J. (2017)

Factors Affecting Code Security in South African Organization

Phindiwe Matiti$^{(\boxtimes)}$ and Salah Kabanda$^{(\boxtimes)}$ (ID)

Department of Information Systems, University of Cape Town, Rondebosch, Cape Town 7700, South Africa

Phindiwe.matiti@alumni.uct.ac.za, Salah.kabanda@uct.ac.za

Abstract. Cybersecurity has become an area that most researchers and practitioners invest their resources in. Yet, cyber related threats remain rampant. This is partly due to vulnerabilities in the systems, specifically in the code, that can be exploited by cyber attackers. Given that cyber related attacks have been more prominent on the African continent, this study seeks to identify and understand the factors affecting code security in South African organizations. The study is informed by a qualitative enquiry. Interviews were used to collect data from nine IT knowledge workers responsible for the development and testing of organizational systems. The findings show that code security should be understood from the context of (1) resource availability, specifically IT professionals with both practical expertise and experience, cyber specific training and adoption and continuous use of security tools; (2) confidence and reliance on IT infrastructure; and (3) work-life balance practice that encourages collaboration between employees.

Keywords: Cybersecurity · code security · vulnerabilities

1 Introduction

Over the past decade, information and communication technologies (ICTs) have exponentially evolved and transformed the world into an information society, communicating through sophisticated and automated information systems, hardware technologies, and other multimedia resources [1]. As a result, organizations have increasingly embraced various kinds of ICTs [2]. This embrace and consequently reliance, has resulted in widespread cybercrime, with criminals targeting corporations and governments through system vulnerabilities, to access valuable data that can then be used for illegal purposes [3]. Vulnerabilities in system applications are code errors commonly caused by neglecting security practices [4, 5]. When these vulnerabilities are exploited, system application developers are frequently blamed and viewed as the weakest link who should do more to protect systems and related technologies [4].

Prior studies have noted that security education, training, and awareness (SETA) programs fails to educate system application developers of pertinent security measures related to the software they develop [36]. The focus of SETA tends to be on all employees

© The Author(s), under exclusive license to Springer Nature Switzerland AG 2023
A. Gerber and M. Coetzee (Eds.): SAICSIT 2023, CCIS 1878, pp. 200–210, 2023.
https://doi.org/10.1007/978-3-031-39652-6_13

in general, and this puts a blind spot on those who really need the training the most – system application developers whose task is to identify and fix the vulnerabilities in the systems. Whilst it is imperative that all employees are informed and trained on cybersecurity issues [6], and have access to and understand security technology tools and methodologies to assist in providing secure system code [7]; it is still not clear what training is provided to the technical team with regards to cybersecurity training [8], given that prior studies have noted how the technical teams receive inadequate training on security matters [9, 10]. Addressing issues of security is paramount in this digital era, specifically in the developing countries of Africa where it is estimated that around 500 million people use the internet and cybercrime attacks are on the increase, with 230 million cybercrime incidents recorded between January 2020 and February 2021 [11]. The impact of cybercrime has been significant. For example, in 2021, the Kenyan IT cybersecurity company further reported that cybercrime reduced the gross domestic product (GDP) by 10%, costing Africa an estimated $4.12 billion USD. Malware attacks have been noted to be one of the growing dangers contributing to the rise in cybercrime in Africa. According to Interpol [11] research, malware is quickly becoming one of the most serious threats facing the African continent, and South Africa is one of the top three countries experiencing the highest number of cybercrime victims. Understanding the factors affecting how organizations in Africa secure their programs, specifically how they secure their code, is important as it can address issues of system vulnerabilities that cybersecurity threats tend to exploit. With this background, this study seeks to respond to the research question what are the factors affecting code security in South African organizations?

2 Literature Review

By the twenty-first century, cyberattacks had spread to various parts of the world, causing organizations to disrupt their normal business processes, lose clients, and negatively impact their image [12]. Cybersecurity is the practice of protecting organizational systems and networks from malicious digital attacks [13]. System application developers tend to be at the fore front of systems development and if they are not security conscious in their practice, this can lead to system vulnerabilities [14]. To mitigate these risks, organizations have spent a significant number of resources to secure their networks by investing in cybersecurity technologies (hardware and software), Information security policy (ISP), and staff training [13]. Cybersecurity measures are part of the organizational security architecture, which is used to map out how to safeguard the enterprise information security of the organization [13]. For example, most organizations use anti-virus and signature-based detection as a means of dealing with software threats by scanning, detecting, and removing malware in the organization's network traffic [15, 16]. However, there are some limitations for example, the signatures used in antivirus can only deal with known attacks in the world of cybersecurity and cybercriminals invent new malware every day [16]. The limitations have the potential to transform from a defensive mechanism to an attack tool, allowing cybercriminals to infiltrate the organization's network and steal sensitive data.

Although the benefits of SETA are well recognized, the programs unfortunately do not always reduce security risks or modify employee behaviour [8]. Also, when implemented, there is always a one-size-fits-all approach that fails to consider the needs of the technical staff [8]. According to Tahaei et al. [17], system application vulnerabilities in system applications arise not because system application developers create new and unique problems that are difficult to detect and fix, but because they lack awareness and/or support in tools that will help them to detect code vulnerabilities. Tahaei et al. [17] have pointed out that organizations do not provide system application developers with the tools and methodology required to become more security conscious during the coding process. It is reported that system application developers find it difficult to use static analysis tools to uncover security vulnerabilities because of the large number of false positives, the lack of collaborative support, and the complexity of the tool output [9]. As a result of the inadequate training and understanding of the static analysis tools, system application developers do not believe that security is part of their responsibilities [9]. Part of the reason for this can be attributed to the fact that to develop a secure internal system application, system application developers must adhere to a Software Development Life Cycle (SDLC) framework and a development model, like agile or waterfall, which usually does not concern itself with issues of security [18]. For example, although aspects of security are touched on, issues of penetration testing or code testing for vulnerabilities in general are not prioritized, making the code become susceptible for cybersecurity attacks. Penetration testing is an essential security measure and it's recognized as one of the best security practices as it focuses on finding vulnerabilities in the operational systems and network infrastructure [19]. Altayaran and Elmedany [20] stated that penetration testing is not fully integrated to the SDLC process, exposing their applications to attacks because of security flaws and bugs that has been made during the development of a system. The penetration testing process makes use of a complex knowledge base to extract the information required in all phases of penetration testing [21]. Penetration testing can be completed using automated tools, the process requires specialized security personnel that has deep knowledge of the possible attacks to carry out and of the hacking static tools that can be used to launch the tests [21].

There has also been the use of the Security-Software Development Life Cycle (S-SDLC) to address security measures in organizations. The S-SDLC is a framework for incorporating security into the SDLC process. According to Aceto et al. [10], it is critical for organizations to invest in the appropriate innovative vulnerability discovery methodology to reduce the risk of unauthorized access to sensitive organizational data. The S-SDLC framework provides system application developers with security features such as coding vulnerabilities, security requirements, and detecting design weaknesses at the early stages of the methodology process [7]. However, the methodology presents some challenges for organizational system application developers because it necessitates the use of a static code analysis tool to detect security vulnerabilities in their code [4]. Given the importance of addressing cyber related security threats in Africa, it is important to identify and understand the factors affecting code security.

3   Methodology

The study is inductive in nature and adopts an interpretivism research philosophy to allow the researcher to gain in-depth understanding, insights, and experience in the areas of system application development, security, training, and education. The research employed purposeful and snowball sampling strategy with knowledge experts contacted via referrals. Knowledge experts in this case were individuals responsible for the development and testing of organizational systems. Data was collected via semi-structured interviews, using an online virtual platform (Teams). Semi-structured interviews allow the researcher to elicit responses and gain a better understanding of the phenomenon, allowing the researcher to investigate subjective viewpoints and collect detailed reports of people's personal views in an interactive manner.

The first phase of analysis began with the process of transcription of each interview, a process that also allows the researcher to immerse themselves in the data. Then, in the second phase of analysis, the researchers reread each transcript to identify ideas and interesting aspect relating to the research study, specifically the key concepts raised in the research questions. During this stage, the researcher developed codes which were useful in summarizing the meaning of that data extract as it related to the phenomenon under investigation. The third stage involves searching for themes, patterns, and relationships among the codes identified from the research data. Searching for themes is part of the overall process of condensing the raw data collected, first by coding them and then grouping these coded data into analytic categories. According to DeSantis and Ugarriza [7], "a theme is an abstract entity that brings meaning and identity to a recurring experience and its variant manifestations. As such, a theme captures and unifies the nature or basis of the experience into a meaningful whole" (362). With this understanding, themes were created for all codes that shared a relationship and were developed in response to the key concepts related to the study.

4   Findings and Discussion

It is argued that qualitative studies have smaller samples than quantitative studies [22]. The research sample consists of nine IT professionals as shown in Table 1 from large organizations, chosen based on their ability to explain the key points raised in the literature. Six participants were interviewed in the oil and petroleum industry, two IT consulting firms, and one freelancer who specializes in penetration testing in various organizations. All the participants in this study have more than seven years of experience in the IT industry.

Table 1. Research Participants

Alias	Participant's Role	Work Experience (Years)	Industry
P1	CyberSecurity Specialist	7	Oil and Petroleum
P2	Team leader for Developers	17	Oil and Petroleum
P3	Manager for Developers	17	Oil and Petroleum
P4	Penetration Tester	11	IT Consultant: Freelancer
P5	Senior System Application Developer	15	Oil and Petroleum
P6	Senior System Application Developer	12	Oil and Petroleum
P7	System Application Developer	12	IT Consultancy
P8	System application tester	7	IT Consultancy
P9	System Application Developer	12	Oil and Petroleum

4.1 The Reliance on IT Infrastructure Affects How IT Practitioners Perceive Code Security

Most participants explained that organizations rely on available IT infrastructure such as web application firewalls, intrusion prevention systems (IPS), application interface layers, and network segregation to protect sensitive data. Participant five stated that *"The security will mostly rely on the company's security firewall to make sure that cybercriminals do not access the data through the in-house developed and stored applications"*(P5). This was further supported by participant one, who further highlighted that *our organization's IT infrastructure provides firewalls, IPS, network segregation, and intrusion detection to protect the systems and data of the system."* (P1). Participants further explained how IT infrastructure assists the organization, making sure that the organization is safe from cyber criminals. Participant five noted the use of access control systems, highlighting that access control systems safeguard the organizational data from unauthorized users and are set up to ensure that the appropriate level of application access is provided. He explains that: *"Not everybody has the same access to the system, and that's how we program the system to make sure that there is no one that gets access to the wrong data".* Participant four's trust in the IT infrastructure was clear, noting that *"when a user inserts their username incorrectly multiple times, it flags them as a potential cyber threat and triggers an investigation" (P4).* In summary, organizations in this study show total reliance on their IT infrastructure which they perceive to be adequately supported in terms of resources to address security incidents. There was no mention of how the IT infrastructure itself was protected which is a concern because any critical infrastructure should be guarded, and cybersecurity risk assessments conducted timeously [23].

4.2 Minimal Adoption of Security Tools Obstructs the Pursuit for Code Security

Although the IT infrastructure provided some security mechanism against cyber threats; participants explained that this was not adequate and talked of the need for up-to-date security tools, specifically vulnerability-checking tools which they all claimed not to have in their organization. Participant one states that they had never been exposed or trained in vulnerability-checking tools and *"there are currently no tools used for checking vulnerabilities of the development team's code"* (P1). Similar sentiments were expressed by participant two, stating that *"at the moment, there is nothing in place to check the code and to know from where a potential threat comes from or will come from"*. Although there was no mention of what type of vulnerability for cybersecurity, they were more concerned about; participants explained the need of having vulnerability-checking tools and *"it is also important to upskill developers with automation tools to be able to have a security mind when coding. This is also an issue because our organization does not have those tools"* (P6). There was evidence of penetration testing in some organizations, however, many reported challenges with it and therefore its use was minimalistic. According to participant four, *"penetration testing is one of the most neglected trades within businesses. "You'll find that it is done on an ad hoc basis. In one big company that I used to work for, there was only one guy that was doing penetration testing within a company that had about seven scrum teams."* (P4). It was emphasized that organizations do not spend enough time and money to invest in the penetration skills required or upskill the system application developers with security penetration testing.

The findings show that code security is affected by the lack of security tools which are key in detecting system vulnerabilities and to bridge this gap, developers are guided by the team policy and guidelines headed by a senior developer. These findings echo prior studies confirming that security tools generally see poor adoption by developers due to among other factors, team policies and lack of organisation support [17] and the fact that most security testing approaches and tools focus on a particular vulnerability making it difficult to be adopted for complex attack scenarios involving several interactions among parties [24]. Meng et al. [25] continues to call for organisational support for developers to carry out security testing to check whether the implemented features work as expected and advises against disabling of security checks to implement a temporary fix in the testing or development environment. Afrose et al. [26] notes the need for organizations to recognize and address these barriers because it plays a significant role in assisting developers with writing and maintaining secure code.

4.3 IT Practitioners' Expertise and Experience with Security Facilitates the Development of Security Code

Due to lack of security tools, most respondents resorted to the adoption of the team's coding rules and guidelines as a component of the current process to minimize security risks within their code. The coding rules and guidelines are used to assist system application developers in ensuring that their *code does not contain hard-coded credentials* (p7). Furthermore, a senior application developer performs the final checks to ensure that no hardcode is exposed to cyber criminals and employees. Senior developers provide guidance to the team regarding for example, *"other optimal ways to better write the code. In short, through the development stages, the code must be reviewed by a senior developer to check for vulnerabilities and to check if the developer followed the coding principles set by the organization"* (P7).

Several participants emphasized the importance of experience in providing secure code while adhering to the established coding rules and guidelines. *"The more years of experience you have writing code, the more you might think about other security strategies for writing code"* (P6). It was further highlighted that new employees are thrown into coding with no experience and are expected to perform and provide safe coding for their systems. Respondent P2 acknowledges the lack of resources as a challenge: *"due to the shortage of resources, we don't have time to train the new system application developers or oversee their coding, which I know it's very risky "*. The findings demonstrate the need for training for junior system application developers. This would alleviate in the long run the workload that senior developers face and also improve on the security and quality of output.

4.4 Overworked Security Personnel Affect Code Security

Despite the availability of policies and having a senior developer performing the final checks, participants commented that additional security measures need to be in place to complement the existing approaches. According to most participants, senior system developers frequently lack the time to review the code created for all system applications due to the number of projects and tasks that are delegated to them. *"Due to the shortage of resources, we don't have time to train the new system application developers or oversee their coding, which I know it's very risky"* (P2). Several participants also emphasized the significance of experience in providing secure code in accordance with the organization's established coding rules and guidelines. *"When you write code, the more years of experience you have, the more you might think about other security strategies for writing code"* (P6). The findings point to the common understanding that 'IT professionals are expected to work long hours and do more with less, while on a constrained budget' [27] as cited by [28]. Such understanding lends the IT professional to work exhaustion, which is likely to influence the quality of output, more specifically in producing secure code, as well as affecting their relationship with the organization [28].

4.5 Organization Support for Cybersecurity Specific Training Facilitate Code Security

Most participating organizations have a program for individual development (IDP) where employees can choose courses based on their individual needs and attend training at their preferred training facility. *"If we believe that a refresher course is required, we have funds available to send to conferences, training, and formal education"* (P5). Managers emphasized that although system application developers use the IDP for educational purposes, such as obtaining a higher degree, they never prioritize security training as a subject they wish to learn (P2). This observation was perceived as a challenge because most developers become trained in other areas, other than the core aspect of security. Most participants emphasized that organizations do not provide formal security specific training specifically for system application developers. All IT staff received generic training, which the entire company also received. According to participant one: *"Most of the time, the training is general and most of the training is focused on phishing" (P1)*. According to participant two, the lack of specialized training was risky and to mitigate the risk, *"new starters with no experience are thrown into small in-house projects while the senior developers support customers with big projects that require intense coding"*.

Only one organization highlighted that their development team receives hands-on training where they learn how hackers attempt to hack the systems, how to spot vulnerabilities, break code, and patch them. Participant 8 explains that *"Every Friday developers have a hackathon designed as an exercise for developers to learn how to spot vulnerabilities in their code. In this exercise, the developers test each other's code as they try to breach and play around with the code.* Given that most developers tend to face tight project deadlines and short product turnaround time, it is important for the organization to support with the resources that allows them to time and effort 'improving their knowledge or hardening their code for long-term benefits' [26].

4.6 Collaboration of IT Practitioners Enables the Development of Secure Code

Most participants emphasized the lack of collaboration among IT teams in organizations particularly between system application developers and the security teams, asserting that this must change to close the security gap in organizations. According to participant six, *"collaboration with all members of the IT team from time to time for knowledge sharing is needed to address cybersecurity in its totality. The issue is that it rarely happens"*. This perception was common from all participants as participant 1 shares: *"The security team have no idea what is going on inside the development space in terms of security. We have developers doing the development work; and then we have the security guys who are not members of the development team who must secure a system they were not part of during development. The two camps do not work together towards addressing security right from the onset of the project and that is a problem"*. This lack of collaboration is exacerbated by the nature of the work the IT practitioner does which is typically undertaken over strict deadlines, 'involves multiple stake holders, requires decision making based on a combination of prior experience and online research' and yet they have no collaborative tools that work well to support teamwork [17]. Nguyen and Dupuis [27] posits that the lack of collaboration is a challenge 'when it comes to introducing code changes or new features to an existing software product/system to ensure that the integrity, functionality, and scalability of the product does not become compromised' (94). The SDLC framework is not concerned with incorporating security within the development framework and penetration testing is not fully integrated into the SDLC process, exposing their applications to attacks because of security flaws and bugs that have been introduced during the development of a system [20]. On the other hand, the Agile methodology is used to develop a functional application in the shortest timeframe while using the fewest resources (24), and penetration testing is not fully integrated into the SDLC process, exposing their applications to attacks because of security flaws and bugs that have been introduced during the development of a system [20].

5 Conclusion

Security has become a sensitive spot for many organizations today. Consequently, organizations have embarked on many strategies to try and identify, understand, and tackle potential areas from which their security can be breached. Most have implemented training and awareness programs to sensitise employees on security related threats. This study presents six factors affecting code security from the system application development team's perspective. The reliance on the organisation's IT infrastructure was perceived to affect how IT Practitioners perceive code security. IT practitioners who perceive the organisation to have control over their infrastructure security tend to have trust in the infrastructure and, as a result, do not invest their time in code security. It is imperative that management conducts regular checks and audits on the IT infrastructure to ensure that indeed it can protect the organisation from cybersecurity threats. Code security efforts were also affected by the minimal adoption of security tools that allows organisation to be proactive in their detection of cybersecurity threats. The lack of readily available expertise and experience with code security hampers the development of secure code. This was further made worse by the fact that most IT practitioners are overworked with minimal cybersecurity specific training or collaboration with other IT Practitioners in the development of secure code (Fig. 1).

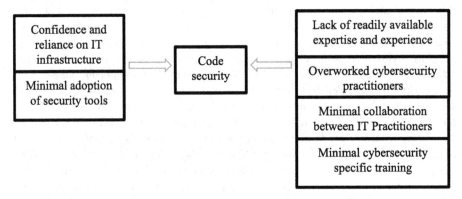

Fig. 1. Factors Affecting Code Security

The findings supported the literature on the lack of IT tool usage among system application developers due to a lack of availability of tools and training. According to Tahaei et al. [17], system application vulnerabilities arise because system application developers lack awareness and/or support in security tools to detect code vulnerabilities. In addition, the findings supported the literature by emphasizing how crucial it is for the technical development team to have access to and knowledge of security technology tools and methodologies to contribute to the creation of secure system code [8]. The technical factor theme is a new finding that participants highlighted as one of the factors affecting cyber-security not having a secure code. Stating that there is reliance on IT infrastructure in place in organizations.

References

1. Santoro, M., Vaccari, L., Mavridis, D., Smith, R.S., Posada, M., Gattwinkel, D.: Web Application Programming Interfaces (APIs): General-Purpose Standards, Terms and European Commission Initiatives. Louxembourg: European Commission (2019). https://doi.org/10.2760/85021
2. David, O.O., Grobler, W:. Information and communication technology penetration level as an impetus for economic growth and development in Africa. Econ. Res.-Ekonomska istraživanja **33**(1), 1394–1418 (2020). https://doi.org/10.1080/1331677X.2020.1745661
3. Aldawood, H., Skinner, G.: Reviewing cyber security social engineering training and awareness programs—Pitfalls and ongoing issues. J. Future Internet **11**(3), 1– 16. (2019). https://www.mdpi.com/1999-5903/11/3/73
4. Assal, H., Chiasson, S.: Think secure from the beginning' a survey with software developers. In Proceedings of the Conference on Human Factors in Computing Systems Proceedings, pp. 1–13. (2019). Association for Computing Machinery, Glasgow, Scotland UK. https://doi.org/10.1145/3290605.3300519
5. Or-Meir, O., Nissim, N., Elovici, Y., Rokach, L.: Dynamic malware analysis in the modern era—A state of the art survey. ACM Comput. Surv. (CSUR) **52**(5), 1–48 (2019). https://doi.org/10.1145/3329786
6. Alshaikh, M., Naseer, H., Ahmad, A., Maynard, S.B. Toward sustainable behaviour change: an approach for cyber security education training and awareness. In: Proceedings of the 27th European Conference on Information Systems (ECIS). Stockholm & Uppsala, Sweden (2019). https://aisel.aisnet.org/ecis2019_rp/100
7. de Vicente Mohino, J., Bermejo Higuera, J., Bermejo Higuera, J.R., Sicilia Montalvo, J.A.: The application of a new secure software development life cycle (S-SDLC) with agile methodologies. J. Electron. **8**(11), 1–28 (2019). https://doi.org/10.3390/electronics8111218
8. Hu, S., Hsu, C., Zhou, Z.: Security education, training, and awareness programs: literature review. J. Comput. Inf. Syst., 752–764 (2021). https://doi.org/10.1080/08874417.2021.1913671
9. Thomas, T.W., Tabassum, M., Chu, B., Lipford, H.: Security during application development: an application security expert perspective. In: Proceedings of the 2018 CHI Conference on Human Factors in Computing Systems. 262, pp. 1–12. (2018). Association for Computing Machinery, Montreal QC, Canada. https://doi.org/10.1145/3173574.3173836
10. Aceto, G., Persico, V., Pescapé, A.: The role of information and communication technologies in healthcare: taxonomies, perspectives, and challenges. J. Netw. Comput. Appl. **107**, 125–154 (2018)
11. Interpol.: African Cyberthreat Assessment Report. Singapore.1–24 (2021). https://www.interpol.int/en/News-and-Events/News/2021/INTERPOL-report-identifies-top-cyberthreats-in-Africa
12. Arnone, R.: Hackers cybercrime-computer security: ethical hacking: learn the attack for better defence. ARIS2-Adv. Res. Inf. Syst. Secur. **1**(1), 50–61 (2021). https://doi.org/10.56394/aris2.v1i1.7
13. Borky, J.M., Bradley, T.H.: Protecting information with cybersecurity. Effective Model-Based Syst. Eng., 345–404 (2019). https://doi.org/10.1007/978-3-319-95669-5_10
14. Braz, L., Aeberhard, C., Çalikli, G.. Less is more: supporting developers in vulnerability detection during code review. In: Proceedings of the 44th International Conference on Software Engineering, pp. 1317–1329. Association for Computing Machinery, Pennsylvania, Pittsburgh (2022). https://doi.org/10.1145/3510003.3511560
15. Kalogranis, C.: Antivirus software evasion: an evaluation of the av evasion tools. Master's thesis for Department of digital systems, pp. 1–21(2018). https://dione.lib.unipi.gr/xmlui/handle/unipi/11232

16. Wressnegger, C., Freeman, K., Yamaguchi, F., Rieck, K.: Automatically inferring malware signatures for anti-virus assisted attacks. In: Proceedings of the 2017 ACM on Asia Conference on Computer and Communications Security, pp. 587–598. Association for Computing Machinery, Abu Dhabi, United Arab Emirates (2017). https://doi.org/10.1145/3052973.305 3002

17. Tahaei, M., Vaniea, K.: A survey on developer-centred security. In: 2019 IEEE European Symposium on Security and Privacy Workshops (EuroS&PW), pp. 129–138 (2019). IEEE, Stockholm. https://doi.org/10.1109/EuroSPW.2019.00021

18. Okesola, O.J., Adebiyi, A.A., Owoade, A.A., Adeaga, O., Adeyemi, O., Odun-Ayo, I.: Software requirement in iterative SDLC model. In: Silhavy, R. (ed.) Intelligent Algorithms in Software Engineering, CSOC 2020, vol. 1224, pp. 26–34. Springer, Cham (2020). https://doi.org/10.1007/978-3-030-51965-0_2

19. Ravindran, U., Potukuchi, R.V., Peng, Y., Li, H., Li, X., Wang, J., Kulkarni, O.K.: A review on web application vulnerability assessment and penetration testing. Rev. Comput. Eng. Stud. **1**, 1–22 (2022). https://doi.org/10.18280/rces.09010

20. Altayaran, S.A., Elmedany, W.: integrating web application security penetration testing into the software development life cycle: a systematic literature review. In: 2021 International Conference on Data Analytics for Business and Industry (ICDABI). IEEE (2021)

21. Casola, V., De Benedictis, A., Rak, M., Villano, U.: Towards automated penetration testing for cloud applications. In: 2018 IEEE 27th International Conference on Enabling Technologies: Infrastructure for Collaborative Enterprises (WETICE), pp. 24–29. IEEE (2018). https://doi.org/10.1109/WETICE.2018.00012

22. Mason, M.: Sample size and saturation in PhD studies using qualitative interviews. In: Forum Qualitative Sozialforschung/Forum: Qualitative Social Research, vol. 11, no. 3 (2010)

23. Roshanaei, M.: Resilience at the core: critical infrastructure protection challenges, priorities and cybersecurity assessment strategies. J. Comput. Commun. **9**, 80–102 (2022)

24. Mai, P.X., Pastore, F., Goknil, A., Briand, L.C.: MCP: a security testing tool driven by requirements. In: 2019 IEEE/ACM 41st International Conference on Software Engineering: Companion Proceedings (ICSE-Companion), pp.55–58 (2019). IEEE, Ontreal, QC, Canada. https://doi.org/10.1109/ICSE-Companion.2019.00037

25. Meng, N., Nagy, S., Yao, D., Zhuang, W., Argoty, G.A.: Secure coding practices in java: challenges and vulnerabilities. In: Proceedings of the 40th International Conference on Software Engineering, pp. 372–383 (2018). https://doi.org/10.1145/3180155.3180201

26. Afrose, S., Xiao, Y., Rahaman, S., Miller, B.P., Yao, D.: Evaluation of static vulnerability detection tools with Java cryptographic API benchmarks. IEEE Trans. Softw. Eng. **49**(2), 485–497 (2022)

27. Armstrong, D.J., Brooks, N.G., Riemenschneider, C.K.: Exhaustion from information system career experience: implications for turn-away intention. MIS Q. **39**(3), 713–727 (2015). https://doi.org/10.25300/MISQ

28. Moquin, R., K. Riemenschneider, C., L. Wakefield, R.: Psychological contract and turnover intention in the information technology profession. Inf. Syst. Manage. **36**(2), 111–125(2019)

Drained and Depleted: The Erosion of Personal and Professional Boundaries of Post-Covid IS Academics

Mufaro Nyangari, Grant Oosterwyk[✉] [iD], and Popyeni Kautondokwa[iD]

Commerce Faculty, Department of Information Systems, University of Cape Town, Cape Town, South Africa

{nynmuf001,ktnpop001}@myuct.ac.za, grant.oosterwyk@uct.ac.za

Abstract. Information Systems (IS) academics were affected by the COVID-19 pandemic resulting in the introduction of a mandatory Work From Home (WFH) norm. This research paper explored the influences of digital technology (DT) use on the Work-Life Balance (WLB) among IS academics in South Africa. Data were collected from eleven IS academics from a higher tertiary institution using semi-structured interviews. The data was analysed using the Gioia methodology. The papers' findings reveal five aggregate dimensions in the form of a data structure that IS academics can use as a guideline to develop a potential grounded theory based on the underlying assumptions on how the phenomenon of DT and WLB amongst IS academics can be further studied.

Keywords: Information Systems Academics · Work-Life Balance · Digital Technology · Post COVID-19 · South Africa

1 Introduction

The working patterns of Information Systems (IS) academics at universities were affected in 2020 by COVID-19 (Sansa 2021), leading to the shift of physical teaching in various departments to move to online synchronous delivery of classes (Crick et al. 2020; Davison 2020; Richter 2020). This shift purported the need and use of Digital Technology (DT) in the home for the daily administration of tertiary education services and content (Adisa et al. 2017; Caroll and Conboy 2020; Elliot et al. 2020; Richter 2020). In addition, this swift shift left academics having to adjust and design online content almost overnight from home (Crick et al. 2020). Work from home (WFH) is not a new phenomenon. Since its inception, there has not been a wide-scale implementation of the WFH program as was seen during the lockdown periods. The increased presence and usage of MT in the home for work led to the digitization of the home (Kusairi et al. 2021). While (Sarker et al. 2012; McDaniel and Coyne 2015) claimed that this increased presence and usage result in the blurring of boundary lines between work and life, causing a work-life conflict (WLC).

For the purposes of this study, Work-Life Balance (WLB) is generally defined as the setting of priorities between work (career & ambition) and life (leisure, family &

© The Author(s), under exclusive license to Springer Nature Switzerland AG 2023
A. Gerber and M. Coetzee (Eds.): SAICSIT 2023, CCIS 1878, pp. 211–227, 2023.
https://doi.org/10.1007/978-3-031-39652-6_14

spiritual development), while a work-life imbalance is an intrusion of work into life hours or vice versa (Putri and Amran 2021; Sarker et al. 2012). While a WLC in this study will refer to the absence of work-life balance as described by Stawarz et al. (2013). Various studies found (Chamakiotis et al. 2014; Kotecha et al. 2014) that academics work more hours than recommended, which highlighted a 56-h working week compared to their professional counterparts who work 40-h weeks, citing DT as the cause. It has been further argued that information and communication technologies (ICT) challenge the concept of WLB due to the increasing requirements for remote working (Chamakiotis et al. 2014). Öksüz et al. (2016) pointed out the irrefutable need for IS academics to use DT in their discipline. A recent study (Caroll and Conboy 2020) has shown the large-scale and rapid movement from the traditional face-to-face setting to working from home, spaces that often lack designated offices. This resulted in academics having to not only redesign and translate content that was being delivered traditionally online but also the design of teaching support had to be reimagined on a broader scale which had not been done before (Abu Talib et al. 2021). Despite the increase in online courses, adequate preparation and planning would have been undertaken to ensure the course was well executed. Hence, we ask: *"What are the influences of digital technology use on the work-life balance among IS academics post-COVID?"*. To address the concerns above, this paper will first look at the problem identified, followed by a narrative review of the literature (Schryen et al. 2020), the chosen research methodology, the findings and analysis followed by the discussion and conclusion.

2 Theoretical Approach

The Boundary theory introduced by (Ashforth, 2000) describes how a boundary separates work and life. This theory was further refined by Clark (2000), who highlighted that not only are work and life separated by a boundary, but this boundary is more like a border between the two domains. Furthermore, it is characterized by *a border crosser* (actor) responsible for moving from one wall to another. Clark (2000) describes work and life as different domains that contain contrasting cultures and purposes with other responsibilities at different times. These domains are divided by demarcating lines known as borders, which are the defining point at which domain-centred behaviours begin or end. These borders are physical, temporal, and psychological. The physical borders are the workplace walls or home walls where domain-relevant behaviour occurs, and temporal borders define when work is done and when family responsibilities are taken up, and the psychological borders are set up by the individual when thinking patterns, behaviour, and emotions are suitable for one domain and not the other Clark (2000). These borders are characterized by permeability and flexibility; permeability is the extent to which elements from one domain can enter another or how easily and readily details from one domain are found in another (Nam 2014). This theory helped guide our understanding of the key factors that blend DT with work-life balance (WLB), further explaining the blurring boundaries in the IS academic profession.

3   Literature Review

The subsequent findings presented originate from various studies with the purpose of summarising prior findings on the phenomenon in the form of a narrative review (Schryen et al. 2020). Importantly, this review does not adhere to the rigorous procedures of a systematic literature review. The authors acknowledge that despite acknowledging the potential adversities associated with DTs, it is crucial not to underestimate the inherent, salient benefits they offer.

3.1   Digital Technology

The term *Digital Technology (DT)* refers to a contemporary wave of interconnected technologies characterized by fundamental features such as cloud computing, wearable devices, mobile technology (MT), social media, business analytics, the Internet of Things, and artificial intelligence. Digital technologies, such as mobile devices, have enabled IS academics to engage in technologically assisted supplementary work (TASW), which can result in longer academic working hours due to the demands of remote work (Kotecha et al. 2014). Technology is an enabler of cognitive work intrusion resulting in the technologically cognitive intrusion of work (TCIW). McDaniel and Coyne (2015) described the presence of mobile devices as embedded and pervasive in everyday life which has resulted in the mobile workforce expressing a sense of intrusion in their personal lives (as referenced by Sarker et al. 2021). Like the lack of a universal definition for WLB, studies have shown that there are no universally accepted patterns of MT use to achieve WLB. However, Sarker et al. (2021) identified three WLB categories that can be applied to MT use: *separation/separate spheres*, *interactive*, and *integration* (Bello and Tanko 2020). Individuals view the importance of each domain as a driver in their use of mobile MT within the WLB. Individuals use MT for work purposes based on how they view the balance within the framework of work and life. McDaniel and Coyne (2015) suggested that individual characteristics also determine how MT is used. Specifically, they were grouped into two clusters: (1) *those who viewed technology as an enabler of their availability* and (2) *those who did not view technology as being central to their lives.*

3.2   Work-Life Balance

Work-life balance (WLB) is a broad concept that involves setting proper priorities between work (career and ambition) and life (happiness, leisure, family, and spiritual development) (Putri and Amram 2020). Work has been operationally viewed as activities undertaken by an individual as purposefully fulfilling specific responsibilities and carrying out duties that require sustained physical or mental effort, often "under compulsion or necessity" (e.g., for wages to sustain life) or paid employment (Bello and Tanko 2020; Sarker et al. 2012).

3.3   Work-Life Conflict

It would not be possible to address WLB without synonymously addressing WLC. Sarker et al. (2012) described WLC as the conflict that arises when work and life pressures are incompatible. Furthermore, Sarker et al. (2012) claim that WLB is low WLC and the converse is true. These constructs exist in the same continuum but on opposing sides. Followed by Stawarz et al. (2013), who claimed that they referred to a poor WLB as WLC. In this paper, the researchers define WLB as the absence of WLC.

3.4   Work from Home

Work from home (WFH) can be referred to as telecommuting or virtual work and is defined as working outside of the conventional office setting, such as within one's home or in a remote office location, often using a form of information communication technology (ICT) to communicate with others (Beckel and Fisher, 2022; Putri and Amran 2021). WFH is not a new phenomenon, its origins can be traced back to the 1970s through a term coined "telecommuting" (Nilles, 1976). However, in practice, before COVID-19, WFH was perceived as a working tradition reserved for 'knowledge workers'. Jamsen et al. (2019) posited COVID-19 as the most significant surge in WFH move as an option to becoming mandatory. Bell et al. (2012) noted that universities had experienced organisational changes leading to increased stress and pressure among academics, and yet there are very few studies concerning DT use influences on WLB among academics. Various studies have reported that academics consider their work stressful (Samaha and Hawi 2016), and literature from Kinman and Wray (2016) indicates that stress is increasing in association with changes taking place at universities (Fotinha et al. 2019).

3.5   Mobile Technology and Work-Life Balance Impacts

MT devices were introduced as luxury devices, but they have now become business tools that allow for work to be done from anywhere and at any time (Stawarz et al. 2013). Raja and Soundarapandian (2022) noted that technology positively and negatively influences and changes the quality of work-life. The presence of MT has altered how work is done and how life is lived (Sarker et al. 2021) but also affected how individuals combine work and personal time (Adisa et al. 2017; Raja and Soundarapandian 2022), thereby impacting WLB. The WLB impacts have been categorized as negative and positive for IS academia. Mobile technologies are another permeation that is now impacting WLB, before MT, work permeations in the home required an individual to physically cross from home to work.

3.6   Negative Technological Impacts

Technoference
Due to the workload of IS academics, working after hours and on weekends has become prevalent among academia, and the flexibility offered by mobile technologies has been pinned as the driver for the interference of work-related activities during non-working hours (Kotecha et al. 2014). Before DT advancements, work-related activities remained in the physical confines of the workspace as the only access to emails was on desktops that needed more portable. Bondanini et al. (2020) referred to the constant connectivity that

invades life as techno-invasions. Sarker et al. (2021) highlighted a sense of helplessness among workers from the constant technological intrusion in their personal lives. It is also during non-working hours that learning materials are prepared and converted to suitable online formats. Technology has been cited as interference because it has turned family spaces meant for relational development and personal 'off time' into inconvenient workspaces and lecture theatres (Toniollo-Barrios and Pitt 2021).

Technologically Driven Cognitive Intrusion of Work

Supplemental work is "a form of distributed work where full-time employees work at home after regular working hours at night or on weekends" (Kotecha et al. 2014, pp. 630). The presence of DT has increased the possibility of supplemental work so much so that it has been referred to as technology-assisted supplemented work (TASW). TASW negatively impacts WLB as IS academics put in more working hours and supplement work performance during non-working hours due to workloads from the university and pressure to publish their work. Stawarz et al. (2013), Cannizzo and Osbaldiston (2016) cited mobile technologies for 'work extensification' of intellectual labour into the personal space continuously until boundary lines are blurred. IS academics struggle with the 'publish or perish' mantra (Lee, 2014; Herndon, 2016), further feeding TASW.

Technostress and Zoom Fatigue

Caroll and Conboy (2020) described the pressure from the COVID-19 lockdown on practitioners' technology-driven work practices as a 'big bang' change as organisations needed more time to adequately plan, train and develop strategies for new technologies. In the context of South Africa, IS academics did not have adequate time to train and develop strategies for technologies such as MS Teams or Zoom. Such a drastic change of completely moving all operations and learning facilities online would require ample planning and training to avoid technology-related stress 'technostress', which has become a significant problem during the pandemic (Zielonka et al. 2022).

Digital Burnout

Increased DT usage due to COVID-19 created another phenomenon of background listening among IS academics, which has negatively impacted WLB. Background listening has resulted from a cyber-based load created by perceived pressure to respond and participate in online meetings and chats for the fear of missing out or getting information leading to technology-related exhaustion known as digital burnout (Sharma et al. 2020). Sharma et al. (2020) noted in a study they conducted that a 1.2-s delay in response to online meetings negatively shaped how others are viewed. This perception leads to increased demand or attention to verbal and non-verbal components which academics cited as being exhausting. Adisa et al. (2017) and Grise-Owens et al. (2018) highlight that burnout is not only digital but physical, if individuals continue to work long hours without taking breaks it can have adverse effects on their health.

Worker Visibility

Workers are no longer physically visible, they look for ways to prove their value by being online more to be seen as being available and engaged (Richter, 2020), this was corroborated by (Jamsen et al. 2022) whose field study highlighted that employees working from home felt more pressure to put more effort to be seen as hardworking and competent. IS Academics are not exempted as they also experience pressure from the cyber-based load to appear as 'good lecturers' by responding quickly to emails or being constantly available for meetings. In trying to be perceived as being available and engaged, academics are permanently online or constantly switched on. Sarker et al. (2012) made note of this phenomenon as '24x7' connectivity and has heightened Cognitive Intrusion of Work (CIW) as academics fail to disengage and unplug from work-related activities.

Blurring of Boundary Lines
Work and life are domains separated by borders that are characterized by permeability and flexibility. When there are high degrees of permeability and flexibility the blurring of boundary lines occurs as highlighted by Stawarz et al. (2013). Before DT, there was no significant integration between work and life as work remained at work and home was for relaxing (Stawarz et al. 2013).

3.7 Positive Technological Impacts

Flexibility
DT allows for work and life to be attended to from anywhere and at any time (Adisa et al. 2017; Nam 2014). Individuals expressed how DT eases the tension and problems that arise from both domains. Kotecha et al. (2014) cited flexibility as one of the major advantages of DT by providing autonomy of working hours for academics, it was also stated that this assisted academics in balancing work and life.

Improved Performance
Improved performance emanates from flexibility and autonomy which enable an individual to schedule their work and manage tasks thereby making them more productive. DT increases worker performance because of fewer interruptions and work independence (Kotecha et al. 2014). Furthermore, DT gives academics autonomy over their working style (Kusairi et al. 2021), for example, an academic who is more nocturnal can use DT to do their work tasks at night when they are more productive. There is increased productivity resulting from flexibility in time management as highlighted by Sarker et al. (2012) that DT offers the availability of multiple media and genres of communication that are suitable for different scenarios, for example, a laptop is suitable for use at home, and an iPad can be carried and used in a meeting.

Improved Coordination
Organisations experience improved coordination because of the increased amount of relational communication from remote working as individuals rely heavily on emails (Jamsen et al. 2022). This makes the organisation's participants more responsible, alert, and proactive in coordination as they know their online commitments. (Richter 2020) stated that DT aids employees to connect in new ways, (Kusairi et al. 2021) noted from

their field research that there was more humour and understanding among co-workers and supervisors.

Potential 24x7 Connectivity
As mentioned before, mobile technologies enable academics to be connected permanently, Sarker et al. (2021) refer to this as the potential for '24x7' connectivity which also improves performance as an individual has unlimited access to information and resources. This also assists in quick decision-making, for example, if one individual in the project needs clarification on certain aspects clarity can be gained quickly, as well as easy access to information needed for collaboration.

4 Methodology

For the primary data source, semi-structured interviews were conducted among eleven IS academics from a single tertiary institution in South Africa. As of 2021, the institution has over 30 000 students and over 1200 full-time academics. Historically, the institution focuses mostly on research (60%) and 40% towards teaching. Initially, the authors correspondent with 16 IS academics, obtaining agreement from 11 individuals to participate. Following ethics approval and participant responses, meetings were scheduled, accommodating each participant's preference for virtual or in-person interaction. In the instance of in-person interviews, arrangements were made for campus meetings. The researchers obtained consent, either verbal or written, to record the interviews. The interview approach focused on straightforward questions, escalating gradually to more intricate and sensitive topics, with definitions provided for any ambiguous terms. The interview duration varied between 30 to 45 min, with follow-up engagement enacted if no response was obtained within a seven-day window. To maintain anonymity, each participant was assigned a pseudonym, designated as 'Participant' followed by a sequential number based on the order of interviews. The participants included academics from all levels: *Professor, Associate Professor, Senior Lecturer and Lecturer.* Table 1 below shows the positions and experiences of the participants. Data were collected during the period of 2022 during the second and third quarters of the year when most universities in South Africa returned to campus. Each participant narrated their experiences and how their use of DT post COVID-19 had influenced their WLB.

An interpretive philosophy employing an inductive approach was used to analyse the observed phenomena. The "Gioia methodology" approach (Gioia et al. 2013) has been chosen as a suitable method for the identification of principal themes by employing an analytical procedure similar to the open and axial coding technique devised by Strauss and Corbin (1998). This process was executed in a systematic and sequential manner, with iterations contingent upon interpretation and preliminary analysis (Bondanini et al. 2020).

Table 1. Participants in this study included their experiences.

Respondent	Position	Experience
Participant 1	Lecturer	9 years
Participant 2	Professor	25 years
Participant 3	Senior lecturer	10 years
Participant 4	Professor	20 years
Participant 5	Associate Professor	22 years
Participant 6	Lecturer	6 years
Participant 7	Professor	22 years
Participant 8	Professor	20 years
Participant 9	Associate Professor	7 years
Participant 10	Lecturer	10 years
Participant 11	Professor	22 years

5 Findings

The papers' findings reveal five aggregate dimensions which IS academics can use as insights based on the underlying assumptions on how the phenomenon of WLB amongst IS academics can be further studied. In this section, we integrate the discussion and findings derived from the study. The themes were in the form of in-vivo codes. Due to their similarities, several first order concepts were merged. Subsequently, the first order concepts were merged into relevant second order concepts followed by aggregate dimensions. Figure 1 below structure captures the relationships among second order themes in conducting the analysis.

5.1 Theme 1: Work-Life Balance

In identifying the lack of WLB among IS academics post-COVID-19, Participant 1 described it as: "*Yeah so and there was no balance at all between work time and personal time. There was so much work, as I said, that moving from face to face to online was quite challenging. It literally meant sacrificing time because at the time we had never done this before*". While Participant 6 expressed it as: "*There's no balance is there such thing as work-life balance? We are just catching up, my dear. I mean, to be honest with you, there is yes, we try our level best but most of the weekends*". Most participants highlighted the need for a WLB to avoid burnout, this supports studies from Kotecha et al. (2014), Crick et al. (2020) and Sarker et al. (2021) who agree that IS academics need a WLB to avoid burning out.

1st Order Concepts   2nd order Themes   Aggregate Dimensions

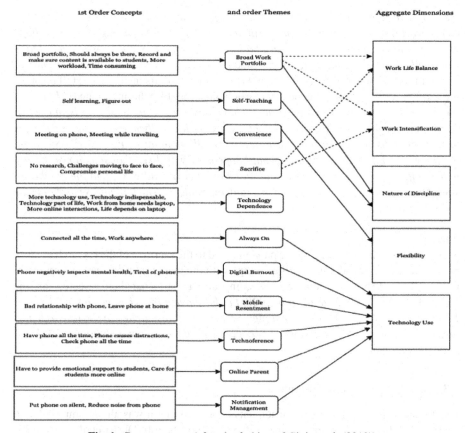

Fig. 1. Data structure (after the fashion of Gioia et al. (2013)).

5.2 Theme 2: Work Intensification

Certain studies (Cannizzo et al. 2019) sustain that DT has led to an increase in the workload faced by academics. COVID-19 increased *work intensification* as IS academics found themselves having to make content available in multiple formats even after COVID-19 thereby increasing the workload. Participant 1 highlighted that, "*So you can't really give students like plus or minus an hour of a lecture because they may not have enough data to download everything, right? So what you did to try and make it easy so that downloading is quick and all of that so it divided into segments of about like 15 min per recording, per lecture. So that was a lot of work. That was a lot of work that took a lot of time that that was really like for me. I could not do anything other than doing that for the whole time when one has to deal with the recording and making sure that students have all the content that they needed in terms of lecturing.*"

This implies that IS academics are facing an increased workload, as highlighted by Bondanini et al. (2020) that DT increases the workload by creating a techno-load. However, the increased workload is not being recorded formally with participant 9 stating it as: "*And, and yeah, so because of also of the COVID-19 thing. So it has necessitated the workload to be a bit dragged on in terms of, you know, if a cause was supposed to be five workshops to six workshops maximum, now that cause is sitting at 10 workshops to allow students to grasp the content. So I mean, if you add six more workshop, that's workload. That's more marking, that, you know, more, more support more everything."*

Our findings so far offer useful insights that while work intensified, the staff resourcing did not match up as explained by participants 3 and 9 who mentioned, *"But well, the way it's happening, or at least how I have observed it, in academia is that when there's more work, it gets absorbed by the same people and then it's as if no one notices there is actually more work, because hey, it's really none anyway, right?" "So, yeah, it's the workload. And I think also what happens is, you'll see that sometimes, we are understaffed at the moment, okay. And that's another difficulty. So, and the number of students are growing. So more and more students come in, which requires more time, be it for marking".*

Sacrifice

The work-intensification during the pandemic led to the sacrifice of the research component with many IS academics failing to cope with the increased workload and research. Others claimed that the increase in teaching directly affected their research, as one claimed: *"No, I didn't, I didn't so in 2020, I didn't have a life what was happening was I remember in addition to all these things, you're doing researcher so the research part died, that I have to be honest. I was not coping with my research in 2020 and 2021 and so something had to go".*

5.3   Theme 3: Nature of Discipline

Our findings showed that some participants expressed that it was almost impossible to separate DT from their work because of the nature of the job (Öksüz et al. 2016). This problematized thereby the relevance pertaining to the inextricable bond between the use of DT and the IS discipline. This was experienced by Participant 10 who claimed: *"Okay, the computer is very important, right? The laptop is very important. This is where you do all your work, you have to look after this thing as is if your life depends on it, because this is what you deliver on the week, and also, this is where your research is, the work is saved in the cloud, but you can access you access it through the device".*

Other participants noted that what makes WLB difficult to attain is the nature of the job with regards to the workload highlighted by Kinman (2014), as Participant 3 explained: *"There's many ways to look into it one way or one side of it is really the lack of and I mean, this is probably also partially a work person's work style, but also, a little bit of it is in the nature of the job because it's affecting most of us so I can see it not just me".* Notably, the authors of this paper agree that academics in IS face the same WLB challenges as their peers in other disciplines. These challenges often stem from the intense 'publish or perish' culture common across academia.

Broad Work Portfolio

Part of the nature of the job is also the kind of work that IS academics have to engage in, most participants explained that being an IS academic consists of two components: teaching and research. However, we argue in this paper that this is the case across most

South African universities. Participant 9 described it as: "*you know, our portfolio of work, right? It's not just teaching. We have to teach obviously, we have to do administration as well. We have convening, obviously, but sitting on committees as well. We have to do research, okay, that also is time consuming supervision, social responsiveness as well. That's quite a broad portfolio*". Sustaining a diverse work portfolio suggests a significant workload for academics, as observed by Fotinha and colleagues (2019). This sentiment was shared by Participant 3 who claimed: "*And then ultimately, that thing will be done well, and it will be delivered. And it will be seen as Oh, everything is fine. But it's not fine. I've had to use so much of my own time to accomplish that.*"

Self-Teaching

There is an expectation for IS academics to have a natural aptitude for technology and knowledge pertaining to technology (Öksüz et al. 2016). A further requirement is a need to dedicate hours beyond their regular work schedule to become proficient in using specific applications or software (Bondanini et al. 2020). For example (Participant 1) claimed: "*So the training for that did not come from the university. It was something that we learnt ourselves. It was really about just, you know, spending whatever time that was needed to be able to do this thing*" [learning to teach online]. *So that when students come back, you have something to offer or to give them.*" These sentiments were echoed by Participant 10 who explained IS academics had to self-learn: "*So by the time they launched the framework, what they called the learning framework we had already figured out or how our own learning will look like*". Participant 10 further claimed: "*that there is an expectation that as a Professor in the IS department you must know the technology and, of course, you also have this imposter syndrome because everybody else that it's sitting on the other side of the teams knows that you are, you know, in quotation, a professor or the doctor in the department, and you know, what must happen? Because doesn't the technology department, but you also don't know?*". While Participant 9 expressed it as: " *I remember, I had to sort of be Oh, my god, this MS Teams, what the hell is that? How do I try and figure out how do you create little rooms and stuff and trying to practice because you're gonna have your students coming in? And you don't know how to share a screen?*". A substantial portion of our data suggests that DT serves a vital role in preserving work-life boundaries while simultaneously facilitating efficient transitions. Conversely, we also identified that technologies engender an atmosphere of constant "knowing how", consequently affecting the perception of WLB among our participants.

5.4   Theme 4: Flexibility

Majority of respondents expressed that though the nature of the job led to an increased workload that there was a lot of flexibility, with Participant 4 citing it as one of the main reasons they became an academic, "*So I became an academic. And at that point, people were saying it's a nice flexible job, you know, you've got young children. And even one of the professors in accounting said to me, yes, you know, nice that, you now, an academic. You know, she's able to attend all her, she's got flexibility.*" DT has further afforded this flexibility by making working from home a possibility and an accepted reality. Adisa et al. (2017) claimed that DT offers both physical and temporal flexibility by allowing academics to connect to work at any time and from any place. Participant 5 went on to explain that: *"With COVID-19, and working from home and things, I was not able to obviously work if I didn't have a laptop. I also tend to work from home more often when I don't need to be on campus, and given the fact that it's become so much more acceptable across a multitude of disciplines to have online interactions".*

Convenience

The role of an academic inherently offers a considerable degree of flexibility. The utilisation of DT enhances this flexibility for information systems (IS) scholars, enabling them to accomplish their work regardless of location and time (Adisa et al. 2017). Participant 2 highlighted that: *"Right. And there was a time where I unfortunately had to be somewhere else and I needed to also have a MS Teams meeting. So what I decided to do is to download MS Teams on my app. I mean on my phone the app on my phone and then I could have this meeting on my mobile app and then I was able to have the meeting because I was travelling."* This constant connectivity served as the impetus for certain participants to transition away from the physical environment to the virtual.

5.5   Theme 5: Mobile Technology Use

Building upon the theme of the nature of the discipline, a key component involves the development and functionality of technological artifacts (Öksüz et al. 2016). Consequently, the utilization of MT becomes an intrinsic component of the IS discipline. This suggests that IS academics are inevitably exposed to the influences of MT, as it constitutes a fundamental aspect of the profession. Participant 5 articulated this notion as follows: *"Absolutely fundamental and if I look specifically at my laptop. With COVID-19, and working from home and things, I was not able to obviously work if I didn't have a laptop ".*

Technology Dependence

The pandemic has resulted in an increased reliance on and usage of DT, (Kotecha et al. 2014). Furthermore, many academics carry DTs with them to guarantee continuous access to work. Participant 5 expressed this development as follows: *"With COVID-19, and working from home and things, I was not able to obviously work if I didn't have a laptop, and then I now use it significantly, because I can actually do like marking I can interact, etcetera, with students having my electronic device there, then I can make sure that I can make notes and things like that. So yeah, it's been fairly indispensable."*

Participant 5's comment indicates an increase in the usage of DT as they noted that they now use DTs significantly compared to before. Participant 7 described their relationship with their DT device as follows: *"I feel like I'm like I am a tortoise and my laptop is my shell, it could never go without me and I can never go to the left. So yeah, so it's part of your life. It's part of your attire.".* This highlighted the extent of dependency on DT. The authors agreed that the onset of the COVID-19 pandemic has indeed intensified the connection between academia and DT. This increased interplay has culminated in an ambiguous boundary, amplifying the challenge for academics (specifically for IS academics in the context) to disengage from work. This theme suggests that the pandemic has expedited the merging of work and personal domains, exacerbating the difficulty in achieving a clear work-life separation.

Always On

Having an increased dependency on mobile devices and always having them on you, may lead to feelings of 'always being connected' (Waller and Ragsdell 2012) as expressed by Participant 8 who noted that *"But on the other hand, it allows you to work anywhere, you know what I mean? Then you connect it all the time, you, you will receive an email on your phone, right"*. Participant 5 confirmed this by stating how the presence of DT makes one always feel connected, *"And then also, it's the always connected. So you never actually are not receiving emails or receiving communication. And you tend to be working all the time"*. Accompanying 'always being on' is also the potential and expectation of 24x7 availability, by continually having DTs available would imply that IS academics don't miss any communication and as stated by the participant. These feelings of 'always being on' feed into technologically driven cognitive intrusion of work.

Digital Burnout

Participant 4 explained their concerns over the increased usage and dependency as well as always being connected regarding the negative mental health impacts due to the consistent and increased usage of DT: *"Because I know it impacts negatively on mental health."* Participant 4 further stated that they took a sabbatical due to a case of burnt out. Furthermore, in a recent study, it was identified that digital burnout along with cases of digital fatigue among IS academics was on the increase (Bondanini et al. 2020). As put by Participant 6: *"I am tired of my phone. I think that I have I would say I have been experiencing this. What do you call it? Digital fatigue is like it is real."* This was found to be related to a case of *'**Mobile device resentment**'* towards MT where Participant 6 claimed: *"I don't have a good relationship with my mobile device. I even forget it at home at times"*.

Technoference

A phrase that appeared among IS academics when describing how they felt about their MT devices was the distracting nature of these devices. This was expressed by participants 1 and 5 respectively: *" a mobile device is something one has all the time, you know, even when you're sitting alone somewhere, you are always tempted to just grab your mobile device and start, going through it, whether you're going to Twitter, whether you're going to Instagram or whatever it is, or even WhatsApp, right, because you are just checking all the time or sometimes it's a lot of distractions"* and Participant 5 who claimed: *"Yes. So the first thing, it's distracting. So I'm supposed to be focusing on their interview? I tend to because I was just finishing up my marks. And I was like, no, let me finish that. And the human brain is not meant it's not meant to actually be multitasking. So it is distracting."* Most participants also claimed that DT is distractive, and some academics highlighted how technology interfered during family time.

Online Parent

The use of DT as an IS academic introduced a role that prior to COVID-19 was not there, with participants 8 and 11 expressing how they had to step in as online parents and offer more than academic support but also emotional support for students who had lost loved ones during the pandemic. Participant 8 described it as: *"I had students who lost a parent and the grandmother. So what do you do? You can't just let them be so there was emotional support involved"*. While participant 11 expressed it as: *"Yeah, very much. So, look, I think COVID has brought that being an online parent because we need to, we need to care more for our students"*. Participant 8 further added that this support was not being recognized by the institution.

Notification Management

Some participants highlighted the need to manage notifications to avoid feeling overwhelmed and distracted, as Participant 2 put it: *"But so the devices themselves don't help you but there are software tools available to block out time'*. While Participant 3 described it as: *"I think the only mitigating factor is I do not have notifications on my phone. So WhatsApp, email, anything that comes they will not be active on my phone. 90% of the time is in silent. So I only use it or only see the email or WhatsApp message when I want to not because I don't like sitting here and my phone is pinging their messages, because then it will distract my mind"*. We found that the use of DT devices, such as smartphones, can have the potential to create novel boundaries or potentially erode pre-existing ones.

6   Discussion and Conclusion

This study aimed to examine the impact of DT usage on WLB among IS academics post the COVID-19 pandemic. As IS practitioners and academics inherently rely on DT, the study sought to explore any potential influences on their WLB. The Gioia methodology facilitated the analysis of qualitative data using semi-structured interviews which resulted in five primary themes: (1) work-life balance, (2) nature of the discipline, (3) flexibility, (4) work-intensification, and (5) mobile technology use.

The findings highlighted the need for further research on WLB among IS academics. A potential contribution of this study is its ability to inform the development of a theory grounded in the data with the goal of building an inductive model, supported by the initial data structure. This model could assist IS academics in achieving a balance between work and life, thereby reducing burnout and staff turnover, while recognising the changes in their academic landscape due to the pandemic.

Due to the nature of the IS discipline, there is an expectation that because IS academics have DT as an inherent part of their discipline, they should be comfortable with the influences of DT. This could be claimed as a reason why there has not been adequate training on how IS academics balance work and life with the presence of DT as expressed by participants. The findings indicate that COVID resulted in IS academics experiencing the negative influences of DT more than the positives. Participants mentioned benefits like convenience and flexibility when asked about their relationship with DT. However, some also had strong negative views, with one participant even stating they were tired of their phone. Furthermore, the findings affirm what Clark (2000) mentioned in the Border Theory that individuals consider work and life to be two separate domains in which the individual is responsible for transferring elements from one domain to the other. This was further supported by Adisa et al. (2017), whose model further developed what Clark (2000) alluded to by highlighting how DT now assisted the border crosser, in this case, the IS academic in moving work-related elements into the home space. Thereby leading to the blurring of boundary lines between work and life, this was corroborated by the findings as participants expressed that there would not have been a possibility of work entering the home without the presence of DT. The additional role of being an online parent and the work that accompanies it created by DT was cited by participants as not being recognized by organisations, resulting in IS academics having dual parental responsibilities both in their personal and academic lives. These findings suggest that there is a need for further studies to be done regarding IS academics and how they can relate to and manage the influences of DT in their lives to avoid burnout and ultimately early resignations from institutions. In addition, the findings highlight the need for higher tertiary institutions to implement policies that reinforce boundaries between work and life for IS academics. This paper provides findings which can be used in the development of a WLB model that is suitable for IS academia. Furthermore, for future research, it would be beneficial to expand the study to identify mechanisms or practices that can help reinforce professional boundaries. This addition would significantly enhance the relevance and impact of the study. While this research provides valuable insights into the impact of DT on the WLB of IS academics, it's important to acknowledge its limitations. The study primarily suffers from a relatively small sample size and predominantly had more female academics, which may not fully capture the diverse experiences in the case. Moreover, the research is based on a single case study. While this approach facilitated a detailed examination of the specific context, it potentially restricts the broad applicability of our findings to other universities. Future research should aim to address these limitations by including more participants and diverse academic profiles to ensure a comprehensive understanding of the phenomena at hand.

References

Abu Talib, M., Bettayeb, A.M., Omer, R.I.: Analytical study on the impact of technology in higher education during the age of COVID-19: systematic literature review. Educ. Inf. Technol. **26**(6), 6719–6746 (2021)

Adisa, T.A., Gbadamosi, G., Osabutey, E.L.: What happened to the border? the role of mobile information technology devices on employees' work-life balance. Pers. Rev. **46**(8), 1651–1671 (2017)

Ashforth, B.: Role Transitions in Organizational Life: An Identity-Based Perspective. Routledge, Milton Park (2000)

Beckel, J.L., Fisher, G.G.: Telework and worker health and well-being: a review and recommendations for research and practice. Int. J. Environ. Res. Public Health **19**(7), 3879 (2022)

Bello, Z., Tanko, G.: Review of work-life balance theories. GATR Glob. J. Bus. Soc. Sci. Rev. **8**(4), 217–227 (2020)

Bondanini, G., Giorgi, G., Ariza-Montes, A., Vega-Muñoz, A., Andreucci-Annunziata, P.: Technostress dark side of technology in the workplace: a scientometric analysis. Int. J. Environ. Res. Public Health **17**(21), 8013 (2020)

Cannizzo, F., Mauri, C., Osbaldiston, N.: Moral barriers between work/life balance policy and practice in academia. J. Cult. Econ. **12**(4), 251–264 (2019)

Caroll, N., Conboy, K.: Normalizing the "new normal" changing tech-driven practices under pandemic work. Int. J. Inf. Manage. **55**, 1–6 (2020)

Chamakiotis, P., Whiting, R., Symon, G., Roby, H.: Exploring transitions and work-life balance in the digital era. In: Proceedings of European Conference on Information Systems, Tel Aviv (2014)

Clark, S.C.: Work/Family border theory: a new theory of work/family balance. Hum. Relat. **53**(6), 747–770 (2000)

Crick, T., Knight, C., Watermeyer, R., Goodall, J.: The impact of COVID-19 and 'emergency remote teaching' on the uk computer science education community. In: Proceedings of the United Kingdom & Ireland Computing Education Research Conference, pp. 31–37 (2020)

Davison, R.M.: The transformative potential of disruptions: a viewpoint. Int. J. Inf. Manage. **55**, 1–4 (2020)

Elliot, A., Adjeley, M., Bibi, D.: The office at home: information technology and work-life balance among women in developing countries. In: Proceedings of the Forty-first International Conference on Information Systems, India (2020)

Fotinha, R., Easton, S., Van Laar, D.: Overtime and quality of working life in academics and nonacademics: the role of perceived work-life balance. Int. J. Stress. Manag. **26**(2), 173–183 (2019)

Gioia, D.A., Corley, K.G., Hamilton, A.L.: Seeking qualitative rigor in inductive research: Notes on the Gioia methodology. Organ. Res. Methods **16**(1), 15–31 (2013)

Grise-Owens, E., Miller, J.J., Escobar-Ratliff, L., George, N.: Teaching note-Teaching self-care and wellness as a professional practice skill: a curricular case example. J. Soc. Work. Educ. **54**(1), 180–186 (2018)

Jamsen, R., Sivunen, A., Blomqvist, K.: "Employees' perceptions of relational communication in full-time remote work in the public sector. Comput. Hum. Behav. **132**, 107240 (2022)

Kinman, G.: Effort-reward imbalance and overcommitment in UK academics: implications for mental health, satisfaction and retention. J. High. Educ. Policy Manag. **38**(5), 504–518 (2016)

Kotecha, K., Ukpere, W., Geldenhuys, M.: Technology and work-life conflict of academics in a south african higher education institution. Mediterr. J. Soc. Sci. **5**(2), 629–643 (2014)

Kusairi, S., Muhamad, S., Raza, N.A.: The role of ICT and local wisdom in managing work-life balance during the COVID-19 pandemic: an empirical study in Malaysia. J. Asian Financ. Econ. Bus. **8**(9), 1–11 (2021)

McDaniel, B.T., Coyne, S.M. : Technoference: everyday intrusions and interruptions of technology in couple and family relationships. Fam. Commun. Age Dig. Soc. Med. (2015)

Nam, T.: Technology use and work-life balance. Appl. Res. Qual. Life **9**(4), 1017–1040 (2013). https://doi.org/10.1007/s11482-013-9283-1

Öksüz, A., Walter, N., Distel, B., Räckers, M., Becker, J.: Trust in the information systems discipline. Trust Commun. Digit. World, 205–223 (2016)

Putri, A., Amran, A.: Employees work-life balance reviewed from work from home aspect during COVID-19 pandemic. Int. J. Manage. Sci. Inf. Technol. **1**(1), 30–34 (2021)

Raja, V.R., Soundarapandian, K.: Impact of factors on work-life balance due to technology transformation with respect to information technology employees. Webology **19**(1), 1–2 (2022)

Richter, A.: Locked-down digital work. Int. J. Inf. Manage. **55**, 102157 (2020)

Samaha, M., Hawi, N.S.: Relationships among smartphone addiction, stress, academic performance, and satisfaction with life. Comput. Hum. Behav. **57**, 321–325 (2016)

Sansa, N.A.: Analysis for the Impact of the COVID-19 to the Petrol Price in China (2020). SSRN 3547413

Sarker, S., Manju, A., Sarker, S., Bullock, K.M.: Navigating Work and Life Boundaries. Palgrave Macmillan, London (2021)

Sarker, S., Xiao, X., Sarker, S., Ahuja, M.: Managing employees' use of mobile technologies to minimize work-life balance impacts. MIS Q. Exec. **11**(4), 143–157 (2012)

Sharma, M.K., et al.: Digital burnout: COVID-19 lockdown mediates excessive technology use stress. World Soc. Psych. **2**, 71–172 (2020)

Schryen, G., Wagner, G., Benlian, A., Paré, G.: A knowledge development perspective on literature reviews: validation of a new typology in the IS field. Commun. Assoc. Inf. Syst. **46**(7), 134–186 (2020)

Stawarz, K., Cox, A.L., Bird, J., Benedyk, R.: I'd sit at home and do work emails how tablets affect the work-life balance of office workers. In: CHI 2013 Extended Abstracts on Human Factors in Computing Systems, pp. 1383–1388 (2013)

Toniolo-Barrios, M., Pitt, L.: Mindfulness and the challenges of working from home in times of crisis. Bus. Horiz. **64**(2), 189–197 (2021)

Waller, A.D., Ragsdell, G.: The impact of email on work-life balance. ASIB Proc.: New Inf. Perspect. **64**(2), 154–177 (2012)

Zielonka, J.T., Heigl, R.M., Rothlauf, F.: Technostress revisited at work-from-home: the impact of technostress creators on the perception of eustress moderated by work-home-conflict and job satisfaction. In: Proceedings of Americas Conference on Information Systems, Minneapolis, USA (2022)

Exploring the Suitability of the TOE Framework and DOI Theory Towards Understanding AI Adoption as Part of Sociotechnical Systems

Danie Smit[1]([✉])(iD), Sunet Eybers[2](iD), Alta van der Merwe[1](iD), and Rene Wies[3](iD)

[1] Department of Informatics, University of Pretoria, Pretoria, South Africa
d5mit@pm.me
[2] School of Computing, Department of Information Systems,
University of South Africa, Johannesburg, South Africa
[3] Bayerische Motoren Werke AG, Munich, Germany

Abstract. Organisations that fail to adopt AI, will lose out on new business opportunities or optimisation and efficiency potential. This study is interested in contributing to increasing the likelihood of achieving the organisational adoption of AI that has a positive outcome. AI is part of complex sociotechnical systems, and an organisation can be seen as a giant cybernetic collective, with a shared objective function. We argue that the technological-organisational-environmental (TOE) framework provides a sound theoretical lens in analysing how an organisation's context influences the adoption and implementation of AI. Furthermore, the diffusion of innovation (DOI) theory is proposed to identify enablers for transforming organisations. Together with the combination of DOI and TOE, the stages of diffusion is proposed as an evaluation paradigm in order to evaluate the effectiveness of the enabling factors. Furthermore, the elements and objectives of AI adoption in the context of data-driven organisations are included. This approach, therefore, caters for both the technical and social AI adoption elements and an organisational environment where complex symbiotic relationships prevail. Additionally, on a theoretical level, it aids in enhancing our understanding of the causal factors behind the successful or unsuccessful adoption of AI within organisations.

Keywords: Technological-organisational-environmental framework ·
diffusion of innovation theory · artificial intelligence adoption

1 Introduction

Herbert Simon, a pioneer in artificial intelligence (AI), in his seminal work, "The science of the artificial", explained the difference between understanding the natural and the artificial world [28]. In the natural world, factual sciences explore, describe, explain, and predict phenomena. Factual sciences can be

© The Author(s), under exclusive license to Springer Nature Switzerland AG 2023
A. Gerber and M. Coetzee (Eds.): SAICSIT 2023, CCIS 1878, pp. 228–240, 2023.
https://doi.org/10.1007/978-3-031-39652-6_15

divided into natural and social sciences [10]. In natural and social sciences, a positivist paradigm can be applied where quantitative research methods are used [23]. A disadvantage of quantitative methods is that it treats many social and cultural aspects of organisations as superficial. The context is seen as noise [23]. This specific study is not concerned with natural phenomena, it is interested in investigating the suitability of two main theoretical underpinnings, the diffusion of innovation (DOI) theory and technology-organisation-environment (TOE) framework, towards understanding AI adoption in an organisational setting, when using a qualitative approach. This is important as the context - often referred to as sociotechnical systems - within which AI systems exist cannot be ignored. Also, the challenges that companies are facing in terms of AI adoption include aspects such as workforce and social challenges [18] which can only be fully explored using a qualitative approach. Much has been published about the adoption of technology, and as a result, many theories, models and frameworks have seen the light. For example, the original technology acceptance model (TAM) [9], diffusion of innovation theory (DOI) [27] and the technology-organisation-environment (TOE) framework [32] are theories that exist. Although there is an overlap between general technology adoption enabling factors and factors related to enabling AI adoption, AI adoption has unique characteristics, making it challenging to use existing technology adoption approaches. For instance, AI is at the frontier of computational advancements as its capabilities are constantly evolving, which leads to higher levels of uncertainty and the notion that AI adoption represents a "moving target" [5]. Therefore, the adoption of AI can be classified as a continuum [19]. Adding to the complexity of adoption is the levels of adoption, which refers to adoption by individuals or adoption by the organisation, where organisational adoption is even more complex [27,34].

Steven Hawking is famously quoted in saying: "AI could be the best or worst thing to ever happen to humanity. We can't ignore it"[1]. This study is interested in contributing to increasing the likelihood of achieving the organisational adoption of AI that has a positive outcome. Furthermore, organisations that fail to adopt AI, will lose out on new business opportunities or optimisation and efficiency potential. Given the importance of AI adoption and the complex sociotechnical environment, the main research question this paper aims to address is - *"how suitable is the TOE theory, and the DOI theory in performing qualitative investigations of organisational AI adoption, given a sociotechnical environment?* This research question is in the context of responsible data-driven organisations. A data-driven organisation can be defined as an organisation that acts on observed data rather than merely gut feeling and do so to achieve financial or non-financial benefits [2]. They effectively use data to enable them to achieve their objectives. Data-driven organisation have the expertise, tools and a culture to make use of data to make decisions [2,38]. Furthermore, in corporate social responsibility (CSR), a responsible organisation is concerned about a

---

[1] The best or worst thing to happen to humanity. Cambridge University [youtube], https://www.youtube.com/watch?v=_5XvDCjrdXs, (accessed 18 April 2023).

positive relationship between global organisations and the local society in which it resides, including their employees [8].

The paper starts with a description of the research paradigm, followed by a discussion on sociotechnical systems. The TOE framework and the DOI theory are discussed and evaluated for suitability. Finally, a conclusion section this paper provides a summary and wraps up the discussion.

2   Research Paradigm

Qualitative research methods are used in some social sciences research; they were developed to study cultural and social phenomena [23]. In qualitative research, qualitative data; for example, documents, interviews and participant observation are utilised. Qualitative research is best if the researcher wants to study a particular subject in-depth [23]. Research in information systems that uses a positivist (natural science) paradigm is primarily reactive. Its goal is to identify emergent properties and laws governing organisational behaviour as it affects and is affected by existing information systems [16]. Additionally, traditional quantitative and qualitative methods have limitations where the goal is to study the design, construction or creation of a new artifact [10].

Given the limitations of positivism and interpretivism on creating artifacts, other options should be considered. Pragmatism is a philosophical framework that embraces a particular ontological perspective, where humans are acting in a world which is in a constant state of becoming, with actions and change as the essence [13]. This perspective contrasts with positivism, where the position is one of realism, and the universe comprises objective, immutable structures, and objects [14]. The difference between pragmatism and interpretivism is not that apparent since pragmatism and interpretivism are both associated with qualitative research [13]. In pragmatism, the human is not merely observing the world and subjectively interpreting it but is also intervening in the world. Besides, positivism and interpretivism have limitations when the research is concerned with transformational change [12].

"The philosophical framework of pragmatism permits the application of empiricism while acknowledging metaphysical influences" [21]. It, therefore, acknowledges that there is both mind and matter, that the world is not just a physical world but also a social world. Although an investigation into AI adoption might include technical aspects (such as which technology to adopt), it is not only concerned with natural phenomena but rather focused on the organisational adoption process. Therefore, enabling the adoption of AI is not only perceived to be about technology but should also consider social constructs that include culture and human capabilities across the organisation. Pragmatism can be a useful framework for information system (IS) research as it allows for a holistic approach which allows the researcher to deal with the rapidly changing IS environment [21] and focuses not only on what is but also on what might be [13]. It is therefore fitting that the philosophical underpinning of this study is pragmatism.

As pragmatism is about being helpful and valuable, DSR can be seen within the pragmatism realm [13]. It is, therefore, appropriate to investigate the use in, for example, "organisational change (as in action research) or building of artifacts (as in design research)" [13]. Considering that this study ultimately wants to explore the suitability of theoretical constructs when considering organisational AI adoption, the appropriate methodology of DSR should be considered and explored by future researchers. In short, DSR is centred around the creation of artifacts [17] and the method that is followed, as it "brings both practical relevance (via its emphasis on useful artefacts) and scientific rigour (via the formulation of design theories)" [4, 358]. DSR not only supports the development of artifacts but also allows for the strengthening of the existing knowledge A further, in-depth evaluation of the suitability of DSR for AI adoption, falls outside the scope of this paper. The philosophical paradigm and practical relevance of the DSR approach is an important background context to the approach of the research paper.

3   Sociotechnical Systems

To ensure a holistic approach where not only technical but also social aspects are considered, this study views the organisational adoption of AI sociotechnical system. "Theories of sociotechnical systems indicate that they are constructed and given meaning in the interplay between technical and social components of the systems" [37]. A sociotechnical system has two subsystems, the technical system, which includes the hardware and software and also the actual tasks needed [25]. The actual tasks might include topics such as operational processes or IT governance. The social system consists of typical soft issues such as organisational structure, people, reward systems, knowledge, skills and attitudes. This human (socio) and technical interaction can lead to unexpected, uncontrolled, unpredictable, and complex relationships [25]. Figure 1 provides a diagram of a sociotechnical system and its relationships. As seen in Fig. 1, the sociotechnical system exists within a complex environment. Achieving human-AI symbiosis involves the harmonious integration of social and technical elements, working collaboratively to accomplish the intended objectives. For example, AI can be used by organisations to assist with quality checks in its production process. The objective function of the AI would be to minimise quality issues in the assembly, which would align with the production manager's objective. The production manager would, for example, support the AI solution by investing in more labelled data, provide more processing power or routinely maintain the AI system by updating its algorithms to reflect any changes in production processes or quality standards. In return, the AI system will decrease rework costs and enable to the organisation to achieve its production targets. In this example, the objective of the AI system and the humans involved are aligned.

As this study is focused on the suitability of two theoretical underpinnings in AI organisational adoption, a focus on sociotechnical aspects can assist change mediators in managing change between the actors such as firms, organisations and technology as well as the adoption as a whole. Gregor [15] defines

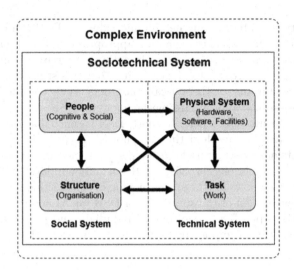

Fig. 1. Sociotechnical systems [25]

"how-to" theories as theories applicable to design and action. The theoretical "how-to" knowledge is required to assist the mediators of the adoption. For changes to sociotechnical systems, mediators are critical actors in promoting system changes, reducing risks, reducing uncertainties, and thereby improving system sustainability [37]. Four reflective elements are identified by Wihlborg and Söderholm, where mediators promote change while developing a system in its social context. They are - translate rather than transfer specific knowledge, function as a single entrance of knowledge, support the selection process through their interpretive components, and bridge knowledge in unforeseen ways. To achieve a holistic approach in investigating the fostering of human-AI symbiosis, sociotechnical theory is employed as the guiding lens.

4   TOE Framework

The TOE framework is an organisational level theory which explains the technology context, the organisational context [32], and the environmental context (see Fig. 2) as the elements that influence a firm's technology innovation adoption decisions [11]. It provides "a useful theoretical lens in analysing the IT (information technology) assimilation, which contends that the adoption, implementation and assimilation of the IS (information systems) in the organisation are affected by factors related to technology, organisation and environment" [40].

The technology context refers to all the relevant technologies to the organisation. Both the technologies that are already in use and those that are not are included in the technology context and influence how organisations can use technology to evolve and adapt [11]. Technology innovations that are not currently implemented in the organisation are categorised into; those that create

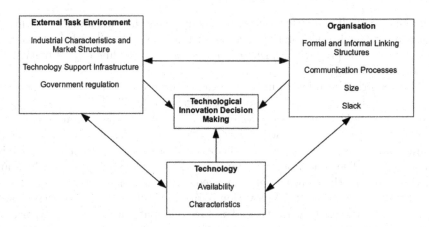

Fig. 2. Technological-organisational-environmental (TOE) framework [32]

incremental change, technologies that trigger synthetic change, and those that are radical and produce a discontinued change [11,33]. The technology innovations that create incremental change require the smallest learning requirements. Technology innovations that produce a discontinued change require a substantial learning requirement and therefore has a substantial and dramatic impact on the organisation [33]. An organisational context is the resources and the characteristics of the organisation, including the firm size, structures between employees, intra-firm communication processes and the level of availability of a resource [11]. The organisational structure (centralised compared to decentralised) and communication processes (management leadership) must be understood to identify the relationship to the innovation adoption process. In the organisational context, the context involves not only the organisation component but also includes the individual in it [36]. The environmental context is the environment in which the organisation exists and includes aspects such as the structure of the industry, the service providers, the regulatory environment [11], competitor pressures, customer pressures, partner pressures and government pressures [6].

As the TOE contexts have a significant effect on adoption, also in the case of analytics [22]. This study uses the TOE framework as a theoretical framework as it caters to external stimuli directly influencing AI adoption and allows researchers to focus on higher-level attributes of AI adoption. Furthermore, the framework complements sociotechnical theory by considering the organisational context of AI adoption.

5 DOI Theory

One theory widely used to understand and explain technology adoption in the context of new innovative approaches is the DOI theory [20,24,27,40]. Because AI is evolving and can be seen as a continuum, it stays an innovation. The

DOI theory is well-suited for studies that emphasise the dissemination of innovation, as opposed to alternative theories such as the TAM [9] and the theory of planned behavior [31], which primarily concentrate on technology or behaviour in a broader sense.

The definition of diffusion in the context of innovation theory is the "process by which an innovation is communicated through certain channels over time among the members of a social system. It is a special type of communication in that the messages are concerned with new ideas" [27, 5]. The idea is that an innovation must widely be adopted until it reaches a critical mass and is self-sustained. The innovation-decision process is the mental process which an individual passes through, namely: knowledge, persuasion, decision, implementation and confirmation [27]. Innovation diffusion theory includes five significant innovation characteristics: relative advantage, compatibility, complexity, trialability and observability. These characteristics are used to explain the adoption of innovations and the decision-making process. In innovation diffusion theory, the degree to which an individual's (or unit's) adoption is relative to other members in the social system is categorised as innovators, early adopters, early majority, late majority and laggards [27].

In this study, the target is to create a theoretical framework to assist researchers in "how-to" knowledge in terms of a theoretical approach to study the enablement of organisational AI adoption. Innovation diffusion theory has widely been used to identify the enablers (variables) of information systems adoption in organisations [24, 26, 40]. When identifying the enablers, organisations need to consider that those that only focus on the technical enablers (variables) tend to neglect transformational approaches required to obtain sustained business value with AI adoption [26]. DOI theory is applied in this study as a mechanism to identify the enabling factors for organisational AI adoption. DOI theory is a suitable mechanism for identifying enabling factors for adopting organisational AI.

6   A Lens for Enabling AI Adoption

On an enterprise level view, the most advanced level of data-driveness and automation, an organisation can be viewed as a giant cybernetic collective [41]. This AI collective exists within an environment and will impact the people and the natural environment.

We propose a framework that considers the sociotechnical nature of AI systems, where social and technical elements connect and collaborate, not in a closed system, but also impacts its environment, and is also impacted by its environment. Furthermore, as the context is in organisational use and adoption of AI, the TOE framework provides an organisational context, where aspects such as ease of use, and achieving organisational goals are important. The combination of DOI theory and a TOE framework is familiar to researchers. DOI theory, together with the TOE framework, have been successfully adopted in several studies [35, 39, 40, 42]. "Business analytics adoption process: An innovation diffusion perspective" is one of the more recent studies. In the study, DOI theory was used to understand the business analytics adoption (initiation, adoption, and assimilation) of organisations and TOE framework to identify its drivers [24].

The TOE and DOI are also used in AI adoption studies, however do not fully allow organisational conclusions in terms of causality [1]. To understand the causality of elements, we propose including the process steps toward adoption as an integral part of theories studying the organisational adoption of AI (See Fig. 3). In DOI theory, the diffusion of innovation takes place involves three main stages: initiation, adoption and assimilation [27]. These phases are critical, the different phases will have different enablement elements and considerations. In the initiation process, the organisation becomes aware of the new innovation, in this case, AI. The second process is the actual adoption process, during this process AI is implemented and confirmed. The last process is the assimilation process. AI becomes an integral part of the organisation's routines and practices during this process. The process is influenced by factors such as AI complexity, trailability, observability, relative advantage and compatibility with the organisation's existing practices [27].

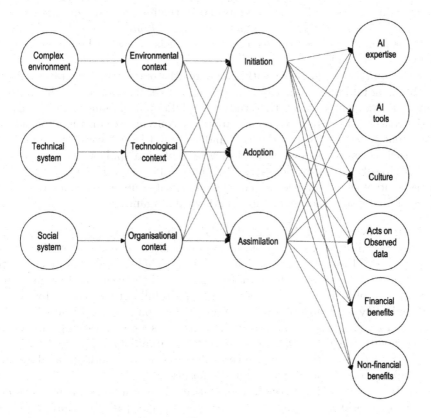

Fig. 3. A theoretical lens for enabling AI adoption

As mentioned in the introduction, a data-driven organisation can be defined as an organisation that acts on observed data rather than merely gut feeling and do so to achieve financial or non-financial benefits [2]. Additionally, a data-driven organisation would AI expertise, tools and a certain culture to adopt and embed AI in the organisation [30]. They effectively use data to enable them to achieve their objectives. Furthermore, by including the environmental context, the impact of AI is recognised. The impact can be extensive and includes social, political, and environmental implications of AI technologies. It can go as be as deep as examining the hidden costs of data extraction and labour exploitation [7].

The proposed theoretical framework is similar to Alsheibani et al. [1], however includes AI expertise, AI tools (including platforms), culture, execution and benefits and benefits of AI. This is included, as a theory should not be limited to the "what", but also includes the "how", "when" or "why " [3], Answering research questions such as *how did the enabling factor contribute to the initiation of the use of AI tools in the organisation?* and *when does the enabling factor contribute to an adoption of a data-driven culture in the organisation?*, can assist in the evaluation of enabling factors and also be used as a step towards understanding of causality in AI adoption. In the first research question example, *how did the enabling factor contribute to the initiation of the use of AI tools in the organisation?*, an example of an enabling factor could be the hosting of technology days [29].

By framing these questions within a pragmatist paradigm, encourages a focus on obtaining information that is of value to practice. We want to emphasise how important pragmatism is for this study as a philosophical foundation, especially in the context of DSR. A pragmatic approach concentrates on the applications and implications of concepts, theories, and deeds in the real world. It emphasises how crucial it is to take into account how valuable and applicable research findings are to solving real-world issues. Pragmatism has several significant benefits in the context of this article, which tries to identify and assess enablers for the successful adoption and application of AI within organisation:

- **Emphasis on practical results:** By taking a pragmatic approach, the research will concentrate on producing information that can immediately be implemented to help organisations adopt AI. This strategy fits in well with the paper's objectives, which are to comprehend the elements that influence the adoption and implementation of AI successfully or unsuccessfully.
- **Flexibility and adaptability:** Pragmatism promotes the blending of various research approaches and methodologies as well as various theoretical viewpoints (such as TOE and DOI). This adaptability fits in well with the paper's strategy, which mixes several theoretical frameworks to analyse and comprehend the adoption of AI in organisations.
- **Problem-focused approach:** Pragmatism places a strong emphasis on tackling real-world issues and difficulties, making it especially appropriate for DSR. DSR attempts to develop and assess artefacts (such as models, frameworks, or tools) to address real-world issues. This study shows a clear commitment to solving the practical issues of AI adoption through the use of the

evaluation methodology for evaluating the efficacy of enabling variables and the focus on the complex sociotechnical systems within organisations.

- **Place an emphasis on context:** Pragmatism recognises the significance of context in comprehending and solving problems. This is especially pertinent to this article because it is believed that the organisational context has a significant impact on the adoption and use of AI. The research can better account for the various and complicated circumstances in which organisations function by adopting a pragmatic approach, which improves the findings' generalizability and application.

Pragmatism enriches the research by focusing on useful results, encouraging methodological flexibility, adhering to the problem-oriented methodology of DSR, and taking context into account. The goals of the article will be met by this philosophical position, which will ultimately contribute to a more thorough and practical understanding of the elements that affect the effective adoption and application of AI within organisations.

7 Conclusion

The main objective of the paper was to explore the suitability of the technological-organisational-environmental (TOE) framework and diffusion of innovation (DOI) theory towards understanding AI adoption as part of sociotechnical systems. This paper explained the requirement of an appropriate theory to assist in identifying enablers for transformations and be useful to support and help the change management and adoption process while having a holistic perspective. Firstly, to allow for a holistic perspective with the target of human-AI symbiosis, sociotechnical theory is introduced as a high-level lens for this study. In the context of sociotechnical theory, the TOE framework is proposed to identify elements that influence an organisation's technology innovation adoption decisions. Secondly, DOI theory is suggested to identify the enablers of AI adoption.

The TOE framework, the DOI diffusion processes (initiation, adoption and assimilation) and the elements of data-driven organisations are combined into one framework. This paper contributes on a theoretical level by providing a framework to also evaluate the possible and impact of the enabling factors and therefore contributing to causality knowledge. It can therefore be used to identify research questions related to the "how", "when" and "why". However, like all studies, this paper also has limitations. The researchers are fully aware that the proposed theoretical model is not close to a grand theory on organisational AI adoption. However, our approach that includes the use of the diffusion processes to evaluate the "how", "when" and "why" the enabling factors can contribute to causality knowledge in the field of AI research in information systems. Future studies will focus on applying the theoretical framework to support the understanding of causality and effectiveness of different enabling factors.

References

1. Alsheibani, S., Cheung, Y., Messom, C.: Rethinking the competitive landscape of artificial intelligence. In: Proceedings of the 53rd Hawaii International Conference on System Sciences (2020)
2. Anderson, C.: Creating a Data-Driven Organisation, 1st edn. O'Reilly, Sebastopol (2015)
3. Bacharach, S.B.: Organizational theories: some criteria for evaluation. Acad. Manag. Rev. **14**(4), 496–515 (1989). https://doi.org/10.5465/amr.1989.4308374
4. Baskerville, R., Baiyere, A., Gregor, S., Hevner, A., Rossi, M.: Design science research contributions: finding a balance between artifact and theory. J. Assoc. Inf. Syst. **19**(5), 358–376 (2018). https://doi.org/10.17705/1jais.00495
5. Berente, N., Gu, B., Recker, J., Santhanam, R.: Managing artificial intelligence. MIS Q. **45**(3), 1433–1450 (2021). https://doi.org/10.25300/MISQ/2021/16274
6. Chen, Y., Yin, Y., Browne, G.J., Li, D.: Adoption of building information modeling in Chinese construction industry: the technology-organization-environment framework. Eng. Constr. Archit. Manag. **26**(9), 1878–1898 (2019). https://doi.org/10.1108/ECAM-11-2017-0246
7. Crawford, K.: Atlas of AI. Yale University Press (2021)
8. Crowther, D., Aras, G.: Corporate Social Responsibility. Bookboon (2008)
9. Davis, F.D.: User acceptance of computer technology: a comparison of two theoretical models. Manag. Sci. **35**(8), 982–1003 (1989)
10. Dresch, A., Lacerda, D.P., Antunes, J.A.V.: Design science research: a method for science and technology advancement. In: Dresch, A., Lacerda, D.P., Antunes, J.A.V. (eds.) Design Science Research, pp. 67–102. Springer, Cham (2015). https://doi.org/10.1007/978-3-319-07374-3_4
11. Dwivedi, Y.K., Wade, M.R., Scheberger, S.L.: Information Systems Theory. Explaining and Predicting Our Digital Society, vol. 1. Springer, New York (2012)
12. Gioia, D.A., Pitre, E.: Multiparadigm perspectives on theory building. Acad. Manag. Rev. **15**(4), 584–602 (1990). https://doi.org/10.5465/amr.1990.4310758
13. Goldkhul, G.: Pragmatism vs interpretivism in qualitative information systems research. Eur. J. Inf. Syst. **21**(2), 135–146 (2012)
14. Goles, T., Hirschheim, R.: The paradigm is dead, the paradigm is dead...long live the paradigm: the legacy of Burrell and Morgan. Int. J. Manag. Sci. **28**, 249–268 (2000). https://doi.org/10.1016/j.biocel.2004.12.003. https://www.markd.nl/content/references/2000Goles.pdf
15. Gregor, S.: The nature of theory in information systems. MIS Q. **30**(3), 611–642 (2006)
16. Hevner, A., Chatterjee, S.: Design science research in information systems. In: Hevner, A., Chatterjee, S. (eds.) Design Research in Information Systems. ISIS, vol. 22, pp. 9–22. Springer, Boston (2010). https://doi.org/10.1007/978-1-4419-5653-8_2
17. Hevner, A.R., March, S.T., Park, J., Ram, S.: Design science in information systems research. MIS Q. **28**(1), 75–105 (2004). https://doi.org/10.2307/25148625
18. Hyder, Z., Siau, K., Nah, F.F.: Use of artificial intelligence, machine learning, and autonomous technologies in the mining industry. In: MWAIS 2018 Proceedings, Saint Louis, Missouri, vol. 43, pp. 1–5 (2018). https://aisel.aisnet.org/mwais2018/43
19. Lacity, M.C., Willcocks, L.P.: Becoming strategic with intelligent automation. MIS Q. Exec. **20**(2), 1–14 (2021)

20. Lee, Y.H., Hsieh, Y.C., Hsu, C.N.: Adding innovation diffusion theory to the technology acceptance model: supporting employees' intentions to use e-learning systems. Educ. Technol. Soc. **14**(4), 124–137 (2011)
21. Litchfield, A.: Holistic pragmatism as a philosophical Framework in Information Systems research. In: 15th Americas Conference on Information Systems 2009, AMCIS 2009, vol. 1, p. 359 (2009)
22. Maroufkhani, P., Wan Ismail, W.K., Ghobakhloo, M.: Big data analytics adoption model for small and medium enterprises. J. Sci. Technol. Policy Manag. **11**(2), 171–201 (2020). https://doi.org/10.1108/JSTPM-02-2020-0018
23. Myers, M.D.: Qualitative research in information systems, pp. 1–19 (2020). https://www.qual.auckland.ac.nz
24. Nam, D., Lee, J., Lee, H.: Business analytics adoption process: an innovation diffusion perspective. Int. J. Inf. Manag. **49**, 411–423 (2019). https://doi.org/10.1016/j.ijinfomgt.2019.07.017
25. Oosthuizen, R., Africa, S., Pretorius, L.: Assessing the impact of new technology on complex sociotechnical systems. S. Afr. J. Ind. Eng. **27**(2), 15–29 (2016)
26. Ransbotham, S., Khodabandeh, S., Fehling, R., Lafountain, B., Kiron, D.: Winning with AI. Pioneers combine strategy, organizational behavior, and technology (2019)
27. Rogers, E.M.: Diffusion of Innovations, 4th edn. The Free Press, New York (1995)
28. Simon, H.A.: The Science of the Artificial, 3rd edn. The MIT Press, Cambridge (2019)
29. Smit, D., Eybers, S., Sibanyoni, N., de Waal, A.: Technology days: an AI democratisation journey begins with a single step. In: Pillay, A., Jembere, E., Gerber, A. (eds.) SACAIR 2022. CCIS, vol. 1734, pp. 335–347. Springer, Cham (2022). https://doi.org/10.1007/978-3-031-22321-1_23
30. Smit, D., Eybers, S., de Waal, A., Wies, R.: The quest to become a data-driven entity: identification of socio-enabling factors of AI adoption. In: Rocha, A., Adeli, H., Dzemyda, G., Moreira, F. (eds.) WorldCIST 2022. LNNS, vol. 468, pp. 589–599. Springer, Cham (2022). https://doi.org/10.1007/978-3-031-04826-5_58
31. Taylor, S., Todd, P.A.: Understanding information technology usage: a test of competing models. Inf. Syst. Res. **6**(2), 144–176 (1995). https://doi.org/10.1287/isre.6.2.144
32. Tornatzky, L.G., Fleischer, M.: The Processes of Technological Innovation. Lexington Books (1990)
33. Tushman, M., Nadler, D.: Organizing for innovation. Calif. Manag. Rev. **28**(3), 74–92 (1986). https://doi.org/10.2307/41165203
34. Van de Ven, A.H.: The process of adopting innovations in organizations: three cases of hospital innovations. People and Technology in the Workplace (1991)
35. Wei, J., Lowry, P.B., Seedorf, S.: The assimilation of RFID technology by Chinese companies: a technology diffusion perspective. Inf. Manag. **52**(6), 628–642 (2015). https://doi.org/10.1016/j.im.2015.05.001
36. Widyasari, Y.D.L., Nugroho, L.E., Permanasari, A.E.: Technology Web 2.0 as intervention media: technology organization environment and socio-technical system perspective. In: Proceedings of 2018 10th International Conference on Information Technology and Electrical Engineering: Smart Technology for Better Society, ICITEE 2018, pp. 124–129. IEEE (2018). https://doi.org/10.1109/ICITEED.2018.8534744
37. Wihlborg, E., Söderholm, K.: Mediators in action: organizing sociotechnical system change. Technol. Soc. **35**(4), 267–275 (2013). https://doi.org/10.1016/j.techsoc.2013.09.004

38. Wixom, B.H., Someh, I.A.: Accelerating data-driven transformation at BBVA. MIT Sloan Center Inf. Syst. Res. **XVIII**(7), 1–4 (2018)
39. Wright, R.T., Roberts, N., Wilson, D.: The role of context in IT assimilation: a multi-method study of a SaaS platform in the US nonprofit sector. Eur. J. Inf. Syst. **26**(5), 509–539 (2017). https://doi.org/10.1057/s41303-017-0053-2
40. Xu, W., Ou, P., Fan, W.: Antecedents of ERP assimilation and its impact on ERP value: a TOE-based model and empirical test. Inf. Syst. Front. **19**(1), 13–30 (2015). https://doi.org/10.1007/s10796-015-9583-0
41. Yolles, M.: Organizations as complex systems: an introduction to knowledge cybernetics. IAP (2006)
42. Zhu, K., Kraemer, K.L., Xu, S.: The process of innovation assimilation by firms in different countries: a technology diffusion perspective on e-business. Manag. Sci. **52**(10), 1557–1576 (2006). https://doi.org/10.1287/mnsc.1050.0487

Key Principles of Ethics in Technology: An Organizational Technology Ethics Checklist

Hanlie Smuts[ID] and Lizette Weilbach[✉] [ID]

University of Pretoria, Private Bag X20, Hatfield, Pretoria 0028, South Africa
{hanlie.smuts,lizette.weilbach}@up.ac.za

Abstract. The evolution of digital technologies enables organizations to optimize business operations through digital transformation programs. The deep integration of technology into organizational processes and ways of work, increases an organization's capacity to act. However, this capacity to act and the powerful digital tools applied in organizations (e.g., artificial intelligence), may place employees in a situation where they must take decisions not required before. Prior to digitalization, decision outcomes were involuntarily constrained by human capability. There is no standardized framework to guide organizations in terms of ethical computing. Hence, the purpose of this paper is to investigate ethics in technology towards defining a checklist for organizations. We extracted 10 key principles from two datasets – a corpus of academic research and a popular press dataset – and categorized it to an ethics framework to derive the checklist. By applying such a checklist, organizations can ensure that they integrate ethics in technology thinking into all digital transformation programs and empower employees with ethical thinking to the practical concerns of technology.

Keywords: Key principles · Ethics in technology · Organizational ethics · Ethics checklist

1 Introduction

We live in a ubiquitous computing world [1] transformed by the evolution of digital technologies [2, 3]. The growing application of digital technologies resulted in a highly integrated cyber-physical space [2, 4]. Some attributes of the cyber-physical space relate to cloud computing (the on-demand availability of computing power and data storage), cognitive computing (artificial intelligence (AI)), internet of things (IoT) (connected world), and computer-based algorithms for control and monitoring (e.g. cyber-physical systems such as autonomous vehicles) [5, 6]. A key enabler to the viability of cyber-physical systems, is the availability of data [7, 8] and the extraction of value from data [9, 10]. Inevitably, data-driven organizations apply data for their decision making, rather than intuition [11, 12].

One of the key demands of the cyber-physical world is the need to provide safety and security for such systems [1]. This requirement is amplified by the aspect that organizations are accelerating their use of disruptive technologies through digital transformation programs [13]. Through digital transformation organizations integrate technology

© The Author(s), under exclusive license to Springer Nature Switzerland AG 2023
A. Gerber and M. Coetzee (Eds.): SAICSIT 2023, CCIS 1878, pp. 241–257, 2023.
https://doi.org/10.1007/978-3-031-39652-6_16

into business processes, products, and services, emphasizing the acknowledgement of potential ethical considerations [14]. The discourse around ethics in technology includes several aspects such as how organizations use information, how employees are engaged and empowered to be able to deal with ethical dilemmas in their day to day work, how organizations manage resources, and how organizations approach sustainability [15, 16]. Therefore, the purpose of our paper is to investigate the key principles of ethics in technology with the aim to create an ethics checklist for organizations by focusing on the primary research question *"What are the key organizational principles of ethics in technology and how may it be categorized into an organization checklist?"*. By applying such a checklist, organizations will be empowered to think about ethics in technology more holistically and ensure that their employees are aware of potential implications as they execute their tasks.

In Sect. 2 we present the background to the study and Sect. 3 highlights the research method. Section 4 contains the data analysis, Sect. 5 the discussion and contribution, and Sect. 6 concludes the paper.

2 Background

Digital transformation in the world of work accelerated transformations in society, highlighting how the application of technology may benefit the environment and society at large [17]. The consideration of benefit in this context, compelled organizations to carefully consider their strategies to fully exploit digital transformational benefits, while preventing digital exclusion and regarding ethical challenges posed by this context [18]. In the next sections we discuss digital transformation, ethics in technology and an information ethics framework.

2.1 Digital Transformation

Digital transformation refers to the *"changes digital technologies can bring about in a company's business model, which result in changed products or organizational structures or in the automation of processes"* [19:124]. It encapsulates an organization's structure, operations, processes, products, and value chains [20] and in an era of rapid technological change, it is changing approaches to strategy formulation [19]. One of the digital transformation strategies that emerged focuses on customer value creation and exceeding customer experiences [21, 22]. The availability of large datasets related to customers enables organizations to take informed decisions in a short period of time, as organizations now have the ability to quickly process large amounts of data [23].

Irrespective of the value of these digital transformation strategies, multiple risks originated from the digital capabilities such as governance risks, legal risks, security and data protection risks [24]. In addition, errors and misuse, such as weaponizing the application of data for malicious intent or for spreading disinformation, while limiting decision-making power, became a reality [25]. However, complexity brought about by digital transformation should not be an excuse to neglect ethical obligations and responsibilities, and existing ethical standards, including implementation mechanisms and instruments, need to be adapted in order to meet new ethical challenges [26].

2.2 Ethics in Technology

The reason technology ethics in organizations is growing in prominence, is driven by key factors such as increased capacity to act and judge [27]. *Firstly*, the diffusion of disruptive technologies in organizations empowers organizations to act, implying that employees have to make choices they did not have to make before [27, 28]. Digital transformation and data analytics enable worker efficiency through automation of repetitive tasks and digitization of work, as well as the delivery of reliable and useful professional work through AI applications [29]. By changing the conventional division of labour between man and machine, employees apply new ways of engaging with customers [30], of deriving insight from patterns in data [31], by applying predictive models to inform business decisions [30] and new business models [32]. With this increased capacity to act, employees are exposed to for example implications of inaccurate recommendations from recommender algorithms that lead to impact on customers, or to make choices regarding using customer information that may have ethical implications [30].

Secondly, prior to digital transformation, employees' actions were involuntarily constrained by their human "weakness" e.g. it was physically impossible – or too time consuming – to manually identify patterns in a big data dataset [33]. With so much technological power, employees have to learn how to be voluntarily constrained by their judgment and their ethics [34, 35]. In order to function effectively, organizations rely on their employees to follow the established rules, policies and procedures [35]. However, based on the increased capacity to act enabled by digital technologies, rules, policies and procedures must be explicit on anonymity breaches, breaches of a user's privacy (employee or customer), the manipulation of behaviour using data or creating recommendation bias – all ultimately leading to a lack of trust [30, 34]. Additionally, employees must be made aware and trained on the implications and courses of action related to these potential outcomes, ensuring a consistent application of ethical decisions (as opposed to each employee taking decisions in this context based on their own judgement and set of values) [36].

2.3 Relationship Framework for Information Ethics

Han [37] developed a relationship framework for information ethics to assist with the education of AI ethics (see Fig. 1). The framework was constructed from a Google Trends analysis and is based on three information and communication technology (ICT) platforms: computing devices without physical interaction (e.g., laptops and smartphones), intermediary platforms (e.g., video conferencing, digital messengers, cyberworld, and metaverse), and computing devices with physical interaction (e.g., wearable robotic limbs, self-driving cars, and robots used in manufacturing). The ethics concerned with these three domains are *computer (internet) ethics* which refers to the more traditional principles that guide computer usage and includes issues such as the illegal cloning of software, the leaking of personal information, hacking, and online abuse. *Internet ethics* is included in this domain as computers are rarely used without being connected. *Computer (internet) ethics* overlaps with *cyber ethics* and encompasses ethical issues occurring in cyberspace, the metaverse, and on social media networks. These include, inter alia, unlawful distribution of works, online slander, social network addiction, and online sexual provocation. *Robot ethics* encompasses *AI ethics* and refers to the ethical considerations needed when implementing softbots (*AI softbot ethics*), or physical bots (*AI (physical) robot ethics*), programmed to perform certain tasks or actions. *Robot ethics* and *AI ethics* overlap with *computer (internet) ethics* and consequently also with *cyber ethics*, which includes issues such as transparency, bias, and accountability around softbots (e.g., chatbots, educational bots, virtual assistants, web crawlers, scrapers, monitoring bots, transaction bots and shopping bots, metaverse and game agents); privacy, control and security around blockchain technology; addiction and potential psychological harm around virtual reality technology; privacy, security and surveillance around IoT technologies; and consent, discrimination and privacy around big data technologies. The overlapping of *robot ethics* with *human ethics* and *computer (internet) ethics* with *human ethics* include issues such as responsibility, safety, and transparency when robots and computers are integrated into human environments and decision-making processes by, inter alia, implanting computer chips or utilizing 'robotic limbs' (*cyborg ethics*). Finally, the overlapping of *robot ethics* and *AI ethics* with *computer (internet) ethics* and *human ethics*, include issues such as the impact of AI on human autonomy and agency, the risks associated with the use of AI in the human body, and the responsibility of individuals and organizations in the development and use of AI cyborg technologies (*AI cyborg ethics*).

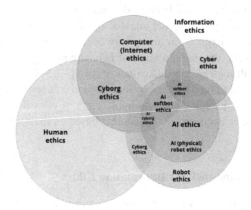

Fig. 1. Han's information ethics framework [37]

3 Methodology

The objective of this paper is to investigate the key principles of ethics in technology with the aim to create an ethics checklist for organizations. In order to achieve this aim, we created two datasets for analysis and categorized the findings. The first dataset was created through a systematic literature review (SLR) aimed at identifying and analyzing the existing body of peer-reviewed papers related to the primary research question [38, 39]. We followed the SLR processes suggested by Rouhani et al. [38], consisting of 3 sequential stages: (1) planning (specifying how the SLR will be carried out), (2) execution (implementing the SLR planning and identifying the corpus for analysis) and (3) results analysis. We executed a search in Google Scholar using the keyword string *"ethics" and ("organisations" or "organizations") and "ethical technology"* and extracted 125 papers. We screened the papers and excluded 12 books or papers that were not available, 5 duplicates, 5 papers not written in English and 11 papers not relevant to our research question. The corpus for analysis consisted of 92 papers for analysis. The corpus was analyzed using Leximancer version 5.00.140 2021/08/25 (www.leximancer. Com) following the methodological procedure applied by Abaimov and Martellini [40] and Khan, Rana and Goel [41]. Leximancer is advanced natural language processing (NLP) software collating frequency of concepts and relationships through an unsupervised iterative process, automatically inferring concepts, themes and report patterns from the data [42].

The second dataset was created by executing a Google search using the same keyword string applied for the SLR. We selected the top 27 news articles and blog posts based on Google's relevance sorted output. As our study focused on a practical contribution in the form of a checklist for organizations, we also wanted to understand the common themes in the popular discourse. The popular press dataset was created by extracting the article text into a MS Word document and imported it into MonkeyLearn, a machine learning platform for text analysis, with a tag cloud feature for data visualization (www. monkeylearn.com). The outcome of the popular press articles was visualized through a weighted list of text data where the frequency of each tag is represented via font size [43]. The relevance score is algorithmically derived by combining key words' frequency with other factors e.g. how descriptive and how long a word is [44].

We then categorized the concepts and themes identified for datasets 1 and 2 against the ethics framework discussed in Sect. 2.3 to develop our ethics in technology checklist for organizations. The results of the academic literature and popular press analyses are discussed in Sect. 4.

4 Data Analysis and Findings

The outcome of the automated content analysis of the first dataset is visualized in a concept map where the concepts identified in the corpus are clustered into heat-mapped themes shown in Fig. 2 [60].

The concept map consisted of 11 themes and 47 concepts depicted in Table 1. The number in square brackets after each theme represents the number of hits. "Hits" refer to the number of text blocks in the corpus associated with the theme [42]. "Key concept description" reflects an abbreviated phrase of the concept identified during the automated content analysis.

The *social* theme focused on key principles when designing policies in different contexts (e.g., countries) in the context of the approach to ethics in technology in organizations [45–48]. Some of these key principles refer to the promotion of human social capital in the context of the advancement of new technologies and the fact that any kind of socialization process, be dominated by human skills [17, 45, 49]. The requirements in this context drive skills training aimed at enhancing and building capabilities and specialized knowledge towards technological advancement, dehumanization, and

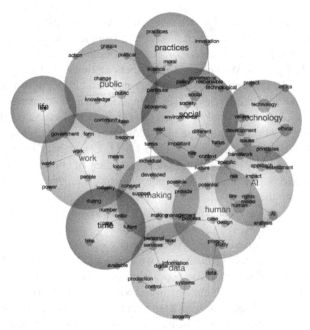

Fig. 2. Key concepts in ethics in technology (Leximancer visualization)

technology focused on serving humanity [50, 51]. Such social actions are shaped by specific institutional and organizational settings, and by the characteristic of relevant technological applications [52].

The *technology* theme incorporates concepts such as ethical issues, development, values, and ethics. Ethical implications for organizations are driven by the widespread deployment of e.g. biometric technologies [53, 54], highlighting the fact that organizations should identify any known ethical issues with a particular emerging technology [24]. This identification may be achieved through various methods such as a bibliometric analysis of existing literature from governments, public reports on a particular technology, or consultation with academics – all with the aim to identify common ethical concerns [24]. The outcome of this identification step must result in explicit action which addresses the ethical issues surrounding the development and use of such systems in organizations [47, 55]. Explicit action should include value-based principles such as transparency and explainability, fairness, human centered values, security and safety, and accountability [40].

The *AI* theme incorporated 10 concepts (refer to Table 1) and focuses on identifying the values to be embedded in AI solutions. These values include safeguarding data protection, the fundamental freedom and rights of natural persons, and specific risk management provisions [56–58]. AI applications and a digital environment have the potential to track, analyze, predict, and even manipulate employees' behaviour. This digital environment therefore impacts autonomy and privacy, and should be applied effectively safeguarding human rights [59, 60].

Table 1. Themes, concepts, and key concept descriptions identified from literature

Theme [Hits]	Concepts	Key concept description
Social [2213]	social, different, responsible, need, role, important, policy, context, society	Policies to be designed for specific social contexts; individuals/communities to leverage new technologies; efforts to enhance collective knowledge, skills and capabilities of individuals/communities to operate in digital economy and address technological challenges; access to education/training programmes on digital literacy; consideration for the potential impact on human society; train individuals on ethical considerations related to technology – ensure development and use to serve humanity
Technology [25040]	technology, ethical, issues, development, values, ethics	Identify known ethical issues and common ethical concerns with emerging technology; use bibliometric analysis of government literature, public reports, and consultation of academics; take action to address ethical issues relating to technology; apply value-based principles
AI [21787]	AI, rights, approach, assessment, impact, risk, framework, model, analysis, specific	Identify values embedded in AI solutions; execute responsible data management and technology development: protect sensitive data and individual rights and freedoms; assess and manage risks associated with the use of technologies; apply in a way which would safeguard human rights: potential to track, analyse, predict and manipulate behaviour
Data [19346]	data, systems, information, services, digital	Approach analysis and use of data critically and carefully to ensure responsible and ethical use; determine who has access to the data and how it is restricted; ethical challenges: sharing of personal information with permission, removal of personal information to protect individuals, protecting data from unauthorizes access, collecting accessing and using of data ethically and legally; data for decision making should not be based solely on quantitative information (neglecting context, culture and individual experiences)
Human [17435]	human, process, design, potential, case	Include human values in technology design; engage with all stakeholders when designing technology

(continued)

Table 1. (*continued*)

Theme [Hits]	Concepts	Key concept description
Making [9643]	making, provide, future, possible	Consider future, past and present scenarios when designing technology; model scenarios to address possible issues pro-actively
Work [6012]	work, people	Digital transformation changes how people work, socialize and engage; new ways of communicating and collaborating; new opportunities for remote work and virtual interaction; impact on physical spaces of work (remote work and changes in office spaces) and communication (social interaction via online communities and social media)
Public	public	Responsible development and use of technology; digitization (AI, biotechnology, and autonomous vehicles) can affect the public more broadly (implications for public safety, public health and the environment); develop and use in responsible way
Practices [9290]	practices, science, innovation	Practices in research, innovation, science and technology to consider ethical implications of their work – reflect on values and actions; take into account potential impact on society (strive to be inclusive, responsive and reflective); training on codes of conduct; awareness of and adherence to ethical and legal frameworks that govern work; adaptability and flexibility to changing circumstances
Time [2988]	time	Consider long-term implications of technology; pace of technological change creates challenges of keeping up (leading to digital divide); technological changes can have a long-term impact on social norms, cultural values and overall quality of life
Life [1997]	life	Consider the impact of digitization on people's well-being and quality of life; use technology in sustainable, responsible and beneficial way

The proliferation of *data* in applications such as IoT, digital twins, and social media, contribute to establishing big data that may be analyzed with machine learning (ML) applications [61]. Data transformation and visualization create visibility of organizational operations such as business processes, production flows and information flows across organizational components, customers and suppliers [62, 63]. Interrogation of this operational data must therefore be considered critically, especially considering who gets access to the data, as the access – or lack of access – matters. Ethical challenges related to this theme includes sharing of personal information without permission, de-identifying information before it is accessed, processed or shared, protection of data from outside threats, the rightful ownership of the data used for analytics, and the application of data for decisions about a population based solely on quantitative information [59, 64, 65].

The *human* theme refers to designing and implementing the digital solutions inclusive of human values, i.e. ethics by design and not bolted on later [24, 66]. Ethics by design also implies the identification of, and engagement with, potential stakeholders. Depending on the context of the organization, stakeholders may include employees, suppliers, professional associations, customers, etc. [45, 48, 56]. *Making* as a theme encompasses scenarios in the context of considering possible outcomes of the future (predictive nature) and reflecting different perspectives of the past and present (descriptive and diagnostic). The purpose of modeling these scenarios, is to enable organizations to predict future risk and to address it pro-actively [59, 63, 64, 67, 68]. The theme, *work*, reflects on the significant change in the way people live, work and play due to the digital transformation [64, 69]. The impact on place, work and people also highlights different ways of engaging and communicating with one another [66, 70]. It is important that this engagement in the ubiquitous computing world, is not just based on technical adequacy, but that a more holistic view should be applied [71–73]. *Practices* refer to research, innovation, science and technology practices with the accountability to reflect on their own value systems, but also to contribute to building reflective capacity in organizational practices [74]. The impact and relation of science on the wider society, in particular the essential notions of inclusion, anticipation, responsiveness and reflection, provides a frame through which fairness may be embedded into practices [54]. It also encompasses training on codes of conduct and the establishment of international governance frameworks, to flexibly and adaptively enable policy safeguards, while enabling organizations to benefit from digital transformation [40, 71].

Three themes are single concept themes, and we discuss them briefly. *Public* focuses on responsible development and application of technology as it relates to the public in general e.g., public safety, public health, etc., while *time* refers to the fast pace of technological change and its long-term potential impact. The theme *life* highlights the impact of digital transformation on people's well-being and quality of life.

The visualization of popular press articles in dataset 2 is shown in Fig. 3 and the relevance score in Table 2.

The most visible themes in the popular press dataset (Fig. 3) and the relevance score (Table 2) are "ethical", "technology" and "data". "Ethics" and "technology" were part of the search words, yet the importance of "data" in the context of ethics in technology is prominent in the popular press articles. Other key themes highlighted by the visualization of popular press includes "information", "privacy", "use" and "trust" within the context of "companies".

Fig. 3. Tag cloud visualization for popular press dataset (MonkeyLearn visualization)

Table 2. Relevance score table (MonkeyLearn)

Theme	Times	Relevance	Theme	Times	Relevance
Ethical	165	1	Use	48	0.36
Technology	144	0.88	Information	48	0.36
Data	94	0.61	People	44	0.34
Ethics	72	0.49	Trust	38	0.3
Companies	70	0.48	Privacy	34	0.28

The themes identified in the second dataset align well with the themes from the first dataset and we applied these findings in the discussion section of the paper towards defining the ethics in technology checklist for organizations.

5   Categorization of Concepts to Information Ethics Relationship Framework and Derivation of Key Principles

A list of key concepts of ethics in technology have been identified (Table 1). To provide an organizational checklist which organizations can use to ensure that they think about ethics in technology in a holistic way, we followed three steps. The first step was to categorize the key concepts identified in the SLR (Table 1), to the four main ethics spheres, as specified by the framework of Han [37], and the technology ethical issues typically encountered in each sphere. In the second step, we derived ten key principles of ethics in technology from the key concepts, linked to the 4 spheres (Table 3). The identified principles were then discussed in more detail. In the final step, the key principles were used to construct a practical technology ethics checklist for organizations (Table 4). The categorization, derivation and construction are discussed in this section.

Table 3. Organizational technology ethics checklist

Ethics Sphere	Key principles of ethics in technology	Yes/No
Computer (internet) ethics	1. *Be ethically driven from the start*: Organizations need to be proactive and stay at the forefront of potential ethical technology challenges. From the start, organizations need to design technology-driven products and services with ethical principles in mind. This can assist them to anticipate and avoid situations, rather than being reactive after the effect	☐
	2. *Embrace an ethical technical technology mindset*: Ethical technology recognition, awareness, and decision-making frameworks should not only be perceived as a compliance or policy action, but it should be inherent to the organization's fabric. Adoption of the technology disruption vocabulary and syntax, is not sufficient; organizations should be aware of the ethical decision-makers' role regarding technology disruptors	☐
	3. *Create a culture of shared responsibility*: Engage all functions and champion it from the top. Leaving shared responsibility to a few teams or departments, promotes the impression that the whole organization is not required to consider it. Organizations need to be able to distinguish the ethical issues technology disruption may introduce and apply consistent means of pinpointing ethical courses of action. By promoting an organizational culture that supports these courses of actions, ethical decision-making will be endorsed	☐
	4. *Ensure an approach that can evolve*: Approaches to ethical technology in organizations should be assessed and revised as needed due to the unpredictable and rapid way in which technology is evolving. Policies developed in recent years, may even no longer directly address current risks based on the rate at which markets are changing, Organizations must therefore develop policies and frameworks to guide technology decisions, with the expectation that they will likely require adjustment and adaptation as markets evolve and technologies change	☐
	4. *Equip employees with the resources to respond*: Employees, teams and departments should have the resources they require to make ethical decisions regarding technology. It is therefore important that organizations provide employees with applicable resources, assets, and tools. These resources will assist employees to recognise ethical dilemmas, to appraise alternatives, to make and to test ethical technology decisions	☐
Cyber Ethics	5. *Moral use of data and resources*: Data is of great value to organizations as they refine product offerings and implement new marketing strategies. However, such strategies can also be invasive in terms of privacy, highlighting many ethical issues. To ensure that data is not leaked or used inappropriately, data protection measures and compliance procedures may be defined and applied in order to guide moral use of data	☐

(continued)

Table 3. (*continued*)

Ethics Sphere	Key principles of ethics in technology	Yes/No
	6. *Design the organization for ethical technology*: Ethical technology policies are not intended to replace business ethics or general compliance, but rather to strengthen them. Hence, avoid creating functional silos in the context of ethics or establish a separate, standalone ethics program; rather expand departments' objectives to include ethical technology considerations. Encourage and teach the organization to distinguish among professional ethics concerns, technology-related ethical issues and broader corporate matters	☐
Robot ethics (Including AI ethics)	7. *Responsible adoption of disruptive technologies*: Digital growth is a business reality, yet such digital transformation should not cause ethical challenges. To ensure that the technologies the organization adopts have ethics considerations and protection in place, organizations should do due diligence prior to technology acquisition. Due diligence may be supported by the development of a guiding framework that is inclusive of technology use cases specific to the organization and aligned to its culture	☐
Human ethics	8. *Respect for employees and customers*: Organizations that engage in good ethical technology practices and that understand that customers and employees are their greatest asset, maintain a strong moral sense of the rights of their employees and the protection of their customers. The value of data is therefore considered within a frame of responsible protection of employees and customers alike	☐
	9. *Make ethical technology part of a holistic, technology know-how approach*: It is important that the whole organization recognises potentially technology-related ethical predicaments. Employees that are not directly involved with or responsible for technology, must be trained and empowered to recognise ethical technology issues; even when these technology issues are less obvious. This may especially be important for less digitally transformed organizations, where the implications of technology for day-to-day operations are less obvious to employees	☐

Ten key principles of ethics in technology were derived through a mapping of the information ethics relationship framework by Han [37] to the key ethics concepts identified in the SLR. Five key principles were derived for the computer (internet) ethics sphere, two for the cyber ethics sphere, one for the robot ethics (including AI ethics) sphere and two for the human ethics sphere. To see the detailed table showing how these the principles were derived, please visit: https://shorturl.at/pO369 (see the 'Linked data' tab).

The key principles of ethics in technology derived from this mapping are expanded on in Table 3 and may be used by organizations as a technology ethics checklist.

The set of 10 key principles for ethics in technology categorized by *computer (internet) ethics, cyber ethics, robot ethics (including AI ethics)* and *human ethics* may be applied as a checklist in organizations. The purpose of this checklist is to enable organizations to integrate ethics in technology thinking into all digital transformation programs and to empower employees with ethical thinking to the practical concerns of technology.

6 Conclusion

The aim of this paper was to examine the key principles of ethics in technology with the aim to create a technology ethics checklist for organizations. The first dataset we analyzed to extract key ethics principles was created through a SLR of 92 academic, peer-reviewed papers. Themes and concepts were extracted with an automated content analysis software tool, Leximancer. We created and analyzed a second dataset of popular press articles to understand the current discourse around ethics in technology in organizations. We aimed to investigate the alignment of the popular press themes to the SLR findings and to establish whether the SLR themes and concepts may be enriched.

The themes and concepts extracted were categorized to four ethics spheres [37] in order to create a checklist that organizations may apply. Our proposed checklist incorporates 10 key principles to enable organizations to apply holistic thinking in the context of ethics in technology. Furthermore, such holistic thinking empowers employees and ensures that they can apply ethical thinking to the practical concerns of technology.

Two objectives guide future research. Firstly, the checklist may be expanded further with a set of guiding questions provided for each key principle. Secondly, the proposed checklist and guiding questions may be tested in an organization as a case study to establish its applicability.

References

1. Qiu, H., Kapusta, K., Lu, Z., Qiu, M., Memmi, G.: All-or-nothing data protection for ubiquitous communication: challenges and perspectives. Inf. Sci. **502**, 434–445 (2019)
2. Vuori, V., Helander, N., Okkonen, J.: Digitalization in knowledge work: the dream of enhanced performance. Cogn. Technol. Work **21**, 237–252 (2018). https://doi.org/10.1007/s10111-018-0501-3
3. Bolisani, E., Bratianu, C..: The emergence of knowledge management. In: Emergent Knowledge Strategies. KMOL, vol. 4, pp. 23–47. Springer, Cham (2018). https://doi.org/10.1007/978-3-319-60657-6_2
4. Sardar, Z.: The smog of ignorance: knowledge and wisdom in postnormal times. Futures **120**, 1–12 (2020)
5. Pfohl, H., Yahsi, B., Kurnaz, T.: The impact of industry 4.0 on supply chain. In: Kersten, W., Blecker, T., Ringle, C. (eds.) Innovations and Strategies for Logistics and Supply Chains, pp. 31–58 (2015)
6. Martinez, F.: Process excellence the key for digitalisation. Bus. Process. Manage. J. **25**, 1716–1733 (2019)
7. Pencheva, I., Esteve, M., Mikhaylov, S.J.: Big data and AI – a transformational shift for government: so, what next for research? Public Policy Adm. **35**, 24–44 (2020)
8. Mandinach, E.B.: A perfect time for data use: using data-driven decision making to inform practice. Educ. Psychol. **47**, 71–85 (2012)
9. Brynjolfsson, E., Hitt, L.M., Kim, H.H.: Strength in numbers: how does data-driven decision making affect firm performance? (2011)

10. Long, Q.: Data-driven decision making for supply chain networks with agent-based computational experiment. Knowl.-Based Syst. **141**, 55–66 (2018)
11. Ghasemaghaei, M., Ebrahimi, S., Hassanein, K.: Data analytics competency for improving firm decision making performance. J. Strateg. Inf. Syst. **27**, 101–113 (2017)
12. Comuzzi, M.: How organisations leverage big data: a maturity model. Ind. Manag. Data Syst. **116**, 1468–1492 (2016)
13. Brown, A.W.: Digital Transformation: Towards a New Perspective for Large Established Organisations in a Digital Age. In: Management and Information Technology after Digital Transformation, pp. 8–19. Routledge, Milton Park (2021)
14. Malnar, D., Olujić, J.: The security challenge of disruptive technologies. Ann. Disaster Risk Sci. ADRS **2**, 37–47 (2019)
15. De Cremer, D., Kasparov, G.: The ethics of technology innovation: a double-edged sword? AI Ethics **2**, 533–537 (2021). https://doi.org/10.1007/s43681-021-00103-x
16. Green, B.: The contestation of tech ethics: a sociotechnical approach to technology ethics in practice. J. Soc. Comput. **2**, 209–225 (2021)
17. Carayannis, E.G., Canestrino, R., Magliocca, P.: From the dark side of Industry 4.0 to Society 5.0: Looking "beyond the box" to developing human-centric innovation ecosystems. IEEE Trans. Eng. Manage. 1–17 (2023)
18. du Plessis, G., Smuts, H.: The diffusion of innovation experience. In: Dennehy, D., Griva, A., Pouloudi, N., Dwivedi, Y.K., Pappas, I., Mäntymäki, M. (eds.) I3E 2021. LNCS, vol. 12896, pp. 318–329. Springer, Cham (2021). https://doi.org/10.1007/978-3-030-85447-8_28
19. Hess, T., Matt, C., Benlian, A., Wiesböck, F.: Options for formulating a digital transformation strategy. MIS Q. Executive **15**, 123–139 (2016)
20. Zimmer, M.P., Järveläinen, J.: Digital–sustainable co-transformation: introducing the triple bottom line of sustainability to digital transformation research. In: Kreps, D., Davison, R., Komukai, T., Ishii, K., (eds.) Human Choice and Digital by Default: Autonomy vs Digital Determination. HCC 2022. IFIP Advances in Information and Communication Technology, vol. 656, pp. 100–111. Springer, Cham (2022). https://doi.org/10.1007/978-3-031-15688-5_10
21. Güler, M., Büyüközkan, G.: Analysis of digital transformation strategies with an integrated fuzzy AHP-axiomatic design methodology. IFAC-PapersOnLine **52**, 1186–1191 (2019)
22. Neumeier, A., Wolf, T., Oesterle, S.: The manifold fruits of digitalization - determining the literal value behind. In: Proceedings der 13. Internationalen Tagung Wirtschaftsinformatik (WI 2017), pp. 484–498 (2017)
23. Hilbert, M.: Big data for development: a review of promises and challenges. Dev. Policy Rev. **34**, 135–174 (2016)
24. Matar, A., de Araujo, M.: D6. 3: methods for translating ethical analysis into instruments for the ethical development and deployment of emerging technologies (2021)
25. Duberry, J.: AI and the weaponization of information: Hybrid threats against trust between citizens and democratic institutions. In: Artificial Intelligence and Democracy, pp. 158–194. Edward Elgar Publishing (2022)
26. Vial, G.: Understanding digital transformation: a review and a research agenda. J. Strateg. Inf. Syst. **28**, 118–144 (2019)
27. Tsamados, A., et al.: The ethics of algorithms: key problems and solutions. In: Floridi, L. (ed.) Ethics, Governance, and Policies in Artificial Intelligence. PSS, vol. 144, pp. 97–123. Springer, Cham (2021). https://doi.org/10.1007/978-3-030-81907-1_8
28. Longo, F., Padovano, A., Umbrello, S.: Value-oriented and ethical technology engineering in industry 5.0: a human-centric perspective for the design of the factory of the future. Appl. Sci. **10**, 4182 (2020)
29. Holford, W.D.: The future of human creative knowledge work within the digital economy. Futures **105**, 143–154 (2019)

30. Milano, S., Taddeo, M., Floridi, L.: Recommender systems and their ethical challenges. AI Soc. **35**(4), 957–967 (2020). https://doi.org/10.1007/s00146-020-00950-y
31. Bangsa, A.B., Schlegelmilch, B.B.: Linking sustainable product attributes and consumer decision-making: insights from a systematic review. J. Clean. Prod. **245**, 118902 (2020)
32. Ferrell, O.C., Fraedrich, J.: Business Ethics: Ethical Decision Making and Cases. Cengage learning (2021)
33. George, G., Haas, M.R., Pentland, A.: Big data and management, vol. 57, pp. 321–326. Academy of Management Briarcliff Manor, NY (2014)
34. Tyler, T.R., Blader, S.L.: Can businesses effectively regulate employee conduct? the antecedents of rule following in work settings. Acad. Manag. J. **48**, 1143–1158 (2005)
35. Kälvemark, S., Höglund, A.T., Hansson, M.G., Westerholm, P., Arnetz, B.: Living with conflicts-ethical dilemmas and moral distress in the health care system. Soc. Sci. Med. **58**, 1075–1084 (2004)
36. Molka-Danielsen, J., Rasool, J., Smith, C.H.: Design and deployment considerations for ethically advanced technologies for human flourishing in the workplace. In: Bhutkar, G., et al. (eds.) HWID 2021. IAICT, vol. 609, pp. 101–122. Springer, Cham (2022). https://doi.org/10.1007/978-3-031-02904-2_5
37. Han, J.: An information ethics framework based on ICT platforms. Information **13**, 440 (2022)
38. Rouhani, B.D., Mahrin, M.N.R., Nikpay, F., Ahmad, R.B., Nikfard, P.: A systematic literature review on enterprise architecture implementation methodologies. Inf. Softw. Technol. **62**, 1–20 (2015)
39. Ramdhani, A., Ramdhani, M.A., Amin, A.S.: Writing a literature review research paper: a step-by-step approach. Int. J. Basic Appl. Sci. **3**, 47–56 (2014)
40. Abaimov, S., Martellini, M.: International Resonance. In: Machine Learning for Cyber Agents: Attack and Defence, pp. 149–202. Springer, Cham (2022). https://doi.org/10.1007/978-3-030-91585-8
41. Khan, S., Rana, S., Goel, A.: Presence of digital sources in international marketing: a review of literature using Leximancer. Int. J. Technol. Mark. **16**, 246–274 (2022)
42. Leximancer: Leximancer User Guide (2021). https://info.leximancer.com/. Accessed 10 Feb 2021
43. Bitzer, S., Thoroe, L., Schumann, M.: Folksonomy: creating metadata through collaborative tagging. In: Handbook of Research on Social Interaction Technologies and Collaboration Software: Concepts and Trends, pp. 147–157. IGI Global (2010)
44. Contreras, D., Wilkinson, S., Balan, N., James, P.: Assessing post-disaster recovery using sentiment analysis: the case of L'Aquila. Italy. Earthq. Spectra **38**, 81–108 (2022)
45. Reijers, W.: Practicing narrative virtue ethics of technology in research and innovation. Dublin City University (2019)
46. Hersee, S.: The cyber security dilemma and the securitisation of cyberspace. Royal Holloway, University of London (2019)
47. Bolland, T.: The construction of the humanitarian UAV: intersections of ethics neoliberalism and biopolitics and resultant implications. Liverpool John Moores University (United Kingdom) (2020)
48. Tõnurist, P., Hanson, A.: Anticipatory innovation governance: shaping the future through proactive policy making (2020)
49. Colli, F., Kerremans, B., Adriaensen, J.: Lobbying the state or the market? A study of civil society organisations' strategic behaviour (2019)
50. Studzieniecki, T.: Wealth or happiness of the European union– the dilemma of the normative economics (2018)
51. Berti Suman, A.: Sensing the risk: a case for integrating citizen sensing into risk governance (2020)

52. Gwala, R.S., Mashau, P.: Corporate governance and its impact on organisational performance in the fourth industrial revolution: a systematic literature review. Corp. Governance Organ. Behav. Rev. **6**, 98–114 (2022)
53. Tambornino, L., Lanzerath, D., Rodrigues, R., Wright, D.: D4. 3: survey of REC approaches and codes for artificial intelligence & robotics (2018)
54. Purvis, B., Celebi, D., Pansera, M.: A framework for a responsible circular economy. J. Clean. Prod. **400**, 136679 (2023)
55. Bryce, V., Stahl, B., Brooks, L.: We need to talk about digital HR ethics! A review of the academic literature on ethical aspects of algorithmic human resource management (HRM) technologies (2022)
56. Mantelero, A.: Beyond Data: Human Rights, Ethical and Social Impact Assessment in AI. Springer (2022). https://doi.org/10.1007/978-94-6265-531-7
57. Gurzawska, A.: Responsible innovation in business: perceptions, evaluation practices and lessons learnt. Sustainability **13**, 1826 (2021)
58. Drobotowicz, K.: Guidelines for designing trustworthy AI services in the public sector (2020)
59. Power, D.J., Heavin, C., O'Connor, Y.: Balancing privacy rights and surveillance analytics: a decision process guide. J. Bus. Anal. **4**, 155–170 (2021)
60. Bringas Colmenarejo, A., et al.: Fairness in agreement with European values: an interdisciplinary perspective on AI regulation. In: Proceedings of the 2022 AAAI/ACM Conference on AI, Ethics, and Society, pp. 107–118 (2022)
61. Flick, C.: A critical professional ethical analysis of non-fungible tokens (NFTs). J. Responsible Technol. **12**, 100054 (2022)
62. Adamik, A., Nowicki, M., Puksas, A.: Energy oriented concepts and other SMART WORLD trends as game changers of co-production—reality or future? Energies **15**, 4112 (2022)
63. Loza de Siles, E.: Artificial intelligence bias and discrimination: will we pull the arc of the moral universe towards justice? J. Int'l. Comp. L. **8**, 513 (2021)
64. Rogerson, S.: The Evolving Landscape of Ethical Digital Technology. CRC Press, Boca Raton (2021)
65. Crawford, K., Gray, M.L., Miltner, K.: Big data—critiquing big data: politics, ethics, epistemology—special section introduction. Int. J. Commun. **8**, 10 (2014)
66. Widdicks, K., Remy, C., Bates, O., Friday, A., Hazas, M.: Escaping unsustainable digital interactions: toward "more meaningful" and "moderate" online experiences. Int. J. Hum. Comput. Stud. **165**, 102853 (2022)
67. Borangiu, T., Trentesaux, D., Leitão, P., Cardin, O., Lamouri, S.: Service Oriented, Holonic and Multi-Agent Manufacturing Systems for Industry of the Future: Proceedings of SOHOMA 2020. Springer, Cham (2021)
68. Ganesh, M.I., Moss, E.: Resistance and refusal to algorithmic harms: varieties of 'knowledge projects.' Media Int. Austral. **183**, 90–106 (2022)
69. Lindhout, P., Reniers, G.: Involving moral and ethical principles in safety management systems. Int. J. Environ. Res. Public Health **18**, 8511 (2021)
70. Stelzer, H.: Responsible innovation and climate engineering. A step back to technology assessment. Philos. Manage. **19**, 297–316 (2020)
71. Arnaldi, S., Ferrari, A., Magaudda, P., Marin, F.: Responsibility in Nanotechnology Development. Springer, Dordrecht (2014). https://doi.org/10.1007/978-94-017-9103-8
72. Zuiderveen Borgesius, F.: Discrimination, artificial intelligence, and algorithmic decision-making. línea], Council of Europe (2018)

73. Banholzer, V.M.: From "Industry 4.0" to "Society 5.0" and "Industry 5.0": value-and mission-oriented policies: technological and social innovations–aspects of systemic transformation (2022)
74. Landeweerd, L., Townend, D., Mesman, J., Van Hoyweghen, I.: Reflections on different governance styles in regulating science: a contribution to 'responsible research and innovation.' Life Sci. Soc. Policy 11(1), 1–22 (2015). https://doi.org/10.1186/s40504-015-0026-y

ChatGPT in Scholarly Discourse: Sentiments and an Inflection Point

Hossana Twinomurinzi(✉) and Sibukele Gumbo

Centre for Applied Data Science, University of Johannesburg, Johannesburg, South Africa
hossanat@uj.ac.za, 222239719@student.uj.ac.za

Abstract. ChatGPT became the most popular Artificial Intelligence (AI) and digital technology platform in history after its launch in November 2022. According to the Diffusion of Innovation Theory, because it reached one million users within five days, and 100 million users within two months, ChatGPT marked an inflection point in society. This study presents a scoping review of the sentiments on ChatGPT in scholarly discourse from 67 publications on the topic. The sentiments were thematically analyzed manually, using ChatGPT and using the new AI function in Atlas.ti®. ChatGPT offered the most comprehensive and versatile analysis even though its results were only used for demonstrative purposes. The key findings reveal a majority positive sentiment from scholars on ChatGPT mainly citing how academia should co-exist with the tool, and for researchers, organizations and society to use ChatGPT to stir greater creativity and productivity. The limited negative and risk sentiments centered around ethical concerns, contradictions, and apprehension about the impact of ChatGPT, through dependency, on human social and cognitive functions in decision-making and judgement. The main recommendations comprise a call for educational reform, training on better usage of ChatGPT, and making the world a better place. The main non-technology focus of ChatGPT research is on "human", "ethics" and "decision-making". The study similarly makes a recommendation for educational reform given the transdisciplinary effect of AI, and for academia, society and organizations to intentionally take advantage of the inflection point to create progressive policies on the maximal use of ChatGPT and other AI tools.

Keywords: Artificial Intelligence · ChatGPT · bibliometric · ethics · scoping review · sentiment analysis · transdisciplinarity

1 Introduction

Machine Learning (ML), Artificial Intelligence (AI), and Natural Language Processing (NLP) have experienced rapid advancements in recent years, leading to the development of powerful tools such as ChatGPT. ChatGPT was launched by OpenAI on November 30, 2022 [1]. It saw over a million users within its first five days of release. A 2022 McKinsey survey shows that AI adoption has more than doubled in the past five years, and there is an increase in AI investment [2]. ChatGPT is powered by the Generative Pre-Trained Transformer (GPT-3) architecture. It is a conversational chatbot that has the potential

© The Author(s), under exclusive license to Springer Nature Switzerland AG 2023
A. Gerber and M. Coetzee (Eds.): SAICSIT 2023, CCIS 1878, pp. 258–272, 2023.
https://doi.org/10.1007/978-3-031-39652-6_17

to revolutionize various sectors due to its wide range of applications. ChatGPT uses deep learning techniques that can generate human-like content and responses, including writing programming code and providing theories based on typed queries [3]. These generative techniques are called Large Language Models (LLMs).

ChatGPT is built on several key building blocks, including the transformer architecture, pre-training process, and fine-tuning process. The transformer architecture of ChatGPT utilizes a neural network that allows for parallel processing of input data. It consists of an encoder that processes input text and a decoder that generates output text [4]. The input is processed as a sequence of tokens, such as words or phrases, which undergo multiple layers of transformation until the decoder generates the final output. Prior to deployment, ChatGPT undergoes an extensive pre-training process, where it is trained on a large amount of text data. This enables it to understand the underlying patterns and structure of languages, equipping it with the capability to generate human-like responses. Following the pre-training phase, ChatGPT undergoes a fine-tuning process to enhance its ability to respond to specific tasks. The model is trained on domain-specific data by providing it with prompts related to the desired task, allowing it to specialize in its responses. The transformer architecture, pre-training process, and fine-tuning process work synergistically to enable ChatGPT to generate relevant responses to text prompts. As a result, ChatGPT is a powerful tool with applications in various areas such as natural language processing, conversational AI, and content generation [1].

ChatGPT and LLMs are versatile and, therefore, extend to a wide range of use cases, including:

1. Chatbots: ChatGPT can create chatbots that provide human-like responses to queries. The capability can be applied in settings where the model has conversations with its users.
2. Content generation: ChatGPT can generate text on a wide range of topics such as generating news articles, essays, and product descriptions. This makes it a valuable tool as it can produce high-quality written content.
3. Text classification: ChatGPT can categorize text into different classes. An example is sentiment analysis, which determines whether the emotional tone of a piece of text is positive, negative, or neutral. This can be useful in scenarios such as customer feedback analysis and social media sentiment analysis.
4. Productivity tool: ChatGPT has features such as text completion of partially written sentences or paragraphs, language translation between different languages, condensing long text into shorter versions, and text editing, for example, proofreading [5].

These use cases highlight the versatility and potential of ChatGPT and other LLMs to enhance productivity, streamline content creation, and improve the efficiency of text-related tasks in various domains. However, to ensure their responsible and ethical deployment in real-world applications, it is important to carefully consider the ethical implications and technological challenges associated with the use of language models like ChatGPT. There are, therefore, divergent discourses surrounding the use of ChatGPT and similar AI. For example, Italy banned ChatGPT citing privacy and data infringement concerns [6].

The main objective of this study, therefore, was to obtain a holistic view of the scholarly sentiment on ChatGPT. A bibliometric analysis was done using the Scopus database, and the identified publications were analyzed and visualized using Bibliometrix® and VOSViewer® tools. Specifically, the study sought to answer the following research question: What are the scholarly sentiments on and recommendations about ChatGPT?

The study contributes to the literature by identifying a possible inflection point in academia and society as a result of ChatGPT and other similar autonomous AI. The key findings point to an overall positive sentiment on the transformation that ChatGPT can bring to academia and society, particularly in stimulating creativity and enhancing productivity. The main concerns, which are limited, center around the likely negative impact on human cognitive and social capabilities.

The remainder of the study is structured as follows: The next section provides an overview of the methodology employed to conduct the study followed by the results and discussion. Finally, we discuss the contributions, limitations and conclusions of the study.

2   Research Methodology

Bibliometric analyses are increasingly popular as a means to identify trends in data, such as the influence of authors, the most cited articles, and top contributing countries [7]. In this study, we employed bibliometric analysis to explore the scholarly discourse on ChatGPT. The process involved collecting, analyzing and visualizing data, and then reporting the findings and inferences. For the data, we conducted a search of Scopus on 17th April 2023 using the keyword "ChatGPT". We retrieved 325 articles but since we preferred peer-reviewed publications, we narrowed down the list to include only refereed journal articles and conference publications. We also included journal articles in press. Additionally, we limited the search to only those in the English language resulting in 107 documents. A further review found 40 documents with missing abstracts or unrelated to ChatGPT leaving a total of 67 documents. Biblioshiny, an online interface for Bibliometrix®, was used to analyze and visually represent the bibliometric data. We also conducted sentiment analysis using three tools: ChatGPT, Atlas.ti [8], and manual thematic analysis. Figure 1 gives a visual representation of the method.

3   Results and Discussion

3.1   Main Information

Table 1. provides the main information in terms of the documents used in the scoping review. These documents, all written in 2023, were from 55 sources and comprised 67 documents. Of the 299 authors, 12 documents were single-authored, while the average number of co-authors per document was 4.71. 33.35% of collaborations involved international co-authorships, which shows the significance of global research collaboration. 95.59% of the documents were articles, while conference papers represented a smaller proportion at 4.41%.

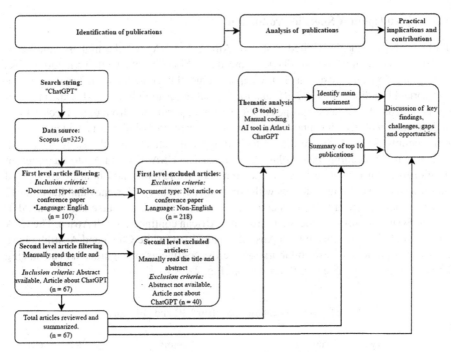

Fig. 1. Schema of identification of research articles and analysis of results

Table 1. Summary of the documents analyzed

Description	Results
Main information about data	
Timespan	2023
Sources (journals, books, etc.)	54
Documents	67
Authors	
Authors	293
Authors collaboration	
Single-authored docs	12
Co-authors per doc	4.63
International co-authorships %	31.34
Document types	
Article	64
Conference paper	3

3.2 Top 10 Country Specific Production

Table 2. shows that the United States of America (USA) has the highest number of authors (86) and total citations (TC), followed by China (40), the United Kingdom (UK) (30), India (18), and Australia (13). We also included the country's 2022 ranking in the Networked Readiness Index (NRI) and the Global Innovation Index (GII) which respectively indicate the country's propensity to exploit opportunities from digital technology, and the national drive for innovation. With the exception of India, it is evident that the same countries that leverage digital technology innovatively, are the same ones with authors who are leading the scholarly discourse. The USA, UK and Australia represent developed countries with well-developed markets, while India and China are considered multifaceted developing countries with emerging economies. Germany and Italy had 12 and 11 articles respectively. This context indicates a global discourse about ChatGPT. The analysis has only one document from the African continent, South Africa. The USA has four collaborations each with Australia and China, while China and Australia have three collaborations. These collaborations across continents are significant in advancing knowledge and expertise in different fields (Fig. 2).

Table 2. Top 10 countries and their NRI and GII positions

#	Country	Continent	Authors	TC	NRI	GII
1	USA	North America	86	15	1	1
2	China	East Asia and Pacific	40	0	23	21
3	UK	Europe	28	6	12	7
4	India	South Asia	18	0	61	42
5	Australia	East Asia and Pacific	13	0	14	19
6	Germany	Europe	12	0	8	12
7	Italy	Europe	11	3	32	31
8	Canada	North America	8	0	11	9
9	France	Europe	8	2	16	13
10	Austria	Europe and Central Asia	7	2	18	17

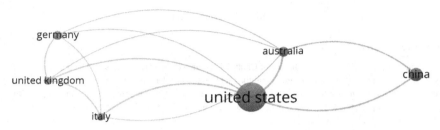

Fig. 2. World map of country collaborations

3.3 Top 10 Cited Articles

Table 3. summarizes the main points from the top 10 cited articles. ChatGPT has been applied in studies in various domains, including the natural sciences [9–11], finance [12], and software development [13]. It also improves teaching and learning [14], and in research, scientific [15] and academic writing quality. There are nonetheless concerns about the credibility and authenticity of generated content [16, 17]. ChatGPT shows great strength in generating ideas and identifying data for finance research but is weak when conducting literature reviews and developing appropriate testing frameworks [12]. In the health sciences, ChatGPT can accelerate scientific literature and generate research hypotheses. However, the health sciences also noted response biases, ethical concerns, outdated training data and low credibility, which may require new policies to prevent misuse. Taecharungroj [18] analyzed tweets about ChatGPT in the first month of its launch to reveal fears about job evolution, and ethical issues together with questions around the concept of Artificial General Intelligence.

Table 3. Top 10 articles

Summary of the top 10 articles
Gilson *et al.* [10] explored the potential of ChatGPT in medical education and knowledge assessments. They used ChatGPT to answer the United States Medical Licensing Examination (USMLE) and compared the responses with that of GPT-3 and InstructGPT. ChatGPT's performance was equivalent to a third-year level medical student score, which revealed implications for medical education and knowledge assessments. ChatGPT was, therefore, recommended as capable of positively augmenting medical education
Pavlik [16] explored the benefits and challenges of using NLP in academic writing. The results show that NLPs have the potential to improve academic writing quality and efficiency. However, the paper questioned the authenticity and credibility of academic writing if used. The paper proposes the need for ethical consideration and caution in the use of these tools for academic purposes
Salvagno *et al.* [15] suggested regulating the use of ChatGPT in scientific writing. The paper also noted that there are no papers written yet in the field of critical care. It recommends that AI chatbot tools should not replace human judgement and output, and highlights the ethical concerns that can arise from their use

(*continued*)

Table 3. (*continued*)

Summary of the top 10 articles
Dowling and Lucey [12] assessed the use of ChatGPT for finance research purposes. The benefits found were mainly from the generation of ideas and the identification of data. Its performance in literature reviews and developing appropriate testing frameworks was, however, not strong. To enhance the quality of ChatGPT outputs, the paper recommends including domain experts in the search process. The paper also highlights ethical concerns
Huh [11] compared the knowledge and interpretation between ChatGPT and medical students in a parasitology examination in Korea. ChatGPT's performance (60.8%) was lower than that of the medical students whose minimum score was 89%. The lower score could have been due to ChatGPT's inability to interpret tables, figures and graphs. Also, some of the data was available only in Korean or was not searchable online. The paper concludes that ChatGPT is not yet sufficient to be used by medical students
Cascella *et al.* [9] discussed the advantages and limitations of LLMs in healthcare. They recognized the benefits of NLP-based models in accelerating scientific literature, generating new research hypotheses and handling large datasets. They, however, also cautioned that some ChatGPT results are biased and untrue. They similarly raised ethical concerns
Lim *et al.* [14] argued for generative AI to be used as a transformative resource for teaching and learning. They argued that the ethical concerns can be addressed with policies and governing frameworks. They identified four paradoxes: generative AI as a 'friend' yet a 'foe', generative AI as 'capable' yet 'dependent', generative AI as 'accessible' yet 'restrictive', and generative AI getting 'popular' even when 'banned'
Ross *et al.* [13] investigated the application of LLMs in software development through their development and use as a conversational assistant. An experiment with 42 participants with varied levels of programming skills showed that LLMs enable emergent behaviors in a co-creative context. While the assistant did not always provide accurate answers, participants had a positive experience and increased productivity
Taecharungroj [18] analyzed tweets about ChatGPT in the first month of its launch. The topics being discussed were news, technology and reactions. The application of ChatGPT was identified in creative writing, essay writing, prompt writing, code writing, and answering questions. Four key issues were also raised: the evolution of jobs, a new technological landscape, questions around artificial general intelligence and ethical issues
Dwivedi *et al.* [17] recognized the use of tools like ChatGPT to increase productivity, teaching, learning and academic research. Their identified concerns included 'biases, out-of-date training data, and lack of transparency and credibility'. They suggested identifying and implementing relevant policies to prevent ChatGPT misuse

3.4 Top 10 Journals

Table 4. shows the top 10 journals revealing multiple disciplines and discourses on ChatGPT, demonstrating its transdisciplinary impact. This means that ChatGPT, as a specific type of AI, has enabled the creation of new bridges between disciplines with different notions of reality [19, 20].

Table 4. Top 10 most relevant journals

#	Journals	Publication focus	No
1	IEEE Transactions on Intelligent Vehicles	Intelligent vehicle research	3
2	Journal of Chemical Education	Chemical education research	3
3	Journal of University Teaching and Learning Practice	Teaching and learning in higher education	3
4	Scientific Reports	Multidisciplinary fields	3
5	CEUR Workshop Proceedings	Computer science	2
6	IEEE/CAA Journal of Automatica Sinica	Control and automation science	2
7	Innovations in Education and Teaching International	Education practices and research	2
8	International Journal of Environmental Research and Public Health	Environmental health	2
9	JMIR Medical Education	Medical education	2
10	Advanced Industrial and Engineering Polymer Research	Industrial and Engineering Polymer Research	1

3.5 Most Frequent Words

Figure 3 highlights the most frequently used words in ChatGPT research based on the keywords. The most frequently used word is 'artificial intelligence', indicating a strong association between ChatGPT and AI. There is also a human-centric focus, with the words 'human' and 'human' being predominant. Overall, there is an intersection between AI, data mining and ML with human-centric focus areas in various domains such as autonomous vehicles, public health, and biotechnology.

Fig. 3. Most frequent words

3.6 Thematic Map

The thematic map shown in Fig. 4 reveals the basic themes as 'chatbots' and 'chat generative pre-trained transformer'. This means that research related to these topics is widespread and well-established. Emerging and declining themes feature 'internet' and 'software' which suggests that interest in these areas may be evolving over time. In the motor themes, the non-technology aspects are 'human', 'ethical' and 'decision making', indicating that ongoing research around ChatGPT is focused on these fields. Finally, in the niche themes, 'autonomous vehicles' and 'computational linguistics' were identified. These topics are highly specialized and less commonly explored. Overall, the thematic map provides insights into the distribution and trends of research themes based on the bibliometric analysis conducted.

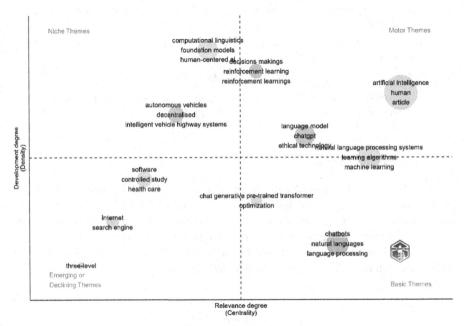

Fig. 4. Thematic map

3.7 Discussion of Findings

Using an emergent open coding regime [21, 22], the sentiments were divided into five themes: positive, negative, balanced, can improve, and risky. A further theme emerged during the analysis of recommendations from the papers. The collection of each sentiment theme and recommendation was then analyzed using thematic analysis in Atlas.ti® version 23 which now has AI thematic analysis built in. This means that we had three alternatives to run a thematic analysis: manually using open coding in Atlas.ti®, using the built-in AI model in Atlas.ti®, and using ChatGPT. For illustrative purposes, we ran all three tools on the positive sentiment theme to observe differences in the results which are shown in Fig. 5.

ChatGPT was able to take on whatever prompting it was given to generate a response, including adopting a critical realist, pragmatist, realist, or interpretivist philosophical lens and generating different comprehensive narratives according to the lens. The AI tool in Atlas.ti®, while useful was not sufficiently comprehensive compared with ChatGPT or the manual analysis. ChatGPT offered the most comprehensive alternatives and analysis as requested or prompted (Table 5.).

The remainder of the analysis followed the manual thematic analysis using an open coding regime (Fig. 5, Fig. 6, and Table 6.).

Table 5. Thematic analysis using different tools on the positive sentiment on ChatGPT

Manual in Atlas.ti®	AI model in Atlas.ti®	ChatGPT using GPT4
8 themes (codes)	**5 themes (codes)**	**7 themes (codes)**
Academic (9)	Productivity (7)	Education and learning (23)
Research improvement (8)	Assessment (6)	Productivity and efficiency (24)
Societal impact (7)	AI (5)	Creativity and originality (11)
Medical (5)	Business efficiency (3)	AI in healthcare and diagnostics (10)
Computer science (2)	Rhetoric (1)	AI limitations and ethical
Enthusiasm (4)		considerations (7)
Organizational efficiency (4)		AI in industry and manufacturing (5)
Manufacturing (3)		AI performance and comparisons (3)
Time: 55 min	Time: ~2 min	Time: Less than 1 min

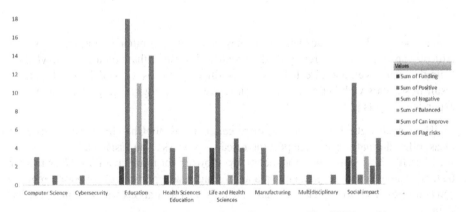

Fig. 5. Overall sentiment in scholarly discourse on ChatGPT by subject

Positive Sentiment. The greatest positive sentiment was for academia to co-exist with ChatGPT, particularly through creating and marking assessments from the teaching side and, from the students' side, creating better learning environments. This would

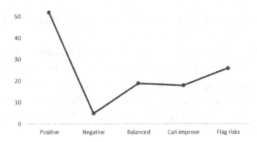

Fig. 6. Sentiment on ChatGPT

Table 6. Detailed sentiment on ChatGPT by subject

Subject area	Funding	Positive	Negative	Balanced	Can improve	Flag risks
Computer science		3			1	
Cybersecurity		1				
Education	2	18	4	11	5	14
Health sciences education	1	4		3	2	2
Life and health sciences	4	10		1	5	4
Manufacturing		4		1	3	
Multidisciplinary		1				1
Social impact	3	11	1	3	2	5
Grand total	**10**	**52**	**5**	**19**	**18**	**26**

reduce the workload for academics so they can focus on other important tasks like critically engaging in research or facilitating learning rather than imparting knowledge. If implemented well and directed towards positive outcomes, ChatGPT can, therefore, result in students with better character who have a more engaged experience and with expanded insights [23].

The second highest sentiment was on research, mainly for ChatGPT to catalyze better ideas, offer alternatives, and support the research process as an assistant.

ChatGPT is seen as a win for society by allowing for more creativity, allowing for better decisions and better judgement, and offering new opportunities for poorer regions and countries. That ChatGPT does make clear its own limitations was seen in a positive light.

There was also a general enthusiasm for ChatGPT to simply offer greater options across any sector regardless of discipline. These papers generally had an optimistic outlook.

The life and medical sectors welcomed ChatGPT for its ability to become a valuable team member that offers better diagnostics and enables the sector to be more efficient.

It can similarly assist with assessments having impressively passed several medical and life sciences exams.

The manufacturing and organizational sectors cited the power to increase productivity, while computer science noted an increase in creativity. ChatGPT also outperformed several existing computer science models.

Negative Sentiment. Contrastingly, the greatest negative sentiment was from the academic sector which expressed concerns about some contradictions in ChatGPT Responses, and it sometimes being unable to resolve the contradictions. This was mainly in the physics subject. It was also claimed that ChatGPT did not exhibit critical thinking capabilities.

The other negative sentiment was an apprehension of the social and cognitive repercussions whereby ChatGPT would weaken human moral judgement and critical thinking, and eventually supplant human agency.

Balanced Sentiment. The balanced call was mainly to conduct due diligence with the results that ChatGPT offers, and to be intentional about ensuring that humans take the lead in the use of ChatGPT. This includes remaining aware of the restrictions around what is being done and taking note of what humans are losing by using the tool.

Flag Risks. The greatest risk flagged was the potential loss of human cognition in terms of a reduction in the ability to be confident about decisions being made stemming from an over-reliance on ChatGPT. Moreover, ChatGPT was feared to threaten privacy and security by making available what should be hidden. Moreover, with a reliance on the tool, existing social traditions are at risk, and these could threaten society as it is understood today.

The other risks included ChatGPT manipulating users through false information and even disinformation, especially in instances where the context is not well understood.

Room for Improvement. The areas for improvement concerned ChatGPT slowing down as more demands are made on it and users needing to be trained to use the tool. Currently, the tool is used without much guidance being provided.

It was also noted that there should be ways in which human existence can be integrated with ChatGPT, which can include training on its usage. It was suggested that what users do with the platform should remain private which would prevent educators from seeing what students have used the platform for.

Sentiment Recommendations. The recommendations were mainly from the academic sector to use ChatGPT as an opportunity for educational reform. This includes rethinking what critical thinking, plagiarism and even assessment mean. A further academic recommendation was to develop clear guidelines for both educators and students on its usage or misuse. There was also a call for publishing houses to reconsider their hard stance on content that is co-authored with ChatGPT in this new era.

The second theme for recommendations was to train users and make ChatGPT a digital literacy. This includes how to prompt ChatGPT for better results and to ensure that the tool is used in an ethical manner.

To avoid ethical issues, it was recommended that all results should be cross-checked and re-evaluated by humans, and to continually monitor humans to measure the extent to which they are affected by the usage of the tool. It was also recommended that the training datasets of ChatGPT need to be improved to prevent bias.

It was finally recommended that ChatGPT be used as a valid tool to make the world a better place by contributing to the Sustainable Development Goals and making health care more accessible.

Limitations. The study was limited in that it performed the sentiment analysis using the abstracts of publications from only one database. The analysis can be extended to more databases and include all the content of a publication.

4 Conclusions

The study investigated the scholarly discourse on ChatGPT since its inception using a bibliometric review and thematic analysis. The reality of the transition from one million "early adopters" in five days to an "early majority" of 100 million users within two months indicates that ChatGPT ushered an inflection point in society [24].

The main findings from the thematic analysis on sentiments towards ChatGPT revealed a widespread positive sentiment about the tool, mainly related to its strong potential in academia, society, and practice to enhance productivity and innovation. This means that educators will need to focus more on being facilitators of learning rather than providers of fundamental knowledge. The move to facilitation has wide-reaching implications for educational pedagogy. It also means that scholars have a broader set of tools to engage in knowledge contribution. In practice, it reveals the greater potential for higher productivity, diagnostic capability and efficient decision-making. It is noticeable that the countries that are driving innovation are the same ones that took the lead in the discourse on ChatGPT. The inclination to innovation has been associated with a higher positive sentiment [25].

The negative sentiments, while limited, underscore the contradictions in some of the responses from ChatGPT and the possible damage to human cognition. The call is for humans to co-exist with ChatGPT with humans providing critical input at key decision points to avoid bias and to ensure the productive usage of ChatGPT. Training on ChatGPT is also called for. This means a transdisciplinary effort from different disciplines is needed to engage with the ethical concerns that are raised, particularly the weakening of human agency through the dependence on the tool, the evasion of privacy and accountability, the loss of jobs, and a widening social divide.

The study contributes to the literature in identifying the emergence of ChatGPT as an inflection point, based on the evidence of the exponential growth of adopters, as well as the overwhelmingly positive sentiment about it. The inflection point is a "good thing" only if academia, society and organizations are intentional about making the world a better place. The implications of ChatGPT for practice, society and academia are, therefore, dependent on how the different sectors respond to it. We recommend progressive and dynamic process-based policies [26, 27] on the use of ChatGPT and a transdisciplinary engagement on the implications of the tool and AI. The question remains as to whether there is a social structural appetite for such reforms.

References

1. OpenAI: OpenAI. https://openai.com/. Accessed 23 Apr 2023
2. What is ChatGPT, DALL-E, and generative AI?—McKinsey. https://www.mckinsey.com/featured-insights/mckinsey-explainers/what-is-generative-ai. Accessed 17 Apr 2023
3. Iskender, A.: Holy or unholy? Interview with open AI's ChatGPT. Eur. J. Tourism Res. 34, 3414–3414 (2023). https://doi.org/10.54055/ejtr.v34i.3169
4. Bhattacharya, K., Bhattacharya, A.S., Bhattacharya, N., Yagnik, V.D., Garg, P., Kumar, S.: ChatGPT in surgical practice—a new kid on the block. Indian J. Surg. (2023). https://doi.org/10.1007/s12262-023-03727-x
5. Adriana, H.: Unpacking ChatGPT: the pros and cons of AI's hottest language model. https://www.ie.edu/insights/articles/unpacking-chatgpt-the-pros-and-cons-of-ais-hottest-language-model/. Accessed 20 Apr 2023
6. McCallum, S.: ChatGPT banned in Italy over privacy concerns - BBC News (2023). https://www.bbc.com/news/technology-65139406
7. Aria, M., Cuccurullo, C.: bibliometrix: an R-tool for comprehensive science mapping analysis. J. Inform. 11, 959–975 (2017). https://doi.org/10.1016/j.joi.2017.08.007
8. TLAS.ti: ATLAS.ti. https://atlasti.com. Accessed 24 Apr 2023
9. Cascella, M., Montomoli, J., Bellini, V., Bignami, E.: Evaluating the feasibility of ChatGPT in healthcare: an analysis of multiple clinical and research scenarios. J. Med. Syst. 47, 33 (2023). https://doi.org/10.1007/s10916-023-01925-4
10. Gilson, A., et al.: How does ChatGPT perform on the United States medical licensing examination? The implications of large language models for medical education and knowledge assessment. JMIR Med. Educ. 9, e45312 (2023). https://doi.org/10.2196/45312
11. Huh, S.: Are ChatGPT's knowledge and interpretation ability comparable to those of medical students in Korea for taking a parasitology examination?: a descriptive study. J. Educ. Eval. Health Prof. 20, 1 (2023). https://doi.org/10.3352/jeehp.2023.20.1
12. Dowling, M., Lucey, B.: ChatGPT for (finance) research: the Bananarama conjecture. Financ. Res. Lett. 53, 103662 (2023). https://doi.org/10.1016/j.frl.2023.103662
13. Ross, S.I., Martinez, F., Houde, S., Muller, M., Weisz, J.D.: The programmer's assistant: conversational interaction with a large language model for software development. In: Proceedings of the 28th International Conference on Intelligent User Interfaces, pp. 491–514. Association for Computing Machinery, New York (2023). https://doi.org/10.1145/3581641.3584037
14. Lim, W.M., Gunasekara, A., Pallant, J.L., Pallant, J.I., Pechenkina, E.: Generative AI and the future of education: Ragnarök or reformation? A paradoxical perspective from management educators. Int. J. Manage. Educ. 21, 100790 (2023). https://doi.org/10.1016/j.ijme.2023.100790
15. Salvagno, M., Taccone, F.S., Gerli, A.G.: Can artificial intelligence help for scientific writing? Crit. Care 27, 75 (2023). https://doi.org/10.1186/s13054-023-04380-2
16. Pavlik, J.V.: Collaborating With ChatGPT: considering the implications of generative artificial intelligence for journalism and media education. Journalism Mass Commun. Educ. 78, 84–93 (2023). https://doi.org/10.1177/10776958221149577
17. Dwivedi, Y.K., et al.: "So what if ChatGPT wrote it?" Multidisciplinary perspectives on opportunities, challenges and implications of generative conversational AI for research, practice and policy. Int. J. Inf. Manage. 71, 102642 (2023). https://doi.org/10.1016/j.ijinfomgt.2023.102642
18. Taecharungroj, V.: "What can ChatGPT do?" Analyzing early reactions to the innovative AI Chatbot on Twitter. Big Data Cogn. Comput. 7, 35 (2023). https://doi.org/10.3390/bdcc7010035

19. Thompson Klein, J.: Prospects for transdisciplinarity. Futures **36**, 515–526 (2004). https://doi.org/10.1016/j.futures.2003.10.007
20. Twinomurinzi, H., Mhlongo, S., Bwalya, K.J., Bokaba, T., Mbeya, S.: Multidisciplinarity in data science curricula. In: African Conference on Information Systems and Technology, pp. 1–8. Kennesaw State University (2022)
21. Glaser, B.G., Strauss, A.: The Discovery of Grounded Theory: Strategies for Qualitative Research. Aldine, Chicago (1967)
22. Owoseni, A., Twinomurinzi, H.: The dynamic capabilities of small and medium - scale enterprises using mobile apps in Lagos, Nigeria. Electron. J. Info. Syst. Dev. Countries **85**, 1–14 (2018). https://doi.org/10.1002/isd2.12061
23. Crawford, J., Cowling, M., Allen, K.-A.: Leadership is needed for ethical ChatGPT: character, assessment, and learning using artificial intelligence (AI). J. Univ. Teach. Learn. Pract. **20**, 2 (2023). https://doi.org/10.53761/1.20.3.02
24. Rogers, E.M.: Diffusion of Innovations (1995). Citeulike-article-id: 126680
25. Saura, J.R., Palacios-Marqués, D., Ribeiro-Soriano, D.: Exploring the boundaries of open innovation: evidence from social media mining. Technovation **119**, 102447 (2023). https://doi.org/10.1016/j.technovation.2021.102447
26. Xivuri, K., Twinomurinzi, H.: A habermasian approach to fair processes in AI algorithms. In: Jembere, E., Gerber, A.J., Viriri, S., Pillay, A. (eds.) SACAIR 2021. CCIS, vol. 1551, pp. 335–343. Springer, Cham (2022). https://doi.org/10.1007/978-3-030-95070-5_22
27. Xivuri, K., Twinomurinzi, H.: A systematic review of fairness in artificial intelligence algorithms. In: Dennehy, D., Griva, A., Pouloudi, N., Dwivedi, Y.K., Pappas, I., Mäntymäki, M. (eds.) I3E 2021. LNCS, vol. 12896, pp. 271–284. Springer, Cham (2021). https://doi.org/10.1007/978-3-030-85447-8_24

The Impact of 4IR Mobile Technologies on Small Businesses in Urban Areas of Pretoria in South Africa

Maria van Wyk and Samuel Ssemugabi[✉] [iD]

University of South Africa, Pretoria, South Africa
ssemus@unisa.ac.za

Abstract. The Fourth Industrial Revolution (4IR) has caused significant disruptions in various aspects of life globally. This pervasive influence of disruptive technologies has compelled reconsideration of the nature of organisations and how they create value. The true potential of 4IR lies in harnessing technologies that can empower a more individuals to positively impact their families, organisations, and communities; with the ultimate goal of building an interconnected society that generates value. The growth and expansion of 4IR has both positive and negative impacts on global technological connectivity services, including South Africa. Connectivity services are crucial for facilitating the flow of digital information and physical products for organisations, including small businesses, which are often the backbone of global economies. The main objective of this study was to investigate the impact of 4IR mobile technologies on small businesses in urban areas of Pretoria in South Africa. Using convenience sampling, data was collected from 35 business owners using interviews with thematic analysis employed to analyse the data. Four key themes emerged in relation to the impact of 4IR mobile technologies on small businesses in urban areas of South Africa. These themes were: the impact/influence of mobile technology, the benefits of mobile technologies, the challenges facing mobile technologies, and knowledge about the Fourth Industrial Revolution.

Keywords: Small businesses · mobile technologies · Social media · Fourth Industrial Revolution · 4IR · South Africa

1 Introduction and Background

The Fourth Industrial Revolution (4IR) is a technology that has disrupted many lives worldwide [1]. The emergence of 4IR and its utilisation of converging technologies to create an inclusive, human-centred future has forced us to reassess the development of countries, the essence of organisations in value creation and the impact it has on human life. According to the World Economic Forum [2], the real opportunities lie in looking into technologies that could enable the most significant number of people to positively

---

This paper is partly based on unpublished student's work

© The Author(s), under exclusive license to Springer Nature Switzerland AG 2023
A. Gerber and M. Coetzee (Eds.): SAICSIT 2023, CCIS 1878, pp. 273–288, 2023.
https://doi.org/10.1007/978-3-031-39652-6_18

impact their families, organisations and communities. The growth and expansion of 4IR globally and in South Africa, could affect technological connectivity services that are crucial for facilitating the flow of digital information and physical products [3].

According to Mbonyane and Ladzani [4], small businesses are the backbone of many economies. The evolution of 41R fourth industrial revolution has brought advanced and virtual technologies to enhance business services and economic growth [1, 4, 5]. Mobile technologies are considered key drivers of 4IR [6], as small businesses are increasingly relying on them to find solutions to their problems. The use of 4IR mobile technologies is forcing both large and small businesses to look at how they conduct their business [1, 6]. Although South African small businesses could use mobile technologies to increase their business success, business owners are unaware of the many opportunities they afford [3]. These 4IR technologies connect, analyse, and respond to information, allowing organisations, customers, and the public to be more responsive, flexible and intellectual. Using social media, small businesses can advertise and market their products and services online to increase their income and render excellent customer service. This would also enable small businesses and their customers to become interconnected, facilitating the creation of a connected society and building inclusive and equitable solutions [4, 7, 8]. While manual businesses, from small to corporate levels, can struggle to sustain themselves, the integration of 4IR in the form of mobile technologies allows businesses to adapt and be more flexible in the way they operate and connect with their customers [9]. According to Muriuki [10], small businesses need to adopt mobile technologies, to reform their operations and realise a return on investment. Mobile technologies are cost-effective and can lead to quick business growth [11]. The main aim of this study is to explore the impact of 4IR mobile technologies on small businesses in urban areas of Pretoria in South Africa.

2   Literature Review

Each successive industrial revolution represents an improvement over its predecessor. The shift in 4IRs has significantly impacted different sectors and human lives [12]. It has impacted how people work, the economy, and our society interacts, as it is a combination of different technologies on the grey lines of physical, biological, and digital spheres. This has impacted positively on small businesses through different aspects of using technology, such as customers shopping online [4]. Integrating mobile and 4IR technologies makes life easier, since people carry this device wherever they go. The use of 4IR technologies such as AI, IoT, 3D printing, and Blockchain in different sectors in South Africa has made significant changes in all sectors of business, as well as economies, and social life [3].

2.1   Fourth Industrial Revolution (4IR)

Klaus Schwab, executive chairman of the World Economic Forum, coined the term 'Fourth industrial revolution", abbreviated to 4IR, to describe the exponential increase in technological developments that impact how we work, the economy, and our society. This technological revolution is characterised by the convergence of digital, physical, and biological technologies [1]. The Fourth Industrial Revolution (4IR) builds upon and extends the concepts of the Third Industrial Revolution (3IR). The 3IR, also known as the Digital Revolution or the Information Age, refers to that period of technological transformation, which occurred in the late 20th century with the widespread adoption of digital technologies, particularly computers and the internet. The 4IR is a technological revolution, characterised by the convergence of digital, physical, and biological technologies [1]. According to Schwab [1] and Moloi [13] what distinguishes 4IR from the previous revolutions are the systems, velocity, scope and impact. The transformation to 4IR has significantly enhanced the capability to store, process, and transmit information in digital form. It has reshaped education, government commerce and every aspect of life [14]. The component of 4IR include artificial intelligence (AI), cloud computing, Internet of Things (IoT), big data analytics, biotechnology, and genetic engineering [15].

2.2 Small Business in South Africa

The definition of a small business varies from country to country. The World Bank defines a small business according to the number of employees, total assets, and annual revenue [16, 17]. Adegbite and Govender [18] contend that a small business should have 10 to 20 employees. However, Serumaga-Zake and Van der Poll [5] state that small businesses could have up to 250 employees. The Republic of South Africa (1996) in the National Small Business Act, No 102 of 1996, published in the Government Gazette No.-17612, of 27 November 1996, defines a *small business* as one with less than 50 employees, privately owned and with a turnover, depending on the Sector; of between 2 and 25 million rand annually [19].

Small businesses form a vital part of the economic growth in South Africa, alleviating poverty, and enhancing job creation [20]. South Africa should adopt 4IR technologies, such as mobile connectivity, the Internet of Things (IoT), and artificial intelligence (AI); this author, Alexander [20], further maintained small businesses play a significant role in the growth and sustainability of a developing economy.

2.3 Improving Connectivity in Small Businesses Through 4IR Mobile Technology

Connectivity is an indispensable characteristic of 4IR mobile technology, serving as a fundamental aspect that enables seamless communication and interaction across diverse platforms and networks. Mobile technologies include devices such as smartphones, tablets, laptops and others that can be accessed when connected to the internet [21]. The user can access nearly all services that were not easily accessed from a fixed-line environment anywhere and at any time [22].

The advent of mobility in networks has paved the way for the development of 4G and 5G networks, which empower users to stay seamlessly connected to the internet [23]. The inherent features of mobile technologies provide numerous avenues for small businesses to enhance their services, for instance: mobile payments, real-time location tracking, mobile banking, mobile advertising, and mobile shopping, while opening up possibilities to improve offerings and engage with their customers in innovative ways [24].

2.4 Opportunities and Challenges of Mobile Technologies in Small Business

Mobile technologies drive the success of a small business in different ways [7]. They simplify administration tasks, like access to financial records and business documents, should the business owner require it. They also make marketing and communication easier and more affordable. Adopting mobile technology in small businesses increases their success [25]. Furthermore, they allow businesses to increase productivity and enhance collaboration with colleagues and with management [26].

Although people find mobile technologies easy to use, it comes with specific challenges. Some challenges users face with mobile technology are sharing personal data and the security of their information when they make online purchases and payments [7, 27]. Schwab [1] states, that ensuring the security of personal information is a significant challenge. Human ability can be affected when it is continuously connected to smartphones or other mobile devices. For example, employees may not participate in meaningful conversations as much as they used to. Users might not be focused and opt to spend time on their social media platforms and personal activities instead of the doing the work they are supposed to do.

2.5 Social Media Platforms to Be Used by Small Businesses

Social media can be defined as a group of internet-based applications that build on the ideological and technological foundations of Web 2.0 and allow the creation of the exchange of user-generated content [28]. However, Hruska and Maresova [29], define *social media* as content from different individuals and organisations. Social media allows small business owners to change the way they do business. Social media allows these owners to communicate directly with their customers [30]. Customers and small business owners can communicate and collaborate on social media networks [31]. Customers may also provide feedback on products and services, and the Company may make changes to products and services based on customer feedback. Different companies can use social media to recruit and hire personnel. For example, LinkedIn, Facebook, and YouTube are among the most professional hiring companies [32, 33].

2.6 Key 4IR Mobile Technologies Utilised in Small Businesses

Small business owners can implement mobile technologies to make online purchases, advertising, online payments, stock ordering, and stock-taking much effectively and efficiently than in the period before 4IR [34]. For example, using social media platforms in small businesses assists with marketing the business services, resulting in increased number of customers [35]. In addition, individuals can share the content to communicate and share their ideas. For instance, social media platforms provide connectivity between consumers and organisations. Businesses can use these platforms like LinkedIn, Twitter, Facebook, YouTube, and WhatsApp to attract customers [36, 37]. Social media has overwhelming benefits that support small business' growth and competitiveness [38].

2.7   The Impact of 4IR on Small Businesses

The Fourth Industrial Revolution (4IR) has caused significant disruptions in various industries' business landscapes [39]. In the perspective of [1], customers used to physically visit stores to make purchases before the advent of the Internet. However, with the advancement of ICTs, especially 4IR technologies, customers can now conveniently shop online from anywhere and at any time [40, 41]. As posted by Sutherland [42] businesses have had to change their customer interactions and marketing strategies to align with this shift. Therefore, it has become imperative for businesses to embrace, adapt, and evolve with the 4IR technologies to remain competitive in today's market.

2.8   Digital Transformation and Small Businesses

Digital transformation (DT) is a multifaceted phenomenon that affects all areas of human activity, including politics, economy, technology, and society [43]. Many small businesses are embracing DT as a new approach, and this is having a positive impact on their performance and productivity while increasing their competitive advantage [44]. Digital transformation not only makes a business more efficient, but it also provides customers with more seamless and intuitive experiences that include endless choices, lower prices, and fast delivery [45].

Unemployment is one of the biggest challenges for young people, both globally and in African countries, especially South Africa. Economic development and job creation have become the main concerns of young people, and the social development and prospects of young people are grim [46]. In this era of 4IR, technology entrepreneurship and the development of small business are seen as channels for promoting sustainable economic growth and self-employment in developing countries. For young people, self-employment offers a dynamic path to income, growth, and human capital development [46].

3   Research Methodology

The main aim of the study was to explore the impact of 4IR mobile technology on small business owners in urban areas of Pretoria in South Africa. To meet this purpose, the researchers adopted qualitative research approach to understand this situation through participants' perceptions. According to Bengtsson [47] the qualitative approach provides detailed information on the phenomenon studied based on people's experiences and interpretations reflecting real life. This encourages participants to broaden their perspectives by describing the context of the study. The research design was a case study. According to Yin [48] a case study seeks to answer the "how" or "why" questions. Case studies in qualitative research focus on explaining or examining situations in everyday life and can be enriched by ensuring their validity and reliability [49, 50].

3.1   Research Method

Interviews were used to collect data in the study area, Pretoria, South Africa. While interviews can be conducted in both structured and semi-structured formats, each having its own advantages [51]. This study primarily employed semi-structured interviews about the impact of 4IR mobile technologies on small businesses in urban areas in Pretoria, South Africa. The utilisation of semi-structured open-ended interviews allowed for a flexible and dynamic approach to data collection [52].

3.2 Data Collection and Sampling

One of the researchers conducted face-to-face interviews with the 35 small business owners located in urban areas in Pretoria. The researcher arranged appointments with the small business owners to invite them to participate in the study. Each interview lasted for 15 to 32 min. During the interviews the researcher requested permission to voice record it for the purpose of data collection. Convenience sampling was used to recruit participants. Convenience sampling is a method of randomly selecting members of population, in this case the public, who meet certain criteria, such as geographic proximity, accessibility and readiness to participate in research at any given time [53].

3.3 Data Analysis Procedure

The recorded data from the 35 participants was transcribed using the Microsoft's Windows Speech Recognition tool. Thematic analysis was employed according to the steps recommended by Braun and Clarke [54], namely, (i) Data familiarisation, (ii) Generation of initial codes, (iii) Identification of themes, (iv) Reviewing themes, (v) Defining and naming themes, and (vi) Producing the report.

3.4 Research Ethics

Ethics clearance from the Ethics Committee of the College of Science, Engineering and Technology of the University of South Africa was granted before data was collected from the participants. This meant that all participants would participate in the study voluntarily and their identity would be kept confidential throughout the study. Personal information or identity were kept confidential in line with the published ethics rules of the University of South Africa. All participants were required to sign a consent form, giving them guidelines about the subject under investigation. They were, however, allowed to withdraw or refuse to participate at any point without negative consequences.

4   Findings and Discussion

4.1 Demographic Information

The following subsections provide the data analysis of the participant's demographic details.

Business Types. These included: Hair salon/Beauty salon, Printing and Internet café, Food and restaurants, Bakery, Clothing shop, Cell phone shop, and others, in descending order of frequency, with the Hair salon/Beauty salon category making up 23%, followed by the Printing and Internet café category with 14%, while the Cell phone shop category made up only 3%. The unspecified category (others) was 34% of the participating small businesses.

Business Employees. Of the 35 businesses, a significant percentage, 83%, of the small businesses in Pretoria's urban areas employed between 1 and 10 staff members. This was followed by 14% between 11 and 50 workers. Only 3% of these businesses had over 50 employees.

Mobile Devices. All businesses that participated used mobile devices. These included mobile phones or smartphones, laptops, tablets, smartwatches, GPS, and others. Smartphone use outweighed other devices (35%), followed by laptops at 13%.

Platforms Used. According to the data collected, the small businesses used Google Maps, social media, QR code readers, contactless payments (tapping), and electronic fund transfer (EFT) technologies to provide services, advertise their businesses, and sell products. Figure 1 shows the proportion of different types of Social Media Platforms used by the participants' small businesses. The results show that most businesses used Facebook (34%) to market their products and services, which had the highest score.

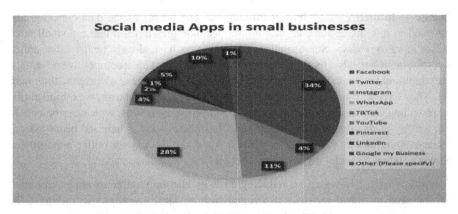

Fig. 1. Social media platforms used by small businesses

WhatsApp followed with a score of 28%, and Instagram and Google My Business (GMB) with scores of 11% and 10% respectively, whereas other social media platforms scored between 1% and 5%. This finding shows that the majority (64%, calculated by adding 34% and 28%) of small businesses in Pretoria adopt Facebook and WhatsApp when operating their businesses.

4.2 Themes

The main aim of this research study was to explore the impact of 4IR mobile technologies on small businesses in urban areas in Pretoria, South Africa. Figure 2 shows the themes that emerged from the analysis of the data collected. The main themes were: Influence of mobile technology, Benefits of mobile technologies, Challenges of mobile technologies,

Knowledge of the Fourth industrial revolution (4IR). Each of the themes is discussed in the following subsections.

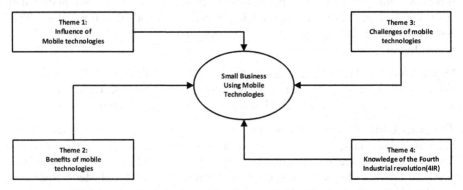

Fig. 2. Themes that emerged from the analysis of the data collected

Theme 1: Influence of Mobile Technologies. The results of the data collected and analysed in this theme indicate that mobile technologies have influenced small businesses in various ways. Some small business owners have already realised that online services, including advertising and online transactions, provide a competitive advantage over traditional methods of doing business, helping small businesses to expend their market. They have also noticed that mobile technologies simplify business administration by providing easy access to documentation and financial records, which can be beneficial for day-to-day operations. For example, businesses such as hair and beauty salons are leveraging mobile technologies through Apps like Booksy for online appointment booking and using social media for reaching a larger target audience.

Additionally, businesses are reducing costs by enabling online meetings, eliminating the need for travel expenses associated with physical meetings. According to the responses of some participants, the influence of mobile technologies in their businesses has had a positive impact since it simplified their businesses practice by enabling them to receive customer comments, complaints, and feedback.

P11 said:

"As far as I know, technology evolves rapidly which means business owners need to budget for upgrading mobile devices". These devices can be very costly". P27 added that *"Implementing mobile payments simplifies transactions as some customers prefer to not carry cash".* In addition, P20 said *"Hair and beauty salon businesses are using the Booksy app for online booking appointments".* Furthermore, P31 stated that *"The use of social media helps my business to reach a bigger target group".* Added to that, P29 stated *"Mobile technologies simplify my businesses administration".*

In summary, this indicated that the influence of 4IR mobile technologies on small businesses in urban areas of Pretoria, South Africa, included improved service delivery, competitive advantages, simplified administration, mobile payments, online bookings, social media, and cost reduction. This meant that small businesses had already been connected to their customers at the time of the research. These perspectives align with those of [36, 55], who highlighted that modern information and communication technologies (ICTs) empower small business employees to collaborate seamlessly, regardless of their physical location, thereby enhancing the potential for improved customer service. Furthermore, they argue that popular social media platforms like Facebook, Twitter, LinkedIn, and YouTube serve as effective communication and marketing tools.

Theme 2: Benefits of Mobile Technologies. This theme highlights the benefits of integrating mobile technology into small businesses. According to the results of this theme, most participants identified a number of advantages of adopting mobile technologies in small businesses. Participants were of the view that the use of mobile technologies streamlines communication with clients and facilitates more efficient collaboration between teams and clients, resulting in increased productivity. For example, P04 stated that:

> "I prefer the use of mobile technologies as it simplifies communication with my clients and allows my business to be more productive", and P6 was of the view that "The use of mobile technologies allows collaboration between teams and their clients". Furthermore, P33 added that "mobile technologies assist my business to reduce costs as I can attend online meetings instead of driving or flying to my meetings".

Another advantage was that mobile technologies such as virtual banking tools, simplified mobile payments while online ordering through mobile applications enables businesses to offer convenient and efficient services to customers, enhancing their overall experience. P13 said:

> "I only know that I can use mobile technology payments to make life easier for the customers".

In addition, P26 stated that:

> "With the use of mobile devices, my customers can place their orders online from a safe environment. Customer can track their order online until the order has been delivered".

Another advantage was that mobile devices also enabled small businesses to reach new customers and expand their target market through easy advertising and promotion on social media, i.e., digital marketing, as well as capturing customer data for specialised marketing efforts. This provides convenience and flexibility to small business owners, allowing them to access business information, check competition marketing materials, and manage their business from anywhere, providing greater flexibility and convenience in managing their operations. P22 mentioned that:

> *"My business can reach new customers with the use of mobile devices". "I can expand my target market".*

Furthermore, P35 added:

> *"I like the convenience of using mobile devices. I can use it from anywhere to access my business information and to check up on the competition marketing materials"*

Moreover, mobile technologies have an advantage that enable customers to place orders online and make payments through mobile applications, providing convenience and safety in the era of 4IR technologies. In addition, businesses and the customers are getting more innovative. For example, P17 stated:

> *"Implementing mobile payments simplifies transactions as some customers prefer to not carry cash" and P08 said "The use of suitable technologies and tools to drive my bakery business. My website allows clients to virtually bake their cake, and cupcakes and select the assorted colours, sizes, and type before they place their order. This is a form of innovation by both my business and the customers".*

Based on the information provided in the last two paragraphs, this theme emphasises the benefits of 4IR mobile technologies in terms of enhanced communication and digitisation, increased productivity, innovation, streamlined payments, and improved flexibility and convenience in business operations. These findings align with several previous studies, such as [15, 21] and [56]. For instance, Gumbi and Twinomurinzi [56] also highlight that 4IR technologies can enhance productivity, quality, delivery, and flexibility of small businesses. Additionally, lsulaimani and Islam [15] propose that innovation is achievable through the synergistic utilisation of various 4IR technological factors.

Theme 3: Challenges of Mobile Technologies. This theme addressed the challenges faced by small business owners, including affordability issues related to the cost of enablers for internet access such as smartphones and data plans. Insufficient funds may also hinder their ability to provide adequate training for employees to understand how to use technology effectively. Moreover, limited funds may result in failure to implement online marketing strategies to stay competitive and may also hinder the adoption of online booking systems and digital payment methods. P03 stated:

> *"Training in new technologies can be very expensive. Not all businesses can afford to upskill their employees when the companies are running on a tight budget".*

In addition, P20 stated that:

> *"Challenges the business is facing are some of the customers who prefer the traditional way of bookings. They refuse to use the online booking system. These same*

customers prefer to pay in cash which is a risk for the business because of theft and robbing of businesses and their customers".

Furthermore, the lack of technological skills and e-skills among employees can result in revenue losses, and some employees may be resistant to working with new technologies due to fear of the unknown. Small businesses are also likely to be concerned about cybercrime that may pose risks to their business or customers. Additionally, poor internet connectivity can be a challenge as it results in unreliable internet access, hindering businesses from operating optimally and conducting online transactions. P04 said:

"The fear of cybercrime and fake proof of payments and fraud. The business did experience fake proof of payment and lost a lot of money". P09 stated that "The cost of mobile devices is expensive. Should they break or get damaged, it can be costly to fix it and, in some instances, replace the device", and P12 said "Employees who are afraid of working with new technologies or different devices. ..... Fear of the unknown". Further to that P08 stated that "Due to the poor internet connection, some users prefer to go to the shop to make their purchases".

In summary, this theme highlights the challenges faced by small businesses in urban areas of Pretoria, South Africa, in adopting and utilising 4IR mobile technologies. These challenges included affordability and cost, technological skills and fear of the unknown, cybersecurity concerns, safety concerns, poor internet connection, hiring skilled personnel, competition and marketing, and employee retention and upskilling. Addressing these challenges would require strategies such as financial planning, training and upskilling programs, cybersecurity measures, robust internet connectivity, and marketing efforts to ensure successful adoption and implementation of 4IR mobile technologies for small businesses in Pretoria. Our findings are corroborated by several other authors, including [15, 18]. For instance, Alsulaimani and Islam [15] discovered that establishing a digital-based business environment can be challenging due to factors such as inadequate internet connectivity and lack of expertise in machine learning and data science. In addition, they discovered that lack of awareness and training to enhance in-house e-skills pose a challenge for small businesses. Furthermore, in their research on the readiness of Botswana's workers for Industrial 4.0, Muchuti and Ebewo [57] found that one specific construct of the Unified Theory of Acceptance and Use of Technology (UTAUT), namely Facilitating Conditions (FC), negatively influenced individuals' intention to adapt to new technologies, including those associated with 4IR. This negative impact was attributed to factors such as insufficient infrastructure for upskilling or reskilling employees by businesses.

Theme 4: Knowledge of the Fourth Industrial Revolution (4IR). This theme highlights the insufficient awareness and knowledge of 4IR technology among certain business owners and their employees. It is evident that they lack familiarity with 4IR components such as artificial intelligence (AI), machine learning, cloud computing, virtualisation, 5G, Internet of Things (IoT), drones, and robotics. Furthermore, some participants were unaware that they were already utilising 4IR technologies. However, there were also participants who recognised the ongoing evolution and the impact of digital transformation on business operations. P1 said:

> "*I know the technologies help human beings to improve their life. I know of Artificial intelligence (AI) and machine learning*".

P3 added that: "*I know about Cloud computing, 5G, and virtualisation. I am currently using virtualisation in my business to assist my customers*". P14 was of the same sentiment and said "*I know about Cloud computing, 5G, and virtualisation. I am currently using virtualisation in my business to aid my customers*".

Furthermore, P02 said:

> "*I would say my knowledge of 4IR is limited. I recently learned that I've been using 4IR technology and was not even aware of it*".

P31 added: "*I believe the Internet of Things (IoT) would be suitable for my business as it is an interconnected web of devices*".

Overall, the findings of this theme suggest that there is awareness and some adoption of 4IR technologies in small businesses in urban areas of Pretoria, South Africa, but there is also a recognition of limited knowledge and potential for further exploration and utilisation of these technologies. These assertions are consistent with the conclusions of several studies, including those by [17, 18, 36]. For instance, Adegbite and Govender [18] argued that SMEs in Africa must capitalise on the 4IR opportunities to expand their businesses, adopt new strategies, and swiftly adapt to digitalisation, computerisation, robotics, and advanced technology across all their operations.

5   Limitations and Future Research

This study was limited to small business owners in urban areas of Pretoria in South Africa. All 35 participants that were invited agreed to participate in the face-to-face interviews. In future research, the population and sample size can be increased to a larger scale, in a similar study, to bring awareness to other small business owners in the rest of South Africa. The research could be extended to different cities in South Africa. This is because many small business owners are aware of 4IR, but they are not utilising its emerging technologies to their full potential, as stated in Theme 4. The findings of the study may be used for future research to bring awareness of the use of mobile technologies in small businesses owners in rural, semi, and peri-urban areas so as to sustain their businesses. They also provide a business opportunity for training small-scale business owners in the application of 41R to business success and increased profitability, particularly in the light of some comments from participants regarding challenges they face, as well as the known phenomenon of rapid updates to 4IR.

6   Conclusion

The study aimed to investigate the impact of 4IR mobile technologies on small businesses in urban areas, specifically in Pretoria, South Africa. The data was collected from 35 small businesses through interviews, and thematic analysis was used to derive the main themes from the data. The demographic data revealed that the majority of small businesses, 60%, were operated by individuals below the age of 40, and various types of businesses such as hair salons, restaurants, and clothing shops were recorded. Additionally, the study found that most small businesses employed one to 10 people and used smartphones, with Facebook and WhatsApp being the dominant social media platforms for business purposes, accounting for 64% of usage.

The thematic analysis of the data identified four main themes related to the impact of 4IR mobile technologies on small businesses in urban areas of South Africa. These themes were: 1) Influence of mobile technology, 2) Benefits of mobile technologies, 3) Challenges of mobile technologies and (4) Knowledge of the fourth industrial revolution (4IR). These themes highlighted that 4IR mobile technologies have positively influenced small businesses in urban areas of Pretoria, South Africa, by improving service delivery, providing competitive advantage, simplifying administration, enabling mobile payments, online booking, and social media, and reducing costs.

However, challenges faced by small businesses in adopting and utilising these technologies include affordability, technological skills, cybersecurity concerns, safety concerns, poor internet connection, hiring skilled personnel, competition and marketing, and employee retention and upskilling. Addressing these challenges would require strategies such as financial planning, training and upskilling programs, cybersecurity measures, robust internet connectivity and marketing efforts. While there is awareness and some adoption of 4IR technologies in small businesses in Pretoria, there is also recognition of limited knowledge and potential for further exploration and utilisation of these technologies. This would enable small businesses and their customers to be interconnected in the service of society.

References

1. Schwab, K.: The fourth industrial revolution: what it means and how to respond. In: World Economic Forum, pp. 1–7 (2016)
2. World Economic Forum (2021). https://doi.org/10.1007/s00146-017-0736-1. Type
3. Alexander, R.: Assessing the ability of the National Innovation System of South Africa to Facilitate the Fourth Industrial Revolution DSI/NRF South African Research Chair in Industrial Development (2021). https://www.uj.ac.za/faculties/college-of-
4. Berce, P.: The fourth industrial revolution. Acad. J. Manuf. Eng. **14**(1), 1–5 (2016). https://doi.org/10.4337/9781786430328.00006
5. Serumaga-Zake, J.M., van der Poll, J.A.: Addressing the impact of fourth industrial revolution on South African manufacturing small and medium enterprises (SMEs). Sustainability (Switzerland) **13**(21), 11703 (2021). https://doi.org/10.3390/su132111703
6. Cowie, P., Townsend, L., Salemink, K.: Smart rural futures: will rural areas be left behind in the 4th industrial revolution? J. Rural Stud. **79**(8), 169–176 (2020). https://doi.org/10.1016/j.jrurstud.2020.08.042
7. Elephant, N., Maphela, B.: An analysis of the importance of mobile technology on small businesses in Noordwyk. J. Legal Ethical Regul. Issues **22**(4), 1–16 (2018)
8. Attaran, M.: The impact of 5G on the evolution of intelligent automation and industry digitization. J. Ambient. Intell. Humaniz. Comput. **14**, 5977–5993 (2021). https://doi.org/10.1007/s12652-020-02521-x

9. Reuschke, D., Mason, C., Syrett, S.: Digital futures of small businesses and entrepreneurial opportunity. Futures **128**(2), 102714 (2021). https://doi.org/10.1016/j.futures.2021.102714

10. Muriuki, N.G.: The role of mobile phone use in the success of small and medium sized enterprises: a Case of SMEs providing financial services in the Kiambu Sub County (2014)

11. Khet, K., Tha, O.: Mobile money affordances: enabling the way for financial inclusion. In: Thirtieth European Conference on Information Systems, Timişoara, Romania (2022)

12. Masabo, T.T.: The readiness of small businesses to embrace the fourth industrial revolution in Mamelodi Township, Thesis (2021)

13. Moloi, T.: Key features of the fourth industrial revolution in South Africa's basic education system. J. Manage. Inf. Decis. Sci. **24**(5), 1–20 (2021)

14. Sutcliffe, M., Bannister, S.: Research on the 4th industrial revolution: implications for local government in the context of skills development, pp. 1–115 (2020)

15. Alsulaimani, B., Islam, A.: Impact of 4IR technology and its impact on the current deployment. Int. J. Comput. Sci. Inf. Technol. **14**(4), 53–67 (2022). https://doi.org/10.5121/ijcsit.2022. 14405

16. Dlamini, B., Schutte, D.P.: An overview of the historical development of small and medium enterprises in Zimbabwe. Small Enterp. Res. **27**(3), 306–322 (2020). https://doi.org/10.1080/ 13215906.2020.1835704

17. Mhlanga, D.: The role of artificial intelligence and machine learning amid the COVID 19 pandemic: what lessons are we learning on 4IR and the sustainable development goals. Int. J. Environ. Res. Public Health **19**(3), 1879 (2022). https://doi.org/10.3390/ijerph19031879

18. Adegbite, W.M., Govender, C.M.: Emerging roles of small and medium enterprises in the fourth industrial revolution in Africa. Mediterr. J. Soc. Sci. **12**(6), 151 (2021). https://doi.org/ 10.36941/mjss-2021-0065

19. The Republic of South Africa. National Small Business Act. Government Gazette, no. 377, pp. 1–20 (1996)

20. Agupusi, P.: Small business development and poverty alleviation in Alexandra, South Africa. In: Second meeting of the Society for the Study of Economic Inequality, no. 9, pp. 1–18 (2007)

21. Arthur-Nyarko, E., Agyei, D.D., Armah, J.K.: Digitizing distance learning materials: measuring students' readiness and intended challenges. Educ. Inf. Technol. **25**(4), 2987–3002 (2020). https://doi.org/10.1007/s10639-019-10060-y

22. Mabinya, B.: The impact of mobile technologies on the business models of SMEs in Pietermaritzburg (2011). http://www.repository.up.ac.za/bitstream/handle/2263/26316/disser tation.pdf?sequence=1

23. Akkari, N., Dimitriou, N.: Mobility management solutions for 5G networks: architecture and services. Comput. Netw. **169**(3), 107082 (2020)

24. Liu, D., Zhao, M., Xu, H., Mehrgan, M.: A new model to investigate the impact of innovative IT services on smart urban growth: the mediating role of urban planners' knowledge. Growth Chang. **52**(2), 1040–1061 (2021). https://doi.org/10.1111/grow.12483

25. Bai, C., Quayson, M., Sarkis, J.: COVID-19 pandemic digitization lessons for sustainable development of micro-and small- enterprises. Sustain. Prod. Consum. **27**(7), 1989–2001 (2021)

26. Ansari, J.A.N., Khan, N.A.: Exploring the role of social media in collaborative learning the new domain of learning. Smart Learn. Environ. **7**(1), 1–16 (2020). https://doi.org/10.1186/ s40561-020-00118-7

27. Thomai, B.: The influence of mobile technology upon dissemination of information for commercial and management purposes (2017)

28. Kaplan, A.M.: Social media, the digital revolution, and the business of media. JMM Int. J. Media Manage. **17**(4), 197–199 (2015). https://doi.org/10.1080/14241277.2015.1120014

29. Hruska, J., Maresova, P.: Use of social media platforms among adults in the United States—Behavior on social media. Societies **10**(1), 27 (2020). https://doi.org/10.3390/soc10010027
30. Taneja, S., Toombs, L.: Putting a face on small business. Acad. Mark. Stud. J. **18**(1), 6867 (2014)
31. Siricharoen, W.V.: Social media, how does it work for business? Int. J. Innov. Manage. Technol. **3**(4), 476 (2012)
32. Chatterjee, S., Kumar Kar, A.: Why do small and medium enterprises use social media marketing and what is the impact: empirical insights from India. Int. J. Inf. Manage. **53**(2), 102103 (2020)
33. Ramnund-Mansingh, A., Reddy, N.: South African specific complexities in aligning graduate attributes to employability. J. Teach. Learn. Grad. Employability **12**(2), 206–221 (2021). https://doi.org/10.21153/jtlge2021vol12no2art1025
34. Putra, P., Santoso, H.: Contextual factors and performance impact of e-business use in Indonesian small and medium enterprises (SMEs). Heliyon **6**(3), e03568 (2020)
35. He, W., Wang, F.-K., Chen, Y., Zha, S.: An exploratory investigation of social media adoption by small businesses. Inf. Technol. Manage. **18**(2), 149–160 (2015). https://doi.org/10.1007/s10799-015-0243-3
36. Appel, G., Grewal, L., Hadi, R., Stephen, A.T.: The future of social media in marketing. J. Acad. Mark. Sci. **48**(1), 79–95 (2019). https://doi.org/10.1007/s11747-019-00695-1
37. Murthy, D.S.N., Nagaraju, E.: Impact of social media on consumer purchase decisions. Int. J. Res. Publ. Rev. **2**(5), 1218–1223 (2022)
38. Kaur, K., Kumar, P.: Social media usage in Indian beauty and wellness industry: a qualitative study. TQM J. **33**(1), 17–32 (2021). https://doi.org/10.1108/TQM-09-2019-0216
39. Asoba, S.N., Mcunukelwa, R.M., Mefi, N.: Elements for a competitive business environment in the context of the fourth industrial revolution: an overview of the South African environment. Acad. Entrepreneurship J. **26**(3), 1–8 (2021)
40. Schutte, F., Edwards, D.: Business model innovation: reinventing the milkman. Int. J. Bus. Manage. Stud. **12**(2), 1309–8047 (2020)
41. Jin, B.E., Shin, D.C.: The power of 4th industrial revolution in the fashion industry: what, why, and how has the industry changed? Fashion Text. **8**(1), 1–25 (2021). https://doi.org/10.1186/s40691-021-00259-4
42. Sutherland, E.: The fourth industrial revolution-the case of South Africa. Politikon **47**(2), 233–252 (2020). https://doi.org/10.1080/02589346.2019.1696003
43. Kraft, C., Lindeque, J.P., Peter, M.K.: The digital transformation of Swiss small and medium-sized enterprises: insights from digital tool adoption. J. Strateg. Manag. **15**(3), 468–494 (2022). https://doi.org/10.1108/JSMA-02-2021-0063
44. Chen, C.L., Lin, Y.C., Chen, W.H., Chao, C.F., Pandia, H.: Role of government to enhance digital transformation in small service business. Sustainability (Switzerland) **13**(3), 1–26 (2021). https://doi.org/10.3390/su13031028
45. Matarazzo, M., Penco, L., Profumo, G., Quaglia, R.: Digital transformation and customer value creation in made in Italy SMEs: a dynamic capabilities perspective. J. Bus. Res. **123**(2), 642–656 (2021). https://doi.org/10.1016/j.jbusres.2020.10.033
46. Masenya, T.M.: Technopreneurship development: digital strategy for youth self-employment in the digital economy, pp. 196–218 (2021). https://doi.org/10.4018/978-1-7998-5015-1.ch010
47. Bengtsson, M.: How to plan and perform a qualitative study using content analysis. NursingPlus Open **2**, 8–14 (2016). https://doi.org/10.1016/j.npls.2016.01.001
48. Yin, R.K.: Discovering the future of the case study method in evaluation research. Am. J. Eval. **15**(3), 283–290 (1994). https://doi.org/10.1177/109821409401500309
49. Creswell, J.W.: Research Design, 3rd edn. Sage Publications, Los Angeles (2009)

50. Leung, L.: Validity, reliability, and generalizability in qualitative research. J. Family Med. Prim. Care **4**(3), 324 (2015). https://doi.org/10.4103/2249-4863.161306

51. Creswell, J.W., Creswell, J.D.: Research Design Qualitative, Quantitative, and Mixed Methods Approach, 5th edn. Sage Publications, London (2013)

52. Kumar, R.: Research Methodology a Step-by-Step Guide for Beginners, 3rd edn. Sage Publications, London (2011)

53. Tullis, T., Albert, B.: Measuring the User Experience. Morgan Hoffman, New York (2014)

54. Braun, V.: Clarke using thematic analysis in psychology. Qual. Res. Psychol. **3**(2), 77–101 (2006). https://doi.org/10.1191/1478088706qp063oa

55. Attaran, M., Woods, J.: Cloud computing technology: improving small business performance using the Internet. J. Small Bus. Entrep. **31**(6), 495–519 (2019). https://doi.org/10.1080/082 76331.2018.1466850

56. Gumbi, L., Twinomurinzi, H.: SMME readiness for smart manufacturing (4IR) adoption: a systematic review. In: Hattingh, M., Matthee, M., Smuts, H., Pappas, I., Dwivedi, Y.K., Mäntymäki, M. (eds.) I3E 2020. LNCS, vol. 12066, pp. 41–54. Springer, Cham (2020). https://doi.org/10.1007/978-3-030-44999-5_4

57. Muchuchuti, S., Ebewo, P.: Jobs 4.0: are Botswana workers ready? Dev. Country Stud. **11**(2), 29–40 (2021). https://doi.org/10.7176/dcs/11-2-05

Author Index

© The Editor(s) (if applicable) and The Author(s), under exclusive license
to Springer Nature Switzerland AG 2023
A. Gerber and M. Coetzee (Eds.): SAICSIT 2023, CCIS 1878, p. 289, 2023.
https://doi.org/10.1007/978-3-031-39652-6

Printed in the United States
by Baker & Taylor Publisher Services